PRODUCTIVITY ISSUES IN SERVICES AT THE MICRO LEVEL

A Special Issue of the Journal of Productivity Analysis

edited by

Zvi Griliches and Jacques Mairesse

Reprinted from the Journal of Productivity Analysis

Volume 4, Numbers 1 and 2 (1993)

KLUWER ACADEMIC PUBLISHERS
Boston/Dordrecht/London

Distributors for North America:
Kluwer Academic Publishers
101 Philip Drive
Assinippi Park
Norwell, Massachusetts 02061 USA

Distributors for all other countries:
Kluwer Academic Publishers Group
Distribution Centre
Post Office Box 322
3300 AH Dordrecht, THE NETHERLANDS

Library of Congress Cataloging-in-Publication Data

Productivity issues in services at the micro level : a special issue of the Journal of productivity analysis / edited by Zvi Griliches and Jacques Mairesse.

p. cm.

"Papers ... first presented at the third Franco-American Economic Seminar"--Introd.

"Reprinted from the Journal of productivity analysis, volume 4, number 1 and 2 (1993)."

Includes bibliographical references.

ISBN 0-7923-9335-X

1. Service industries--Case studies--Congresses. 2. Industrial productivity--Case studies--Congresses. 3. Service industries--France--Case studies--Congresses. 4. Industrial productivity--France--Case studies--Congresses. 5. Service industries--United States--Case studies--Congresses. 6. Industrial productivity--United States--Case studies--Congresses. I. Griliches, Zvi, 1930- . II. Mairesse, Jacques.

HD9980.5.P76 1993
331.11'8--dc20 93-20547
CIP

Printed on acid-free paper.

Printed in the United States of America

JOURNAL OF PRODUCTIVITY ANALYSIS
Vol. 4, Nos. 1/2, June 1993

PRODUCTIVITY ISSUES IN SERVICES AT THE MICRO LEVEL

A Special Issue of the Journal of Productivity Analysis

9780128164150

The Journal of Productivity Analysis, 4, 5–8 (1993)

Editors' Introduction

This special issue of the Journal of Productivity Analysis (JPA) focuses on the empirical analysis of productivity in services at the firm level. It consists of 11 papers, which were first presented at the third Franco-American Economic Seminar.[1] Productivity studies are still relatively scarce in services, especially in view of the major role of this sector in our modern developed economies and the increasing concern about its performance. We thus deemed it worthwhile to ask the contributors to the seminar to revise thoroughly their papers and submit them to the JPA.[2]

To provide a brief overview of the papers (and avoid rephrasing the terse account of their main findings given in the abstracts), we have summarized some of the characteristics of the sample, data, model and type of estimates they use in the accompanying table.

The service industries investigated in these studies are quite diverse, although financial services are overrepresented. The first two papers and the fifth deal with banks (Humphrey, Dietsch, Parsons et al.), the third with both banks and savings institutions (Muldur and Sassenou), the fourth with insurance firms (Fecher et al.). The next two papers relate to airlines and railroads, respectively (Good et al., Berndt et al.), while the following two concentrate on day care centers (Mukerjee and Witte, Preston). The last two consider a variety of services: banking, courts, and urban transit (Tulkens), and restaurants, hotels, engineering, computer programming, computer processing, legal services, accounting, and building cleaning (Mairesse and Kremp).

All the analyses are performed at the micro level, being based on cross-sectional or panel data for samples of firms of widely varying sizes, and in two extreme instances on time series data for one firm only.[3] They focus on a variety of topics, which range from comparing the efficiency of different categories of service firms (such as for-profit and not-for-profit day care centers) or exploring the impact of mergers and deregulation on productivity performance (of banks, airlines, or railroads), to assessing the magnitude of returns to scale and scope (in banking) or investigating the properties of different parametric or nonparametric methods to estimate cost and production functions (or frontiers).

Although emphasizing such diverse issues, all studies adopt similar frameworks, following the so-called primal and dual general approaches to productivity analysis—that is, specifying and estimating production or cost function models. Thus, five studies resort to the estimation of a translog cost function together with the corresponding factor share equations (three a total cost function, one a variable cost function, and one both), while two others are based on a slightly generalized Cobb-Douglas (total) cost function. Among the four remaining ones, two rely on straight Cobb-Douglas production functions, and the other two on nonparametric production frontiers (one of which also experiments with the Cobb-Douglas).

The estimates of these cost and production models are obtained either by econometric methods or by now more or less familiar data envelopment analysis (DEA) techniques. Most such estimates are of a cross-sectional nature, though a number of authors try to

Summary of the various studies' characteristics

Articles	Sample	Data	Model	Estimates
Humphrey	683 banks 1977–1978 U.S.	5 outputs 4 inputs	Translog total cost function and share equations	Cross-sectional Average and "thick frontier" estimates
Dietsch	343 banks 1987 France	4 or 3 outputs 3 inputs	Translog total cost function and share equations	Cross-sectional
Muldur and Sassenou	59 banks and 249 savings firms 1987 France	3 outputs 3 or 2 inputs	Translog total cost function and share equations	Cross-sectional
Fecher et al.	347 insurance firms 1984–1989 France	1, 2, or 3 outputs 2 inputs	Nonparametric and Cobb-Douglas production function	Cross-sectional Average and DEA estimates Efficiency analysis
Parsons et al.	1 bank 1974–1987 Canada	2 outputs 4 inputs	Translog total cost function and share equations	Time series
Good et al.	12 air carriers 1976–1986 U.S. and Europe	1 output 3 inputs	Cobb-Douglas production function	Panel data Efficiency analysis
Berndt et al.	27 railroads 1974–1986 U.S. and Europe	1 output 5 inputs	Translog variable cost function and share equations	Panel data
Mukerjee and Witte	80 day care centers 1987 U.S. (Massachusetts)	1 output 3 inputs	Generalized Cobb-Douglas total cost function	Cross-sectional
Preston	2707 day care centers 1977 U.S.	1 output 2 inputs	Generalized Cobb-Douglas total cost function	Cross-sectional
Tulkens	3 different samples Belgium	Various outputs and inputs for 3 samples	Nonparametric production function	FDH and DEA estimates Efficiency analysis
Mairesse and Kremp	1790 firms for 8 service industries 1984–1988 France	1 output 2 inputs	Cobb-Douglas production function	Panel data

Tulkens is interested in comparing the free disposal hull (FDH) method and other data envelopment analyses (DEA) in measuring efficiency. He considers three different applications: the first to 773 branches of a public bank and 991 branches of a private bank in 1987, with eight outputs and three inputs; the second to 187 courts from 1983 to 1985, with three outputs and one input; the third to one urban transit company with monthly data from 1977 to 1989 for one output and three inputs.

Mairesse and Kremp try to account for part of the extreme dispersion of labor productivity differences and changes among firms and investigate the divergence between cross-sectional and time-series-type estimates of the production function.

take advantage of the panel structure of their data to control for possible errors of specification in their models. It is interesting to note that the econometric and DEA methods may be closer than some of their respective advocates seem to believe. Several of the studies show that the former as well as the latter can be effectively used to assess the relative efficiency of groups of firms or individual firms, and one of them explicitly compare results arising from both (Fecher et al.). Econometric techniques can also be nonparametric and applied to estimating cost or production frontiers (and not only "average" functions), while ultimately DEA should be amenable to statistical inference.

Perhaps the most valuable feature of all the analyses is their care and ingenuity in putting together the data, measuring variables, and pulling out relevant information. Many of them are not content with an overall output measure, but endeavor to manage with less aggregated measures. Nearly all also include in the estimated models a number of auxiliary variables intended to control for specific attributes of outputs, inputs, or production techniques, and other characteristics of firms.

After reading this wide-ranging set of articles, one is inclined to consider that services, after all, may not be all that different from goods, and that productivity analyses raise similar difficulties for both. One also gets the same feeling from the two important recent publications on output and productivity measurement problems in the service sectors, and this is in fact a major conclusion reached by Robert Solow and Zvi Griliches in their respective introductions to these publications.[4] A number of difficulties that are thought to be intrinsic to analyzing productivity in service industries are brought about by a deceptive sense of familiarity arising from the many studies in agriculture and manufacturing industries, and they largely proceed from the general fallacy of misplaced concreteness. One advantage of tackling productivity issues in services is that it makes us also more critical and demanding about how more traditional goods producing sectors are to be analyzed.

Zvi Griliches, Harvard University and NBER
Jacques Mairesse, INSEE (Paris) and NBER

As we go to press, we mourn the death of Professor Ann Friedlander. Nan, as she was known to most people, made valuable contributions to productivity analysis, especially in the transportation sector. She was also an inspiring teacher and colleague. We shall miss her.

Notes

1. The third Franco-American Economic Seminar was held in July 1990, as part of the National Bureau of Economic Research (NBER) Summer Institute. The Franco-American Economic Seminar has been launched under the auspices of the French Ministry of Foreign Affairs, in association with the NBER, in order to promote cooperation and exchanges between economists of the two countries in applied topics of importance.
2. Papers at the Franco-American Economic Seminar are given without any commitment for publication; they usually report on research in progress and are discussed in detail. Most of the remarks and suggestions of the discussants at the seminar have been taken into account in the completed and revised versions of the papers submitted to the JPA. Hence, with the exception of Frank Wykoff on Muldur and Sassenou, the discussant comments are not included, but their role and contributions are most gratefully acknowledged.

3. Parsons et al. and Tulkens third application.
4. See Solow [1992] and Griliches [1992]. For a thought-provoking conceptual analysis stressing on the contrary important differences between services and goods (and among services themselves), see Hill [1977]. This author, however, recognizes that similar processes are involved in the production of both services and goods.

References

Griliches, Zvi. (1992). "Introduction." In Zvi Griliches (ed.), *Output Measurement in the Service Sectors*. Chicago: National Bureau of Economic Research and University of Chicago Press, 1–22.

Hill, T.P. (1977). "On Goods and Services." *Review of Income and Wealth* 123(4), 315–338.

Solow, Robert. (1992). "Introduction." *The Scandinavian Journal of Economics* 94, suppl., 5–7.

The Journal of Productivity Analysis, 4, 9–34 (1993)

Cost and Technical Change: Effects from Bank Deregulation

DAVID B. HUMPHREY
Department of Finance, Florida State University, Tallahassee, FL 32306

Abstract

Banks were substantially deregulated during the 1980s. This altered the cost-minimizing mix between deposit interest payments and operating expenses (capital and labor for branch convenience and "free" deposit services). Measured bank output was relatively unaffected by these changes. The proportion of deposits receiving higher interest rates increased more rapidly than factor quantities were reduced, so unit deposit costs rose. Consumers benefited, but the measured net effects for banks were negative, averaging −0.8% to −1.4% a year in net technical change from 1977 to 1988. These influences were measured three different ways and for both equilibrium and disequilibrium factor input specifications. All three approaches—a standard time trend, a time-specific index, and shifts in cross-sectional cost functions—gave consistent results. The results were robust whether measured at the banking firm or branch office level or on the cost frontier.

1. Introduction

U.S. banking activities were substantially deregulated during the 1980s. Most of this activity took place on the liability side of the balance sheet where deposit interest rate ceilings were removed and new types of interest bearing transactions accounts were authorized. At the same time, expenditures on information technology were rising. Industrywide, these expenditures comprised perhaps as much as 20% of total (noninterest) operating costs or around $20 billion annually (Cooper [1989]).

Both of these events would be expected to be associated with significant technical change and productivity growth in banking. Yet from 1977 to 1986, the Bureau of Labor Statistics (BLS) measured an 11.1% increase in bank (single factor) labor productivity, or only 1.2% per year (BLS [1989, p. 170]). But even this growth is seen to be overstated when it is (crudely) transformed into a more comprehensive multifactor measure, giving only 0.5% a year over this period. Many researchers find such a low growth (in either measure) surprising given the very significant expenditures on information technology which have occurred (Baily and Gordon [1988]). The basic question addressed in this paper is why has measured bank productivity growth been so low? The culprit seems to be the negative, cost-increasing response by the banking industry to the recent deregulation, an event in banking not unlike the negative productivity effects of mandating pollution control restrictions in the electric utility industry.

The net effects of deregulation and technical change in banking are investigated using a panel of 683 of the largest banks in the United States in a pooled time-series, cross-sectional analysis from 1977 to 1988. Only 5% of all banks are represented, but they comprise

$2 trillion of the $3 trillion of U.S. banking assets. Three alternative methods of estimating net technical change econometrically are utilized: the standard time trend approach, a time-specific index (Caves, Christensen, and Swanson [1981]; Baltagi and Griffin [1988]), and annual shifts in cross-section cost functions (Berger and Humphrey [1992]). These three approaches, along with their equilibrium/disequilibrium specifications, serve to demonstrate the robustness of our results. Net technical change at both the average banking firm and branch office level are derived. This is also done for the set of "best practice" banks on the cost frontier. On the frontier, technological change can be identified separately from the diffusion of existing technology to nonfrontier banks, a separation not possible in existing studies which combine the two influences.

In what follows, the bank regulatory changes occurring during the 1980s and the nature of the industry's response are outlined in Section 2. In Section 3, the three alternative modeling structures for estimating bank technical change are derived, compared, and adjusted for possible disequilibrium behavior when dereguation occurred. The results of these alternative methodologies for net technical change are presented and discussed in Section 4. Existing estimates of bank technical change and productivity growth are then presented in Section 5, and reasons offered as to why they differ from those estimated here. Lastly, the paper is summarized in Section 6, and conclusions are drawn as to why banking has experienced such a low rate of technical change. Implications for the future are also noted.

2. Background of Bank Regulatory Change and Response

2.1. Deregulation Legislation

The Depository Institutions Deregulation and Monetary Control Act (DIDMCA) was passed in late 1980. In addition to improving monetary control by making reserve requirements universal, the DIDMCA (a) established interest bearing NOW (negotiable order of withdrawal) consumer checking accounts; (b) phased-out Regulation Q interest rate ceilings on savings and small denomination (less than $100,000) time deposits; and (c) required pricing for previously free Federal Reserve payment services (in order to maintain U.S. Treasury revenues as reserve requirements were reduced). While the first change had already been successfully implemented for New England bank and thrift institutions as a regional experiment, a major impetus for this (and later) deregulation was the tremendous rise in market interest rates and the corresponding explosive growth in money market mutual funds (MMMF). MMMFs were uninsured and had very limited check writing privileges, but were viewed as a strong substitute for bank consumer deposits, mostly time and savings (not demand).

In late 1982 the Garn–St Germain Depository Institutions Act was passed. This Act authorized the establishment of a money market deposit account (MMDA), which was the equivalent of a MMMF account. MMMFs, which started in 1973, grew to be close to 15% of household deposits by 1982 ($211 billion), but fell by 27% in 1983 as depository institutions offered MMDAs [Fraser and Kolari, 1985, Table 2-3, p. 31].

2.2. *Time Pattern of Interest Rates and Other Bank Costs*

The climb in market rates (90-day Treasury bills) over the entire period 1977 to 1988 is shown by the solid line in Figure la. This fluctuation is closely followed by the change in the average rate paid on bank purchased funds (bold dashed line).[1] The change in the average rate paid on demand, savings, and small time deposits (combined) had considerably less fluctuation (dashed line).[2] Importantly, however, the *spread* between these controlled rates and purchased funds before and after decontrol was narrowed substantially—falling by 44%.[3]

For the panel data set, 49% of assets are currently funded by produced deposits (demand, savings, and small time deposits) while 45% are funded by purchased funds. The remainder is comprised of equity capital and long-term debit, subject to regulatory imposed minimums. Because these funding shares are similar and have not been subject to dramatic fluctuation,

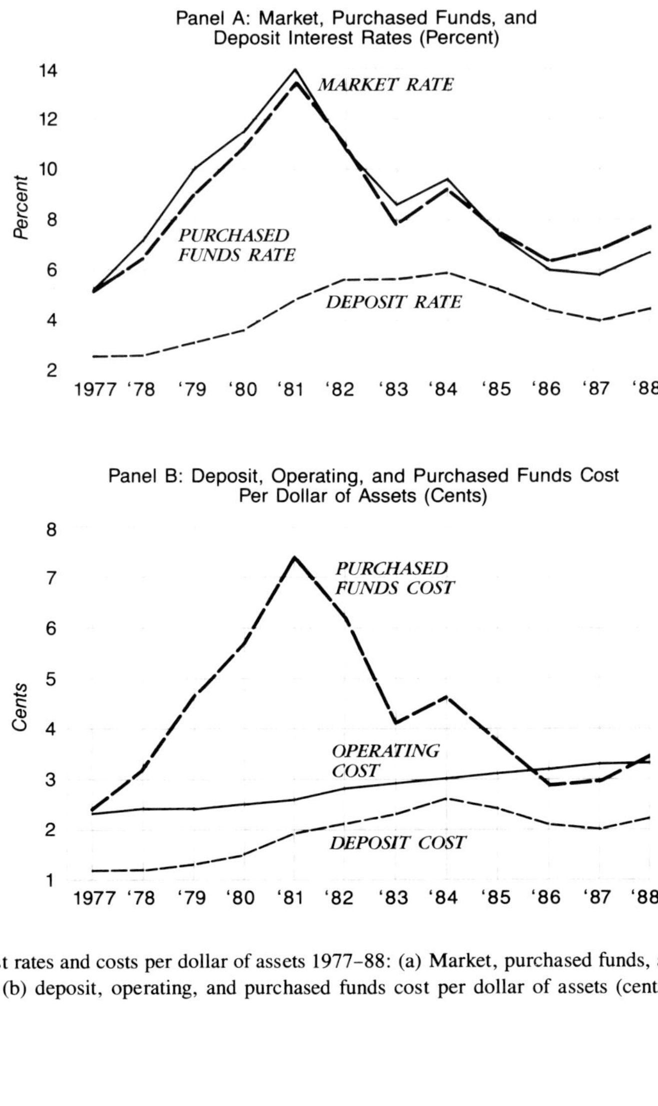

Figure 1. Interest rates and costs per dollar of assets 1977–88: (a) Market, purchased funds, and deposit interest rates (percent); (b) deposit, operating, and purchased funds cost per dollar of assets (cents).

the effects from changing rates (Figure 1a) are largely duplicated in the funding costs per dollar of assets (Figure 1b).

Currently, interest costs represent 68% of total costs, while operating costs make up the remainder. On average, half (49%)[4] of operating costs (solid line) are used to "produce" deposits, through the application of physical capital and labor (and related expenses), while virtually no operating costs are used to produce purchased funds. The prices of capital and labor rose by 113% and 133%, respectively, over 1977–1988—faster than the GNP deflator (80%)—and so rose in real terms.[5]

Comparing pre- and postderegulation periods, it is seen that the cost of purchased funds per dollar of assets rose by 14% between 1977 and 1978 and 1987 to 1988 while operating costs (capital, labor, and related expenses) rose by 40%. Importantly, deposit interest costs per dollar of assets rose by 75%, showing the relative impact of deregulation. Thus, interest rate decontrol on deposits and the establishment of interest-earning checking accounts have significantly increased the long-term cost of an important component of loanable funds in the banking system.

2.3. Banking Industry Response

Some of the increased cost of loanable funds was passed on to borrowers through floating rate loans. Other borrowers had few alternative funding sources (e.g., consumer installment credit, small business loans, and credit card and home loans).[6] However, large bank business borrowers were not so constrained; they have increasingly dealt directly with large lenders using the commercial paper market (lowering funding costs by leaving out the bank intermediary).[7]

A second response to deregulation has been to cut back on the growth of operating costs. Many banks have sold or closed hundreds of branch offices, and labor has been redeployed or laid off.[8] Instead of providing new branch offices at a rate equal to or greater than that at which deposits grew, so that the real deposit/branch ratio would remain roughly constant or fall as it did prior to deregulation, banks slowed their rate of branch expansion and raised the real deposit/branch ratio by 27% over 1982 to 1988. This conserved physical capital, leading to more intensive use of bank offices.

3. Three Econometric Models of Bank Net Technical Change

With this brief background, three ways of measuring the net effects of deregulation and ongoing technical change are specified: a standard time trend, a time-specific index, and shifts in cross-section cost functions. Alternative equilibrium/disequilibrium versions of these models, concerning the factor inputs, are also developed.

3.1. Technical Change from a Time Trend

A basic problem with measuring technical change in a service industry like banking is that there is no unique indicator or proxy for measuring technical progress, such as the average age or vintage of capital equipment used in manufacturing studies to capture (embodied) technical progress. Thus, it is not surprising that all but one banking study has chosen to model technical change as a simple time trend. Within the context of a general translog cost function, the time trend model we estimate is as follows:

$$\ln TC = \alpha_0 + \sum_i^5 \alpha_i \ln Q_i + \sum_k^4 \alpha_k \ln P_k + \alpha_B \ln B + \alpha_M M + \alpha_U U + \alpha_T T$$

$$+ \frac{1}{2} \sum_i^5 \sum_j^5 \delta_{ij} \ln Q_i \ln Q_j + \frac{1}{2} \sum_k^4 \sum_l^4 \gamma_{kl} \ln P_k \ln P_l + \beta_{BB} \frac{1}{2} (\ln B)^2$$

$$+ \beta_{TT} \frac{1}{2} (T)^2 + \sum_i^5 \sum_k^4 \rho_{ik} \ln Q_i \ln P_k + \sum_i^5 \theta_{iB} \ln Q_i \ln B + \sum_i^5 \theta_{iM} \ln Q_i M$$

$$+ \sum_i^5 \theta_{iU} \ln Q_i U + \sum_i^5 \theta_{iT} \ln Q_i T + \sum_k^4 \phi_{kB} \ln P_k \ln B + \sum_k^4 \phi_{\kappa M} \ln P_k M$$

$$+ \sum_k^4 \phi_{kT} \ln P_k T + \pi_{BM} \ln BM + \pi_{BU} \ln BU + \pi_{BT} \ln BT + \rho_{MT} MT + \rho_{UT} UT + \epsilon, \tag{1}$$

$$S_k = \alpha_k + \sum_l^4 \gamma_{kl} \ln P_l + \sum_l^5 \rho_{ik} \ln Q_i + \phi_{kB} \ln B + \phi_{kM} M + \phi_{kT} T + \mu, \tag{2}$$

where

- TC = total cost (interest and operating expenses)
- Q_i = real output (i = value of demand deposits, small time and savings deposits, real estate loans, installment loans, and commercial and industrial loans, all deflated by the GNP deflator in order to approximate the underlying transaction service flows)
- P_k = input prices (k = labor, physical capital, deposit interest rate, purchased funds interest rate)
- B = number of branch offices (an alternative way to expand bank output)
- M = bank merger dummy variable, to capture the cost effects of a merger in the year it occurs
- U = unit bank dummy variable, to capture the effects of moving from unit banking to intrastate branching in eight states over 1977–88
- T = a time trend dummy variable, $T = 1, 2, \ldots, 12$ for the 12 years
- S_k = input cost share $\partial \ln TC / \partial \ln P_k$ (only $k - 1$ shares are used in estimation)
- ϵ, μ = error terms.[9]

Technical change in a multiproduct framework represents the common rate of input reduction holding outputs fixed and is expressed as $-(\partial \ln TC/\partial T)$ or[10]

$$TREND = -\left[\alpha_T + \beta_{TT}T + \sum_i^5 \theta_{iT} \ln Q_i + \sum_k^4 \phi_{kT} \ln P_k + \pi_{BT} \ln B + \rho_{MT}M + \rho_{UT}U\right]. \quad (3)$$

The growth in technical change arises from the pure effect of technical advance which saves or uses inputs in constant proportions (neutral technical change or $\alpha_T + \beta_{TT}T$), effects associated with saving or using inputs in nonconstant proportions (nonneutral technical change or $\Sigma_k^4 \phi_{kT} \ln P_k$), effects associated with changes in outputs (scale augmenting technical change or $\Sigma_i^5 \theta_{iT} \ln Q_i$), and regulatory changes. A number of recent studies in the electric utility area have suggested that, while the rate of technical change obtained using the time trend is probably accurate when evaluated at the mean of a time series data set, it will poorly reflect the year-to-year variation in technical change when this process is not constant or smoothly increasing or decreasing (Kopp and Smith [1983]; Nelson [1986]). Thus, two other alternative representations of technical change are also estimated.

3.2. An Index of Technical Change

The index approach effectively permits technical change to be nonsmooth, so that substantial year-to-year variations can occur if they exist in the data. This approach, initiated in Caves, Christensen, and Swanson [1981] and developed more completely by Baltagi and Griffin [1988], is a generalization of Solow's index of technical change $A(t)$. Our approach utilizes a time-specific shift variable (D_t) which enters by itself as an intercept (for neutral technical change) as well as interacting with outputs (for scale augmentation) and input prices (for nonneutral change).[11] As applied in this comparative study, the cost function system (1) and (2) is rewritten as

$$\begin{aligned}\ln TC = &\sum_t^{12} n_t D_t + \sum_i^5 \sum_t^{12} \alpha_{it} D_t \ln Q_i + \sum_k^4 \sum_t^{12} \alpha_{kt} D_t \ln P_k + \sum_t^{12} \alpha_{Bt} D_t \ln B + \alpha_M M + \alpha_U U \\ &+ \frac{1}{2} \sum_i^5 \sum_j^5 \delta_{ij} \ln Q_i \ln Q_j + \frac{1}{2} \sum_k^4 \sum_l^4 \gamma_{kl} \ln P_k \ln P_l + \beta_{BB} \frac{1}{2} (\ln B)^2 \\ &+ \sum_i^5 \sum_k^4 \rho_{ik} \ln Q_i \ln P_k + \sum_i^5 \theta_{iB} \ln Q_i \ln B + \sum_i^5 \theta_{iM} \ln Q_i M \\ &+ \sum_i^5 \theta_{iU} \ln Q_i U + \sum_k^4 \phi_{kB} \ln P_k \ln B + \sum_k^4 \phi_{kM} \ln P_k M \\ &+ \pi_{BM} \ln BM + \pi_{BU} \ln BU + \epsilon, \end{aligned} \quad (4)$$

$$S_k = \alpha_{k1} + \sum_{l}^{4} \gamma_{kl} \ln P_l + \sum_{i}^{5} \rho_{ik} \ln Q_i + \phi_{kB} \ln B + \phi_{kM} M + \mu, \tag{5}$$

where D_t = a time-specific dummy variable which equals 1.0 in period t and zero in other periods, $t = 1, 2, \ldots, 12$ years.

In this specification the growth rate of technical advance is expressed yearly as $-(\partial \ln TC/\partial D_{t+1} - \partial \ln TC/\partial D_t)$:

$$INDEX = -\left[n_{t+1} - n_t + \sum_{i}^{5} \ln Q_i(\alpha_{it+1} - \alpha_{it}) + \sum_{k}^{4} \ln P_k(\alpha_{kt+1} - \alpha_{kt}) + \ln B(\alpha_{Bt+1} - \alpha_{Bt})\right]. \tag{6}$$

The index for period 1, the base period, is zero so the estimated parameters n_1, α_{i1}, α_{k1}, and α_{B1} do not reflect technical change but represent, respectively, the overall equation intercept (α_0) and slope parameters for each output and input price plus the branching variable.[12] In period 2, *INDEX* is positive or negative, reflecting technical advance or retrogression, and equals

$$-\left[n_2 - n_1 + \sum_{i}^{5} \ln Q_i(\alpha_{i2} - \alpha_{i1}) + \sum_{k}^{4} \ln P_k(\alpha_{k2} - \alpha_{k1}) + \ln B(\alpha_{B2} - \alpha_{B1})\right],$$

and so on for later periods.

3.3. Technical Change from Shifts in Cross-Section Cost Functions

In the time-specific index approach to technical change it was maintained that technical change is only reflected in pure intercept shifts and possible interactions with outputs, input prices, and number of branch offices. A more general approach, possible when there are sufficient cross-section observations, would be to allow all cost function parameters to be affected by technical change (Berger and Humphrey [1992]). Because all parameters are permitted to vary over time, the time-specific index approach using D_t above is essentially nested within it. The model is equivalent to the equation system (1) and (2) with all time variables set to zero and the resulting specification separately estimated for each cross-section time period.[13] The growth rate of technical change is reflected in the percentage difference in predicted average costs ($\widehat{AC}$) using the estimated parameters from periods t_{t+1} and t but evaluated using data only from the base period t:

$$SHIFT = -(\widehat{AC}^{*}_{t+1} - \widehat{AC}_t)/\widehat{AC}_t, \tag{7}$$

where

$\widehat{AC}_t$ = $\exp(\hat{\beta}_t(X_t))/TA_t$ or predicted average total cost per dollar of assets
$\hat{\beta}_t$ = estimated cost function parameters of period t
X_t = data from period t (in logs) used to evaluate the parameters
TA_t = total value of bank assets
$\widehat{AC}^*_{t+1}$ = $\exp(\hat{\beta}_{t+1}(X_t))/TA_t$ or predicted average total cost using parameters from $t + 1$ evaluated with t period data

In effect, these three models range from specifying a smooth rate of technical advance (*TREND*) to a rate of advance that can be quite discontinuous (*SHIFT*), with the middle ground covered by a model that blends elements of both approaches (*INDEX*).[14]

3.4. *Equilibrium versus Disequilibrium Specifications*

Equilibrium models are probably appropriate as long as changes in output demand and/or input prices are relatively small and/or smooth, and therefore forecastable. But such a situation clearly does not apply to the 1980s when banking deregulation occurred. The value of funds in the new and decontrolled accounts rose from \$165 billion in 1980 (and were located only in New England) to almost \$500 billion three years later. They leveled off at \$677 billion by 1988 and funded almost one-fourth of all bank assets.

The cost functions specified above have assumed that all inputs were fully utilized and reflected equilibrium usage. But, after deregulation, banks found themselves "overbranched" and cut back on their earlier rates of office expansion. This allowed deposit growth to exceed that of branches so that the real deposit/branch ratio rose, reducing—but not eliminating—excess branch capacity. One way to model disequilibrium behavior uses a restricted cost function where capital is treated as a quasi-fixed input and variable costs are minimized subject to the level of capital in place.[15] The quantity of the capital input replaces the price of capital in the equilibrium total cost functions above and this quantity enters the equation as a separate argument (with own, squared, and interaction terms with the other variables). When bank physical capital is treated as a quasi-fixed input in the time trend model above we have

$$\ln VC1 = (1)^* + \alpha_F \ln F + \beta_{FF} \frac{1}{2} (\ln F)^2 + \sum_{k}^{3} \gamma_{kF} \ln P_k \ln F$$

$$+ \sum_{i}^{5} \rho_{iF} \ln Q_i \ln F + \phi_{FB} \ln F \ln B + \phi_{FM} \ln FM + \phi_{FT} \ln FT, \qquad (8)$$

$$S1_k = (2)^* + \gamma_{kF} \ln F, \qquad (9)$$

where

$VC1$ = variable cost (total cost minus expenditures on capital)
F = quasi-fixed input, capital K
$S1_k$ = input cost share in variable cost (not total cost) for the variable inputs

The asterisk indicates that all summations in equations (1) and (2) are now done over three input prices rather than four (as the price of capital has been deleted). Similar adjustments to the equilibrium index and shift models will transform them into disequilibrium specifications. The three technical change measures now reflect changes in variable cost *VC1* and have a correction factor which permits the technical change measure from *VC1* to equal that from a total cost function (e.g., Equations (3), (6), or (7)) if total costs—not just variable costs—are being minimized. These variable cost measures of net technical change when capital is the quasi-fixed input are *TREND1*, *INDEX1*, and *SHIFT1*.[16]

Because labor is used along with capital to provide branch services, it is possible that labor should also be treated as quasi-fixed. With both factor inputs treated as quasi-fixed, the specification is the same as (8) except that F refers to two quasi-fixed inputs (involving a summation over capital and labor whenever F is specified); *VC2* replaces *VC1* and only contains interest expenses; and all summations for the variable input prices are done over only the two interest rates.[17]

4. Estimates of Bank Net Technical Change

The three alternative specifications of bank net technical change, for both the equilibrium and disequilibrium models, were all estimated using an iterative, seemingly unrelated regression procedure. For the time trend and index models, an autocorrelation correction was necessary.[18] Variable definitions and parameter estimates are shown in the Appendix.

4.1. A Comparison of Results for the Banking Firm

Net technical change can be derived for the banking firm as well as for the average branch office. The former is more interesting as it recognizes that bank output can be expanded in two different ways: (1) more output can be supplied when real deposits and loans grow at each existing branch; and (2) real deposits and loans can grow if new branches are added in new market areas. To examine technical change at the level of the banking firm, the number of branches should not be held constant. Thus the branching variable (B) is set to zero in all of the above equations, permitting the results to reflect the variation in B as well as the variation in output per branch.

Indices of bank technical change for the banking firm over 1977 to 1988 are shown in Figure 2, where the *TREND*, *INDEX*, and *SHIFT* technical change specifications are each contrasted across three model types. Thus, Figure 2a shows the time trend results for the equilibrium model where all factor inputs are presumed to be variable (*TREND*), the model where capital is the single quasi-fixed input (*TREND1*), and the model where both capital and labor are assumed to be quasi-fixed (*TREND2*).

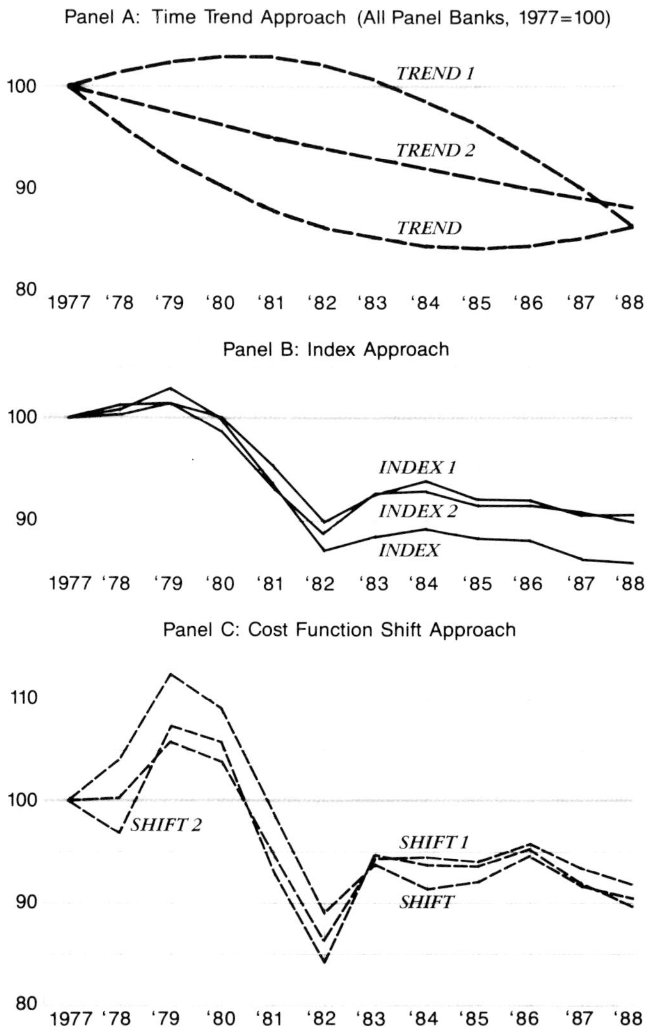

Figure 2. Indices of bank net technical change 1977–88: Comparison of time trend, index, and cost function shift. (a) Time trend approach (all panel banks, 1977 = 100). (b) Index approach. (c) Cost function shift approach.

Overall, there is a basic similarity in the banking firm results: net technical change was generally positive during the prederegulation period 1977–1980, turned strongly negative when deregulation was initiated in 1981, adjusted somewhat two years later, but flattened out from 1983 to 1988 to finish up the period in an overall negative position. This pattern, with some variation, holds for all of the models used.[19]

As would be expected if some inputs were in disequilibrium during this period, the model which presumes equilibrium usage of all inputs typically shows a larger reduction in net technical change during the period of adjustment than models which explicitly account for the possibility of disequilibrium behavior. For the *INDEX* and *SHIFT* approaches, the

Table 1. Average yearly rates of bank net technical change (1977–88).

Model	Time Trend	Index	Cost Function Shift
Equilibrium	−1.4%	−1.4%	−0.9%
Disequilibrium			
K quasi-fixed	−1.3	−0.9	−0.8
K, *L* quasi-fixed	−1.2	−1.0	−1.0

Computed from Figure 2. K = book value of physical capital in constant dollars, L = number of employees.

close correspondence between the two disequilibrium specifications suggests that capital was the factor input most in disequilibrium. Our preferred model is thus the one where capital is quasi-fixed (*TREND1, INDEX1, SHIFT1*).[20]

In Table 1 the results in Figure 2 are expressed as a single number—the average yearly rate of net technical change. All the rates shown have the same sign and a similar value for each of the equilibrium or disequilibrium models estimated.[21] Overall, net technical change in banking was negative and ranged from −0.8% to −1.4% a year from 1977 to 1988.[22] These results were robust to a number of different specifications and variable definitions including (a) specifying firm-specific effects;[23] (b) using a different price of capital;[24] (c) using a different definition of operating cost;[25] and (d) adjusting for deposit service charge and fee revenues.[26]

4.2. Net Technical Change at Large versus Small Banks

The pattern of net technical change by bank size class mirrors that shown in Figure 2. The only difference lies in the levels of technical change achieved and is seen in Table 2, which presents only the results where capital is quasi-fixed (our preferred model). Large banks (with assets more than $10 billion) experienced far less negative net technical change than did small banks (with assets of $100–$200 million).[27] Two reasons may contribute to this difference. First, large banks derive a smaller proportion of their loanable funds from those deposits that were deregulated than do smaller banks. Thus the negative effects on total costs at large banks should be less. Second, large banks typically experience more

Table 2. Average yearly rates of bank net technical change at large and small banks (1977–88).

Disequilibrium *K* Quasi-Fixed	Time Trend	Index	Cost Function Shift
Large banks	−0.9%	−0.5%	−0.6%
Small banks	−1.5	−1.2	−1.4

Computed from Figure 2 and evaluated at means of size class data. Large banks had assets greater than $10 billion; small banks had assets of $100–$200 million.

rapid deposit growth than small institutions and also have much larger branch networks which could be cut back and/or restructured. Thus large banks are better able to reduce operating costs through more intensive use of branch offices.[28]

4.3. Net Technical Change for the Average Branch Office

At the branch level, net technical change is somewhat improved but still negative.[29] The range for the time trend and index models is −0.6% to −1.2% a year (compared to −0.8% to −1.4% for the banking firm). For the cost function shift model, the improvement was larger; the average growth rate was zero (or very close to it) rather than negative. The difference between the branch and firm level results is that net technical change for the average branch office will not reflect output expansion from adding new branches, only by adding more output at each existing office. The results indicate that too little bank output emanates from the average branch office and the net effect over 1977 to 1988 has been negative or zero technical change. At the firm level, an additional negative effect is added, namely, too many branches in the highly disaggregated U.S. banking system.

This conclusion has support in the industry. A recent consultant study for the American Bankers Association concluded that about half of all bank branches are not profitable (Booz-Allen and Hamilton [1987]). Sometimes this results from keeping unprofitable branches open in areas where they meet "community needs," and if they were closed would lead to a low regulatory rating under the Community Reinvestment Act (CRA) guidelines. But mostly this results from an emphasis on market share and firm size to the detriment of current profits (discussed below).

4.4. Cost Frontier versus All Banks

The results so far apply to all 683 banks in the panel data set, which account for two-thirds of all assets at U.S. banks. But all banks are not equally cost efficient; some of the variation in measured net technical change may have come from changes in the diffusion of existing technology from the most efficient banks to all the others, rather than reflecting new technical change. To account for this possibility, all the above estimations at the level of the banking firm were redone using only the quartile of banks which experienced the lowest average cost of the entire 1977–1988 period. In effect, this set of "best practice" banks is used to estimate a thick cost frontier, as opposed to a frontier edge as is typically done in the frontier literature (e.g., Ferrier and Lovell [1990]). The logic of this approach has been discussed elsewhere (Berger and Humphrey [1991]).

The cost differences observed between banks in the lowest and highest average cost quartiles in the panel data set averaged 24%.[30] These cost differences are not temporary or random since they refer to the same set of low- and high-cost banks over the 12-year period, and thus the chance effects which temporarily raise or lower costs should have been averaged out. These persistent cost differences are strongly related to persistent differences in bank profits. Fully 47% of the banks in the lowest cost quartile were also in the highest profit quartile over the entire period. As well, 72% of these lowest costs banks had profits above the median; only 8% had profits in the lowest quartile.[31] These differences in cost efficiency and profits raises the possibility that low-cost banks may have experienced different rates of technical change compared to the other banks in the panel.

Upon investigation, this possibility was not realized. The technical change results for the time trend and index models using the lowest cost quartile of banks were so similar to those shown in Figure 2 that it is not worth graphing the results (the overlap would be too great). This similarity covers both the levels of net technical change as well as their turning points for all three of the equilibrium/disequilibrium specifications.[32] The same holds for the shift approach, but only after data on banks in the largest size class were deleted prior to evaluating (7).

4.5. Other Measures of the Effects of Deregulation

Perhaps a more direct measure of the cost effect of deregulation is the value of total deposit balances which had their interest ceiling lifted plus the balances of newly authorized interest earning checking accounts (e.g., NOWs and MMDAs).[33] When deregulation was still essentially a regional experiment in New England (1980), the extra interest expenses on deregulated balances (shown in Table 3, column 1), raised the total cost of banks in this panel data set by an estimated 1.0%. Thus, if ongoing technical change in the banking system was, for example, 2.0% of total cost, then *net* technical change measured in a statistical model would have been only half as large. Estimated extra interest expenses rise sharply up to 1986 and then level off.[34] Considering that bank profits (net income) as a percent of total costs only averaged 7.0% over the entire period, the cost impact of deregulation is seen to have been quite large.

The bank response—more intensive use of branch office and labor inputs—is seen in the last two columns. While the total number of branches continued to grow in the aggregate, the rate of increase was reduced. From 1982 to 1988, each branch supported a larger value of real deposits, and the ratio rose by 27%. Labor intensity also increased: the labor/branch ratio fell by 21% over 1980 to 1988, partly by shifting many full-time branch positions to part-time status to only cover peak use. While one can argue that the cost impact of deregulation could have been minimized if all banks had pared their branch operations

Table 3. Effects of bank deregulation.

Year	Estimated Cost of Deregulated Balances (% of total cost) (1)	Real Deposit/ Branch Ratio ($ million) (2)	Number of Employees/ Branch Ratio (3)
1980	1.0%	$33.0	44.8
1982	1.5	27.9	42.0
1984	2.6	31.7	40.5
1986	3.8	36.1	38.3
1988	3.6	35.5	35.2

more rapidly and to a greater degree, market share concerns apparently inhibited this response. Since choice of a bank by a depositor is largely based on convenience (according to industry surveys), a dramatic and profitable reduction in one bank's branching network would serve also to expand market share and profits at competing banks which retained their branch networks. In the end, both sets of banks would have been more profitable in the short run but market shares would have been redistributed away from those banks which cut their branch networks the most. Thus most banks seemingly chose to sacrifice short-term profits in order to maintain market share and hope that long-term profit would follow as deposit growth continued to exceed the establishment of new branches.

4.6. A Common Sense Explanation of the Results

Prior to deregulation, banks substituted convenient branch offices, service personnel, and nonpriced services (e.g., free checking) for their inability to pay something close to a market rate on demand, savings, and small time deposits (Evanoff [1988]).[35] Once interest rate ceilings were removed and consumer interest checking was offered, banks quickly paid the higher rates. From a cost standpoint, they subsequently found themselves to be "overbranched" and the profitability of their deposit base fell from $61 billion in 1980 to $4 billion in 1988 (Berger and Humphrey [1992]). In effect, deregulation removed banks' virtual monopoly control over zero interest checking accounts and low interest small consumer savings deposits. Subsequent competition "forced" banks to shift from low-interest cost funds inputs to higher interest cost funds inputs without a fully cost offsetting reduction in factor inputs used to provide branch convenience and other low-priced deposit services. Since the deposit services provided were largely unchanged as consumers shifted from one type of checking account to another, measured bank output (an approximation of transactions flow) would have been stable even as the price and the *quantity* of interest earning checkable deposits rose. Thus costs per unit of (measured) output should rise, even when corrected for input price changes.[36]

This analysis, we believe, explains why we (and others) have failed to observe much positive net technical change in banking during the 1980s. Going beyond this explanation, however, it is seen that another part of the problem lies in the inability to accurately capture all potentially important aspects of bank output. If branch convenience and the continued provision of underpriced deposit services are valued by users, then certainly some of the (now extra) costs incurred by banks in providing "unnecessarily" high levels of these services after deregulation has served to increase the quality of bank output. If one adopts this view, then what appears to be measured technical "retrogression" may instead be due to understating output growth as benefits received by bank depositors rose relative to their prederegulation level.

An analogous situation occurred in the electric utility industry during the 1970s. Expensive pollution control restrictions were mandated for electric utilities and, although these costs were largely made up by rate increases, measured output of this industry—kilowatt hours—did not rise commensurately. As a result, total factor productivity was seen to fall (e.g., Gollop and Roberts [1983]). But if cleaner air resulted, then the quality of this industry's output actually rose but will not be captured in the output measure used. It is argued here that the same sort of thing occurred in banking. And, to the degree that the banks' real deposit/branch and labor/branch ratios continue to improve in the future, then unit costs will fall without causing a reduction in measured bank output. Thus productivity will be seen to rise even though branch convenience will have fallen.

5. Existing Bank Productivity Estimates and Why They Are Overstated

In a recent study of (large bank) net technical change over 1980 to 1986, Hunter and Timme [1991] find a positive 1% annual growth rate using a time trend in a cost function model.[37] Since our model and data set are similar to theirs, it is useful to determine the likely reason for these different results. Hunter and Timme (a) use a shorter time period, (b) exclude money center banks, and (c) use the interest rate of purchased funds to capture the variation in both purchased funds and deposit interest rates. Adjusting the *INDEX* model to account for (a) and (b) still gave a negative estimate for net technical change (a −2.0% annual rate). Adjusting for (c) as well yielded a positive 1.0% result, and would appear to be an important reason for the different results. Use of a purchased funds rate, which generally fell over 1980 to 1986, may not also well reflect the rate on deposits, which rose slightly over the period (see Figure 1a).

In contrast, the annual single factor (labor) productivity estimate provided by the BLS for the 1980 to 1986 period is 3.3%.[38] But technical change is effectively a multifactor measure, covering the contribution to output of both capital and labor (as well as other inputs). If these factor inputs grow at the same rate, then the single factor measure will equal the multifactor measure. However, since the growth of real capital (39.9%) exceeded that of labor (13.8%) over 1980 to 1986, the BLS measure is seen to be overstated. When (crudely) transformed into a multifactor measure,[39] a 1.5% annual average rate of growth is obtained. For a time period closer to that used in this study (1977–86), the transformed BLS measure is only 0.5% a year, as was noted in the introduction.

5.1. *Total Cost versus Operating Cost Net Technical Change*

Two other econometric studies determined net technical change from a model employing a time trend but looked only at *operating*, not total, cost (Evanoff, Israilevich, and Merris [1990]; Hunter and Timme [1986]).[40] When the *INDEX* model is run with operating cost replacing total cost (and deleting the two interest rate input prices), a −1.2% annual rate of net technical change is estimated. When capital is treated as quasi-fixed in this model, the rate becomes positive at 1.1% a year.

There are two reasons why total cost is preferred over operating cost in these analyses. First, expressing technical change in terms of total cost is the appropriate multifactor measure when deposited and purchased funds are considered to have input characteristics, along with capital and labor. This is true today when interest costs are such a large component (68%) of total costs and would hold even if all banks were aggregated together and purchased funds were zero (since deposits would still exist). Second, use of operating cost by itself distorts other measures of bank efficiency, such as scale economies. Such a specification neglects the fact that purchased funds and produced deposits are substitutes, so that the true input-output cost structure will not be captured by looking at factor inputs alone.[41] A similar argument can be made for the proper specification of net technical change.

6. Conclusions

The banking deregulation of the 1980s established new interest-earning checking accounts and removed interest rate ceilings on time and savings deposits. This altered the cost-minimizing mix between interest payments and operating expenses, which comprised capital and labor for branch convenience and the provision of underpriced deposit services. Banks incurred higher interest costs more rapidly than operating expenses were reduced, leading to a substantial net increase in costs. Consumers benefited, because they now received higher interest without a fully offsetting reduction in branch convenience, but the measured net effect on banks was negative (more than offsetting any underlying positive influence of technical advance). At the firm level, banks experienced a *negative* measured average rate of net technical change of between −0.8% and −1.4% a year.

Three alternative approaches to determining net technical change were estimated. The standard time trend approach, which has been the typical approach used to date in banking, was used along with two others. Unlike the time trend, these other approaches can display substantial year-to-year variation in technical change if it exists in the data. One alternative was a time-specific index of technical change (Caves, Christensen, and Swanson [1981]; Baltagi and Griffin [1988]) and the other relied on shifts in separately estimated cross-section cost functions (Berger and Humphrey [1992]). On a yearly average basis, the three approaches yielded the range of results noted above, while the latter two methods identified similar year-to-year variations in net technical change. Specifically, prior to deregulation, technical change was positive at perhaps 1% to 2% a year. This turned strongly negative in 1981 and 1982 when, first, new interest-earning checkable accounts were established and, second, interest rates were decontrolled. Net technical change improved the following year as operating costs—labor and capital—were more intensively used and output expanded as banks became more competitive with money market mutual funds. Thereafter, technical change was essentially flat and ended the period in 1988 in an overall position lower than where it started in 1977.

In general, greater negative technical change was measured when all factor inputs were assumed to be fully utilized (an equilibrium model) than when either one or both of the capital or labor inputs were permitted to be quasi-fixed (a disequilibrium model). The most likely situation following deregulation is that capital was quasi-fixed. Qualitatively, however, the conclusions noted above are robust to the equilibrium/disequilibrium specifications, although the level of measured negative technical change did differ in a manner consistent with the existence of excess capital capacity in banking.

Large banks experienced less negative technical change than did smaller ones. Larger banks experienced greater deposit growth and had larger branch networks, both of which offer greater opportunities for (relative) cost reductions through more intensive use of factor inputs (e.g., a higher real deposit/branch ratio, which is roughly equivalent to a higher output/capital ratio in banking). As well, technical change at the average branch office was somewhat less negative than that for the entire banking firm. The branch measure reflected the low (but improving) deposit/branch ratio while the firm level measure reflects this influence and plus the negative effect of having too many branches (postderegulation).

While there are substantial and persistent cost differences among similarly sized banks, averaging 24% between banks in the lowest and highest cost quartiles over 1977 to 1988, these differences did not bias the estimates of net technical change. That is, these results were very similar whether all 683 banks in the panel data set were used or whether the estimates were from those banks in the lowest cost quartile. Put differently, the dispersion of technical change from the "best practice" banks to all the others apparently proceeded at a constant enough rate so that the technical change experienced for the set of most efficient banks was essentially the same as that experienced by all banks.[42]

The banks in the panel data set account for $2 trillion out of the $3 trillion of U.S. banking assets. Thus our results regarding negative technical change following deregulation may generalize to the banking industry as a whole. These results, however, conflict with those of other banking studies (Hunter and Timme [1986, 1991]; Evanoff et al. [1990]) as well as with the single factor (labor) productivity series computed by the Bureau of Labor Statistics [1989]. Some reasons for these differences are offered in the text.

In the future, there will be new shocks associated with the rapid pace of interstate merger and acquisition activity expected to occur as barriers to such combinations are removed in most states. This restructuring should lead to a continuation of disequilibrium behavior in banking. On the positive side, current levels of overbranching and overstaffing will fall as deposit growth continues to exceed that of new branches. These improvements, although evident during the 1980s, should accelerate as branching networks of merged/acquired banks are increasingly consolidated in overlapping market areas. The end result, over the next decade, will likely be a more competitive and cost-efficient banking system but one that need not be associated with large positive net technical change during the transition.

Appendix

Means and standard deviations of the variables are shown in Table A1.[43] Parameter estimates are in Table A2.[44] All data are from the Consolidated Report of Condition and Income (Call Reports) except as noted.[45] Major changes in these reports made it advisable to start the study in 1977 rather than earilier. Only banks that were in continuous operation over the 12-year period were used. Banks with assets less than $100 million were excluded; although numerous (over 11,500), they account for a small portion of bank output.

Only banks in states that permitted some form of intrastate branching (limited or statewide) during any year over 1977 to 1988 were chosen for the panel. As of 1988, there were only four unit banking states (Colorado, Illinois, Montana, and Wyoming). Bank mergers were treated as the acquisition of new deposits, assets, and factor inputs by the larger of the institutions involved,[46] and a dummy variable was added to account for the one-year potential cost effects of these (391) mergers. Banks were placed in size classes consistent with their average size over the 12-year period.

Table A1. Summary of data (all 683 panel banks, 1988).

		Mean	Std. Dev.
Cost variables			
TC	Total cost (as a percent of assets)*	8.4%	1.3%
S_L	Labor share of total costs (percent)	18.6	4.5
S_D	Deposit share of total cost (percent)	40.1	11.8
S_p	Purchased funds share of total cost (percent)	19.0	12.9
$S1_D$	Deposit share in variable cost *VC1* (percent)	51.6	14.1
$S1_p$	Purchased funds share in variable cost *VC1* (percent)	24.2	15.4
$S2_p$	Purchased funds share in variable cost *VC2* (percent)	31.5	18.8
Other cost variables of interest			
OC	Operating cost (as a percent of assets)*	3.5	1.1
ID	Interest on deposits (as a percent of assets)*	3.3	0.9
IPF	Interest on purchased funds (as a percent of assets)*	1.6	1.1
Output variables			
DD	Demand deposits (as a percent of assets)*	16.7	5.5
TS	Retail (small) time and savings deposits (as a percent of assets)*	52.9	14.5
RE	Real estate loans (as a percent of assets)*	24.0	10.2
CI	Commercial and industrial loans (as a percent of assets)*	20.8	9.1
IN	Installment loans (as a percent of assets)*	13.4	8.1
Other variables (not in percent)			
B	Number of banking offices	40.3	70.2
P_L	Price of labor, $000 per year, 1988 dollars	27.1	7.4
P_k	Price of physical capital, 1988 dollars (assumed to be proportionate to the per square foot replacement cost of office space in the region, taken from F.W. Dodge)	84.3	11.4
P_D	Interest rate on deposits	4.8	1.4
P_F	Interest rate on purchased funds	6.5	1.2

*Numbers are expressed relative to assets for exposition only. Regressions are based on raw data in $000.

All value data were put into real terms (using the GNP deflator) prior to estimation; real bank costs are dependent on real input prices and real output levels. The five bank deposit and loan output categories chosen reflect 71% to 80% of bank value added during the 1980s (see Berger and Humphrey [1992] for details). When the value of deposits and loans grow, they reflect (a) more checks being written and processed and more loans being made as well as (b) the fact that average deposit and loan balances rise as the prices of the goods purchased with these funds increase over time. The wide range of goods and services purchased out of deposit and loan funds suggested that deflating these balances with the GNP deflator[47] would approximate the unobserved underlying transaction flows for individual banks, flows that are captured for all banks by the BLS in their index of aggregate bank output.

On an aggregate basis, there was a good correspondence between our deflated output series and that of the BLS, which is based on actual physical measurements of checks

Table A2. Parameter estimates.

TREND1		*SHIFT1*	(1977)	(1988)
INTERCEPT	−2.021**	INTERCEPT	0.928	0.869
DD	−0.563**	DD	0.179	0.403**
TS	1.392**	TS	0.612**	−0.075
RE	−0.004	RE	0.217*	0.320**
CI	0.265**	CI	0.443**	0.911**
IN	−0.038	IN	−0.115	−0.169
K	0.042	K	−0.406**	−0.356**
PL	0.931**	PL	−0.181**	−0.140*
PD	0.059**	PD	0.305**	0.924**
PF	0.010**	PF	−0.125*	0.216**
T	−0.037**	M	−0.034	−0.146
M	0.054	DD2	0.134**	0.166**
U	0.481**	TS2	0.197**	0.378**
DD2	0.074**	RE2	0.006	−0.012
TS2	0.115**	CI2	0.038*	0.113**
RE2	0.004**	IN2	0.110**	−0.018
CI2	0.092**	DDTS	−0.143**	−0.128**
IN2	0.079**	DDRE	−0.019	−0.059**
DDTS	0.019*	DDCI	0.051*	0.028*
DDRE	−0.043**	DDIN	−0.029	0.001
DDCI	−0.014*	TSRE	0.026	−0.021
DDIN	0.032**	TSCI	−0.060**	−0.236**
TSRE	0.045**	TSIN	−0.049**	0.040**
TSCI	−0.083**	RECI	0.013	0.056**
TSIN	−0.088**	REIN	−0.019	−0.011
RECI	0.0008**	CIIN	−0.030	0.008
REIN	−0.022**	K2	0.010	0.029*
CIIN	−0.022**	PL2	0.105**	0.077**
K2	0.013	PD2	0.163**	0.155**
PL2	0.017**	PF2	0.065**	0.109**
PD2	0.091**	KPL	0.013	0.022*
PF2	0.099**	KPD	−0.006	−0.011*
KPL	0.006	KPF	−0.006	−0.011*
KPD	−0.003	PLPD	−0.101**	−0.062**
KPF	−0.003	PLPF	−0.004	−0.016
PLPD	−0.005**	PDPF	−0.062**	−0.093**
PLPF	−0.013**	DDK	0.036	−0.021
PDPF	−0.086**	DDPL	−0.005	0.022**
T2	0.004**	DDPD	−0.019*	−0.050**
DDK	0.014**	DDPF	0.025	0.028
DDPL	0.008*	TSK	0.032	0.017
DDPD	−0.035**	TSPL	−0.041**	−0.010
DDPF	0.027**	TSPD	0.097**	0.150**
TSK	−0.061**	TSPF	−0.055**	−0.140**
TSPL	−0.130**	REK	−0.031**	0.035**
TSPD	0.164**	REPL	−0.004	−0.006
TSPF	−0.034**	REPD	−0.001	−0.020**
REK	0.022**	REPF	0.005	0.026**
REPL	−0.017**	CIK	−0.019	0.017
REPD	0.004**	CIPL	−0.043**	−0.044**
REPF	0.013	CIPD	−0.052**	−0.072**
CIK	0.012*	CIPF	0.096**	0.116**
CIPL	0.018**	INK	0.002	−0.015
CIPD	−0.061**	INPL	0.070**	0.005
CIPF	0.043**	INPD	−0.035**	−0.003
INK	0.007	INPF	−0.035**	−0.003

Table A2. Continued.

TREND1		*SHIFT1*	(1977)	(1988)
INPL	0.044**	DDM	0.057	−0.015
INPD	−0.022**	TSM	0.017	0.056
INPF	−0.022**	REM	0.015	−0.000
DDT	−0.009**	CIM	−0.002	−0.028
TST	0.001	INM	−0.058	0.002
RET	−0.003	KM	−0.049	−0.008
CIT	0.000	PLM	0.025	−0.001
INT	0.010**	PDM	−0.013	0.000
DDM	−0.005	PFM	−0.013	0.000
TSM	−0.002			
REM	−0.001			
CIM	−0.002			
INM	0.006			
DDU	0.055**			
TSU	−0.117**			
REU	0.028**			
CIU	−0.021*			
INU	0.013			
KT	0.000			
PLT	0.004**			
PDT	−0.002**			
PFT	−0.002**			
KM	−0.006			
PLM	0.013**			
PDM	−0.006**			
PFM	−0.006**			
TM	−0.002			
TU	0.009**			
R^2 = .996 (data transformed using $\hat{\rho}$ = .87)			R^2 = .983 (data not transformed)	R^2 = .989

INDEX1

D1	0.901**	DDD10	−0.064	RED7	−0.018	IND4	0.038
D2	1.054**	DDD11	−0.065	RED8	−0.041	IND5	0.073
D3	1.381**	DDD12	−0.071	RED9	−0.048	IND6	0.117**
D4	1.516**	TSD1	0.530**	RED10	−0.033	IND7	0.108*
D5	1.628**	TSD2	0.545**	RED11	−0.021	IND8	0.096*
D6	1.542**	TSD3	0.548**	RED12	−0.025	IND9	0.113*
D7	1.311**	TSD4	0.538**	CID1	0.373**	IND10	0.116**
D8	1.362**	TSD5	0.529**	CID2	0.356**	IND11	0.107*
D9	1.266**	TSD6	0.518**	CID3	0.350**	IND12	0.111*
D10	1.216**	TSD7	0.555**	CID4	0.340**	KD1	−0.049
D11	1.275**	TSD8	0.577**	CID5	0.348**	KD2	−0.054
D12	1.288**	TSD9	0.577**	CID6	0.353**	KD3	−0.058
DDD1	0.023	TSD10	0.565**	CID7	0.346**	KD4	−0.057
DDD2	0.037	TSD11	0.539**	CID8	0.360**	KD5	−0.058
DDD3	0.029	TSD12	0.556**	CID9	0.371**	KD6	−0.064
DDD4	0.049	RED1	0.004	CID10	0.376**	KD7	−0.059
DDD5	0.030	RED2	−0.008	CID11	0.388**	KD8	−0.054
DDD6	−0.006	RED3	−0.013	CID12	0.383**	KD9	−0.052
DDD7	−0.022	RED4	−0.011	IND1	0.034	KD10	−0.055
DDD8	−0.030	RED5	−0.021	IND2	0.033	KD11	−0.051
DDD9	−0.052	RED6	−0.013	IND3	0.040	KD12	−0.052

Table A2. Continued.

			INDEX1				
PLD1	0.133**	PFD2	0.038	TSIN	−0.075**	REPD	−0.001
PLD2	0.113**	PFD3	0.077**	RECI	0.009**	REPF	0.007**
PLD3	0.082**	PFD4	0.091**	REIN	−0.018**	CIK	0.005
PLD4	0.061**	PFD5	0.117**	CIIN	−0.035**	CIPL	−0.028**
PLD5	0.040**	PFD6	0.102**	K2	0.019*	CIPD	−0.058**
PLD6	0.056**	PFD7	0.047*	PL2	0.028**	CIPF	0.085**
PLD7	0.084**	PFD8	0.052*	PD2	0.098**	INK	−0.004
PLD8	0.073**	PFD9	0.039	PF2	0.079**	INPL	0.004
PLD9	0.091**	PFD10	0.029	KPL	0.009**	INPD	−0.002
PLD10	0.107**	PFD11	0.031	KPD	−0.005**	INPF	−0.002
PLD11	0.118**	PFD12	0.048*	KPF	−0.005**	DDM	0.008
PLD12	0.104**	M	−0.006	PLPD	−0.024**	TSM	0.006
PDD1	0.860**	U	0.259**	PLPF	−0.004**	REM	−0.001
PDD2	0.849**	DD2	0.001	PDPF	−0.074**	CIM	−0.012**
PDD3	0.840**	TS2	0.144**	DDK	0.023**	INM	0.000
PDD4	0.848**	RE2	0.009**	DDPL	0.028**	DDU	0.008
PDD5	0.844**	CI2	0.101**	DDPD	−0.044**	TSU	−0.070**
PDD6	0.842**	IN2	0.063**	DDPF	0.016**	REU	0.043**
PDD7	0.869**	DDTS	−0.012	TSK	−0.057**	CIU	0.005
PDD8	0.874**	DDRE	−0.049**	TSPL	−0.016**	INU	−0.004
PDD9	0.869**	DDCI	−0.007	TSPD	0.097**	KM	−0.004
PDD10	0.864**	DDIN	0.069**	TSPF	−0.081**	PLM	0.006**
PDD11	0.852**	TSRE	0.037**	REK	0.024**	PDM	−0.003**
PDD12	0.848**	TSCI	−0.071**	REPL	−0.006**	PFM	−0.003**
PFD1	0.007						

$R^2 = .998$
(data transformed using $\hat{\rho} = .88$)

**(*) Parameter significant at 99% (95%) confidence level.

processed, deposit and withdrawal activity, number of new loans made, and trust accounts serviced. Over 1977 to 1986, the BLS series on bank output rose by 40.4%. The aggregate, cost share weighted series for the panel data set showed an increase of 43.8% over the same 10-year period.

Acknowledgment

The opinions expressed do not necessarily reflect those of the Board of Governors, the Reserve Banks, or their staffs. Comments by Allen Berger, Ernst Berndt, Dennis Fixler, Melvyn Fuss, Zvi Griliches, Denis Kessler, Jacques Mairesse, Nancy Rose, Jack Triplett, Frank Wykoff, and other members of the Franco-American Economic Seminar on Productivity Issues in Services at the Micro Level are appreciated, although they bear no responsibility for errors. Research assistance by Alex Wolman has been outstanding.

Notes

1. Purchased funds include federal funds, large denomination (more than $100,000) CDs, Eurodollars, and other liabilities for borrowed money.
2. Interest expenses are not allocated between these three types of deposits in the report forms used.

3. The average market rate in 1977–78 and 1987–88 was 6.25%, while the average deposit rate was 2.6% and 4.2%, respectively. The spread fell from 3.65 to 2.05 percentage points, a reduction of 1.6 percentage points or 44%.
4. The operating cost allocations are for large banks in the *Functional Cost Analysis* reports for 1980, 1984, and 1988 (Board of Governors of the Federal Reserve System).
5. Factor quantities rose as well. The real value of bank capital (book value divided by the GNP deflator) expanded by 68%, while the number of employees rose by 34%.
6. By 1983–84, one-third of all bank loans were tied to a floating rate. The other loans carried a fixed rate, although their average maturity was short—only 15 months.
7. Commercial paper is an effective substitute for bank commercial and industrial (C&I) loans and by 1988 was 76% of the value of these loans.
8. For example, Bank of America has cut staff by 34% and number of branches by 27% (or 350 offices). Manufacturers Hanover has cut staff by 24%. Many other large banks have implemented similar, if less drastic cuts (Bennett [1987]; Weiner [1989]).
9. The standard symmetry and homogeneity of degree 1.0 in input prices restrictions are imposed in estimation, as are the cross-equation coefficient equality restrictions between (1) and (2). It was maintained, because of competitive factor markets and a lack of any strong monopsony power by banks, that the movement from unit to intrastate branching was unlikely to affect input prices. Thus the interaction between $\ln P_k$ and U is not specified, nor is there an interaction term between M and U.
10. The negative sign transforms technical progress into a positive value. As shown in Caves, Christensen, and Swanson [1981], technical change can alternatively be expressed as the common rate of output expansion holding inputs fixed or $-(\partial \ln TC/\partial T)/\Sigma(\partial \ln TC/\partial \ln Q_i)$. If banking experiences constant returns to scale (i.e., $\Sigma(\partial \ln TC/\partial \ln Q_i) = 1.0$), then the two expressions are the same. In our analysis, these two measures typically differ by only 5%, which reflects the range of scale economies or diseconomies found for different sized banks.
11. This follows Caves, Christensen, and Swanson [1981]. Baltagi and Griffin [1988] extended this approach by specifying numerous nonlinear restrictions in order to obtain the same $A(t)$ effect for neutral, nonneutral, and scale augmenting technical change, in a manner similar to that for T in the time trend model above. When the nonlinear restrictions were used here, estimation was quite time-consuming. Importantly, the results were almost identical with or without these restrictions and we elected to stay with (4).
12. Thus $n_1 = \alpha_0$ and the slope parameters are $\Sigma\alpha_{i1} \ln Q_i$, $\Sigma\alpha_{k1} \ln P_k$, and $\alpha_{B1} \ln B$ in period 1 and all following periods.
13. The cross-section model also equals Equations (4) and (5) with α_0 replacing $\Sigma_t^{12} n_t D_t$, $\Sigma_i^5 \alpha_i \ln Q_i$ replacing $\Sigma_i^5 \Sigma_t^{12} \alpha_{it} D_t \ln Q_i$, $\Sigma_k^4 \alpha_k \ln P_k$ replacing $\Sigma_k^4 \Sigma_t^{12} \alpha_{kt} D_t \ln P_k$, and $\alpha_B \ln B$ replacing $\Sigma_t^{12} \alpha_{Bt} D_t \ln B$. In estimation, the variables U and $\ln Q_i U$ were deleted because of collinearity problems in the smaller sample set when each cross section was separately estimated.
14. In *TREND*, all estimated parameters are stable over time, while in *SHIFT* all parameters can change at each point in time. In *INDEX*, the D_t parameters change at each point in time while all other parameters are stable over time (hence the "blend").
15. Such a model, as shown by Berndt and Fuss [1986] for U.S. manufacturing, can significantly affect estimates of productivity (accounting for between one- and three-fifths of this sector's conventionally measured decline in total factor productivity). In banking, capital costs are only 15–20% of total costs, so the effects of excess capital capacity, and other potential capital measurement problems, may be expected to be correspondingly smaller.
16. As shown in Caves, Christensen, and Swanson [1981], technical change in the time trend model ($TREND = -(\partial \ln TC/\partial T)$) becomes

$$TREND1 = \frac{-(\partial \ln VC1/\partial T)}{1.0 - \partial \ln VC1/\partial \ln K}.$$

As well, the index measure becomes

$$INDEX1 = \frac{-(\partial \ln VC1/\partial D_{t+1} - \partial \ln VC1/\partial D_t)}{1.0 - \partial \ln VC1/\partial \ln K}$$

and the shift measure

$$SHIFT1 = \frac{-(\widehat{AC1}^*_{t+1} - \widehat{AC1}_t)/\widehat{AC1}_t}{1.0 - \partial \ln VC1_t/\partial \ln K_t},$$

where $\widehat{AC1}$ is predicted average variable cost from *VC1*. In general, the term in the denominator is .90 and raises the estimate of technical progress in a variable cost function by around 10%.

17. Correspondingly,

$$TREND2 = \frac{-(\partial \ln VC2/\partial T)}{1.0 - \partial \ln VC2/\partial \ln K - \partial \ln VC2/\partial \ln L},$$

$$INDEX2 = \frac{-(\partial \ln VC2/\partial D_{t+1} - \partial \ln VC2/\partial D_t)}{1.0 - \partial \ln VC2/\partial \ln K - \partial \ln VC2/\partial \ln L},$$

and

$$SHIFT2 = \frac{-(\widehat{AC2}^*_{t+1} - \widehat{AC2}_t)/\widehat{AC2}_t}{1.0 - \partial \ln VC2_t/\partial \ln K_t - \partial \ln VC2_t/\partial \ln L_t}.$$

18. The autocorrelation parameter ρ was estimated using the pooled 683 cross section by 12 time-period panel data set, but excluding the relation between $\epsilon_{i,12}$ and $\epsilon_{j,1}$ when the data shifts from an observation on bank i in year 12 to bank j in year 1. The data were transformed using the standard generalized differences approach (see Wonnacott and Wonnacott [1979, pp. 216–218]). The resulting $\hat{\rho}$, a slightly different one for each of the three models, was around .87. The same $\hat{\rho}$ was used for all equations in each system estimated (following Berndt and Savin [1975]).
19. On average, the terms reflecting nonneutral and scale augmenting technical change were offset by the terms reflecting pure or neutral technical change, which showed retrogression.
20. The estimated models were not always well behaved. In some instances, negative predicted marginal costs were observed and the second order condition for cost function convexity was not met. While troubling, these problems are not rare events in multiproduct banking data sets. However, the technical change results seem to be little influenced. For example, the equilibrium *INDEX* model met the second order condition while the disequilibrium *INDEX1* did not but the technical change results are quite similar (see Figure 2b).
21. Similarly, in the Baltagi and Griffin [1988] study of electric utilities, the average yearly rates of technical change for the time trend and (more general) index specifications were almost identical.
22. The alternative definition of net technical change in the time trend models—the common rate of output expansion holding outputs fixed—yielded −1.5%, −1.2%, and −0.9% in place of the three figures shown in column 1 of Table 1. Thus the two alternative definitions give very similar results.
23. The yearly rate of net technical change was −0.6% with firm-specific dummies in *INDEX1* (versus −0.9% in Table 1). The small influence of firm specific effects on these results mirrors that shown below when net technical change is measured using a thick frontier cost function.
24. The price used—new contract cost per square foot of office space in nine U.S. regions—was replaced with furniture, equipment, and structure expenses divided by book value of physical capital. The former, observable only over nine regions, rose by 113% over 1977–88. The latter, observable for each bank, rose by only 19%. Since the GNP deflator rose by 80%, the capital price used is likely a more accurate measure of the replacement cost of capital. Even so, the *INDEX* model results are virtually identical to either capital price.
25. Excluding "other noninterest expenses"—a hodgepodge of data processing expenses paid to subsidiaries (74%), management fees paid to the holding company (17%), and other expenses (9%)—from operating costs altered the *INDEX* model results from −1.4% to −0.7%. Banks are required to name expenses which make up 25% or more of the total; the composition noted above reflects that of 70 of the largest 200 banks which did so.
26. Reflecting the view that deposit service charge revenues offset deposit interest expenses, including these revenues will lower total costs and the (net realized) deposit interest rate paid. This adjustment in the *INDEX* model had almost no effect on the net technical change results. Minimum balance requirements, largely implemented

after deregulation, can raise (idle) deposit balances and implicit revenues, with no increase in costs. This effect is already captured in the model.

27. While the table shows only the results for large and small banks using the disequilibrium model where capital is quasi-fixed, the same divergence by size class is also evident in the other two models. Hunter and Timme [1991] also found that larger banks experienced greater technical change than smaller banks, although their study concerned banks with assets greater than $750 million.
28. The results shown in Table 2 were based on estimates where large and small banks are pooled together. When the data are not pooled and the index model was reestimated using only banks with more than $1 billion in assets, the −0.5% figure for the largest sized banks shown in the table rises slightly to −0.6%, while the average for all of the large banks in the sample is −1.2. Thus, pooling small with large banks or using large banks separately still yields the conclusion that the very largest banks experienced greater net technical change.
29. The branch level results were obtained by estimating all equations with the branching variable (B) included, so the partial derivative of cost with respect to time gives results where B is held constant.
30. The cost differences over eight size classes of banks (from $100 million to over $10 billion in total assets) ranged from 11% to 41%.
31. A very similar relationship exists between high-cost banks and low-profits.
32. An alternative to the thick frontier approach used here would be to specify firm-specific effects using the entire panel data set. This was done and the results, which were very similar, were noted above.
33. This measure was initially used in the regression analysis but had to be dropped because of high collinearity with time.
34. The ratio of deregulated balances to total savings and small time deposit (TS) at all banks was applied to TS balances for the panel data set. The higher interest rate resulting from deregulation was set equal to 1.6 percentage points, which is the actual reduction in the spread between 1977–78 and 1987–88 for the market and deposit rates shown in Figure la (see note 3). Column 1 is the product of deregulated balances and the increased spread, expressed as a percent of total cost.
35. The case of airlines was similar. Competition prior to deregulation took the form of providing more frequent flights for customer convenience, rather than lowering fares, which were regulated (Sickles, Good, and Johnson [1986, p. 145]).
36. During this inflationary period, bank costs would have risen even without deregulation, but not nearly as much as occured with it. Some low-cost time and savings deposits would have continued to shift to MMMFs and been replaced by higher cost bank CDs sold to the MMMFs. The limited check-writing arrangements adopted by MMMFs to control operating costs, which both restricted the number of checks written per month and specified high minimum amounts, would have prevented any significant disintermediation of demand deposits and thereby continued to keep these bank costs low. Since over 80% of the deregulated bank balances were composed of NOW and MMDA deposits, and these experienced the largest rate increases following deregulation, it is clear that the great majority of the negative effects measured above would not have occurred in the absence of deregulation.
37. This is from estimating a third-order translog cost function using total bank costs (all operating and interest expenses). When a (more standard) second order function is used, the rate of estimated net technical change falls to 0.4% annually.
38. The BLS data do not permit a comparison over 1977–1988, the time period of this study.
39. The single factor BLS measure can be alternatively derived by subtracting the log of the BLS labor input index over the six years 1980–1986 (109.2) from their output index (132.3), with 1980 = 100.0, and solving for the implied compound annual growth rate (giving 3.3% a year). In our panel data set, the number of employees rose by 13.8% while the real (GNP "price" deflated) book value of bank capital stock grew by 39.9%. The cost share weighted average growth rate of these labor and capital inputs over 1980–1986 is 20.8% (= 13.8%(.73) + 39.9%(.27)). The implied annual growth in multifactor productivity is thus only 1.5% (= exp((ln 132.3 − ln 120.8)/6) − 1.0).
40. If the 68% of total costs which comprise interest expenses is assumed to experience no technical change, then the annual net technical change associated with total cost in these two studies will only be around 32% as high as the technical change associated with the operating costs, or 0.6% and 0.4%, respectively.
41. Flat or slightly U-shaped average cost curves are evident for banks when total (operating plus interest) costs are used in estimation. However, cost curves based only on operating costs typically yield significant scale economies. This is because larger banks rely more on purchased funds so that operating costs per dollar

of assets (an approximation to average costs) will necessarily fall for this reason alone. When total costs are used, incorporating as they do the substitution of purchased funds for produced deposits, scale economies for large banks typically disappear (see Hunter and Timme [1986, pp. 163–164] for an example).

42. Similar results for all banks and those with the lowest costs were shown to also occur for scale and product mix efficiency measures (Berger and Humphrey [1991]).
43. These means are for the average bank in the data set. They will differ from some values shown in Figure 1 which reflect asset share weighted averages and, in effect, treat all the banks as a single entity.
44. The basic parameters are defined in Table A1. Squared terms, like DD times DD, are expressed as DD2 while an interaction between DD and TS becomes DDTS. The remaining parameter names are self-evident.
45. The flow figures are the annual totals from the year-end (December) Call Report, while the stock figures are averages of the December and June Calls from a current year plus the December report of the immediately preceding year (to avoid biases from growth or decline over the year).
46. This follows the treatment of airline mergers in Sickles, Good, and Johnson [1986, p. 151].
47. No price index for bank output exists for the 1977–88 period.

References

Baily, Martin N., and Robert J. Gordon. (1988). "The Productivity Slowdown, Measurement Issues, and the Explosion of Computer Power." In William Brainard and George Perry (eds.), *Brookings Papers on Economic Activity*, Vol. 2, Washington, DC: The Brookings Institution, 347–420.

Baltagi, Badi H., and James M. Griffin. (1988). "A General Index of Technical Change." *Journal of Political Economy* 96, 20–41.

Bennett, Andrea. (1987). "Banks with Foresight Trim Branches in Initial Volleys of Cost-Cutting War." *American Banker* 1.

Berger, Allen N., and David B. Humphrey. (1991). "The Dominance of Inefficiencies Over Scale and Product Mix Economies in Banking." *Journal of Monetary Economics* 28, 117–148.

Berger, Allen N., and David B. Humphrey. (1992). "Measurement and Efficiency Issues in Commercial Banking." In Zvi Griliches (ed.), *Output Measurements in the Service Sectors*, Studies in Income and Wealth, vol. 56, National Bureau of Economic Research, Chicago, IL: University of Chicago Press, 245–279.

Berndt, Ernst R., and Melvyn A. Fuss. (1986). "Productivity Measurement with Adjustments for Variations in Capacity Utilization and Other Forms of Temporary Equilibrium." *Journal of Econometrics* 33, 7–29.

Berndt, Ernst R., and N. Eugene Savin. (1975). "Estimation and Hypothesis Testing in Singular Equation Systems with Autoregressive Disturbances." *Econometrica* 43, 937–957.

Board of Governors of the Federal Reserve System. (various years). *Functional Cost Analysis*. National Average Report, Commercial Banks, Washington, DC.

Board of Governors of the Federal Reserve System. (various years). *Consolidated Report of Condition and Income*. Washington, DC.

Booz-Allen and Hamilton. (1987). "Managing Delivery System Economics." Bank Branch Profitability Study for the American Bankers Association.

Bureau of Labor Statistics. (1988). U.S. Department of Labor, *Productivity Measures for Selected Industries and Government Services*. Bulletin 2322, 170.

Caves, Douglas W., Laurits R. Christensen, and Joseph A. Swanson. (1981). "Productivity Growth, Scale Economies, and Capacity Utilization in U.S. Railroads, 1955–74." *American Economic Review* 71, 994–1002.

Cooper, Jeanne D. (1989). "Banks' Data Technology Outlays Climb to $20 Billion Annually. *American Banker* 1.

F.W. Dodge Division. (various years). *Dodge Construction Potentials Bulletin*, Summary of Construction Contracts for New Addition and Major Alteration Projects, New York: McGraw Hill.

Evanoff, Douglas D. (1988). "Branch Banking and Service Accessibility." *Journal of Money, Credit and Banking* 20, 191–202.

Evanoff, Douglas, D., Philip R. Israilevich, and Randall C. Merris. (1990). "Relative Efficiency Technical Change, and Economics of Scale for Large Commercial Banks." *Journal of Regulatory Economics* 2, 281–298.

Ferrier, Gary, D., and C.A. Knox Lovell. (1990). "Measuring Cost Efficiency in Banking: Econometric and Linear Programming Evidence." *Journal of Econometrics* 46, 229–245.

Fraser, Donald R., and James W. Kolari. (1985). *The Future of Small Banks in a Deregulated Environment.* Cambridge, MA: Ballinger.

Gollop, Frank M., and Mark J. Roberts. (1983). "Environmental Regulations and Productivity Growth: The Case of Fossil-Fueled Electric Power Generation." *Journal of Political Economy* 91, 654–674.

Hunter, William C., and Stephen G. Timme. (1986). "Technical Change, Organizational Form, and the Structure of Bank Productivity." *Journal of Money, Credit and Banking* 18, 152–166.

Hunter, William C., and Stephen G. Timme. (1991). "Technological Change and Production Economies in Large U.S. Commercial Banking." *Journal of Business* 64, 339–362.

Kopp, Raymond, and V. Kerry Smith. (1983). "An Evaluation of Alternative Indices of Technological Change." *Scandinavian Journal of Economics* 85, 127–146.

Nelson, Randy A. (1986). "Capital Vintage, Time Trends, and Technical Change in the Electric Power Industry." *Southern Economic Journal* 53, 315–332.

Sickles, Robin C., David Good, and Richard L. Johnson. (1986). "Allocative Distortions and the Regulatory Transition of the U.S. Airline Industry." *Journal of Econometrics* 33, 143–163.

Weiner, Lisabeth. (1989). "First Bank May Pare 20% of Jobs as Part of Major Restructuring." *American Banker* Sept., 1.

Wonnacott, Ronald J., and Thomas H. Wonnacott. (1979). *Econometrics*, 2nd ed., New York: Wiley.

The Journal of Productivity Analysis, 4, 35–50 (1993)

Economies of Scale and Scope in French Commercial Banking Industry

MICHEL DIETSCH
F-67082 Université Robert Schuman-Strasbourg

Abstract

This paper presents estimations of economies of scale and scope in the French banking industry. Using a translog model of bank costs, the paper demonstrates the existence of economies of scale for French banks, particularly in what concerns operating costs. Economies of scale are observed in all classes of bank size. Results also suggest that cost subadditivity exists in the French banking industry.

1. Introduction

The main object of this paper is to present estimations of economies of scale and scope in the French banking industry. In the past few years, major changes in financial products and markets have strengthened competition between banks which compels bank managers to focus on cost control more than in the past and regulatory authorities to introduce the efficiency of banking industry as an objective of regulation besides the traditional objectives of safety and soundness. In the French banking industry, major questions about bank costs and competition are, Do "universal" large banks suffer from costs advantages or disadvantages as compared with the small or medium-sized specialized banks? Are small local and regional banks competitively viable? Will they have to merge in the next few years? And, more generally, will the unification of the European market in 1992 produce major changes in the structure of banking industry?

Previous study of economies of scale (Levy-Garboua and Renard [1977]) has shown that French banks exhibit economies of scale. Unfortunately, like all studies of economies of scale made in the 1970s, that study was limited in important respects essentially because of the incapacity of the functional form used (Cobb-Douglas) to capture the multiproduct nature of the banking firm and to fit a cost curve which could take a U shape over the full range of banks. The present study avoids these pitfalls by using a translog cost function for the estimation of the form of the cost curve.

Before presenting the translog model of bank costs we shall describe in the first section the structure by size of costs for French banks. The object of this section is to present some results which can have some importance for the explanation of the results of the econometric study. The second section discusses the question of the choice of bank outputs and then presents estimations of economies of scale and economies of scope in French banking industry. The results presented here differ noticeably from the results generally obtained in American banking industry, particularly in what concerns the existence of economies of scale.

2. Structure of Costs in French Banking

This study uses an exhaustive basis coming from the Commission Bancaire which supervises the banks in France. Data include all commercial depository banks. The object of this section is to describe the structure of activities and cost in French commercial and mutual depository banks. There are two main categories of depository banks in France: the *banques AFB* (which have a status of corporation and are members of the Association Française des Banques) and the *banques mutualistes* (which are mutual banks and must not be confused with savings and loans). In this section, we present no other depository institutions, particularly savings and loans, because of the peculiarities of their status and of their activities in France. In other words, in this section the focus is on the activities and costs of these banks which are or tend to be "universal." They represent the main part of the French banking system.

The contents of this section are constructed largely in the same way as in Humphrey (1985) in order to allow a comparison between American and French banking industries. Two criteria of analysis are used to study the composition of bank assets and liabilities and their costs of production: the size of the bank, measured by the number of employees, and the "category" to which it belongs.

To determine the "category" to which a bank belongs, we used the classification proposed by the Commission Bancaire (1986). This classification is the result of the application of a principal components analysis using about 100 financial ratios of French banks. Each class is composed of the closest banks in terms of the structure of assets and liabilities. For instance, the class denominated "three largest banks" groups the more universal banks in nature. Five categories of banks are distinguished:

1. The three largest (in terms of assets size) French commerical banks
2. National banks, which are universal AFB-banks of medium-large size
3. Regional banks, which are universal AFB-banks of medium-size located in regional banking markets
4. Local AFB banks which restrict their activities to a local market
5. Mutual banks, which are small- or medium-sized banks located in local and regional banking markets and are affiliated to a network of mutual banks.

As we will see in what follows, the combination of these two criteria, size and category, is useful to explain the form of the cost curve in the banking sector. We will consider total cost and its components: operating costs and financial costs. When possible, we will relate costs to products. But, in absence of a functional cost analysis data basis, this attempt is quite limited.

2.1. Total Costs of Production, Bank Size, and Bank Category

Total cost is the sum of operating costs and financial costs. Operating costs comprise all expenses related to the use of physical and labor factors. Financial costs comprise interests paid to all depositors and to other creditors of the bank (interests on bonds and on interbank loans).

The ratio of total cost per borrowed funds (borrowed funds include deposits, long-term debt and interbank loans) measures the total cost per dollar borrowed by the banks. This cost is decreasing with the size of banks at a decreasing rate, as shown in table 1. This shape of the ratio was valid in 1989 as well as in the early 1980s. Table 1 shows equally that the ratio is lower in large banks and in mutual banks. Consequently, there is no "apparent" U-shaped cost curve concerning total costs in French banking industry.

It is interesting to observe the structure of total banking costs. On the average, financial costs represent about 45% of total costs and operating costs represent about 55%. Interests on deposits represent an average 51% of the total of interests, interests paid on interbank liabilities represent about 40% of all interets paid by banks and interests on long-term debt 9%.

Table 1 shows that operating costs vary more with the bank size than do interest costs. The ratio of "frais généraux" (overheads, which regroup main variable costs except interest: labor costs, corporate taxes, and other operating expenses) per borrowed franc tends to decrease with the size of banks. This ratio is more than two times lower in the largest banks than in the smallest ones. Other operating costs (depreciation charges) tend also to decrease with bank size, but their amount is small compared to frais généraux. This result is similar to those obtained for U.S. banking industry.

In contrast, the ratio of interests paid per borrowed franc tends to show a U-shaped cost curve. The interest costs per franc are higher in the smallest and largest banks. This observation is valid for 1989 as well as for 1980. The ratio of other financial costs (provisions and losses on loans) per borrowed franc is higher too in small banks and in the largest ones.

Table 1. Percentage total, financial and operating costs per borrowed franc 1980 and 1989.

Employee-Size Classes*	Total**		Operating		Wages		Physical Capital		Provisions		Interests	
	80	89	80	89	80	89	80	89	80	89	80	89
Under 50	14.7	16.0	6.6	6.6	4.1	3.7	2.0	2.6	1.7	1.6	6.4	5.8
50–250	14.0	12.3	6.6	5.7	4.4	3.1	1.8	2.2	1.2	1.4	6.2	5.2
250–500	13.4	10.8	6.7	4.4	4.5	2.4	1.8	1.6	1.0	1.1	5.8	5.3
500–750	13.4	10.6	5.3	4.0	4.7	2.3	1.3	1.5	1.1	1.0	5.9	5.6
750–1000	14.0	10.4	6.9	3.8	4.8	2.0	1.3	1.5	1.2	1.0	5.8	5.7
1000–1500	14.3	11.2	6.9	4.2	4.7	2.4	1.9	1.5	1.3	1.2	5.6	5.8
1500–10,000	13.5	11.2	5.7	4.0	4.0	2.4	1.3	1.3	1.2	0.9	6.6	6.3
> 10,000	13.2	11.3	4.1	2.9	2.9	1.8	0.9	0.9	1.0	1.3	8.1	7.1
Total	14.1	11.5	6.4	4.6	4.2	2.5	1.8	1.7	1.3	1.3	6.4	5.6
Category of banks												
Mutual	NA	10.5	NA	3.8	NA	2.0	NA	1.5	NA	2.4	NA	5.7
Local	14.6	14.0	6.7	6.2	4.3	3.4	2.0	2.4	1.6	1.0	6.3	5.4
Regional	13.9	12.2	6.9	5.6	4.6	3.4	1.9	1.9	1.1	1.3	6.0	5.3
National	13.4	11.8	5.4	4.1	3.9	2.7	1.2	1.2	1.1	1.2	6.9	6.6
3 Largest	12.9	11.3	3.5	2.9	2.4	1.8	0.9	0.9	1.1	0.9	8.3	7.1
Total	14.1	11.5	6.4	4.6	4.2	2.5	1.8	1.7	1.3	1.7	6.4	5.6

*AFB banks only. Source: Commission Bancaire.

**Total cost is the sum of all operating costs, provision, and interests.

All costs are expressed in percentage of borrowed funds: deposits + CDS + interbank habilities + bonds and other long-term debt.

The specific form of the total cost curve can then be explained. As we saw before, the total cost tends to decrease with a decreasing rate when the size of banks increases. This decrease is mainly the result of the decrease in operating costs with bank size. Even if interest costs are higher in the largest banks, this increase in interest is insufficient to produce an increase of total costs in this class of banks. For that reason, total cost function is not U-shaped.

An analysis by category of banks shows that the level of operating costs is higher in local and regional AFB banks and lower in the largest banks. But the former seems to have cheaper source of funds, as their lower level of interests per borrowed franc tends to show.

The decrease of level in operating costs with bank size cannot be explained by a decrease of the level of wages (including taxes). The ratio of wages per worker seems quite independent of size (Table 1). The decrease in operating costs is the result of the decrease in other operating expenses. These expenses regroup variable costs associated with the use of capital equipment such as office rentals and such expenses as advertising and transport. They also include the rentals coming from lease financing, which are important especially concerning computer and telecommunication equipment. To evaluate more precisely the cost of physical capital used in banking production we regrouped all the expenses tied with the use of different kinds of equipment in banking, particularly depreciation and rentals of lease financing. The ratio of these expenses per borrowed franc appears in Table 1 (cost of physical capital). Observation shows that this cost diminishes regularly with size. It is about three times higher in the smallest banks than in the largest ones. This decrease is, in great part, the result of the decrease of expenses and other operating expenses related to computer and telecommunication equipment use. Moreover, the ratio of depreciation charges per borrowed franc is decreasing with bank size. These elements of observation allow us to conclude that the decrease of operating costs with size in French banking are essentially the result of the decrease of expenses associated with the use of equipment.

2.2. *Costs per Factor*

Here the analysis concerns essentially the financial costs. We calculate average costs by dividing interests on each source of funds by the amount in francs of this source. Results appear in Table 2. Three main sources of funds are distinguished: deposits (including CDs), interbank liabilities, and long-term debt. Table 2 shows in addition the average cost of labor measured by the ratio of wages per worker.

Some remarks can be made about the variation of average financial costs with the size of banks. First, the average cost of deposits is (for all kinds of deposits) lower in medium-sized mutual banks than in the smallest and largest AFB banks. This result comes from the difference of behavior between banks concerning the collect of deposits we noted previously. Mutual banks hold more demand deposits than other banks. Note that the function of average cost of deposit tends to have a U-shaped form. Second, the average cost of interbank market funds has in contrast an inverse U-shaped form. The cost is higher in medium-sized banks than in small and large banks. The large banks have a better access to the interbank market than other banks. As shown, the small banks are creditors on this market. Third, largest banks have a greater access to the financial market too, but they borrowed

Table 2. Average cost of alternative sources of funds and average cost of labor in French banking.

	Deposits		Interbank		Long term		Wages/Worker	
Employee-Size*	1980	1987	1980	1987	1980	1987	1980	1987
Under 50	6.1	4.7	10.0	8.6	11.2	8.8	12.9	19.0
50–250	6.0	3.6	9.7	8.5	10.4	9.1	12.8	20.5
250–500	5.6	2.8	9.9	9.2	11.1	5.7	12.6	21.0
500–750	5.4	2.1	10.0	8.5	12.0	6.6	13.2	21.3
750–1000	4.7	1.9	11.7	9.3	11.6	6.9	13.8	20.8
1000–1500	5.3	2.2	8.2	8.6	12.0	8.0	12.0	21.3
1500–10,000	5.5	3.7	9.2	8.8	11.2	11.1	13.3	21.7
> 10,000	6.0	3.7	11.3	7.5	11.5	9.1	13.2	22.5
Total	5.8	2.9	9.7	8.6	11.5	7.5	12.9	21.5
Categories								
Mutual	NA	2.6	NA	9.1	NA	6.7	NA	21.1
Local	5.9	3.7	10.6	7.8	11.3	8.8	12.8	21.5
Regional	5.5	3.2	8.0	7.0	11.3	10.6	12.7	21.8
National	5.7	3.5	9.4	7.8	11.8	10.5	13.4	23.3
3 Largest	6.0	3.7	11.3	7.5	11.8	9.2	13.2	22.5
Total	5.8	2.9	9.7	8.6	11.5	7.5	12.9	21.5

*1980 AFB banks only. Source: Commission Bancaire.

more on this market in a period (beginning of 1980s) of higher loans rate. It is the reason why their average cost of long-term debt is higher than that of medium-sized banks. We can see that long-term debt of mutual banks is relatively cheap. This result can be explained by the fact that they borrow minor funds on the financial market and more from their associates via the center of the federation.

It is interesting to note that the structure of interest costs is very different among bank size classes and among categories of banks. The share of interests paid to owners of interbank market securities is more important than the one of interest on deposits in each class or category of banks. But, in the medium-sized (mutual) banks, the share of interest paid on deposits is particularly high, compared to the share which is observed in other classes. This result comes from the decentralized organization of these banks. The share of deposit interest is relatively high in small banks. The reason is that these banks, as we have shown, are relatively specialized in deposits, while national and large banks have a more diversified structure of liabilities.

Finally, the observation of the ratio of wages per worker (table 2) shows that the average cost of labor tends to increase slightly with size. This result can be explained by different factors: location, qualification of workers, differences in the structure of activities.

3. Estimation of Economies of Scale and Economies of Scope

3.1. The Definition of Bank Outputs and Inputs

As is well known, one of the main problems to solve before estimating the form of bank costs function is to define bank outputs and to choose measures for them. The conventional literature on the banking firm offers two separate views of bank production which have been used in most of the previous cost studies. Recent developments of the theory of financial intermediation and of the theory of dynamic contracts offer a new view of bank activities which can be used for solving those problems.

3.1.1. Real approach versus portfolio approach. One of the most frequently used methods for choosing bank outputs is to consider a bank as a firm which looks like other firms, which is like a non-financial firm. In this approach bank assets, and especially bank loans, are treated as outputs and liabilities or deposits as inputs. This method comes from an approach of the banking firm which finds its roots in the traditional theory of the firm. In this approach (Klein [1971]; Sealey and Lindley [1877]; Sealey [1980]) the banking firm "transforms" deposits into loans in the same way as automobile industry transforms steel and other raw materials into cars. But this approach neglects fundamental functions of banks, that is to say to offer deposits the value of which is certain for the wealth holders and to provide depositors with transaction and liquidity services.

Alternatively, in a portfolio approach of the banking firm, the function of banks is to hold simultaneously assets and deposits (Pyle [1972]; Hart and Jaffee [1977]; Santomero [1984], for instance). Following this approach, deposits as well as assets must be defined as bank products. In the portfolio approach of the banking firm the inputs are labor force and real capital used in the conception and application of assets and liabilities diversification and assets-liabilites management which allow to transform the risk and liquidity characteristics of funds intermediated by the bank.

These two approaches of the bank products have roots in two separate theories of the banking firm which, in short, do not focus on the specificity or "specialness" of the banking firm. But banks are not firms like other firms. They do not hold the same portfolio as do other non-bank financial intermediaries. However, recent developments of the theory of dynamic long-term contracts as well as recent developments of the theory of financial intermediation offer methods to choose bank outputs and inputs which take into account the "special" characteristics and the optimality of bank products.

3.1.2. Optimal bank contracts and intermediation. The traditional reason for considering banks as "special" comes from the liquidity of bank deposits. Wealth holders can think that banks offer a guarantee that deposits can be withdrawn on demand or at short notice at a fixed price. In this way, banks are supposed to provide liquidity insurance to the owners of the deposits. In the old literature (Edgeworth [1888]), the provision of these liquidity services relied on the fact that only a small fraction of depositors withdrew funds. It was then possible to estimate that fraction and to satisfy liquidity needs while making illiquid investments. Another conventional view is that the bank deposits are "special" because they offer an access to the guarantee of the lender of last resort. In these views deposits are the specific products of the bank.

Recent literature shows that the existence of the bank itself can be explained as an optimal response to individual choices of consumption. As showed by Diamond and Dybvig [1983], in writing demand deposit contracts and holding illiquid assets the bank satisfies the desires of consumers of improving the terms under which they can withdraw funds for consumption. Diamond [1984] gives another explanation of the existence of a banking firm. When the information structure is characterized by difficulties in observing the returns of the projects of the borrowers, the optimal financial arrangment is a risky debt contract, under which the banks monitor the borrowers in the event of default. In order to economize on monitoring costs it is optimal for a competitive financial firm to assume a function of intermediation between savers and borrowers. The banking firm appears as an endogenous response to the incentive problems which exist in the relationships between savers and borrowers because of asymmetries of information. The nature of the banking firm is the following: it contracts with borrowers and monitors them, the bank transforms the characteristics of assets for ultimate wealth holders—in short, it transforms loans into deposits—and it holds a diversified portfolio, what permits it to assume credit risks and also eliminates the need for depositors to monitor the bank as it allows the bank to offer liquidity to depositors. In such an explanation of the existence and of the economic role of banks, the deposits as well as the loans and other investments of banks must be chosen as the bank products.

3.2. The Model

3.2.1. The translog functional form. In a multiproduct industry, the analysis of competition between firms is more complex than in a monoproduct context. The minimum average cost function is not a sufficient concept. Observation of this cost does not allow to conclude that the structure of the industry is competitive. As shown by recent development of industrial organization theory (Baumol, Panzar, and Willig [1982]), the relevant concept is the one of cost subadditivity. Cost subadditivity exists if the cost of production of a vector of products by a firm is lower than the cost of production of the same vector by a set if independent firms, given the price of real factors and the state of technology. In this context, competition may exist between firms with very different scales of operation and very different output mix combinations. Cost subadditivity may come either from economies of scope (which result from joint production and related cost complementarities of products) or from ray scale economies (which come from differences of scale for firms using the same product mix). Recently, Berger, Hanweck, and Humphrey [1987] have developed this approach to take account of changes of scale and product combination simultaneously.

To estimate economies of scale and economies of scope, we use a translog cost function. This model allows to enter the various banking products as separate variables and, contrary to the Cobb-Douglas or CES functions, does not impose homogeneity and constant elasticity of substitution of the production function. The translog function permits us to determine the characteristics of the underlying production function simply by analyzing the form of the related cost function, provided that costs are a positive homogeneous, nondecreasing, concave function of factor prices and that the firm minimizes costs. The translog cost function is a general representation of the cost function:

$$\ln C = \alpha_0 + \sum_{i=1}^{4} \alpha_i \ln y_i + \sum_{j=1}^{3} \beta_j \ln p_j + \frac{1}{2} \sum_{i=1}^{4} \sum_{k=1}^{4} \sigma_{ik} \ln y_i \ln y_k$$

$$+ \frac{1}{2} \sum_{j=1}^{4} \sum_{h=1}^{4} \gamma_{jh} \ln p_j \ln p_h + \sum_{i=1}^{4} \sum_{j=1}^{3} \delta_{ij} \ln y_i \ln p_j, \tag{1}$$

with C = total cost of banking production including operating costs and interest paid

y_i = quantity of ith output

x_j = quantity of jth factor input

p_j = price of the jth factor input

The function must be linearly homogeneous in input prices, concave in p_j and increasing in y_i and p_j. The standard homogenous conditions are imposed through the use of the following restrictions:

$$\Sigma \beta j = 1, \tag{1a}$$

$$\Sigma \delta\, ij = 0, \tag{1b}$$

$$\Sigma \gamma\, jh = 0. \tag{1c}$$

Global economies of scale, that is to say economies of scale resulting from an increase in all outputs by a common factor k, are measured by differentiating equation (1) with respect to all products y_i:

$$e_g = \frac{d \ln C}{k} = \sum_{i=1}^{4} \frac{\partial \ln C}{\partial \ln y_i}$$

$$e_G = \sum_{i=1}^{4} \alpha_i + \sum_{i=1}^{4} \sum_{j=1}^{4} \sigma_{ik} \ln y_k + \sum_{i=1}^{3} \sum_{j=1}^{3} \delta_{ij} \ln p_j \tag{2}$$

where

$$e_G \begin{cases} <1 & \text{implies economies of scale,} \\ 1 & \text{implies constant costs,} \\ >1 & \text{implies diseconomies of scale.} \end{cases}$$

In this formulation e_G is made a function of differences in output mix as well as differences of factor prices.

Scope economies exist if the costs of the joint production are less than the costs of separate production of the same level of output for each product. Scope economies are determined, following Panzar and Willig [1977], by the condition

$$\frac{\partial^2 C}{\partial y_i \, \partial y_k} < 0, \qquad i = k.$$

In terms of translog function, this condition can be approximated to

$$\alpha_i \, \alpha_k + \sigma_{ik} < 0, \tag{3}$$

where the products y_i and the input prices p_j have been normalized at their sample means.

3.2.2. The measure of bank outputs. As we showed before, one difficult issue in analyzing economies of scale is the choice of bank outputs. Another difficulty is to measure these products. Two approaches are used in the literature: production and intermediation. According to the production approach, banks produce transactions on accounts by processing loans and deposits and using labor and real capital. In this approach, output is measured in terms of number of transactions or number of accounts or in terms of franc volume of accounts. Detailed data on accounts are not available in the data basis we use. For this practical reason we cannot try to estimate a production approach cost function using number of accounts. Here, we only use the amounts in francs of the different banking products. According to the intermediation approach, the banks which assume intermediation function offer different kinds of assets, using different kinds of liabilities. They produce amounts in francs of loans and other assets. While in the production approach, costs are operating costs only, in the intermediation approach, costs include financial costs as well as operating costs. This approach is consistent with the fact that the objective of banks is to minimize total costs, not only operating costs.

The consensus emerging from the necessity to recognize the multiproduct nature of the banking firm brought several authors to measure bank output as a vector of a small number of deposit and loan categories. For instance, Berger, Hanweck, and Humphrey (1987) used a vector of five products: demand deposits, time and saving deposits, real estate loans, commercial loans, and installment loans. As we saw before, one reason for using loans and deposits as bank products comes from the nature of the financial intermediation function. In depository institutions like banks, lending implies automatically that costs will be incurrred to raise deposits or other resources for funding loans. Alternatively, the costs for managing the payment system and raising deposits include costs entailed by finding efficient use for these funds. But, in recent years the activities of banks on the money and financial markets have been growing in an impressive manner, so that, beside their "classical" intermediation function, banks have reinforced their role in equilibrating money and financial markets by making arbitrages. These new developments of bank activities induce us not to restrict the analysis to loans and deposits, even if these products consume most of labor force and real capital of banks. Consequently, in this study, we consider four bank outputs:

1. Deposits: total of demand, term, and saving deposits
2. Loans: total of loans to firms and households
3. Long-term securities (assets)
4. Interbank market activity (interbank liabilities net of interbank assets).

We restrict in some cases the specification of the cost function to the first three categories of products.

3.2.3. Factor inputs and factor input prices. Three factors of production are identified in this study: labor services, real capital, and financial capital. For each of them, the factor price is determined by dividing the total cost associated to the holding or the use of the factor by a measure of the real quantity of the factor or a proxy. Following this method the price of labor services is measured by the average wage in each bank: ratio of wages (including taxes) divided by number of employees. The cost of financial capital is determined by the average cost of borrowed funds measured by the ratio of interests paid per borrowed franc (the denominator of this ratio includes all borrowed funds: deposits, long-term debt, and interbank liabilities). It is more difficult to obtain an unambiguous measure of the price of real physical capital. In some studies the price of capital is measured by the rental cost of office space in geographical areas of the bank. This type of measure is inadequate in the case of French banks. We constructed instead a crude measure of price of capital by dividing the sum of physical capital expenses by the franc value of borrowed funds (the same variable as the one used in the definition of cost of financial capital).

Other variables have been included in the analysis to take account of some specificities of banks: degree of risk exposure, structure of deposits, and structure of loans.

3.3. The Results

We present now the estimation of economies of scale and economies of scope in French banking using the translog model. The interest of these estimates is that the estimation uses an exhaustive data basis. Former study of economies of scale in French banks used a Cobb-Douglas function (Levy-Garboua and Renard [1977]). They concluded that there are economies of scale for French banks during the 1970s. It is a well-known fact that this methodology does not allow to test for economies of scope. The Muldur and Sassenou study (1992) (in this volume) uses also a translog model. The sample of medium-sized banks used in this study differs from ours.

The translog model was estimated using the 1987 data for 343 French banks. While more specialized banks—such as investment banks or money market banks—were not included in the descriptive analysis of bank activities and costs in the previous section, these banks were included in the data basis used for the estimation. The methodological reason is to test for the existence of economies of scale taking into account banks which are more specialized in the production of one product, for instance, long-term loans or trading in market securities. However, all banks collect deposits, so that the more specialized banks also produce (at lower level) the other banking products. The y_i are then everywhere different from zero.

To estimate the cost function, we used extra information coming from a set of derived cost share equations. Indeed, it is possible to derive a system of cost share equations directly from the translog cost function (Shephard's lemma). This is done by differentiating (1) with respect to p_j:

$$\frac{\partial \ln C}{\partial \ln p_j} = \frac{p_j x_j}{C} = S_j = \beta_j + \sum_{h=1}^{4} \gamma_{jk} \ln p_h + \sum_{i=1}^{3} \delta_{ij} \ln y_i, \tag{4}$$

where x_j is the quantity of factor j and S_j is the cost share of the jth input.

The use of the cost share equations permits us to gain additional degrees of freedom by estimating the cost function and the derived cost share equations using iterative Zellner seemingly unrelated regressions (SUR). This system is estimated together with the cross equations restrictions implied by Shephard's lemma and the linear homogeneity restrictions in prices (1a) to (1c) which establish consistency between the production function and the dual cost system. Since the sum of the cost shares must be equal to one, one equation is redundant. The equation deleted is the cost share of capital equation. From this system we can derive estimates of economies of scope and global economies of scale.

We estimate four alternative cost systems specifications. The first two utilize total costs (financial plus operating costs) as dependent variable. They differ only by the number of products considered. One model considers only three products: loans, deposits, and investment in long-term securities. It excludes net interbank activity. The other model includes the latter product in addition to the other three. The last two models utilize operating costs only as dependent variable. They differ by the number of products as in the precedent case. In addition, when we used the fourth product, we included in the total cost function financial costs net of financial revenues on interbank loans.

3.3.1. Translog cost function estimates. Table 3a highlights the results of the SUR estimation of the cost system when total cost is the dependent variable. Table 3b shows the results when operating costs is the dependent variable. On the whole the explanatory power of the model is quite good. Most of the estimates are statistically significant and carry the expected signs. Moreover, the joint significance of the large majority of the cross-product terms suggests that more restrictive production functions (such as the Cobb-Douglas or CES function) would be rejected. Many of these terms are significantly different from zero, probably by reason of economies of scope or diseconomies of scope.

After imposing linear homogeneity on costs with respect to prices, we tested whether the cost function could be explained by homothetic technologies. CES production function requires that each parameters σ_{ij} (homogeneity) and δ_{ij} be restricted to zero and that $\beta_1/\beta_2 = \gamma_{13}/\gamma_{23}$ and $\beta_1/\beta_3 = \gamma_{12}/\gamma_{23}$ (Denny and Fuss [1977]). Cobb-Douglas function requires in addition that the parameters γ_{ij} be equal to zero. *F*-tests of the cost function all rejected these restricted conditions at the 1% level. That implies that cost complementarities between products probably exist.

The esimated cost system is monotonic and concave. The estimated own-price elasticities of demand for inputs are negative. The estimates fit well for both the total cost equation (Table 3a) and the operating cost equation (Table 3b). Estimates were made also for each class of size. We use these results for calculus of economies of scale and economies of scope.

Table 3a. Parameter estimates from the cost system (total cost, four products).

Variable	Coefficient	t of Student
Constante	−3.567	−18.170
DEPOSITS	0.084	2.328
LOANS	0.600	7.658
SECURITIES	0.037	2.146
INTERBANK	0.519	9.023
WAGES	1.420	13.722
CAPITAL	0.338	3.560
INTEREST	−0.758	−18.220
$DEPOSITS^2$	0.072	12.462
$LOANS^2$	0.068	8.366
$SECURITIES^2$	0.007	4.885
$INTERBANK^2$	0.008	12.239
$WAGES^2$	−0.421	−25.703
$CAPITAL^2$	0.210	14.719
$INTEREST^2$	0.0002	0.053
DEP*LOA	−0.073	−8.054
DEP*SEC	−0.025	−5.759
DEP*INTBK	0.007	−0.823
LOA*SEC	0.043	6.979
LOA*INTBK	−0.137	−8.896
SEC*INTBK	−0.027	−6.116
DEP*WAGES	0.063	4.941
DEP*CAP	0.126	1.103
DEP*INTER	−0.076	−8.503
LOA*WAGES	−0.233	−12.556
LOA*CAP	0.047	3.020
LOA*INTER	0.186	18.618
SEC*WAGES	0.007	0.941
SEC*CAP	0.003	1.558
SEC*INTER	−0.007	−1.846
INTBK*WAGES	0.026	3.901
INTBK*CAP	0.056	−11.077
INTBK*INTER	−0.082	−1.846
WAGES*CAP	0.211	6.916
WAGES*INTER	0.632	100.884
CAP*INTER	−0.633	−51.809
BRANCHES	−0.102	−9.774
RISK	−0.011	−0.925

$R^2 = 0.885$.
345 French banks. Source: Commission Bancaire.
Year 1987.

Table 3b. Parameter estimates from the cost system (total cost, three products).

Variable	Coefficient	t of Student
Constante	−3.385	−16.971
DEPOSITS	0.085	0.751
LOANS	0.873	8.771
SECURITIES	0.121	3.002
WAGES	0.195	3.899
CAPITAL	0.804	16.033
DEPOSITS^2	0.195	6.319
LOANS^2	0.033	6.508
SECURITIES^2	0.009	2.424
WAGES^2	0.116	25.190
CAPITAL^2	0.115	13.122
DEP*LOA	−0.212	−4.220
DEP*SEC	−0.083	−5.613
LOA*SEC	−0.062	−5.496
DEP*WAGES	−0.169	−10.748
DEP*CAP	0.169	10.758
LOA*WAGES	0.134	10.639
LOA*CAP	−0.141	−13.324
SEC*WAGES	0.006	5.072
SEC*CAP	−0.028	−5.409
WAGES*CAP	0.025	0.718
BRANCHES	−0.123	−8.562
RISK	−0.119	−0.139

$R^2 = 0.982$.
345 French banks. Source: Commission Bancaire.
Year 1987.

3.3.2. Economies of scale. Economies of scale are observed in all classes of banks size whatever the form of the esimated cost model (Table 4a for total cost and Table 4b for operating costs). Three classes of size were considered here: small banks with no more than 1000 employees, medium banks with between 1000 and 10,000 employees, and large banks (the three largest banks) with more than 10,000 employees. Overall economies of scale are calculated using equation (2) holding factor prices and output constant at the sample means of each class. The value of e_g in each class and in the whole sample is lower than 1, which indicates economies of scale. In addition, economies of scale increase with the size of banks. Because large banks are more universal than medium- or small-sized banks, these scale economy results suggest that universal banking possess a cost advantage compared with specialized banking. On the basis of these results concerning economies of scale competitive viability of small banks is not guaranteed for the future.

Results show that economies of scale exist for operating costs as well as for total costs. But the effect of scale seems lower when considering total costs than when we consider operating costs only in the case of the three products model excluding interbank activity

Table 4a. Estimation of economies of scale (total cost).

	Three-Products Model	Four-Products Model
Small banks	0.973	0.991
Medium banks	0.950	0.979
Three largest banks	0.899	0.946
Total	0.953	0.961

All coefficients significant at the 1% level.

Table 4b. Estimation of economies of scale (operating costs only)

	Three-Products Model	Four-Products Model
Small banks	0.959	0.938
Medium banks	0.893	0.924
Three largest banks	0.914	0.906
Total	0.963	0.927

All coefficients significant at the 1% level.

which does not require so much capital and labor as other productions as well as in the case of the four-products model. The fact that economies of scale are lower when we consider total costs than when we consider operating costs only demonstrates that use of financial capital, probably because of a long history of interest rates regulation, does not favor the extraction of economies of scale, especially for the medium and large banks. Conversely, use of labor and capital could favor the extraction of such economies. In the case of the four-products model, we observe that, as in the case of the three-products model, economies of scale are higher when we consider operating costs only.

Otherwise, calculus (not shown here) of specific economies of scale associated with each product demonstrates that there are such economies of each product considered in this study. In particular, the results demonstrate that there exist specific economies of scale when the estimated cost system retain only operating costs as dependent variable. Moreover, one counterintuitive empirical result relates to the coefficient on the variable "branches." The coefficient is negative, which seems surprising. The explanation comes from the fact that large banks have the highest number of branches. As shown before, these banks have lower unit costs per france.

3.3.3. Cost complementarities. One advantage of the translog cost system is that it permits estimation of any cost complementarities which might appear among the different products in a multiproduct firm. Equation (3) gives the formula employed for the calculus of economies of scope. The results appear in Table 5 for operating costs. We retain here for comments the values of the estimation including operating costs only for the reason that cost complementarities are more related to the use of labor and physical capital than to the use of financial capital. (As we argued before, regulation of interest rates hindered the extraction of economies of scale in French banking industry.)

Table 5. Estimation of economies of scope (operating costs).

	Three-Products Model	Four-Products Model
Deposits-loans	−0.058	−0.055
Deposits-investments	0.018	0.009
Deposits-interbank	—	0.012
Loans-investments	0.093	−0.028
Loans-interbank	—	−0.066
Investments-interbank	—	−0.134

All coefficients significant at the 1% level.

Results show that cost complementarities exist for the following couples of products:

- Deposits and loans
- Investment of long-term securities and activity on interbank market
- Loans and activity on interbank market

These results are consistent with the realistic approach of the conduct of a universal bank. These results reinforce the conclusion that universal banks have no cost disadvantage compared with specialized banks. Note that if we take into account financial costs, most of these economies disappear. That can be due to the regulation of interest rates.

Our results suggest that cost subadditivity exists in French banking industry, particularly when the cost system estimation retains the operating cost as the dependent variable. In that case, indeed, the results show simultaneous product specific economies of scale and economies of scope. However, economies of scope are not observed at a high level for all combinations of products. There is no strong cost complementarity. In addition, even if product scale economies of scale appear when we estimate the system with total costs as the dependent variable, we do not find in that case economies of scope because of the apparent inverse link between cost of liabilities and size of banks.

4. Conclusion

The results of this study tend to demonstrate the existence of economies of scale and economies of scope in the French banking industry. But these economies are not large in magnitude. These results are different from those obtained by American studies which generally verify the absence of economies of scale for large banks in the United States. It would be interesting to know if the differences of results might be explained by some differences between the two banking industries, such as differences in the organization of banks, differences in the qualification of employees, difference in the concentration level, and so on. For the French banking industry, our results tend to demonstrate that universal banking gives an advantage compared to specialization and that competition between banks in the future must be analyzed on the ground of imperfect competition theory.

Acknowledgment

The research was supported by the Conseil National du Crédit and the research department of the Association Française des Banques. Data and computer time were provided by the Commission Bancaire. This paper has benefited from a presentation at the Franco-American Economic Seminar on Productivity Issues in Services at the Micro Level–National Bureau of Economic Research, July 1990. The author thanks Allan Berger, Melvyn Fuss, Jack Triplett and two anonymous referees for helpful comments. Errors are the responsibility of the author alone.

References

Baumol, W., J. Panzar, and R. Willig. (1982). *Contestable Markets and the Theory of Industry Structure.* New York: Harcourt Brace Javanovich.

Berger, A., G. Hanweck, and D. Humphrey. (1987). "Competitive Viability in Banking: Scale, Scope and Product Mix Economies." *Journal of Monetary Economics* 20, 501–520.

Commission Bancaire. (1986–1990). Rapports annuels.

Denny, M., and M. Fuss. (1977). "The USE of Approximation Analysis to Test for Separability and the Existence of Consistent Aggregates." *American Economic Review* 67, 404–418.

Diamond, D. (1984). "Financial Intermediation as Delegated Monitoring." *Review of Economic Studies* 51, 353–414.

Diamond, D., and P. Dybvig. (1983). "Bank Runs, Deposit Insurance and Liquidity." *Journal of Political Economy* 91, 401–419.

Dietsch, M. (1988). "Economies d'Échelle et Économies d'Envergure dans les Banques de Dépôts Françaises." Miméo, Institute d'Etudes Politiques de Strasbourg.

Edgeworth, F. (1988). "The Mathematical Theory of Banking." *Journal of the Royal Statistical Society* 51, 113–127.

Hart, O., and D. Jaffee. (1974). "On the Application of Portfolio Theory to Depository Financial Intermediaries." *Review of Economic Studies* 41, 129–174.

Humphrey, D. (1985). "Costs and Scale Economies in Bank Intermediation." In R. Aspinwall and R. Eisenbeis (eds.), *Handbook for Banking Strategy.* New York: Wiley, pp. 745–783.

Klein, M. (1977). "A Theory of the Banking Firm." *Journal of Money, Credit and Banking* May, 205–218.

Levy-Garboua, V. and F. Renard. (1977). "Structure et Rentabilité des Banques." *Banque* Sept./Oct.

Pyle, D. (1972). "On the Theory of Financial Intermediation." *Journal of Finance* June, 734–747.

Santomero, A. (1984). "Modeling the Banking Firm." *Journal of Money, Credit and Banking* June, 567–602.

Sealey, C. (1980). "Deposit Rate Setting, Risk Aversions, and the Theory of Depository Financial Intermediaries." *Journal of Finance* Dec. 1139–1154.

Sealey, C., and J. Lindley. (1977). "Inputs, Outputs and a Theory of Production and Cost at Depository Financial Institutions." *Journal of Finance* 32, 1251–1266.

The Journal of Productivity Analysis, 4, 51–72 (1993)

Economies of Scale and Scope in French Banking and Savings Institutions

UGUR MULDUR
Commission of the European Communities, Bruxelles, Belgique

MOHAMED SASSENOU
Department of Economic and Financial Analysis, Caisse des Dépôts et Consignations, Paris, France

Abstract

In this study, we analyze the costs incurred by French commercial banks and savings institutions. One of the main distinctions between these two types of financial entities concerns management costs, which are higher for commercial bank demand deposits than for the savings institutions' tax-free "livret A" passbook accounts. Taking this differential into consideration by constructing separate models based on different principles, we find that the average overall and operating costs of the savings institutions are half those of commercial banks. As regards operating costs, small savings institutions enjoy a significant cost advantage over small commercial banks, but this cost advantage is smaller when one compares the performance of large savings institutions to the large banks. The results of our econometric estimates suggest a possible explanation, as we find increasing returns to scale for the banks and diminishing returns for the savings institutions. The value of the returns-to-scope parameter at the mean point appears to indicate a complementarity between certain pairs of outputs. Therefore, ouptut diversification appears to have a positive impact on cost levels for both savings institutions and commercial banks; while institution size, measured by the total assets, has a different impact in these two industries.

1. Introduction

This article is part of a series of studies on the structure and performance of French financial institutions being conducted by the Caisse des Dépôts et Consignations. Following our earlier papers on the subject (Muldur and Teston [1988]; Muldur and Sassenou [1989]; Sassenou [1990]; Muldur, Sassenou, and Heringer [1990]), our aim here is to use two models—Cobb-Douglas and translog—to estimate parameters from data on costs and output of banks and savings institutions. For each of these institutional categories, the results obtained provide a distinctive evaluation of economies of scale and scope. Our findings do not, however, allow systematic interinstitutional comparisons. Overall the approaches used are different.

We adopt the production approach for the savings institutions (caisses d'épargne) and the intermediation approach for the commercial banks. This a priori choice was dictated by the difference in status between the two types of entities. Unlike the banks, the savings institutions do not turn their deposits into credits, since they hand over the funds gathered to a central institution—Caisse des Dépôts or Sociétés Régionales de Financement (SOREFIs)—in exchange for a commission. We therefore regard deposits as outputs for the savings institutions and as inputs for the commercial banks. This precludes comparing the orders of magnitude of the estimated parameters. In addition these two specifications cannot be compared in terms of quality of fit. The Cobb-Douglas function supposes a single aggregated output—the balance-sheet total—while the translog function takes into account three disaggregated outputs.

We begin by surveying the changes in regulations governing the two industries. We then present the theoretical framework, the sample, and variables. The econometric results are presented in the last section.

2. Historical Survey of the Regulation of French Banks and Savings Institutions

Government has long played a major role in the French banking system. In the aftermath of the First World War, the French government strictly defined the role assigned to each banking institution in the economy. The 1945 Banking Act created five circuits specializing in the supply of subsidized loans to distinct economic activities such as agriculture, public housing, exports, industrial development, and local development. The activities of commercial (i.e., deposit) banks and investment banks were separated, and their diversification and intensive development were prohibited by a series of regulatory and economic measures including quantitative credit controls, rediscounting policy, and a ban on the opening of branches.

Within this compartmentalized system, savings institutions were assigned the task of collecting private savings, mainly by offering in return a capped, tax—exempt savings product, the "livret A" savings passbook. The savings institutions were not free to use the funds collected through the "livret A" at their discretion. By law, these funds were centralized in the hands of a public institution, the Caisse des Dépôts et Consignations (CDC), which was given responsibility for using the funds—initially to finance the public-sector debt and subsequently to finance public housing and local government.

France began introducing reforms to deregulate the banking system in 1965–1967. The regulatory frontiers between deposit banks and investment banks were made more flexible. Commercial banks were allowed to open branches throughout the country. To compensate the free services on checking accounts (for example, no charge for checks), a system of nonremuneration of demand deposits was instituted.

Commercial banks took advantage of deregulation to compete for liquid savings on a large scale, expanding their share of that market from 24% in 1965 to 53% in 1970. They rapidly enlarged their branch networks, practically doubling the total number of bank branches from 4849 in 1967 to 9543 in 1975. Savings institutions, on the other hand, expanded their branch networks rather more slowly, from 5127 in 1967 to 5977 in 1975.

To offset the advantages of these two categories of banks, the authorities allowed savings institutions to offer their customers uncapped, non-tax-exempt savings products ("livret B" in 1966), unit trusts or mutual funds (1967), certificates of deposit, personal loans (1969), and subsidized loans (1972). On the other hand, permission to open checking accounts was withheld from the savings institutions; all they could do was to offer customers access to credits and standing orders.

The process of turning the savings institutions into banks has advanced steadily over the past two decades. New regulations have allowed the savings institutions to distribute current accounts and charge cards (from 1978) and foreign exchange services (1980). At the same time, savings institutions gradually lost their monopoly of tax-exempt savings accounts. A variety of new special-regime, high-interest tax-exempt savings accounts (PEL 1970, LEP 1982, CODEVI 1983, LEE 1984, PEP 1989) began to be distributed by all financial institutions, banks as well as savings institutions. The steady abolition of regulatory barriers between activities has brought these two categories of banking institution into increasingly direct competition, chiefly in the field of retail banking.

A fresh wave of deregulation swept the French banking system in the mid-1980s. The 1984 Banking Act now applies to all French financial institutions. It acknowledges the savings institutions as full-fledged credit institutions, subjecting them to the same prudential standards as the commercial banks.[1] Practically all regulatory restrictions on the development and diversification of French commercial banks were abolished in the second half of the 1980s with the exception of those concerning remuneration of demand deposits and charges for written means of payment. The leading French banks are turning into German-style "universal" banks and are active in all banking, financial and insurance markets (Muldur [1990]).

French savings institutions still have a monopoly of the "livret A." But that monopoly, increasingly challenged by the commercial banks, is also under threat from financial innovations and the effects of recent European Community banking regulations, which will allow foreign European banks to offer interest-bearing demand deposits. Having already considerably broadened their product range, the savings institutions are now preparing to cope with the probable decline of "livret A" balances in the 1990s. After many years as single-product firms, the savings institutions are swiftly evolving into multiproduct ones. But, for the time being, this diversification is confined essentially to retail banking.

3. The Structure of the Banking and Savings Institutions Industries

Despite the gradual unification of regulations governing commercial banks and savings institutions, the two industries still have very different structures. In 1987, there were 394 banks totaling 9939 branches. French commercial banks are either publicly or privately owned companies. They are also multiproduct firms. With the exception of tax-exempt savings, they enjoy a dominant position in all banking and financial markets (see Table 1).

Table 1. Commercial banks and savings institutions' market shares in 1987.

Markets	Commercial Banks (%)	Savings Institutions (%)	Mutual and Cooperative Banks (%)	Other Institutions (%)*
All lending (except interbank)	47.7	4.5	21.7	26.1
Securities	79.4	2.5	17	1
Demand deposits	40.8	9.3	24.2	25.7
Term deposits	63.8	6.7	15.2	14.3
Savings accounts	6.3	48	18.1	27.6
Certificates of deposit	52.4	0.5	33.5	13.6
Unit trusts or mutual funds	48	10.8**	24	17.2

*"Crédit Municipal," financial companies, specialized financial institutions.
**Including CDC and Post Office.

The French banking industry is one of the most concentrated in Europe. The largest three banks (BNP, Credit Lyonnais, and Société Génerale) hold 42% of total assets in France, against 26.5% in the United Kingdom and 21.5% in Germany. These three leading French banks account for 54.5% of total deposits and 49.2% of total lending. The French savings industry is the most unconcentrated in Europe after than of Germany. In France, the three leading savings institutions have 14.8% of the market, while the top 10 institutions account for only 25% (Muldur, Sassenou, and Heringer [1990]).

The average size of a French commercial bank is five times greater than that of a savings institution. The total assets of the largest bank are 20 times greater than those of the leading savings institution. But concentration in the savings industry gathered pace in the late 1980s. The total number of these mutual institutions fell from than 460 in 1985 to 224 at the beginning of 1990. Mergers are set to continue until the total number falls to around 30. See Table 2.

The relatively low degree of concentration among savings institutions is due essentially to a specific regulation governing their territorial scope. Each savings institution is confined within its home region, and inside each region each savings institution is assigned a narrow geographic development area. This regulation helps to account for the extremely small size of savings institutions relative to the banks.

The structural differences observed between the two industries may be accounted for either by the different regulations governing their activities, or by their relative cost efficiencies. Given the trend to uniformity in their respective regulations and the increasing interpenetration of their markets, the problem of cost efficiency and, consequently, the nature of returns to scale prevalent in each industry are becoming daily more important in France.

Moreover, in order to investigate the impact of deregulation on the financial services industries, we must determine the cost structure of each industry. Section 4 seeks to build simple models suited to the specific characteristics of these two financial services industries in order to estimate the reciprocal importance of economies of scale and scope.

4. The Choice of Models for the French Commercial Banking and Savings Institution Industries

With the accelerating process of bank deregulation in all the advanced countries, there is a growing body of research in Europe that attempts to estimate economies of scale and scope in financial intermediaries. In the past, most studies of this type were conducted

Table 2. Characteristics of banks and savings institutions in 1987.

	Savings Institutions	Banks
Average size (total assets in FRF billion)	2.4	12.2
Number of institutions	365	394
Total number of branches	4356	9939
Number of branches per institution	12	25
Number of accounts per institution	106×10^3	108×10^3
Number of employees per institution	81	651

in the United States. In the embryonic stages, the pioneering works of Gramley [1954], Alhadeff [1954] and Horvitz [1962] stand out. From the mid-1960s onwards, the "BBM" methodological approach developed by Benston [1965a, 1965b] and Bell and Murphey [1967] dominated the literature on banking costs for more than 15 years. These studies estimated banking cost functions using Cobb-Douglas technologies. Much of the debate focused on the definition of bank output.

In the 1980s, a new "BHH" model replaced the primitive Cobb-Douglas specification with a more generalized functional form. Benston, Hanweck, and Humphrey (1982) estimated a translog function with a composite output index. Authors adopting this model found a significant U-shaped average cost curve, casting considerable doubt on the earlier Cobb-Douglas specification. But the very small optimal size resulting from these studies failed to account for the presence of large firms in the banking sector. Researchers therefore directed their investigations to the existence of economies of scope.

Many authors explicitly or implicitly take into account the multiproduct nature of the firm by using the theory developed by Baumol, Panzar, and Willig [1982]. But the evidence on cost complementarity in banking has yet to be proven. Most of the previous studies have either proxied the multiple output by creating a composite commodity using scalar indices, or treated the bank as a collection of separate production functions. While certain investigators such as Murray and White [1983] and Gilligan, Smirlock, and Marshall [1984] reported significant economies of scope, others such as Benston et al. [1983] and Le Compte and Smith [1985] found no significant economies of scope.

The methodology used in these studies, encompasses two major debates. The first concerns the economic definition of a banking firm, which involves determining the choice and specification of the outputs and inputs of banking activity. The second concerns the choice of prevalent technologies in the banking industry.

4.1. Definition of a Bank

In the production approach, banks are defined as providers of services that can be divided into major groups: those that generate funds (demand deposits, term deposits, etc.) and those that apply funds (such as commercial lending, hire purchase and securities transactions).

From the point of view of costs, all these services are regarded as distinct outputs and the unit of measure generally used is the number of accounts. Logic demands that interest expenses necessarily be excluded from the scope of the analysis; consequently, a bank's operating costs alone are taken into account. This definition of a bank, adopted by advocates of the production approach, therefore implicitly regards a bank's asset management as independent of its liabilities management, which itself gives rise to the production of other services.

Moreover, a bank wishing to improve its competitiveness would seek to minimize all its costs regardless of its output level. It is therefore difficult to justify the elimination of financial costs from the scope of analysis. According to the relatively more recent intermediation approach, a financial institution's production process necessarily entails financial intermediation, that is, the taking or borrowing of funds, which are then lent or invested. This model treats deposits, labor and capital as inputs (Mester [1987]). The explained variable therefore includes both financial and operating costs.

Before choosing between the production and intermediation approaches, which are based on different concepts of banking activity, we have sought to define clearly the inputs and outputs of French financial institutions. This required an understanding of the banking production process, in particular the role of deposits. As Frish [1965] points out, a production process has two dimensions, one technical (transformation process), the other economic (creation of outputs of higher value than the inputs). The application of this approach to banking, as proposed by Sealey and Lindley [1977] for the United States, is useful in determining outputs and inputs.

Viewed from this angle, commercial bank production can be treated as a multistage process. In the first stage, the French banks produce a series of payment services and exchange them for the use of customer deposits. In France, demand deposits are not interest-bearing and payment services are free—a sort of barter arrangement between banks and their customers. In a second step, the commercial banks transform these deposits, with the aid of other inputs—labor and capital—into outputs such as loans and securities.

From the point of view of the French system, the intermediation approach seems better suited to the commercial banks. Given the relative importance of interbank activity, interest costs are substantial, representing on average more than 60% of their total costs. Moreover, practically all their deposit-taking services, and particularly their payment services, are provided free of charge, and no interest is paid on checking accounts. The commercial banks treat deposits as if they were an input and seek to offset the cost of deposit-taking services via fee cross-subsidization. For these reasons, we have decided to treat the funds taken or borrowed by the commercial banks as raw material and to analyze all costs, both operating and financial.

On the other hand, this approach is not suited to the analysis of French savings institutions, in particular because of the different role of deposits there. The savings institutions do not transform deposits into commercial loans. With the exception of savings institutions in the Alsace-Moselle region and a quota set by the Minjoz Act, savings institutions centralize their deposits with the SOREFIs (regional credit institutions) and the CDC, which are responsible for reallocating them to public projects defined by Parliament. The fixed interest paid by savings banks to depositors is identical to that applied by the CDC in remuneration of the funds held centrally by it. But the CDC also pays savings institutions a fixed commission representing on average more than a third of their net bank income. In that sense, deposits represent an output for the savings institutions, allowing them to write off their deposit-taking costs and generating a profit margin. In this case, we obviously cannot regard deposits as raw materials or inputs. Rather, they are an input that procures a major share of the institutions' income.

The same goes for lending by the savings institutions. Such loans are generally funded in full by the SOREFIs, which also bear the corresponding interest rate risk. Savings institutions are paid by the SOREFIs for expenses incurred in their intermediation activities with customers. In a sense, the French savings institutions operate as a tax-exempt deposit-taking and loan-placement network, without directly engaging in bank transformation. Consequently, each product or financial service represents a distinct output for the savings institutions. As a result, where the savings institutions are concerned, we have decided to adopt the classic production approach, in which deposits are treated as outputs and the unit of measurement generally used is the number of credit or debit accounts.[2]

By choosing two different models, each suited to the specific characteristics of each industry, we are aware of having reduced the scope for a systematic comparison of our findings. But the opposite choice would have meant deliberately ignoring the basic distinctiveness of the two branches. The ultimate aim of banking industry models, however, should be to describe as realistically as possible the actual behavior of different types of banks with regard to costs and risk.

4.2. Prevalent Technologies

The second major debate in the literature (see Gilbert [1984] and Muldur and Teston [1989] for a complete survey) concerns the choice of prevalent technologies in the banking industries. The abandonment of the Cobb-Douglas specification in the 1970s was due to the model's technical inability to deal with variable returns to scale and the complementarity of banking costs. While the translogarithmic functions help solve these problems, they raise new ones of their own. First, the translog function is not defined at point 0. Second, aggregation of the different outputs into a single composite index raises difficulties, and as Kim [1985] has suggested, the cost function needs to be as disaggregated as possible in order to obtain the most reliable estimates. A third problem relates to output endogeneity, a prospect made more likely by the wave of deregulation in recent years.

More recently, Clark [1984] and Kilbride, McDonald, and Miller [1986] specified a special version of a generalized functional form in which all variables underwent a Box-Cox transformation. The authors claimed that a primitive Cobb-Douglas specification of banking costs captures the data adequately. Lawrence [1989] demonstrated that the rejection of their postulated flexible functional form is a necessary, but not sufficient, condition to justify a Cobb-Douglas specification in the banking industry, and found that the sufficient conditions are usually not met.

In the absence of detailed studies on the best choice of specification for French banks and savings institutions, we have decided to test both Cobb-Douglas and translog technologies for the two industries. To answer the question of the existence of returns to scale, as in our first study (Muldur and Sassenou [1989]), we consider a model based on a Cobb-Douglas cost function. To determine the existence of returns to scope, we adopt a more complex model based on a translog function. The forms and underlying hypotheses of the two models are outlined below.

4.3. Cobb-Douglas Model

The model is written as

$$C = AQ^{\alpha} S^{\beta} h^{\lambda} S^{\delta} w_1^{\alpha 1} w_2^{\alpha 2},$$

where

C = costs
Q = output
h = homogenization variable
S = structural variable
w_1 = unit cost of labor
w_2 = unit cost of physical capital

C's elasticity relative to Q constitutes the returns-to-scale parameter. For the cost variable, depending on the approach selected, we consider either operating costs or total costs. For output, we treat total assets and the number of accounts respectively for banks and savings institutions as a homogeneous product. The homogenization variable will be proxied by the number of branches for banks, and by the average deposit per account for savings institutions.

Preliminary studies revealed the dependence of savings institutions on the "livret A," accounting for approximately 70% of deposits, whereas for the deposit-taking banks demand deposits occupy a preponderant position. As our structural variables, we therefore take the share of "livret A" in total deposits for savings institutions, and the share of demand deposits in capital committed for banks.

4.4. Translog Model

Depending on whether we are looking at banks or savings institutions, we use a different variable to measure costs and the number of inputs. For banks, we consider the total cost of production factors as an endogenous variable. For explanatory variables, in addition to the price of production factors, we include the main financial products offered by French financial institutions. The production factors included are labor, physical capital (such as buildings and equipment), and financial capital. The latter consists of all the financial resources available to the financial institution demand deposits, term deposits, and interbank and bond borrowings.

For savings institutions, we initially treat operating costs as an endogenous variable. Because we have adopted the production approach for these institutions, only unit labor costs and unit physical capital costs are included in the list of explanatory variables with pure denoted w_i. Particularly, interest paid by the savings institutions in order to hold these deposits is not included as an explanatory variable.

We define the following outputs denoted y_i:

- For banks: commercial loans, interbank loans, securities transactions
- For savings institutions: customer deposits, commercial loans, securities and cash management transactions

The cost function is in the form

$$\text{Log } C = \alpha_0 + \sum_{i=1}^{3} \alpha_i \text{ Log } y_i + \sum_{j=1}^{3} \beta_j \text{ Log } w_j$$

$$+ \frac{1}{2} \sum_{i=1}^{3} \sum_{j=1}^{3} \delta_{ij} \text{ Log } y_i \text{ Log } y_j + \frac{1}{2} \sum_{j=1}^{3} \sum_{k=1}^{3} \gamma_{jk} \text{ Log } w_j \text{ Log } w_k$$

$$+ \sum_{i=1}^{3} \sum_{j=1}^{3} \varepsilon_{ij} \text{ Log } y_i \text{ Log } w_j + u,$$

$$S_j = \beta_j + \sum_{i=1}^{3} \gamma_{ij} \text{ Log } w_i + \sum_{i=1}^{k} \varepsilon_{ij} \text{ Log } y_j + e_{\dot{\gamma}}.$$

with the following constraints:

Symmetry $\quad \delta_{ij} = \delta_{ji}, \quad \gamma_{ij} = \gamma_{ji},$ (3)

Homogeneity $\quad \sum_k \gamma_{ik} = 0, \quad \sum_j \varepsilon_{ij} = 0, \quad \sum_j \beta_j = 1.$

The returns-to-scale parameter is defined with this translog function by

$$\text{SL} = \left[\sum_{i=1}^{k} (\alpha_i + \sum_{j=1}^{k} \delta_{ij} \text{ Log } y_j + \sum_{l=1}^{3} \varepsilon_{il} \text{ Log } w_l) \right]^{-1}. \quad (4)$$

To evaluate the economies of scope between two outputs, we use the finding of Baumol, Panzar, and Willig [1982]: "the complementarity of outputs is a sufficient condition for the existence of economies of scope,"[3] namely

$$\frac{\partial^2(C)}{\partial y_i \partial y_j} < 0,$$

which, with the translog function, gives

$$\delta_{ij} + \left(\alpha_i + \sum_{j=1}^{k} \delta_{ij} \text{ Log } y_j + \sum_{j=1}^{3} \varepsilon_{ij} \text{ Log } w_j \right) \left(\alpha_j + \sum_{j=1}^{k} \delta_{ij} \text{ Log } y_j + \sum_{j=1}^{3} \varepsilon_{ij} \text{ Log } w_j \right) < 0. \quad (5)$$

As in most econometric studies, we evaluate (4) and (5) at the mean point ($y_j = 1$, $w_i = 1$), which gives[4]

$$SL = \left[\sum_{i=1}^{k} \alpha_i \right]^{-1}, \tag{4'}$$

$$SC = \alpha_i \alpha_j + \delta_{ij} < 0. \tag{5'}$$

4.5. Variables and Samples

Initially, we have two samples covering 129 commercial banks and 282 savings institutions. To arrive at homogeneous populations, we have eliminated investment banks and financial companies from the first sample, keeping only 59 deposit and lending banks with branch networks. In the case of savings institutions, we have selected only 247 entities unaffected by merger operations. While this effort to build homogeneous files has enabled us to pare the number of homogenization variables to a minimum, it has reduced the size of our samples. Nevertheless, the commercial banks remaining in our final sample account for 54% of total assets of all banks, and for 73% of the total number of bank branches in metropolitan France. The corresponding representativity ratios for the savings institutions are approximately 86% and 84%.

To test for the existence of a "size effect" for scale, we have distinguished three sizes, defined in Table 3, for each category of financial institution.

4.5.1. Cost factors: labor, physical capital, financial capital.

Labor. In the absence of precise data as to the aggregate number of hours worked by personnel, we have selected the number of employees as our labor variable. This variable is designated by the letter L.

Physical capital. Bank balance sheets contain information on fixed assets and leasing operations. We used income statements to assess the stock of depreciated capital. The definition of physical capital adopted here is K = net fixed asset + stock of depreciated capital + leasing transactions.

Table 3. Sizes of financial institutions.

	Banks			Savings Institutions		
Size	Assets (FRF billion)	Number	Relative Importance of Assets in (%)	Assets (FRF billion)	Number	Relative Importance of Assets (%)
Small	< 5	17	2.89	< 1.5	113	13.39
Intermediate	5 ≤ × < 20	23	11.00	1.5 ≤ × < 4	92	30.83
Large	> 20	19	86.11	> 4	42	55.77

Financial capital. By financial capital we refer to credit accounts held by the Treasury, banks, financial companies, and customers; certificates of deposit; bonds; securities transactions; equity loans; and securities given or received as collateral.

As the balance sheet provides an instantaneous (year-end) picture of the bank's assets, it does not reflect variations in financial capital items over the year. To take these movements partially into account, we have based our calculation of financial capital on the average values at the start and end of the period, rather than the end-of-period position only. F denotes this computed value of financial capital.

4.5.2. Factor costs.

Cost of labor (CT) = personnel expenses.

Costs of physical capital (CK) = purchases of good and services from outside suppliers
+ appropriations to depreciation of fixed assets rented out.

Cost of financial capital (CF) = expenses incurred in cash management and interbank operations
+ expenses incurred in customer transactions
+ interest paid out on bonds
+ interest on equity loans and long-term securities.

The total cost of factors (CTF) is the sum of the three costs defined above:

$$CTF = CT + CK + CF.$$

Unit costs of factors are defined as

$$W_1 = \frac{\text{personnel expenses}}{\text{number of employees}} = \frac{CT}{L}.$$

$$W_2 = \frac{\text{cost of physical capital}}{\text{physical capital}} = \frac{CK}{K}.$$

$$W_3 = \frac{\text{cost of financial capital}}{\text{financial capital}} = \frac{CF}{F}.$$

4.5.3. Outputs. Bank outputs comprise customer loans, interbank loans, and securities transactions. For the savings institutions, we have selected three representative aggregates: customer deposits, customers loans, and securities and cash management transactions. Table 4 shows the mean and standard deviation of each output's share of total assets.

Table 4. Outputs as a percentage of total assets: mean and standard deviation (%).

	Commercial Banks						Savings Institutions		
	Loans to Customers								
Samples	Consumer Loans	Loans to Unincorporated Business	Corporate Loans	Interbank Loans	Securities Transactions	Off-Balance Sheet Items	Deposits	Loans	Capital Market Transactions
Total sample	11.1	4.6	21.4	22.6	1.6	1.4	69.6	26.5	1.965
	(4.9)	(6.6)	(15.3)	(15.3)	(2.8)	(3.3)	(8.1)	(6.8)	(6.6)
Size 1	10.3	4.7	28.4	22.5	1.0	2.1	69.0	26.8	2.3
	(14.9)	(7.8)	(20.5)	(19.7)	(2.4)	(5.0)	(9.9)	(7.7)	(9.8)
Size 2	10.7	3.1	(16.8)	23.4	1.2	1.0	69.2	27.1	1.6
	(17.5)	(15.0)	(11.4)	(14.1)	1.6	(1.5)	(6.4)	(6.2)	(1.6)
Size 3	4.5	2.4	13.9	(30.8)	2.2	1.6	72.1	24.4	1.9
	(15.2)	(3.4)	13.6	(15.4)	3.3	1.4	(5.5)	(4.9)	(1.8)

5. Main Findings

5.1. Cobb-Douglas Specification

5.1.1. In French banks, savings on operating costs are offset by diseconomies on financial costs. To estimate the Cobb-Douglas specification, we take into account total assets, unit factor costs, homogenization variables, and structural variables. This estimation, however, fails to yield statistically more accurate results than the specification where the explanatory variables include only total assets and the number of branches (see comments on Table 5). We have therefore adopted the latter specification as a base model for banks.

Table 5. Estimates of a Cobb-Douglas type cost function* (59 Retail banks 1987).

		Basic Model		Model Taking Account of Number of Branches		
	Sample	Log (*TA*)	R^2 (SSE)	Log (*TA*)	Log (*Na*)	R^2 (SSE)
Total cost	Sample	0.98	0.97	0.97	0.01	0.97
	Total 59 banks	(0.02)	(0.24)	(0.03)	(0.03)	(0.24)
	Size 1	1.23	0.84	1.21	0.03	0.84
	17 banks	(0.14)	(0.30)	(0.16)	(0.08)	(0.30)
	Size 2	1.13	0.83	1.11	-0.07	0.85
	23 banks	(0.11)	(0.20)	(0.11)	(0.04)	(0.17)
	Size 3	1.05	0.96	0.99	0.05	0.97
	19 banks	(0.05)	(0.22)	(0.06)	(0.03)	(0.20)
	Total sample	0.84	0.87	0.69	0.27	0.94
		(0.04)	(0.49)	(0.04)	(0.04)	(0.35)
Operating costs	Size 1	1.08	0.63	0.87	0.27	0.74
		(0.21)	(0.46)	(0.20)	(0.11)	(0.40)
	Size 2	0.63	0.20	0.70	0.26	0.43
		(0.27)	(0.48)	(0.24)	(0.09)	(0.41)
	Size 3	0.97	0.79	0.65	0.33	0.97
		(0.12)	(0.55)	(0.06)	(0.03)	(0.22)

*We began by estimating the Cobb-Douglas specification with all the explanatory variables listed in the text. The results of the Fischer test, which allows a comparison between two interlocking models, led us to accept the model that explains total cost by the total-assets variable alone. For the model in which operating costs are an endogenous variable, the number of branches constitutes a statistically significant explanatory variable along with the total assets. The estimations performed on the entire sample yield

$$\text{Log (total cost)} = \underset{(0.03)}{0.96}\ \text{Log}\ (TA) + \underset{(0.03)}{0.04}\ \text{Log}\ (Na) - \underset{(0.03)}{0.02}\ \text{Log}\ (TVD) + \underset{(0.11)}{0.12}\ \text{Log}\ (w_1) + \underset{(0.11)}{0.12}\ (w_2)$$

and

$$\text{Log (operating costs)} = \underset{(0.05)}{0.72}\ \text{Log}\ (TA) + \underset{(0.04)}{0.27}\ \text{Log}\ (Na) + \underset{(0.04)}{0.07}\ (TDV) + \underset{(0.07)}{0.03}\ \text{Log}\ (w_1) + \underset{(0.04)}{0.08}\ \text{Log}\ (w_2)$$

where TA = total assets
Na = number of branches
w_1 = unit cost of labor
w_2 = unit cost of physical capital

Estimated standard deviations are given in parentheses.

In the case of banks, returns to scale are practically constant when all banking costs are taken into account. Conversely, the hypothesis of increasing returns to scale is verified when the analysis is framed in terms of operating costs. Introducing the "number of branches" variable into the model does not affect the elasticity of total cost to assets. Because the elasticity of total cost to the number of branches is nonsignificant, we obtain a different result for the specification when we treat operating costs as an endogenous variable. Economies of scale relative to this cost component become more significant.

These results show that the economies of scale obtained on operating costs are more than offset by diseconomies on financial costs (Table 5). Some American authors have observed a similar phenomenon case in the U.S. banking industry. Hunter and Timme [1986] show, for example, that the inclusion of interest cost eliminates the economies of scale observed for operating costs. Benston, Hanweck, and Humphrey [1982] find that the economies of scale for operating costs observed for branch state banks are also reduced when interest cost is included and the SCEs lose their significance for the larger banks.

On the other hand, in some countries like Belgium this relation is reversed. Pacolet [1989], finds that the diseconomies of scale for operating costs observed for the largest Belgian banks are compensated by the economies in the interest costs. These differences may be explained by the effects of each country's distinctive regulatory system.

We do indeed find decreasing returns to scale when financial costs are taken into account as an explanatory variable. Our econometric tests lead us to reject the two extreme hypotheses: strict complementarity or infinite substitutability between operating costs and interest costs. The intermediate hypothesis of unit substitutability between these two components of total cost appears more appropriate. This suggests that commercial banks are not bound by a rigid breakdown of these two cost components, nor are they in a position to combine them at will (Muldur and Sassenou [1989]).

The interest-cost diseconomies result from the differences in financing procedures according to the size of French banks. The larger banks raise far more of their capital on the interbank and bond markets than do the small deposit-taking banks and regional banks, which prefer to collect cheap resources such as non-interest-bearing demand deposits (see Table 6).

5.1.2. Total impact of an increase in the number of branches. We have also sought to assess the impact of an increase in the number of branches on banking costs. Here, we observed a beneficial effect on financial costs and a negative effect on operating costs. Our tests show that a high number of branches tends to reduce the financial costs of liabilities by increasing the proportion of demand deposits in capital committed. The combined impact of the two effects on total cost depends on the relative share of each component. Using the cost structure set out in Table 7, we have calculated the average total effect of a 1% increase in the number of branches. The effect appears to be positive for the small banks, weak for the medium-sized banks and negative for the big ones (see Muldur and Sassenou [1989]). Unless they modify their cost structure by reducing the relative share of operating costs, the big banks have nothing to gain from increasing their number of branches. For the small banks, on the other hand, a rise in the number of branches would reduce their total cost.

Table 6. Estimated Cobb-Douglas cost function taking into account the number of branches and structure of deposits. (59 commercial banks 1987)

	Operating Costs				Financial Cost of Liabilities			
Samples	Log (*TA*)	Log (*NA*)	Log (*TDV*)	R^2 (SSE)	Log (*TA*)	Log (*NA*)	Log (*TDV*)	R^2 (SSE)
Total sample	0.90	—	0.17	0.90	1.03	—	-0.18	0.95
59 banks	(0.04)		(0.05)	(0.45)	(0.03)		(0.04)	(0.33)
	0.72	0.27	0.06	0.94	1.06	-0.04	-0.17	0.95
	(0.04)	(0.04)	(0.04)	(0.35)	(0.04)	(0.04)	(0.04)	(0.33)
Size 1	0.74	—	0.49	0.63	1.29	—	-0.03	0.60
17 banks	(0.50)		(0.32)	(0.46)	(0.47)		(0.30)	(0.50)
	0.44	0.39	0.33	0.72	1.60	-0.39	0.13	0.80
	(0.41)	(0.22)	(0.28)	(0.40)	(0.40)	(0.19)	(0.25)	(0.40)
Size 2	0.80	—	0.10	0.60	0.97	—	-0.19	0.63
23 banks	(0.20)		(0.04)	(0.28)	(0.29)		(0.06)	(0.41)
	0.88	0.07	0.07	0.62	0.97	0.03	-0.18	0.63
	(0.21)	(0.09)	(0.04)	(0.28)	(0.30)	(0.13)	(0.06)	(0.42)
Size 3	0.94	—	0.29	0.86	1.00	—	-0.18	0.94
19 banks	(0.07)		(0.08)	(0.20)	(0.45)		(0.05)	(0.28)
	0.72	0.27	0.10	0.93	1.02	-0.02	-0.17	0.94
	(0.07)	(0.05)	(0.07)	(0.33)	(0.06)	(0.04)	(0.06)	(0.28)

TDV = demand deposits as a percentage of capital committed.

Table 7. Costs structure in banks and savings institutions.

	Commercial Banks				Savings Institutions			
Percent	Total Sample 59 Banks	Size 1 17 Banks	Size 2 23 Banks	Size 3 19 Banks	Total Sample 247 Institutions	Size 1 113 Units	Size 2 92 Units	Size 3 42 Units
Financial costs as percentage of total cost	65	59	66	69	73	80	78	76
Operating costs as percentage of total cost	35	41	34	31	27	20	22	24
Total costs/ total assets	11.1	11.6	11.7	9.9	5.6	5.3	5.8	5.9
Operating costs/ total assets	3.8	4.5	3.8	3.0	1.2	1.1	1.3	1.4
Financial costs/ per total assets	7.3	7.1	7.9	6.9	4.4	4.2	4.5	4.5

Another factor may be that the ATM networks have yet to prove their worth in terms of cost savings over the period studied. This result seems to be confirmed by the strategies currently being pursued by the big banks, which are exchanging part of their branch networks for those of non-French European banks, or else modifying their national spread without increasing their total number of branches. Big banks also have greater scope for spreading personnel among their many branches. Our figure for the elasticity of costs to the number of branches (0.27 in 1987, and 0.34 in 1982) confirms the results of studies carried out on French data more than 15 years ago (Levy-Garboua and Levy-Garboua [1975]).

If, on the other hand, France were to completely deregulate interest rates on lending, particularly on demand deposits, the operating cost economies obtained by big banks might no longer be eliminated by financial cost diseconomies. In this new competition, the big banks could potentially pass on their operating cost advantages to their offered lending rates and thus attract more demand deposits. However, the small local and regional banks would not be entirely penalized, as they could continue to exploit their advantages in terms of local presence and specialization to counter competition from the large institutions.

5.1.3. Absence of economies of scale in terms of total and operating costs in the savings institutions. In Table 8, we report the estimates of the model for the total sample and by size category. We comment only on the results obtained for three size categories, since the Chow tests leads us to reject the hypothesis of the overall sample's homogeneity.

Table 8. Estimates of a Cobb-Douglas type cost function: operating costs as an explained variable (247 savings institutions 1987).

Samples	Log (*NC*)	Log (*TMD*)	Log (w_1)	Log (w_2)	Log (*PLA*)	R^2 (SSE)
Total sample	1.10	1.06	0.23	0.05	—	0.95
247 institutions	(0.02)	(0.03)	(0.06)	(0.06)		(0.23)
	1.07	1.04	0.23	0.08	-1.02	0.96
	(0.02)	(0.03)	(0.06)	(0.06)	(0.27)	(0.22)
Size 1	1.21	1.02	0.25	-0.02	—	0.83
113 institutions	(0.08)	(0.14)	(0.09)	(0.11)		(0.28)
	1.21	1.04	0.24	0.03	-1.19	0.84
	(0.07)	(0.13)	(0.09)	(0.11)	(0.49)	(0.27)
Size 2	1.19	1.18	0.01	0.13	—	0.76
	(0.07)	(0.08)	(0.09)	(0.07)		(0.17)
	1.18	1.17	0.02	0.15	-0.99	0.79
	(0.07)	(0.07)	(0.09)	(0.06)	(0.30)	(0.16)
Size 3	0.97	0.97	0.20	0.11	—	0.95
42 institutions	(0.04)	(0.04)	(0.19)	(0.11)		(0.15)
	0.97	0.97	0.20	0.11	0.03	0.95
	(0.04)	(0.09)	(0.19)	(0.11)	(0.64)	(0.16)

NC = number of accounts
TMD = ratio of total deposits to number of accounts
PLA = "livret A" as a percentage of total deposits taken
w_1 = unit cost of labor
w_2 = unit cost of physical capital

Small savings institutions seem to exhibit dimishing returns to scale. A 1% increase in the number of accounts drives up operating costs by 1.21%. We regard the significance of the unit labor cost parameter as a possible explanation of these diseconomies. Indeed, the smaller savings institutions manage their labor costs rather well, but soon as they reach a sightly higher output level their unit labor costs rise faster than their output. This may be due to hirings of more qualified staff.

For medium-sized savings institutions, we also observe diminishing returns to scale. By contrast, the explanation for these diseconomies is different. As Table 8 indicates, the labor cost elasticity is not significant but the cost-of-capital elasticity is. When institutions in this size category reach a certain output level, their investments rise more than proportionally to the number accounts. We suggest two explanations for this phenomenon: oversized computer systems relative to business volume; and the fact that larger savings institutions tend to be located in urban areas where pay scales and building costs are higher.

In the biggest size category, we find no diseconomies of scale. Unlike their smaller counterparts, these savings institutions seem to adapt their equipment and workforce size more closely to their business volume.

We observe the positive effect of regulated deposits (livret A) on savings institutions' operating costs. A 1% increase in livret A deposits as a share of total funds gathered enables the institutions to cut their operating costs by an average 1%, except for the larger entities, which are beginning to diversify and are thus reducing their dependence on the livret A. This finding also underscores the fragility of the savings institutions' cost efficiencies in the event of deregulation. As already noted, the decline in livret A funds gathering in recent years has begun to destabilize the financial equilibrium of savings institutions.

5.2. Translog specification

Table 9 lists the results of our translog function estimates for the total bank sample. The figures show the existence of economies of scale for the three output pairs simultaneously. Moreover, we find economies of scope for the securities transactions-interbank loans pair, both in operating costs and total cost. However, when we take into account the estimates of the approximate standard deviations, our conclusions need to be adjusted. The statistical tests seemingly reject the hypotheses of diminishing overall returns to scale and diminishing returns to scope for the securities transactions-interbank loans pair; the assumption of increasing returns to scope for the other two pairs also appears to be rejected.

Table 9. Estimated coefficients of returns to scale and scope for commercial banks ($w_i = 1$, $y_i = 1$).

	Total Returns to Scale	Cost Complementarities between Commercial Loans and Interbank Loans	Cost Complementarity between Interbank Loans and Securities Loans Transactions	Cost Complementarity between Commercial Loans and Securities Transactions
Total costs	2.50	–0.01	–0.36	–0.08
	(2.07)	(0.14)	(0.49)	(0.31)
Operating costs	2.38	0.56	–1.20	0.83
	(1.60)	(0.45)	(1.13)	(0.99)

Table 10. Estimated coefficients of returns to scale and scope for savings institutions with operating costs ($w_i = 1$, $y_i = 1$).

	Total Returns to Scale	Cost Complementarities between Deposits and Loans	Cost Complementarities Deposits and Securities Transactions	Cost Complementarities between Loans and Securities Transactions
Total France	0.65	–0.97	–0.76	0.03
247 institutions	(0.42)	(2.36)	(1.24)	(0.40)
France hors	0.68	–1.79	0.19	0.17
Alsace-Lorraine	(0.50)	(2.70)	(0.13)	(0.30)
227 caisses				

For the savings institutions,[5] the first statistical analysis identified three broad types of activity: deposits, lending and securities trading. The table shows the relative share of the three outputs in total assets. Clearly, with 69% of assets, deposits are the most important activity of these financial institutions.

Overall returns to scale seem diminishing. This finding is consistent with those obtained using a model based on a Cobb-Douglas cost function. When we take into account the estimates of the approximate standard deviations, the hypothesis of increasing returns to scale is rejected.

With regard to returns to scope, we generally find a complementarity between deposits and lending, and between deposits and securities and cash management activities. Conversely, there is a noncomplementarity between lending and securities and cash management activities. This noncomplementarity appears to be attributable to savings institutions in Alsace and Lorraine. In most cases, the relatively high values for estimated standard deviations leave no choice but to reject the hypothesis of decreasing returns to scope.

Thus—as with the banks—the estimated parameters generally suggest the existence of returns to scope between the product pairs considered, except for the (customer loans-securities and cash management activities) pair, but statistical tests based on approximate standard deviations do not allow us to confirm these conclusions. Three main reasons may underlie the imprecision of these parameters:

1. The small scale of the bank sample: an increase in its size could reduce the estimated standard deviations.
2. The strong multicolinearity between bank outputs, which increases the imprecision of estimators. One way to remedy this problem might be to use the instrumental-variables technique.
3. Sample heterogeneity: the parameters of returns to scale and scope estimated on a cross-section may be regarded as the average parameters of returns for the banks estimated on time-series (Mairesse and Griliches [1989]). Estimating these models on a panel over a sufficiently long period would allow us to test the heterogeneity hypothesis.

6. Conclusion

In this study, we have constructed separate models, based on different principles, to study the costs incurred by French commercial banks and savings institutions. Because of the differences in structure, specialization and regulations between the two categories, we decided to adopt different analytical approaches for each. Choosing a single approach and model for both would certainly have facilitated a direct comparison of results, but these would have been of little significance owing to the structural and behavioral distinctions noted above.

We find that the average total costs and average operating costs of the savings institutions are twice as small as those of commercial banks. The main reason is that commercial banks incur higher costs in managing their demand deposits than savings institutions in managing livret A accounts. However, the operating cost gaps between the two institutional categories diminish with size. This suggests that the structure and behavior of the larger savings institutions resemble those of commercial banks.

The results of our econometric estimates give a likely explanation for the phenomenon. Using the Cobb-Douglas specification, we observe increasing returns to scale for banks and diminishing returns for savings institutions. The estimation of a more flexible cost function corroborates these findings. The value of the returns-to-scope parameter at the mean point seems to indicate a complementarity between certain pairs of outputs.

However, when we take into account the estimates of the approximate standard deviations, the hypothesis of diminishing returns to scale and scope is rejected. The fragility of the results obtained with the translog function is partly due to the relatively small size of the French bank population compared with that of U.S. banks. In 1988, France had about 1000 financial institutions of which 394 commercial banks, 190 mutual or cooperative banks, 285 savings institutions, and 21 municipal credit institutions, compared with over 14,000 banking institutions in the United States.

The differences in cost efficiency arise mainly from the specific provisions of French banking rules, which forbid banks from gathering the liquid, tax-exempt types of deposits virtually monopolized by the savings institutions and the post office. Conversely, the same regulations forbid the savings institutions from allocating funds at their discretion: by law, the funds must be centralized by the Caisse des dépôts et Consignations and used in the public interest. For their funds-gathering activity, the savings institutions receive a 0.75% commission on livret A deposits taken. In other words, while the rules make it easier for savings institutions to gather funds cheaply, they oblige them to accept a low rate of return (see Muldur, Sassenou, and Heringer [1990]).

The cost efficiency of the savings institutions is offset by the allocation efficiency of the banks which, moreover, specialize in high-profitability markets. If we take into account cost efficiency and allocation efficiency simultaneously, the operating costs incurred by savings institutions appear to be high relative to their profit margins.

The decline in livret A deposits, under pressure from new high-yield products, or the possible deregulation of the livret A, would undermine the savings institutions' relative cost efficiency. To counter this trend, the savings institutions have embarked on an accelerated merger policy. If this strategic choice does not allow them to expand their market share in competitive, high-yield sectors, they will risk losing their cost advantage without improving their allocation efficiency.

Our findings also have major implications at the European level. The expected positive effects of financial integration in the EEC seem to be overestimated in certain studies such as the Cecchini's report on the "cost of non-Europe," which sees potential welfare gains from increased competition and economies of scale. Our results, as well as those of Pacolet's analysis of the Belgian banking system [1989], definitively disprove the notion that the more diversified big banks operating on the greater scale of a single European market would gain in efficiency (Muldur and Pacolet [1990]). This conclusion highlights the urgent need for a competitive banking policy, which at present is virtually nonexistent in a certain number of countries and at EEC level.

Acknowledgment

An initial version of this paper was presented at the Franco-American Economic Seminar on Productivity Issues in Services at the Micro Level, National Bureau of Economic Research, Boston, July 23–26, 1990. The authors wish to thank E.R. Berndt, D.B. Humphrey, J. Mairesse, C. Morrison, and F.C. Wykoff for their suggestions on the first version of this paper, but accept responsibility for any remaining errors. The opinions expressed in this document are not necessarily those of the Caisse des Dépôts et Consignations.

Notes

1. The 1988-06 regulation obliges savings institutions to maintain the same equity levels as banks.
2. In Muldur and Sassenou [1989] we estimate a Cobb-Douglas cost-function using data from 59 commercial banks. The results differ according to the choice of financial costs versus operating costs as the endogeneous variable. In the first case we find near constant returns to scale, whereas in the second case returns are largely increasing.
3. This system is estimated together with the equations implied by Shephard's lemma and the linear homogeneity restriction in prices. We use Zellner's seemingly unrelated regressions (SURs) for the estimates. The variables are normalized to 1.
4. We are aware of the limits of the functional forms adopted here, in particular for assessing economies of scope. Our paper, however, does not seek to offer more flexible forms of the kind found in the literature, notably the generalized CES quadratic form tested by Röller [1990] on time series for the U.S. telecommunications industry. Rather, our aim is to estimate the standard forms on French data. While very common in the United States, this type of study is very seldom undertaken in France.
5. For the Cobb-Douglas specification, we have adopted the number of bank accounts as an output indicator. The main advantage of the translog specification is that it allows a test of the existence of economies of scope by taking into account three disaggregated outputs. To preserve consistency, it would have been preferable to use the number of accounts or transactions for each of the three financial instruments chosen. As this type of data is unavailable for France, we proxied these physical variables by the corresponding value variables.

References

Alhadeff, D. (1954). *Monopoly and Competition*. Berkeley and Los Angeles: University of California Press.

Baumol, W., Panzar, and R. Willig. (1982). *Contestable Markets and the Theory of Industry Structure*. New York: Harcourt Brace Jovanovich.

Bell, W., and B. Murphy. (1967). "Bank Service Charges and Costs." *National Banking Review* 4, June.

Benston, G. (1965). "Branch Banking and Economies of Scale." *Journal of Finance* 20, May.

Benston, G. (1967). "Economies of Scale and Marginal Costs in Banking Operations." *National Banking Review* 2, June.

Benston, G., A. Berger, A. Hanweck, and D. Humphrey. (1983). "Economies of Scale and Scope in Banking." *Proceedings of a Conference on Bank Structure and Competition*, Chicago, Ill. Federal Reserve Bank of Chicago.

Benston, G., G.A. Hanweck, and B. Humphrey. (1982). "Scale Economies in Banking: A Restructuring and Reassessment." *Journal of Money, Credit and Banking* 14, Nov.

Bernard, A. (1977). "Le Coût du Capital Productif: Une ou Plusieurs Mesures?" *Annales de l'INSEE* 28.

Chajaï, M. (1986). "Modèles de Fonctions de Production et Substitutions entre Facteurs: Une Étude Économétrique sur Données de Panel." Thèse de doctorat de l'EHESS, Paris.

Clark, J.A. (1984). "Estimation of Economies of Scale in Banking Using a Generalized Functional Form." *Journal of Money, Credit and Banking*.

Colin, L. (1989). "Banking Costs, Generalized Functional Forms and Estimation of Economies of Scale and Scope." *Journal of Money, Credit and Banking* 3, Aug.

Cuneo, P. (1982). "Productivité et Recherche-Développement: Une Étude Économétrique sur Données de Panel." Thèse pour le doctorat de troisième cycle de l'EHESS, Paris.

Dietsch, M. (1993). "Returns to Scale and Returns to Scope in French Banking Industry." This volume.

Dormont, B. (1983). "Modèles de Demande de Travail: Une Comparison France-RFA sur Données de Panel." Thèse pour le doctorat de troisième cycle de l'EHESS, Paris.

Frisch, R. (1965). *Theory of Production*. Rand McNally.

Gilbert, A.R. (1984). "Bank Market Structure and Competition: A Survey." *Journal of Money, Credit and Banking* Nov.

Gilligan, T., M. Smirlock, and W. Marshall. (1984). "Scale and Scope Economies in the Multiproduct Banking Firm." *Journal of Monetary Economics* 13.

Gramley, E. (1962). "A Study of Scale Economies in Banking." Federal Reserve Bank of Kansas City.

Horvitz, P. (1965). *Economies of Scale in Banking in Private Financial Institutions*. Englewood Cliffs, NJ: Prentice Hall.

Hunter, W.C. and T.S.G. Timme. (1986). "Technical Change, Organizational Form and the Structure of Bank Production." *Journal of Money, Credit and Banking* 2, May.

Ivaldi, M., and Alii. (1990). "Estimation de la Forme de Fourier Flexible sur Données individuelles." Cahier 9001, Gremaq Toulouse.

Kilbride, B., Bill McDonald, and R. Miller. (1984). "A Reexamination of Economies of Scale in Banking Using a Generalized Functional Form." *Journal of Money, Credit and Banking* 18, Nov.

Kim, Y. (1986). "Economies of Scale and Economies of Scope in Multiproduct Financial Institutions: Further Evidence of Credit Union." *Journal of Money, Credit and Banking* 18, May.

LeCompte, R., and S.D. Smith. (1985). "An Empirical Analysis of Scale and Scope Economies in the Savings and Loan Industry." Working Paper, Texas Christian University.

Levy-Garboua, L., and V. Levy-Garboua. (1975). "Les Coûts Opératoires des Banques Françaises: Une Étude Statistique." *Revue d'Economie Politique*, Feb.

Mairesse, J. (1972). *L'évaluation du Capital Fixe Productif: Méthodes et Résultats*. Paris: Collection de l'INSEE série C, no. 18–19.

Mairesse, J., and Z. Griliches. (1989). "Hétérogénéité et Panels, y-a-t-il des Fonctions de Production Stables." NBER Working Paper.

Mairesse, J., and M. Sassenou. (1989). "Les Facteurs Qualitatifs de la Productivité: Un Essai d'évaluation." *Revue Economie et Prévision* 91, May.

Mester, L.J. (1987a). "A Multiproduct Cost Study of Saving and Loan." *Journal of Finance* 42, June.

Mester, L.J. (1987b). "Efficient Production of Financial Services: Scale and Scope." *Business Review*, Federal Reserve Bank of Philadelphia, Jan.–Feb.

Muldur, U. (1990). "Restructurations et Stratégies dans le Secteur Financier Européen." *Revue d'Economie Financière* 12.

Muldur, U., and J. Pacolet. (1990). "Economies of Scale in European Financial Institutions." Paper for the New European Financial Market Place Colloquium organized by the Centre for European Policy Studies, Brussels, Nov. 29–30.

Muldur, U., and M. Sassenou. (1989). "Structure des Coûts et Efficacité des Banques Françaises." *Revue d'Analyse Financière* 79, Dec.

Muldur, U., M. Sassenou, and S. Heringer. (1990). "Structures et Performances Financières des Caisses d'Épargne Françaises." Internal report, Caisses des Dépôts et Consignations.

Muldur, U., and P. Teston. (1989). "Bilan Critique sur la Littérature en Matière d'Indicateurs de Coût et Rendements d'Échelle dans la Banque." Document de travail 1989-07, Caisse des Dépôts et Consignations.

Murray, D., and R. White. (1983). "Economies of Scale and Economies of Scope in Multiproduct Financial Institutions: A Study of British Columbia Credit Unions." *Journal of Finance* 35, June.

Pacolet, J. (1989). "Market Structur en Operation de Efficientic in de Belgische Financiele Sector." Doctoral dissertation, Leuven, KU Leuven.

Röller, L.H. (1990). "Proper Quadratic Cost Functions with an Application to the Bell System." *Review of Economics and Statistics.*

Sassenou, M. (1988). "Recherche-Développement et Productivité dans les Entreprises Japonaises: Une Étude Économétrique sur Données de Panel," Thèse pour le doctorat, EHESS, Paris.

Sassenou, M. (1990). "Accroissement d'Activité, Diversification des Produits et Intéractions entre facteurs de coût dans la Banque Française." Document de travail 1990-09/T, Caisse des Dépôts et Consignations.

Sealey, C.W., and J.T. Lindley. (1977). "Inputs, Outputs and a Theory of Production and Cost at Depository Financial Institutions." *Journal of Finance* 32, Sept.

Sibjorn, A.R., Forsend, and S. Jansen. (1989). "Bank Output Measurement and the Construction of Best Practice Frontiers." Papier présenté au 16ème Congrés du European Finance Association, Stockholm.

Szymczak, P. (1988). "Essai sur la Rentabilité Bancaire." Thèse pour le doctorat, Université de Paris I.

The Journal of Productivity Analysis, 4, 73-76 (1993)

Comments on "Economies of Scale and Scope in French Banking and Savings Institutions" by Ugur Muldur and Mohamed Sassenou

FRANK C. WYKOFF
Pomona College and the Claremont Graduate School, Claremont, CA 91711

Formation of a unified European common market is one of the most exciting economic developments of the late twentieth century. But successful unification will depend crucially on financial integration, because both monetary and fiscal policy operate through the underlying financial structure. Yet financial institutions designed to perform specific social objectives in support of policy may not survive the competitive pressures of integration without an increasingly Byzantine regulatory structure which itself could defeat the original purpose of integration. It is hard to imagine an effective, fully integrated European Economic Community (EEC) in which individual countries each shelter radically different financial structures. As in agriculture, public and private planners, who are considering the optimal design of the financial system, will need to address several knotty issues relating to structure. How many different types of financial institutions will there be? What will be the functions, product mix, and scale of each type? Will unification accelerate deregulation or lock in existing designs and structures? Will current activities, some of which are still protected by tight regulation and close integration of public and private institutions, continue to be served or will these institutions buckle under more powerful international competitive forces? Muldur and Sassenou implicitly address these questions for France by analyzing the scope and scale properties of the French financial system. Anyone who wishes to understand the French financial system, which for better or worse, will play a major role in European financial policy, will find this analysis helpful. Muldur and Sassenou (MS) provide a very useful historical perspective on the post-World War I evolution of the French system followed by a careful cost function analysis of the scope and scale properties of two rather distinct types of French financial institutions that have survived up to this point—savings institutions and commercial banks.[1] Analytically, rather than trying to forecast continued evolution of the French system, MS provide a cost-function snapshot of this vintage 1990 French bimodel system. Whereas their approach seems to imply a distinct bimodel system, their scope and scale results seem to suggest further integration of the two systems unless natural competitive forces are somehow restrained in the future by regulatory barriers.

I would like to consider the MS snapshot from the more dynamic historical perspective provided in the MS paper. As one considers the evolution of a financial system in the post-World War II period, whether it be French, European, or American for that matter, two extremes might be considered—varied and homogeneous. The varied system might consist of many different institutions, each filling a unique niche specializing on both asset and liability sides of the balance sheet. Both French and American systems in the immediate post-World War II period were designed to have different niches filled by different types of institutions restrained and insulated in their niches from outside pressures by a variety of carrot-and-stick regulations. Both countries had very active and complex regulatory mechanisms controlling the financial sector. While credit unions, savings and loans, mutual savings banks, investment banks and commercial banks populated the U.S. system, five distinct types of lending institutions characterized France with distinctions based on both liability characteristics and loan purpose.

Deregulation during the 1960s to 1980s on both sides of the Atlantic combined with technological innovation, maturation, and internationalization of financial markets and with competitive forces to blur the lines between various forms. By the 1990s it became clear that both European and U.S. systems were evolving toward a single, complex, and concentrated financial system. This nearly integrated system is characterized by significant cross over activity among apparently different institutions in which "commercial banks" buy government securities, "security dealers" issue money market check-writing accounts while "savings institutions" issue checking accounts and make commercial loans. The regulatory walls between financial institution types seem simply to be dissolving in the fact of new computer processing systems, faxes, instantaneous telecommunications, and other advanced technologies as well as new financial instruments and inventive and aggressive entrepreneurship. Some partitions remain held in place mainly by regulations designed to protect low-cost funds for the public sector or to support certain social goals such as low-cost housing.

MS focus on two principal French financial institutions circa 1990—savings institutions and commercial banks. Though quite different from banks in 1947, savings institutions now have more in common legally with commercial banks. Still the savings institutions retain their original purpose as their primary activity—to seek out savings from the private sector which can be used to fund public debt. These funds are put into tax-exempt interest-bearing passbook savings accounts, called Livret A, that are passed along to centralized public French agencies, the SOREFIs (regional credit unions) and the Caisse des Depots et Consignations (CDC). The private savings institutions are compensated with commissions by the government for placing funds in these savings accounts. The funds are then used to finance public spending. About 70% of savings institutions' deposits consist of these Livret A accounts. French regulators are evidently trying to sustain this niche in order to protect low-cost sources of funds for public expenditure, even as, according to Muldur and Sassenou, "the steady abolition of regulatory barriers between activities has brought these two categories of banking institutions into increasingly direct competition, chiefly in the field of retail banking." Despite apparent concern in France, the European community appears to be moving toward a German model, the "universal" bank—a homogeneous banking system in which one type of institution dominates the entire sector, serves as a holding type company for management of many firms, owns controlling stocks in many firms, and provides all types of financial services.

Still, circa 1991, the French savings institutions, essentially simple collection agencies for the government, make loans to finance public projects according to guidelines set by Parliament. These savings institutions are basically different, according to MS, from private commercial banks that attract deposits and make loans according to their own private optimization calculus. Given these two distinct institutional forms, MS use two different models to analyze the cost functions of the two institution types.[2] Liabilities of savings institutions, principally the Livret A accounts, are an end of themselves for savings institutions. Saving banks act like bounty hunters who bring in accounts and receive a commission accordingly from the CDC. Thus these liabilities are outputs along with the public loan eventually made to public needs. For commercial banks, however, MS side with Sealey and Lindley [1977], who treat liabilities as inputs that are transformed by banks, which act as intermediaries into loans (the outputs). MS note that little direct income is generated by deposit accounts of banks because deposits bear no interest to the depository by regulatory law.

MS find that small savings institutions can thrive in competition with small commercial banks due to the former's legal monopoly advantage of low-cost, tax-exempt Livret A accounts. However, as size and scope increase, private banking scale and scope economies begin to offset advantages of low-cost Livret A accounts available only to savings institutions. Then the savings institutions, constrained to making public loans only, cannot take advantage of the lucrative private loans available to their commercial bank competitors. Thus French regulators can continue to insulate small savings institutions by preventing private commercial banks from competing for tax-exempt Livret A type savings accounts, and these same regulators can still prevent large savings institutions from making profitable private loans. The CDC forces them to make low-yielding public interest loans as defined by Parliament. How long can this artificial institutional arrangement survive? MS seem to think that French regulation can continue to survive since they do not detect significant scale and scope advantages to larger and larger European private banks. Nonetheless, one must wonder how long these unique French financial institutions, that serve as low-cost collection agencies for the public fisc, can continue to survive in the face of growing international competitive presssures.

Notes

1. Using cost function methodology, based on duality theory, MS estimate Cobb-Douglas and translog functions, well within the established methodology used in modern analysis of the efficiency of financial institutions. Basically the natural log of total costs is regressed against the natural logs of output, or outputs for a multiproduct model, and the natural logs of input prices. The translog model is the Cobb-Douglas model with additional cross-product terms for interaction effects. A producer enjoys economies of scope in two product lines if their cross price elasticity indicates that they are complements. In this case the producer can lower costs by jointly producing the two goods. A producer enjoys increasing returns to scale if an equaproportional increase in all inputs leads to a greater than proportional increase in output. See Hancock [1991] for an excellent discussion of the methodology.
2. The most serious maintained hypothesis in these models is the selection of inputs and outputs, because, while the cost function methodology is widely adopted, there is no consensus among researchers on which activities of financial institutions are inputs and which are outputs. The choice of least consensus is in the treatment of liabilities. MS follow Sealey and Lindley [1977] for commercial banks by treating liabilities as inputs. They follow Berger and Humphrey [1991] and others for savings institutions by treating their liabilities as outputs. Both choices are by and large made arbitrarily, though MS justify their choices by reference to the principal income earning activity of the two different types of financial institutions.

References

Berger, Allen N., and David B. Humphrey. (1990). "Measurement and Efficiency Issues in Commerical Banking." In *Output Measurement in the Service Sector.* National Bureau of Economic Research, Proceedings of the Charleston Conference, South Carolina, forthcoming.

Hancock, Diana. (1991). *A Theory of Production for the Financial Firm.* Boston: Kluwer Academic.

Sealey, C.W., and J.T. Lindley. (1977). "Inputs, Outputs, and A Theory of Production and Cost at Depository Financial Institutions." *Journal of Finance*, 32, 1251–1266.

The Journal of Productivity Analysis, 4, 77–93 (1993)

Productive Performance of the French Insurance Industry*

F. FECHER
Department of Economics, University of Liège, B-4000 Sart Tilman, Liège 1, Belgium

D. KESSLER
EHESS, 42 Bd. Raspail, 75007 Paris, France

S. PERELMAN
Department of Economics, University of Liège, B-4000 Sart Tilman, Liège 1, Belgium

P. PESTIEAU
CORE, University of Louvain, and Department of Economics, University of Liège, B-4000 Sart Tilman, Liège 1, Belgium

Abstract

The purpose of this paper is to provide for both life and non-life insurance an assessment of the relative productive performance of French companies. We use parametric and nonparametric approaches to construct a frontier to be used as a yardstick of productive efficiency. Our data basis covers 84 life and 243 non-life companies for the period 1984–1989. The main findings show a high correlation between parametric and nonparametric results and a wide dispersion in the rates of inefficiency across companies. This dispersion can be reduced when controlling for variations in scale, ownership, distribution, reinsurance, and claims ratios.

1. Introduction

Over the last years the European insurance market has been subject to various challenges and made aware of the need of improving its performance. In the famous report on the "Cost of Non-Europe" (Emerson et al. [1988]) one finds a quite striking price comparison for life and non-life insurance across eight EEC countries. It appears for example that the price of a basket of insurance services is on the average rather higher in France than in the Netherlands or the United Kingdom, even after controlling for differences in taxation. Within the French market, one also finds discrepancies, though less dramatic, across companies (50 Millions de Consommateurs [1988, 1989]). Many objections have been raised toward such results. We all know how much caution is needed for a meaningful price comparison. It remains that such discrepancies cannot but call for some explanation pertaining to national regulation, scale economies, market structure and productive efficiency.

Most of the research in this area has dealt with issues of optimal scale and competitiveness as well as with the role of regulatory intensity. Recently, Finsinger [1989] has noted some close correlation between the regulatory intensity and the price level of life and non-life insurance in seven European countries. The issue of scale economies has been widely studied in a number of countries without conclusive results (see, e.g., Finsinger and Pauly [1986]). The issue of productive inefficiency has often been raised in particular lately in relation to the segmentation and regulation of most European insurance markets. It has however been rarely studied and the few existing works are even based on the concept of partial labor productivity or that of average cost (Finsinger [1984]; Finsinger et al. [1985]).

In this paper, we use the measure of productive inefficiency which is more general than that of partial productivity. It rests on the concept of the production frontier, that is the maximum possible outputs which can be produced from given quantities of a set of inputs (see Forsund et al. [1980]). The indicator of productive, also called technical, inefficiency gives the distance between this frontier and the input-output vector of actual production in a given firm at a given period in time. The production frontier approach has been used lately for a wide range of activities (see Pestieau and Tulkens [1990]). It is considered as particularly appropriate for the major service industries.

We shall use alternative measures of outputs which are related to the French franc volume of gross premiums. For life insurance, we also use financial returns. For inputs, we use labor including commissions and a composite variable consisting of various outlays. The data covers 84 life and 243 non-life companies for the period 1984–1989. Two methods are adopted to measure technical efficiency having each their own strength: a stochastic frontier model based on a Cobb-Douglas production function and data envelopment analysis (DEA). DEA has been widely used in previous efficiency studies of financial services (Sherman and Gold [1985]; Rangan et al. [1988]); it consists of a linear programming technique for constructing a nonparametric, piecewise linear envelope to the observed data. As an alternative, a stochastic parametric frontier is estimated; it is expected to be relatively superior to DEA if the flexible functional form of production so estimated is close to the true underlying technology of the insurance industry (Gong [1987]; Gong and Sickles [1989]). As additional explanatory variables, various key characteristics of insurance companies are introduced: the reinsurance ratio, the distribution ratio, the legal status, the scale of operations, and the claims ratio (e.g., the ratio of claims to gross premiums).

2. Productive Efficiency

2.1. The Concept

The basic problem with measuring productive efficiency of microunits such as insurance enterprises is to establish benchmarks. The seminal article by Farrell [1957] introduced the concept of the best practice reference frontier which delineates the technological limits of what an enterprise can achieve. This best practice frontier, also called the production or the efficiency frontier specifies for an enterprise the maximum quantities of outputs it can produce given any level of inputs and, for any levels of outputs, the minimum quantities of inputs it needs for producing. From that tool, one defines the concept and the index of production inefficiency. An enterprise is deemed inefficient if its outputs and inputs are below the frontier. That is, it could produce more outputs with the available inputs or decrease its levels of inputs while keeping production unchanged. The indicator of inefficiency is given by the relative distance between the actual observed production and the nearest benchmark production.

Figure 1 represents such a production frontier for the one-input one-output case. If an enterprise yields an input-output vector equal to E, it is inefficient and its degree of productive efficiency can be given either by an input based indicator $\alpha'\alpha/E\alpha$ or by an output-based indicator $E\beta/\beta'\beta$. Either indicator would be equal to 1 when the actual production Pies on the frontier.

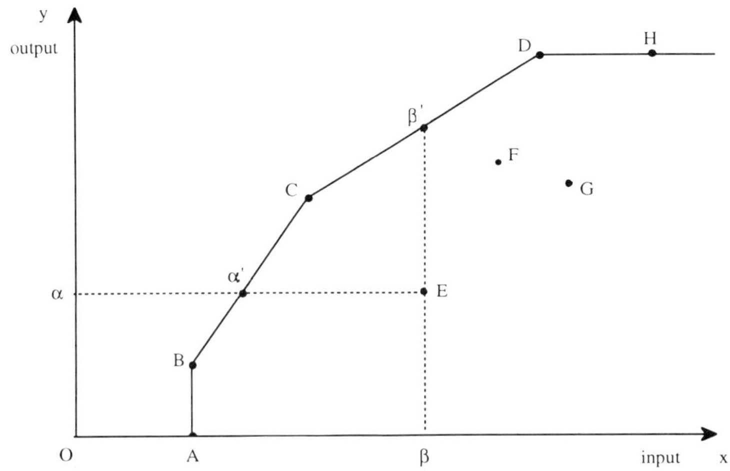

Figure 1. Efficiency frontier constructed from observed data by means of the DEA-V method.

2.2. The Parametric versus the Nonparametric Method

To construct such a production frontier, one distinguishes two main alternative approaches depending on whether or not the frontier can be specified as a function with constant parameters. When making a choice between parametric and nonparametric frontiers one should keep in mind what we know about the underlying technology at hand. For example, in the agriculture and manufacturing branches, one has quite a clear-cut idea of the underlying technology and the econometric estimation of parametric production functions makes a lot of sense. On the other hand, when dealing with service industries, a nonparametric approach such as the DEA seems at least as appropriate as it does not rely on an explicit assumption as to the technology and it applies to activities with both multiple outputs and multiple inputs.

In a recent study, Gong and Sickles [1990] address this question utilizing Monte Carlo techniques which enable them to theoretically control the structure of both technology and efficiency. Unfortunately, most empirical work such as the present one are hindered by the lack of knowledge of the true structure of production and efficiency. One can just hope that both parametric and nonparametric approaches provide quite similar results, saving the researcher the embarrassment of having to select one approach over the other without solid arguments.

As a representative of nonparametric approaches, we adopt the DEA developed by Charnes, Cooper, and Rhodes [1978], which uses linear programming techniques to envelope observed input-output vectors as tightly as possible without requiring a prior specification of functional forms. DEA requires only an assumption of convexity of the production possibility set and disposability of inputs and outputs. It employs a postulated minimum extrapolation from observed data in the application. Here, we allow for variable elasticity of scale (the so-called DEA-V) which implies with one output y and one input x, the frontier technology given by *ABCD* and the horizontal line to the right of *D* in Figure 1 where the dots represent the observed activities. Activities *B*, *C*, and *D* are all fully efficient while *E*, *F*, and *G* are inefficient. *H* is output efficient and input inefficient.

One of the main advantages of DEA is that it allows for considering at the same time several inputs and several outputs. In that case, efficiency is measured in terms of inputs or outputs along a ray from the origin. In this paper, DEA efficiency measure is expressed in terms of inputs.

Formally, the efficiency frontier is constructed by solving a linear programming problem which amounts to finding for each firm the maximum of a ratio of weighted outputs (plus some scalar reflecting the intercept—point A in Figure 1) to weighted inputs subject to the condition that the similar ratio (that is using the same weights) for every firm be less than or equal to unity. The weights vary for each firm and are chosen in the most favorable way that the constraints allow.

With panel data, one has input-output observations for each firm and each year of the period considered. Then, to construct an index of firm-specific technical efficiency, we have taken the mean values over time periods.

Let us now turn to the parametric approach and more particularly to the stochastic frontier model. In such a model, output is bounded above by a stochastic production frontier that is stochastic in the sense that its location is allowed to vary randomly. We may represent it by

$$y_s = f(x_s; \alpha) + \epsilon_s,$$

where y is the *single* output of firm s, x_s is a vector of observations on its input levels, α is a vector of unknown production parameters. The term ϵ_s is a composed error term, $\epsilon_s = \nu_s - \mu_s$ with ν_s, a symmetric normal term capturing randomness outside of the control of the firm and μ_s (≥ 0), a one-sided component capturing randomness assumedly under the control of the firm. This later term is used to derive the indicator of technical efficiency.

With panel data as used here, there are two ways of measuring efficiency. First, one can follow Jondrow et al. [1982] and estimate a measure for each year and for each firm. But, this raises some statistical problems as the term μ_s is contaminated by the presence of the error term ν_s. This is why it is often judged preferable to use alternative firm-specific measures assumed to be constant over time, as suggested first by Schmidt and Sickles [1984].

In this paper we choose the maximum likelihood (ML) procedure proposed by Battese and Coelli [1988]. Specially designed to deal with panel data, this procedure amounts to estimating the conditional expectation of the individual efficiencies μ_s assumed to follow a normal distribution, $N(m, \sigma^2)$, with truncation at zero. Compared with the traditional half-normal distributional hypothesis this maximum likelihood procedure[1] allows a more flexible modeling of inefficiencies, including the half-normal distribution as a special case corresponding to $m = 0$.

3. Measuring the Output of the Insurance Industry

The data requirement of productive efficiency measurement is rather minimal: a set of input-output vectors, each characterizing the actual operations of a number of production units. In particular, it does not impose comparability of inputs and allows for introducing qualitative aspects. When studying the insurance industry input data does not seem to raise any problem but of availability. Insurance companies mainly use various skills of labor, equipment and buildings.

The real difficulty, both conceptual and statistical, lies in measuring the production of the insurance industry (O'Brien [1991]; Hornstein and Prescott [1991]; Hirshorn and Geehan [1977]). In the case of a typical manufacturing industry, real ouptut in a given year is measured by taking the number of various types of products produced. If one wants to aggregate them in a single output indicator, one takes a weighted average of those quantities with the respective product prices in some designated base year being used as a weight. The productive efficiency approach at least in its nonparametric version allows for foregoing the question of aggregation but not the initial problem of defining the different outputs of the industry.

The first to be interested by the issue of ouptut measurement are the national income accountants. In a number of countries, insurance production is no more than an index of labor input. Needless to say that as a direct implication calculation of productivity change then turns out to be a tautological exercise. Academic research has rarely dealt with the mere issue of output measurement. It has rather concentrated on the estimation of scale economies and more recently of scope economies. In most studies, premiums earned and/or claims paid are used as a proxy for output. One also finds as indicator of output, often in combination with the above, the number of policies in force.

On what grounds other than that of availability could we use the premiums paid to companies as a measure of their output? After all, these represent the value that free willing consumers attribute to the insurance service they are seeking (let us, however, note that insurance coverage is often compulsory). If the contingencies against which they seek protection do not occur, they will be satisfied and yet they would then receive nothing back from their insurance company. Naturally, this view contradicts the national income accounting approach which would at the same time add premiums paid but subtract all payments dependent on contingencies such as fire, death, crash, sickness, thus avoiding double counting.

Premiums collected directly concern the technical activity of an insurance company. It reflects the ability of an insurance company to market products, to select clients, and to accept carrying risks. It does not, however, reflect its financial activity, in other words its ability to invest the necessary reserves in a proper manner. Assets management represents quite a large part of a company's activities, and the returns of these investments are a proxy for their quality. The returns can be computed in a number of ways: (1) the returns in the forms of dividends, coupons, rents, . . . plus possibly (2) realized capital gains net of capital losses, plus possibly (3) unrealized capital gains on stocks, bonds, and real estate.

In this study, the output of insurance companies is measured by (1) gross premiums, (2) gross premiums (disaggregated by sectors), (3) gross premiums along with financial returns (dividends, coupons, rents, . . .).

Whatever the output variable chosen, one should be very cautious in analyzing the results of an insurance company: due to the fact that an insurance company—especially in the life sector—rests upon a package of long-term contracts, the different items in the loss and profit account as well as in the balance sheet can be related to phenomena that took place much earlier or will take place much later. The claims paid in a given year can correspond to a contract signed 10 years before, and which entailed administrative costs for the last 9 years. Premiums collected in a given year will in most cases entail large distribution cost that might not be amortized throughout the entire lifetime of the contract. The intertemporal nature of an insurance company makes annual accounts quite unfit, but it seems today impossible to adopt another approach in which a cohort of contracts would be followed along with premiums paid, incurred losses, costs of all kinds, and returns on the various investments backing up technical reserves.

4. Data and Results

4.1. Data

Table 1 and Table 2 give a description of the main data used in this study.[2] They come from both profit and loss accounts and balance sheets sources. The main output variable is gross premium. When using DEA, the non-life insurance gross premiums are decomposed either in three classes: civil liability, fire and property damages, accident and health or in two categories: motor and non-motor insurance. In the case of life insurance, the net returns on financial investment are used as an additional output along with gross premiums. This reflects the two main functions of a life insurance company: to service the insurance contracts of its policyholders and to manage the savings entrusted to it. We also decompose premiums into those related to group life insurance and those related to all other types of life insurance.

The wage bill (labor costs) is used as proxy for the labor force. It has been checked from a richer but narrower sample of companies so that this is a quite good approximation.

Table 1. Structure of non-life insurance in France (average values for 1984–89 in millions FF or in percent).

Firm Characteristics	Firm Number	Gross Premiums	Wage Bill	Other Outlays	Distribution Ratio (%)	Reinsurance Ratio (%)	Claims Ratio (%)
Institutional form							
Foreign	78	112.9	37.8	9.2	74.7	34.8	52.2
Mutual	86	737.3	157.5	62.6	39.7	36.9	47.4
Public	4	11,949.8	3,292.7	800.2	54.3	15.9	68.8
Stock	75	863.5	259.3	74.2	54.0	36.5	43.9
Total	243	760.4	202.1	61.1	55.6	35.8	48.2
Scale*							
5–30	55	15.5	5.0	1.3	68.7	37.5	48.8
30–150	80	80.7	26.9	8.3	56.2	41.6	40.5
150–400	44	258.3	71.8	23.7	47.1	38.9	48.6
400–	64	2,596.4	680.4	204.7	49.1	25.0	57.0
Total	243	760.4	202.1	61.1	55.6	35.8	48.2

*Measured by gross premium income in million FF.

Table 2. Structure of life insurance in France (average values for 1984–89 in millions FF or in percent).

Firm Characteristics	Firm Number	Gross Premiums	Wage Bill	Other Outlays	Distribution Ratio (%)	Reinsurance Ratio (%)	Claims Ratio (%)
Institutional form							
Foreign	15	224.8	48.7	28.1	25.3	7.4	56.8
Mutual	13	998.9	110.2	46.3	28.3	16.3	43.7
Public	4	8,628.9	1,004.1	504.8	25.2	4.7	73.2
Stock	52	929.0	93.1	42.7	34.6	9.1	33.9
Total	84	1,180.7	131.2	62.7	31.4	9.7	41.3
Scale*							
5–100	23	35.7	8.3	4.1	29.6	12.0	39.7
100–300	16	178.4	49.5	20.9	34.3	17.1	42.9
300–1000	20	573.4	70.6	41.3	29.4	4.1	40.5
1000–	25	3,361.6	345.0	160.2	32.8	7.2	42.4
Total	84	1,180.8	131.2	62.7	31.4	9.7	41.3

*Measured by gross premium income in million FF.

We include in that labor input variable the amount of commissions paid to intermediaries, brokers or tied agents and their staff, who sell insurance without being employed by the company. As an additional input, we use a composite input consisting of various outlays such as capital consumption, purchase of equipment and supplies. Four main institutional forms, the reinsurance ratio (proportion of reinsurance ceded to total gross premiums), the distribution ratio (proportion of commissions paid to total costs incurred), the claims ratio (proportion of claims to gross premiums), and the scale (proxied by the level of gross premiums) are introduced as characteristics of insurance companies, which might have some effect on their level of performance.

Public companies in either property-liability or life insurance have on the average a disproportionate size relative to the stock, mutual, and foreign companies. Not surprisingly the distribution ratio is the lowest for mutual non-life companies and is higher in non-life than in life companies. The reinsurance ratio decreases with scale in life insurance companies. Further, it is particularly low in public companies, which is expected as these are state-backed.

Those ratios can hide features which cannot be controlled for by lack of data. For example, the distribution ratio in life insurance is particularly low in companies which are linked to banks and can thus use their network. In life insurance which has lately experienced a rapid growth, the claims ratio can be viewed as a proxy for maturity.

If one looks at the distribution of these ratios across companies as given in Figures 2 and 3, one cannot be but surprised by their wide dispersion which reveals an insurance market both heterogeneous and segmented. As shown, this feature explains for a great part the low efficiency levels that we obtain.

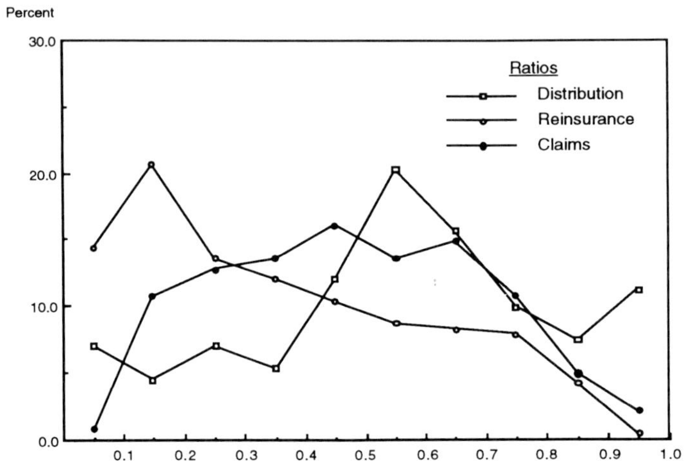

Figure 2. Frequency distribution of firm-specific characteristics (non-life insurance).

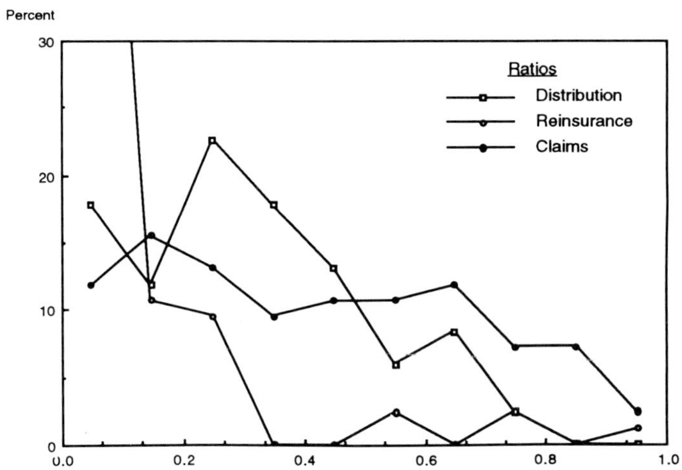

Figure 3. Frequency distribution of firm-specific characteristics (life insurance).

4.2. Firm-Specific Productive Efficiency in Non-Life Insurance

On the basis of those unbalanced panel data,[3] we first analyze the productive efficiency of non-life insurance on the basis of a stochastic production frontier (ML) and of DEA. With DEA, we allow for variable elasticity of scale and consider three alternative sets of output variables: aggregate gross premiums (DEA1), gross premiums in three branches (civil liability, fire-property, accident-health) (DEA3), gross premiums in motor and non-

Table 3. Firm-specific average efficiency measures in non-life insurance: alternative approaches.

Institutional Form	Number	Nonparametric Frontiers DEA1	Nonparametric Frontiers DEA2	Nonparametric Frontiers DEA3	Parametric Frontier ML
Foreign	78	0.493	0.493	0.499	0.493
Mutual	86	0.535	0.544	0.563	0.477
Public	4	0.923	0.972	0.974	0.574
Stock	75	0.457	0.506	0.524	0.386
Total	243	0.504	0.523	0.537	0.412
Standard deviation		0.203	0.252	0.236	0.154
Range		0.13–1.0	0.01–1.0	0.01–1.0	0.18–0.97
Kendall's rank correlation with DEA1		1.0	0.69	0.62	0.74

motor branches[4] (DEA2). Further, we focus on firm-specific inefficiency which implies that we average the efficiency measures over the period covered. The results are given in Table 3 for the whole sector and with a distinction according to the institutional type of company. Overall, efficiency is quite low and hence our results ought to be interpreted with caution and by focusing on comparison rather than on absolute levels of efficiency. We shall come back to this. Efficiency is of course relatively higher with three rather than with one or even two outputs. Note that the correlation between those measures is high.[5]

What clearly appears is that public companies are the most efficient with the three other institutional types close to each other.[6] The superiority of public companies ought to be interpreted with caution as there are only four of them with a quite high scale.

To estimate the stochastic production frontier model, we represent the production frontier by the following Cobb-Douglas function:

$$\ln y_{st} = \alpha_0 + \alpha_1 \ln x_{1,st} + \alpha_2 \ln x_{2,st} + \epsilon_{st},$$

where y_{st} represents the output of the sth firm in year t, x_{ist} ($i = 1, 2$) denotes input i, α_0, α_1, and α_2 are constants.[7] One defines $\epsilon_{st} = \nu_{st} - \mu_s$, ν_{st} being the usual random term, and μ_s, independent of ν_{st}, being obtained by truncating the normal distribution above zero and representing the firm-specific degree of inefficiency. Within this approach only a single output is considered. The efficiency measure of firm s is estimated as a conditional expectation, $E[\exp(-\mu_s)|\epsilon_{st}]$, following Battese and Coelli [1988]. In Table 3, under the heading of ML is given the efficiency measure when the output variable is gross premiums.[8]

Overall the dispersion of all these efficiency measures is wide as can be seen from the standard deviation or the range values. This variability can be explained in part by the yearly nature of the data sources, namely, the annual accounts of individual insurance companies. Efficiency dispersion is also due to the volatility of the insurance market. In our sample, there are a number of companies which either started or disappeared during 1984–1989.

To compare DEA with stochastic frontier results, we ought to focus on the one-output case. The rank order correlation coefficient between the DEA1 and the ML efficiency

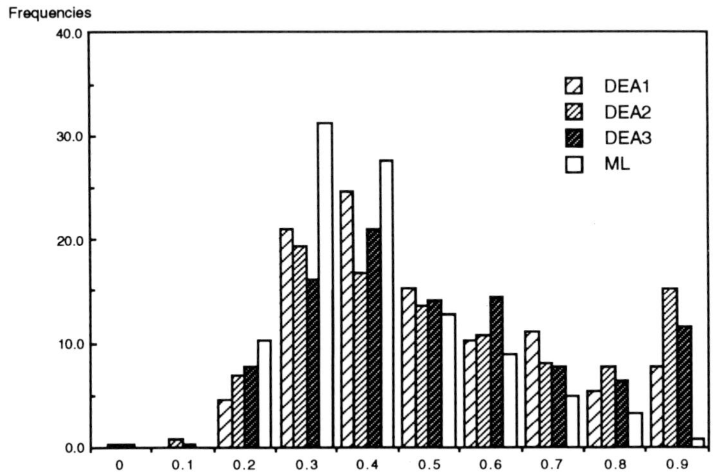

Figure 4. Frequency distribution of firm-specific efficiency measures in non-life insurance.

measures is rather high (0.74). This indicates that the two approaches are rather converging, which is an interesting result. In previous works, one often noticed that parametric and nonparametric techniques led to contrasted results. Figure 4 provides the graphical distribution of DEA and stochastic frontier efficiency measures. The general pattern is the same. The measure based on the stochastic approach has a distribution to the left of the other with a strong concentration in the range 0.3 and 0.4.

We now try to see whether some characteristics of insurance companies can account for differences in efficiency. To do so, we focus on two efficiency measures: those based on DEA with three types of premiums (DEA3) and on the stochastic frontier with gross premiums (ML). Table 4 shows how those two efficiency measures vary with the distribution ratio, the reinsurance ratio, the scale, and the claims ratio of the companies studied. It clearly appears that efficiency increases with size and this is not just due to the large size of public companies. Efficiency seems to decrease with the commission ratio. Reinsurance seems to have depressive impact on efficiency whereas the claims to premiums ratio has on the contrary a positive effect. The latter result is not surprising. One must realize that in a steady-state world, the difference between premiums and claims should just include costs and profits, which both are minimized in a competitive, efficiency aimed setting. As to the link between efficiency and reinsurance, it can be interpreted in two ways: an inefficient firm tends to seek coverage through reinsurance and a firm with much reinsurance could lack incentives to be efficient.

4.3. Firm-Specific Productive Efficiency in Life Insurance

We proceed with life insurance companies in the same way as with non-life insurance companies. That is, we use both DEA and stochastic frontier to estimate firm-specific technical efficiency in our panel data of 84 companies covering the period 1984–1989. With DEA,

Table 4. Efficiency measure and firms' characteristics in non-life insurance.

			Efficiency Measures (average values)	
Characteristics	Number	Range	DEA3	ML
Distribution ratio (%)	86	0–50	0.576	0.477
	102	50–75	0.507	0.373
	105	75–100	0.533	0.382
Reinsurance ratio (%)	85	0–20	0.624	0.466
	86	20–50	0.532	0.404
	72	50–100	0.440	0.359
Scale (millions FF)	55	5–30	0.479	0.347
	80	30–150	0.422	0.351
	44	150–400	0.573	0.465
	64	400–	0.706	0.509
Claims ratio (%)	58	0–30	0.410	0.337
	72	30–50	0.479	0.381
	88	50–75	0.622	0.449
	25	75–100	0.701	0.550
Total	243		0.537	0.412

we consider three alternative definitions of output: gross premiums (DEA1), both gross premiums and investment returns (DEA2), gross premiums both in collective insurance and in other types of life insurance (DEA3). As to the stochastic frontier approach, we derive firm-specific productive efficiency for gross premiums (ML). The efficiency measures so derived are presented in Table 5 in terms of overall average values, average values per institutional type, standard deviations, and range values.

Table 5. Firm-specific average efficiency measures in life insurance: alternative approaches.

		Nonparametric Frontiers			Parametric Frontier
Institutional Form	Number	DEA1	DEA2	DEA3	ML
Foreign	15	0.106	0.110	0.157	0.076
Mutual	13	0.327	0.348	0.401	0.250
Public	4	0.474	0.582	0.607	0.183
Stock	52	0.381	0.414	0.451	0.293
Total	84	0.328	0.357	0.398	0.242
Standard deviation		0.288	0.315	0.302	0.239
Range		0.04–1.0	0.05–1.0	0.05–1.0	0.04–0.95
Kendall's rank correlation with DEA1		1.0	0.92	0.81	0.72

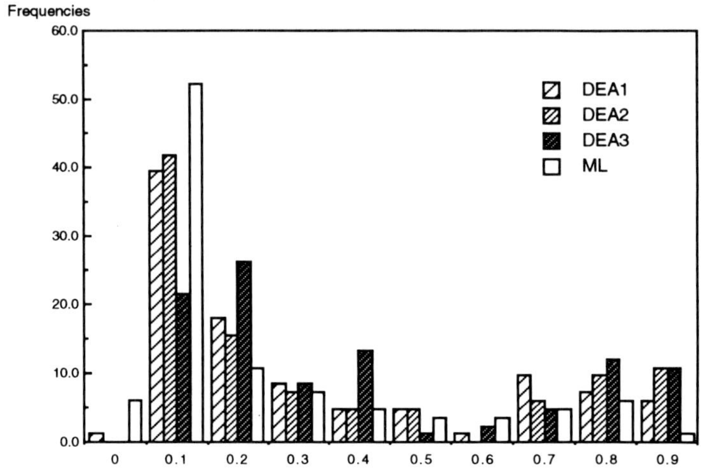

Figure 5. Frequency distribution of firm-specific efficiency measures in life insurance.

Again, efficiency is higher with two outputs rather than one. Kendall's rank correlation between DEAl and ML is equal to 0.72, which indicates that both these parametric and nonparametric approaches yield similar pattern of results. In all the cases studied, the dispersion of estimates is large with companies ranging from almost complete inefficiency to full efficiency. This appears in Figure 5 where the four indicators are depicted.

With regard to the institutional form, public life insurance companies are the most efficient though in a less striking way than for non-life insurance. In fact, with the stochastic frontier (ML), mutual and stock companies perform even better than the public ones.

In Table 6, we can see the effects on efficiency of other characteristics of life insurance companies. We have kept two measures, that is DEA2 and ML, as in the non-life insurance case. We find the following patterns: (i) efficiency increases with scale and with the ratio of claims to premiums; (ii) it decreases with the reinsurance ratio; (iii) it first decreases and then increases as the commission ratio increases.

The effect of scale is the same as in non-life insurance. This is an interesting result particularly if we note that productive scale effects are already taken into account in constructing the efficiency frontier. The effect of the claims to premiums ratio is totally different from that observed in non-life insurance. In fact, this ratio reflects two opposite characteristics: the pressure on costs and on profits as observed before and the maturity of the company. The latter characteristic is particularly important in life insurance where the time gap between paying premiums and getting benefits can be long. In this particular instance, this is the dominant characteristic. Young companies which cash in premiums and hardly pay any claims are unexpectedly "more efficient." To put it another way, if we used claims as a measure of the output, that effect would disappear.

Efficiency decreasing with reinsurance might pertain to issues of self-responsibility and incentives. These factors can also explain the ambiguous relation between efficiency and the cost ratio.

Table 6. Efficiency measure and firms' characteristics in life insurance.

			Efficiency Measures (average values)	
Characteristics	Number	Range	DEA2	ML
Distribution ratio (%)	23	0–20	0.376	0.260
	34	20–40	0.269	0.181
	27	40–100	0.454	0.304
Reinsurance ratio (%)	17	0–1	0.656	0.507
	29	1–5	0.414	0.246
	25	5–20	0.194	0.135
	15	20–100	0.156	0.095
Scale (millions FF)	23	5–100	0.261	0.117
	16	100–300	0.184	0.144
	20	300–1000	0.349	0.320
	25	1000–	0.564	0.359
Claims ratio (%)	23	0–20	0.541	0.426
	18	20–40	0.414	0.265
	18	40–60	0.219	0.131
	25	60–100	0.247	0.138
Total	84		0.357	0.242

4.4. Scale Economies

In this subsection, we cope with a side issue linked to our efficiency measures: the existence of increasing returns to scale.

One of the most lively areas of applied academic research on the insurance industry concerns the estimation of returns to scale using cross-sectional data and cost functions. In such a study of the French insurance industry, Lahaye et al. [1990] show that there are slight economies of scale in the French life and non-life insurance industry. With the stochastic frontier approach, we were able to compute the scale elasticities. They amount to 0.92 and 1.01 for non-life and life, respectively.

5. Explaining the Dispersion of Efficiency Indicators

The efficiency indicators obtained for both types of insurance are rather low and dispersed, those two features being closely related. Were the dispersion narrower, the average efficiency would be higher. One can thus safely conjecture that such important levels of inefficiency cannot be exclusively attributed to poor management but to various characteristics of the companies studied and of the overall insurance market.

We can explain part of the variance of our efficiency indicators with the characteristics used above, that is, scale, distribution, reinsurance, claims ratios and also the structure

Table 7. Determinants of the dispersion of efficiency indicators: Coefficient estimates and *t*-tests of independent variables.

Sector	Efficiency Indicator	Scale	Reinsurance Ratio	Commission Ratio	Claims to Premiums Ratio	Output Structure*	R^2
Non-life	ML	0.03 (6.35)	0.30 (5.46)	−0.20 (6.27)	0.48 (8.00)	−0.003 (0.09)	0.49
	DEA3	0.05 (6.27)	0.29 (3.12)	−0.001 (0.01)	0.62 (6.07)	−0.06 (1.14)	0.37
Life	ML	0.04 (3.79)	−0.51 (4.34)	0.001 (0.01)	−0.51 (6.76)	0.14 (2.19)	0.55
	DEA2	0.06 (4.05)	−0.71 (4.48)	0.11 (0.78)	−0.57 (5.59)	0.09 (1.01)	0.50

*For non-life insurance, this variable is the ratio of fire and property damages insurance premiums to all premiums; for life insurance, it is the ratio of collective insurance premiums to all premiums.

of premiums. For this purpose, we simply use the OLS technique, the results of which are given in Table 7.

From this table, one clearly sees that half of the variance of efficiency indicators can be explained by those five characteristics. Within that multivariate analysis, the bivariate relations noted above do not always hold. In particular, the reinsurance ratio now seems to have a positive effect on the efficiency of non-life insurance companies. It is also interesting to note that in life insurance, collective contracts induce efficiency.

This table leaves us with a puzzling question: why are most determinants of efficiency of opposite signs for life and non-life companies? One of the reasons for this might be that our indicators of output for the two sectors do not have the same implications in terms of two basic dimensions of the product of insurance: probability of a loss and size of a loss. Then what is being viewed as efficiency differences would simply be differences in output mix which are explained by characteristics such as the claims to premiums ratio or the ratio of reinsurance.[9] Another reason which has been alluded to earlier is that those characteristics do not have the same meaning in life and in non-life insurance. In non-life insurance, the claims to premiums ratio basically reflects the pressure of competitive forces on costs and profit margins. Thus, it is not surprising that it is positively related to efficiency. In life insurance, it also denotes the maturity of companies which face very few claims when newly established. This maturity effect seems to dominate the other effect and explains the negative sign. The reinsurance ratio has also an opposite sign in life and non-life insurance. In Tables 4 and 6, bivariate analysis yields a negative link between reinsurance and efficiency, and this was then interpreted in terms of incentives. In a multivariate approach, such as presented in Table 7, the interaction with other variables might explain the shift in sign observed in non-life insurance.

Even though we can explain part of the variance of our efficiency indicators, we are left with another puzzling question: how do companies with such poor performance survive in the market? Answers to that question pertain to the specifics of the French insurance market. First, there is no such thing as a unique price of insurance. A young driver has on the average to pay a higher premium than on old driver; a firm having experienced heavy damages has to pay a higher price for a given coverage than a luckier firm. Clearly, prices differ according to characteristics of the insured.

Second, the insurance market is very segmented. Companies tend to cover specific categories of clients. This is the outcome of adverse selection. Priests do not drive the same way as taxi drivers. Hence, there are in France two mutual insurance companies covering only priests and taxi drivers respectively. One can easily imagine that the types of services provided to those two groups differ markedly. More generally, looking at the portfolio of a number of companies, one easily realizes that they tend to specialize more or less explicitly.

Third, insurance companies use contrasted marketing channels. Some use tied agents networks; others prefer brokers or rely on banks networks. In fact, most companies use their own blend of these commercial devices. Insurance production technology can thus be expected to vary a lot across companies as the marketing of services is part of that technology.

For all these reasons, one should not be too surprised to find such lasting differentials in the levels of measured efficiency.

6. Conclusions

In this paper, we have used two different approaches to efficiency estimation of the French insurance sector. They don't seem to lead to very different findings and this is an interesting result on its own. Those findings can now be summarized. First, in both life and non-life insurance, there is a wide dispersion of efficiency, average efficiency being about 50% for non-life and 30% for life insurance; second, efficiency seems to depend on various characteristics of insurance companies. It is relatively higher in public companies. Efficiency appears to be higher, the larger the scale of operations and the lower the reinsurance ratio. The effect of the distribution ratio is unclear and that of the claims ratio is contradictory: it is positive for non-life and negative for life insurance.

The indicators we derived are very low and widely dispersed, and yet they are not particularly striking with respect to other efficiency studies.[10] It remains that we feel uncomfortable toward them as we realize that alternative definitions of output should be at least tested. To do so, we want to use output variables pertaining to the number and the main types of insurance contracts as well as incorporating a better treatment of the dynamic dimension of insurance activities. For this, we cannot count on published data but we hope to conduct a survey of our own. It will be interesting to see when this task is completed whether or not it yields a much different picture of the productive performance of the insurance industry.

In conclusion, a final caveat is in order which is also an invitation for further research. The tests presented in this paper have been restricted to the French insurance market. To conduct a truly comparative efficiency study which would tell us more about the capacity of the French insurance industry to face European competition, the same tests should be applied within and across other countries. Especially given the 1993 deadline for the single market, comparative research on the insurance industries in the whole EEC would be highly desirable.

Acknowledgment

Financial support from the Belgian Science Foundation (FRFC n° 2.4537.90) and the Geneva Association are acknowledged. We are grateful to Roger Betancourt, Rolf Färe, Shawna Grosskopf, Knox Lovell, Chantal Pirard, Henry Tulkens, and Edward Wolff for their comments.

Notes

*Paper presented at the Franco-American Economic Seminar on Productivity Issues in Services at the Micro Level. NBER, Cambridge, MA, July 23–26, 1990.

1. To estimate this model we use the econometric package FRONTIER written by Coelli [1989] and specially conceived to deal with unbalanced panel data.
2. The data were available from the French Federation of Insurance Companies (FFSA). From an original sample of 104 life insurance and 331 non-life insurance companies we have come down to 84 and 243 companies respectively, dropping observations which looked unreliable or which concern too small companies (gross premiums below 5 million FF).
3. We have a balanced panel for just 48 life and 164 non-life companies.
4. This distinction takes into account the case of compulsory motor insurance.
5. We used the Kendall rank correlation coefficient instead of the more traditional Pearson's coefficient because we are particularly interested by the comparison of efficiency ranking and not of efficiency values.
6. This finding is analogous with that of Finsinger [1984] for the German insurance market.
7. We have not introduced here a time variable. In previous tests, it did not appear significant which is consistent with the finding of Fecher and Pestieau [1993] and Wolff [1991], for whom there is hardly any technical progress in the insurance industry.
8. The regression estimates are given the Appendix.
9. This interpretation was suggested by one of the referees.
10. See, e.g., Caves and Barton [1990]. See also Kremp and Mairesse [1991], who observe in nine French service industries a wide dispersion of firm individual productivity and profitability rates even when accounting for various sources of heterogeneity.

Appendix: Estimation of Cobb-Douglas Stochastic Production Frontiers for Non-Life and Life Insurance*

Variable	Intercept	Labor	Composite Input			
Parameter	α_0	α_1	α_2	$\sigma^2_{(\nu+\mu)}$	λ**	m
Sector						
Non-life	0.32	0.72	0.20	0.153	0.927	0.981
	(43.9)	(55.6)	(16.7)	(10.0)	(162.5)	(16.5)
Life	4.27	0.40	0.61	1.06	0.97	1.53
	(17.1)	(13.9)	(16.4)	(8.2)	(330.7)	(10.9)

*The *t*-tests are given in parentheses.
**$\lambda = \sigma^2_\mu/(\sigma^2_\mu + \sigma^2_\nu)$.

References

Assurances automobile-habitation. (1989). *50 Millions de Consommateurs*. No. 40.

Battese, G.E., and T.J. Coelli. (1988). "Prediction of Firm-Level Technical Efficiencies with a Generalized Frontier Production Function and Panel Data." *Journal of Econometrics* 38, 387–399.

Bien choisir votre assurance: vie-décès-retrait. (1988). *50 Millions de Consommateurs*. No. 34.

Caves, R.E. and D.R. Barton. (1990). *Efficiency in U.S. Manufacturing Industries*. Cambridge, MA: The MIT Press.

Charnes, A., N.W. Cooper, and E. Rhodes. (1978). "Measuring Efficiency of Decisions Making Units." *European Journal of Operation Research* 2, 429–449.

Coelli, T.J. (1989). "Estimation of Frontier Production Functions: A Guide to the Computer Program Frontier." Working Paper #34, Department of Econometrics, University of New England.

Emerson, M. et al. (1988). "The Economics of 1992." *European Economy* No. 35.

Farrell, M.J. (1957). "The Measurement of Production Efficiency." *Journal of the Royal Statistical Society*, Series A, 120, part 3, 253–281.

Fecher, F. and P. Pestieau. (1993). "Performance and Regulation in Financial Services." in H.O. Fried, C.A.K. Lovell and S.S. Schmidt (eds.), *The Measurement of Productive Efficiency*. Oxford: Oxford University Press, pp. 374–385.

Finsinger, J. (1984). "The Performance of Public Enterprises in Insurance Markets." In M. Marchand, P. Pestieau, and H. Tulkens (eds.), *The Performance of Public Enterprise, Concepts and Measurement*. Amsterdam: North-Holland, pp. 223–241.

Finsinger, J. (1989). "European Integration of Insurance Markets. Preliminary but Novel Perspectives." Working Paper #15, University of Luneburg.

Finsinger, J., E. Hammond, and J. Tapp. (1985). *Insurance: Competition or Regulation*. London: IFS.

Finsinger, J., and M. Pauly (eds.) (1986). *The Economics of Insurance Regulation*. London: MacMillan Press.

Forsund, F.R., C.A.K. Lovell, and P. Schmidt. (1980). "A Survey of Frontier Production Functions and of Their Relationship to Efficiency Measurement." *Journal of Econometrics* 13, 5–25.

Gong, B.H. (1987). "Finite Sample Evidence on the Performance of Stochastic Frontier and Data Envelopment Models in the Estimation of Firm-Specific Technical Efficiency Using Panel Data." Ph.D. thesis, Rice University.

Gong, B.H., and R.C. Sickles. (1989). "Finite Sample Evidence on the Performance of Stochastic Frontier and Data Envelopment Analysis Using Panel Data." *Journal of Productivity Analysis* 1, pp. 229–261.

Hirshorn, R., and G. Geehan. (1977). "Measuring the Real Output of the Life Insurance Industry." *Review of Economics and Statistics* 59, 211–219.

Hornstein, A., and E. Prescott. (1991). "Measures of the Insurance Sector Output." *The Geneva Papers* 59, 191–206.

Kremp, E., and J. Mairesse. (1991). "Dispersion and Heterogeneity of Firm Performances in Nine French Service Industries, 1984–1987." NBER Working Paper #3665.

Jondrow, J., C.A.K. Lovell, I.S. Materov, and P. Schmidt. (1982). "On the Estimation of Technical Inefficiency in the Stochastic Frontier Production Function Model." *Journal of Econometrics* 19, 233–238.

Lahaye, J.M., S. Perelman, and P. Pestieau. (1990). "Les Économies de Dimension dans l'Assurance Francaise." *Revue d'Economie Financière* 11, 105–111.

O'Brien, C.D. (1991). "Measuring the Output of Life Insurance Companies." *The Geneva Papers* 59, 201-235.

Pestieau, P., and H. Tulkens. (1990). "Assessing the Performance of Public Sector Activities: Some Recent Evidence from the Productive Efficiency Viewpoint." Core Discussion Paper #9060.

Rangan, N., R. Grabowski, H.Y. Aly, and C. Pasurka. (1988). "The Technical Efficiency of U.S. Banks." *Economics Letters* 28, 169–175.

Schmidt, P., and R.C. Sickles. (1984). "Production Frontiers and Panel Data." *Journal of Business and Economic Statistics* 2, 367–374.

Sherman, H.D., and F. Gold. (1985). "Bank Branch Operating Efficiency. Evaluation with Data Development Analysis." *Journal of Banking and Finance* 9, 297–315.

Wolff, E. (1991). "Productivity Growth, Capital Intensity, and Skill Levels in the U.S. Insurance Industry, 1948–86: A Preliminary Look." *The Geneva Papers* (forthcoming).

The Journal of Productivity Analysis, 4, 95–113 (1993)

Productivity and Computers in Canadian Banking

DARRELL PARSONS AND CALVIN C. GOTLIEB
Department of Computer Science, University of Toronto, Toronto, Ontario, Canada M5S 1A1

MICHAEL DENNY
Department of Economics, University of Toronto, Ontario, Canada, M5S 1A1

Abstract

Canadian banks have invested millions in computer systems in the last two decades. Yet the banks and outside observers have been uncertain that these investments have had net benefits. In this paper, unique data collected directly from a bank is used to investigate the impact of these investments on bank output, input and productivity. Using data from 1974–1987, a translog cost model is estimated. Both capital and labor are divided into information and noninformation inputs. The results are generally consistent with economic theory. The attempt to separate technical change from possible scale effects is very sensitive to alternative specification. Overall there has been some productivity growth associated with the changing computer technology. However, many of the benefits seem to have accrued to the customer and have not directly lead to gains for the bank.

1. Introduction

Since the introduction of computers four decades ago contradictory beliefs about their economic effectiveness have persisted. The belief that widespread use was inevitable has been largely borne out. Yet, despite explosive growth in use of computer and communications based information technology (IT) serious doubts persist concerning its actual net economic benefits (Binhammer and Williams [1976, p. 143]; Yap and Walsham [1986]). These worries have persisted from early centralized, mainframe EDP applications (Hoos, [1982]), through widespread personal computer (PC) use (Bowen [1986]).

This research attempts to measure the growth in productivity in Canadian banking and compare this growth with the IT investment in the Canadian banking industry. Banking was chosen in part because it was felt that this industry is a very large user of IT. In banking, communication and records keeping are prime activities and thus the application of IT should be natural and useful in this industry. That the banking industry has been a leading user of IT supports this intuition.

The effect of large-scale IT investment in banking, as in other areas, has been difficult to demonstrate conclusively (McQueen and Savary [1977]; Gotlieb [1985]). The current trend in banking technology is to build large-scale distributed transaction systems and, unlike centralized mainframe systems and PCs, these systems are generally believed to be very successful.[1] Notable examples are the SWIFT international banking network and, outside banking, the airline reservation systems. Yet there is concern in the banking industry about the net benefits from large IT investments in on-line teller terminal networks and automated teller machine (ATM) networks (Touche Ross [1984]).

This paper reports the results of investigating the productivity impact of IT investment. The results are based on extensive data collected in one of the five large Canadian Chartered Banks, supported by the internal systems business case documentation from that bank and case studies from a second of the five banks. Previously data at this level of detail on a Canadian bank were not available and there is at present no similar data available for a larger cross section of Canadian banks.

Section 2 will discuss the development of the data in a form that is useful for productivity analysis. The following section will present the estimates of productivity growth in relation to the investment in IT. Sections 4 and 5 develop and estimate an econometric cost model. This is a simple exploratory model which provides some evidence on the role of scale economies and the possibility of sharp changes in the technology as the IT investment was undertaken. We conclude with a brief summary.

2. Productivity and Investment in IT

If measures of the benefits of information technology investment were readily available, a direct cost benefit analysis could be undertaken. While this would be feasible for some specific IT investments, data are not available for the complete range of these investments at the level of the firm. As an alternative, we will consider the growth of total factor productivity in relation to IT investment. By proceeding in this fashion, we are not considering the benefits that accrue to consumers or to firms in the IT industries.

Suppose the production technology can be represented by a production function

$$Y = f(K, L, M, t), \tag{1}$$

where output Y is produced using capital, K, labor, L, and materials, M. Then total factor productivity, TFP, can be calculated as a residual, from the relationship

$$\dot{Y} = S_K\dot{K} + S_L\dot{L} + S_M\dot{M} + TFP, \tag{2}$$

which states that the rate of growth of output, $\dot{Y}$, is the cost share weighted sum of the rates of input growth plus TFP growth.

Our data set contains considerable detail for each six-month period but does not cover a very long time period. This will restrict our ability to estimate complex econometric models later in the paper. We must aggregate the data in order to succinctly discuss and evaluate the productivity changes. However, we have tried to do this in a manner that retains some of the richness of the raw data.

The input data are organized into four aggregate inputs. There are two capital inputs and two labor inputs. We have included measures of information capital and labor as explicit inputs in the bank production model.[2] Any large-scale use of IT requires a specialized labor force. To investigate this aspect, we have disaggregated labor as well as physical capital.

Total labor is separated into two categories: (a) *production labor* (traditional production and support personnel) and (b) *information labor* (systems personnel). The former are bank product and service specialists and general support staff. They include all branch personnel and most head office personnel, excluding those of the systems department and data centers. The latter, information system personnel, are all those involved in the design, implementation, and (the largest group) operation of telematics based systems for production activities. This group includes the personnel of the systems and operations departments, and the central and regional data centers. Employees who use the information system to carry out their standard banking functions, such as tellers using the on-line banking terminals, are not information labor by this definition.

The capital data is divided into *information capital* and *production capital*. Information capital includes all production computer systems, peripherals, communication systems, and software. Rental costs include the actual costs of equipment rented and the imputed rental on owned equipment.[3] The cost of system development, physical operation, and maintenance is included in information capital.[4] Production capital includes the rental costs of all premises, non-data-processing office fixtures and equipment, and all other miscellaneous operating expenses.[5] Premises costs for systems and data centers could not be separated from other premises costs and are included in production capital.

Tables 1 and 2 show the total costs, prices, quantity indices, and cost shares of the four major inputs.[6] The actual number of employees is also shown for the two labor inputs.[7] For notational simplicity the four factors will be labeled K for production capital, L for production labor, M for information capital, and E for information labor.[8]

The growth of bank production labor[9] leveled off in the late 1970s, started to grow again in 1979, peaked early in 1982, then dropped to remain stable at around 25,000 to 26,000 employees. The prior long-term trend of employment growth and the pattern of information system implementation that is evident in internal bank studies strongly suggest that automation has allowed output growth without employment growth in certain bank outputs from about 1979. The leveling-off of staff growth in the late 1970s corresponded to effective completion of the on-line teller network. Subsequently new network applications were added in the early 1980s.

The information labor, particularly in the regional data centers, declined significantly after 1982, likely due to IT applications reducing centralized manual operations such as on-line data capture eliminating much data entry work. Data center staff remained about constant from 1985 while the later growth in the number of information workers came mainly in the systems department as new applications development accelerated in the latter part of the decade. As will be seen, there is no evidence of productivity improvement from this later investment in IT systems development.

The price series for both production (P_L) and information (P_E) labor categories are constructed from bank data.[10] The price series for production (P_K) and information (P_M) capital are each constructed from a weighted aggregate of their component prices. The price series for the components are mainly taken from data published by Statistics Canada.[11]

Information capital's component prices are derived in a similar way. The price series for the mechanical equipment component of M (e.g., ATMs) is the fixed capital stocks and flows price index for the finance, insurance and real estate, mechanical equipment (D883290). In the absence of better price indices, the consumer price index for telephones (D484188) is used for data communications, and the P_E index, developed above for the price of E, is used for the labor related components of M (maintenance and repair, consulting).

Table 1. Production inputs: total value and price ($000).

Period Apr/Oct	Production Capital and Other Exp. K: Value V_K	Price P_K	Quantity Index	Cost Share (%)	Production Labor L: Value V_L	Price P_L	Number X_L	Quantity Index	Cost Share (%)
1974 A	51231	1.000	100.0	35.6	81311	1.000	19711	100.0	56.5
O	58960	1.116	103.1	36.4	90360	1.059	20677	104.9	55.7
1975 A	62171	1.142	106.3	34.5	102774	1.156	21544	109.3	57.1
O	66489	1.197	108.4	34.4	110643	1.202	22322	113.2	57.2
1976 A	74279	1.275	113.7	34.6	120484	1.262	23151	117.5	56.2
O	78530	1.342	114.2	33.7	133743	1.327	24423	123.9	57.4
1977 A	86519	1.351	125.0	34.0	145067	1.391	25284	128.3	56.9
O	83186	1.380	117.6	32.2	151119	1.484	24693	125.3	58.4
1978 A	94833	1.450	127.7	33.9	157825	1.551	24667	125.1	56.5
O	99679	1.569	124.0	33.7	167035	1.584	25560	129.7	56.5
1979 A	122121	1.781	133.9	35.7	186446	1.730	26127	132.6	54.5
O	130209	1.938	131.1	36.0	195396	1.765	26830	136.1	54.0
1980 A	146537	2.206	129.6	36.8	210560	1.914	26667	135.3	52.9
O	135674	2.034	130.2	33.6	223370	1.998	27095	137.5	55.4
1981 A	168771	2.607	126.4	36.9	237520	2.165	26596	134.9	51.9
O	197109	3.109	123.7	39.3	250274	2.234	27155	137.8	49.9
1982 A	193236	2.831	133.3	36.6	271867	2.426	27165	137.8	51.5
O	198383	2.954	131.1	36.7	278868	2.564	26361	133.7	51.7
1983 A	176321	2.519	136.6	34.4	272262	2.574	25636	130.1	53.2
O	170690	2.520	132.2	33.2	278902	2.580	26205	133.0	54.3
1984 A	161386	2.612	120.6	32.0	276717	2.682	25007	126.9	54.8
O	167521	2.833	115.4	32.2	284709	2.723	25343	128.6	54.7
1985 A	167359	2.724	119.9	31.2	297282	2.822	25535	129.5	55.5
O	171187	2.684	124.5	31.2	305908	2.851	26012	132.0	55.7
1986 A	185859	2.806	129.3	32.1	313422	2.933	25901	131.4	54.2
O	180906	2.729	129.4	31.1	320645	2.942	26422	134.1	55.1
1987 A	188307	2.744	133.9	30.9	331836	3.116	25817	131.0	54.5
O	200144	2.860	136.6	31.4	347458	3.210	26240	133.1	54.4

Source: Internal bank data adjusted for confidentiality.

For the information technology (computers, peripherals) price series we adopt the new hedonic price index for computer equipment introduced by the U.S. Bureau of Economic Analysis (BEA) in 1985.[12] The prices series used is that developed by Gordon [1989] (extended from 1985) for office computing and accounting machinery (OCA) that combines the BEA revised index for computers with the price index of other types of OCA. This index is based on the U.S. computer market but no similar Canadian index is available. As rented and owned IT is the major component of M, the aggregate price P_M declines throughout most of the period studies. The effect of this can be seen in the huge growth in the information capital input quantity. The cost share for M grows from 4% to 9% of total costs (peaking at 9.5% in April 1987), while the quantity of M grows by almost 1800% in the period.

Table 2. Information inputs total value and price ($000).

	Information Capital M				Information Labor E				
Period Apr/Oct	Value V_M	Price P_M	Quantity Index	Cost Share (%)	Value V_E	Price P_E	Number X_E	Quantity Index	Cost Share (%)
1974 A	5766	1.000	100.0	4.0	5520	1.000	1167	100.0	3.8
O	6418	1.019	109.3	4.0	6376	1.057	1275	109.2	3.9
1975 A	7372	0.941	135.8	4.1	7781	1.176	1399	119.9	4.3
O	7694	0.865	154.2	4.0	8505	1.217	1477	126.6	4.4
1976 A	9016	0.858	182.3	4.2	10753	1.387	1638	140.4	5.0
O	9545	0.841	196.8	4.1	11285	1.378	1732	148.4	4.8
1977 A	11001	0.807	236.6	4.3	12234	1.383	1870	160.3	4.8
O	11560	0.783	256.2	4.5	12816	1.521	1781	152.6	5.0
1978 A	12995	0.711	316.9	4.7	13722	1.567	1852	158.7	4.9
O	14275	0.658	376.3	4.8	14689	1.652	1880	161.1	5.0
1979 A	17083	0.588	503.8	5.0	16459	1.816	1916	164.2	4.8
O	19458	0.511	661.0	5.4	16928	1.857	1927	165.2	4.7
1980 A	22018	0.507	753.3	5.5	18937	1.998	2004	171.7	4.8
O	24208	0.485	865.1	6.0	20227	2.043	2093	179.3	5.0
1981 A	29796	0.506	1021.7	6.5	21838	2.209	2090	179.1	4.8
O	30903	0.541	991.3	6.2	23080	2.322	2101	180.1	4.6
1982 A	36731	0.521	1222.0	7.0	26171	2.569	2154	184.6	5.0
O	36617	0.504	1261.3	6.8	25950	2.688	2041	174.9	4.8
1983 A	38057	0.526	1254.1	7.4	25520	2.712	1989	170.5	5.0
O	39425	0.564	1213.3	7.7	25014	2.859	1849	158.5	4.9
1984 A	42490	0.591	1246.9	8.4	23942	2.897	1747	149.7	4.7
O	44911	0.552	1412.0	8.6	23772	2.885	1742	149.3	4.6
1985 A	46405	0.617	1303.9	8.7	24701	2.978	1753	150.2	4.6
O	46720	0.593	1367.4	8.5	25649	3.051	1777	152.3	4.7
1986 A	51123	0.576	1539.7	8.8	27739	3.140	1867	160.0	4.8
O	51345	0.561	1586.4	8.8	29339	3.192	1943	166.5	5.0
1987 A	57754	0.583	1719.5	9.5	30866	3.355	1945	166.6	5.1
O	57524	0.526	1897.8	9.0	33113	3.463	2022	173.3	5.2

Source: Internal bank data adjusted for confidentiality.

2.1. Measuring Bank Output

The general problem of output measurement in service industries, and in banks in particular, is an old problem of productivity measurement (Marimont [1969]; Gorman [1969]; Berger and Humphrey [1990]; Fixler and Zieschang [1990]). In banking, many different services are provided to the public, but direct fees are charged for only some of these services. The fees do not necessarily cover the direct cost of providing the service. While fee income is becoming much more important, most bank revenue is derived from the spread between the interest paid on deposit accounts and interest charged on loans.

In this study, bank output is measured as an index of the quantitites of each major service provided, weighted by the bank internal unit cost of providing each service, measured in a base year.[13] Services include the number of checks processed, debits and credits against accounts, loans, term deposits, travelers' check sales, and other similar transactions. If the volume of such "services" has increased then output has increased. This approach is consistent with other studies (Daly, Rao, and Geehan [1985]; Geehan and Allen [1978]) but there is substantial disagreement on how to measure bank output.

The internal bank unit costs are used as a proxy for the value of each bank service. The unit costs for one base year, 1974, are used as the value of each output service in every period. Output is measured in constant 1974 dollars. The base-year (1974) value for services introduced after 1974 is estimated by extrapolating backwards, based on comparisons with other similar services. The internal, bank calculated, unit costs that are used are based on internal allocation of shared and overhead costs. Due to the difficulties in accurately allocating joint costs to joint products, they are not guaranteed to reflect the true cost of providing each service. However, in any given period, they reflect the firm's own best guess and these comparative costs are calculated with a consistent set of assumptions. For these reasons they are the best estimates available of value of services. It is impossible to know how these values relate to long-run or short-run marginal cost which is the theoretical measure that we would like to observe.

The number of service transactions in banking changes significantly as the patterns of use of financial services change. Deposit account activity has grown due to the introduction of daily interest accounts, no-fee transactions with minimum deposit balances, and ATM networks. There is more transaction activity without there necessarily being an increase in the level of "financial intermediation" or deposit balances. Yet, clearly, there are many value enhanced banking services. Customers' access to their accounts has greatly improved. ATMs (usually) allow unrestricted access outside banking hours to a subset of banking services. The distribution of ATMs and the on-line teller terminal network which allow banking at any branch bring bank services closer to customers, wherever they may be. Customers can more effectively manage personal finances. There are a greater variety of financial deposit instruments and more ready access to information from the ATM or branch network and, eventually, by telephone. Individuals can hold less cash, reducing their personal risk of loss and leaving the surplus to earn interest, by making smaller, more frequent ATM withdrawals as required.

The primary components of bank output are liabilities (services related to deposits), assets (services related to loans), and other services (related to safekeeping and exchange). There are, respectively, 14, 8, and 20 subcategories of service for each of these major categories included in our bank output measure. Table 3 shows the aggregate quantity, growth, and share of total output for each output category. The lowest growth in output occurs in the other output category of services. This category includes services which are still largely manual, such as the sale of travelers' checks, bill payments receipt, and safety deposit box services, and the newest automated services, such as current account reconciliation, preauthorized payments, payroll accounting, and direct deposits.

3. Total Factor Productivity

Table 4 shows the growth of bank output and the portion of that growth attributable to the growth of each input and to TFP for three subperiods. The calculated value for TFP

Table 3. Aggregate output and three main output components.

	Total Output		Aggregate Output Services ($000) based on 1974 unit costs)								
	Y		Asset Services			Liability Services			Other Services		
Period Apr/Oct	Quant.	Growth	Quant.	Growth	Percent of Total	Quant.	Growth	Percent of Total	Quant.	Growth	Percent of Total
1974 A	135842	1.000	37022	1.000	27.3	81505	1.000	60.0	17316	1.000	12.7
O	139491	1.027	35984	0.972	25.8	84444	1.036	60.5	19064	1.101	13.7
1975 A	148902	1.096	50222	1.357	33.7	81324	0.998	54.6	17356	1.002	11.7
O	161249	1.187	55731	1.505	34.6	86062	1.056	53.4	19456	1.124	12.1
1976 A	172763	1.272	60306	1.629	34.9	93835	1.151	54.3	18622	1.075	10.8
O	167484	1.233	50966	1.377	30.4	95493	1.172	57.0	21025	1.214	12.6
1977 A	168151	1.238	53304	1.440	31.7	96186	1.180	57.2	18661	1.078	11.1
O	173586	1.278	53370	1.442	30.7	100355	1.231	57.8	19861	1.147	11.4
1978 A	185194	1.363	54358	1.468	29.4	110704	1.358	59.8	20132	1.163	10.9
O	192146	1.414	55259	1.493	28.8	115557	1.418	60.1	21329	1.232	11.1
1979 A	192986	1.421	56336	1.552	29.2	117145	1.437	60.7	19505	1.126	10.1
O	200837	1.478	56974	1.539	28.4	120893	1.483	60.2	22970	1.327	11.4
1980 A	201422	1.483	57048	1.541	28.3	122740	1.506	60.9	21634	1.249	10.7
O	212596	1.565	58037	1.568	27.3	132684	1.628	62.4	21876	1.263	10.3
1981 A	210364	1.549	57090	1.542	27.1	131391	1.612	62.5	21884	1.264	10.4
O	217762	1.603	57488	1.553	26.4	135579	1.663	62.3	24696	1.426	11.3
1982 A	215626	1.587	52849	1.427	24.5	139187	1.708	64.6	23590	1.362	10.9
O	221232	1.629	53615	1.448	24.2	141199	1.732	63.8	26418	1.526	11.9
1983 A	224987	1.656	58790	1.588	26.1	143148	1.756	63.6	23049	1.331	10.2
O	235902	1.737	59588	1.610	25.3	150267	1.844	63.7	26046	1.504	11.0
1984 A	228751	1.684	56487	1.526	24.7	148358	1.820	64.9	23906	1.381	10.5
O	230552	1.697	56955	1.538	24.7	147305	1.807	63.9	26292	1.518	11.4
1985 A	234003	1.723	62239	1.681	26.6	149007	1.828	63.7	22757	1.314	9.7
O	239781	1.765	63186	1.707	26.4	151718	1.861	63.3	24878	1.437	10.4
1986 A	239351	1.762	65776	1.777	27.5	149035	1.829	62.3	24539	1.417	10.3
O	250718	1.846	69247	1.870	27.6	155769	1.911	62.1	25701	1.484	10.3
1987 A	248849	1.832	71999	1.945	28.9	152264	1.868	61.2	24586	1.420	9.9
O	255531	1.881	74931	2.024	29.3	154685	1.898	60.5	25915	1.497	10.1

Source: Internal bank adjusted for confidentiality.

for each half-year is also shown, in the first column. TFP increased by 18.0% from October 1974 to October 1987 which averages about 1.5% per year (pa). In the first five-year period (May 1974 to April 1979) output grew significantly and all inputs grew. Most of this growth is attributable to growth in the two production inputs although the contribution of information capital is large considering its cost share (see Table 2). TFP actually declined by about 0.1% per year despite output growth of over 35%. The productivity decline that occurred in 1976–1977 and 1979 could be related to heavy investment in IT that had not yet yielded sufficient efficiency gains. The major productivity gains came in the second five-year period (May 1979 to April 1984). Output growth slowed to 18% but all inputs except one declined in the period. Again information capital (*M*) grew significantly. There was a net productivity improvement of 19.1% or about 3.5% pa. The more detailed data shows a productivity decline during this period in early 1981 and 1982. The large decline in April 1982 appears anomalous from inspection of the detailed expense categories contributing to *K*.

Table 4. Total factor productivity calculated as a residual.

Period Apr/Oct		TFP (semi-annual)
1974	A	
	O	-1.84%
1975	A	1.88%
	O	4.52%
1976	A	2.00%
	O	-6.89%
1977	A	-5.78%
	O	6.45%
1978	A	2.67%
	O	1.78%
1979	A	-4.97%
	O	3.37%
1981	A	-0.04%
	O	3.37%
1982	A	-5.31%
	O	4.76%
1983	A	1.84%
	O	5.27%
1984	A	2.53%
	O	0.41%
1985	A	0.52%
	O	-0.23%
1986	A	-2.41%
	O	3.07%
1987	A	-1.29%
	O	0.05%

Growth in Output, Inputs, and TFP

Period	May 1974 to April 1979	May 1979 to April 1984	May 1984 to Oct 1987
Output growth	40.5% (7.0%)	18.0% (3.4%)	11.3% (3.2%)
Growth of prod capital, *K*	11.6% (2.2%)	-4.7% (-0.9%)	4.1% (1.1%)
Growth of prod labor, *L*	18.9% (3.5%)	-3.3% (-0.7%)	2.7% (0.8%)
Growth of info labor, *E*	2.5% (0.5%)	-0.6% (-0.1%)	0.7% (0.2%)
Growth of info capital, *M*	8.1% (1.6%)	7.5% (1.5%)	3.9% (1.1%)
TFP	-0.6% (-0.1%)	19.1% (3.5%)	0.0% (0.0%)
TFP 1974–1987	18.0% (1.5%)		

Annual growth rate shown in parentheses.

subcategories of property taxes, property maintenance and security, publicity, stationery, and other (unspecified) operating expenses all show an anomalous increase. These may have been one-time charges related to the change to consolidated annual reporting imposed by the Bank Act of 1980. The April 1981 decline was due to a decline in total output likely related to the severe economic downturn at that time. Subsequently there was strong growth in output while the reductions in input use continued. Extensive operational rationalization was planned in this period based on the IT infrastructure that had been built up in the 1970s. The economic decline of the early 1980s may have helped motivate this rationalization and it certainly made it easier to carry out. The next major automation stage, involving "smart," multiple-function, personal-computer-like banking terminals, was planned for this period but mass implementation did not take place until after 1984—after the period of highest productivity growth.

From the bank documentation available, there is no evidence of specific large-scale innovation in automation that could account for the decline in labor that took place from 1979 to 1984. The decline is due in part to the accumulation of a number of smaller technical innovations and a reduction in the number of branches. The restructuring of branches, aided by the initial implementation of ATMs, was likely a factor in the decline of production capital that occurred in this period as well. It has already been indicated that the decline in data center staff (part of *E*) resulted from the decentralization and automation of data capture via the on-line network.

A closer look at the pattern of output growth (Table 2) during 1979–1984 is helpful. The liability, other, and asset component of output grew by 27%, 23%, and 3% respectively over the five years. Almost 75% of the growth in *other* outputs was due to increased volume of automated banking services (particularly direct deposits and payroll accounting). Liability service volumes are primarily a measure of the number of transactions against various accounts. These types of activities are precisely those that are most impacted by branch automation and are most likely to be characterized by economies of scale when produced with the aid of IT. On the other hand, asset related services have been least affected by automation. For example, an internal bank study at another bank concluded that there was no net productivity improvement in consumer loans processing during the period 1971–1983. Investment in IT has increased fixed costs absolutely and relatively, thus reducing the banks' ability to adjust costs to changes in output. Binhammer and Williams [1976] suggest that it is likely this makes the banks more innovative in introducing services with high transaction volumes that have economies of scale in utilizing the IT networks. This is supported by our data. This evidence suggests that there are economies of scale, due to automation, in some bank services.

It was just before (1978) this period of high productivity growth, many of the new, more flexible products were introduced: daily interest savings, daily interest checking, variable-rate mortgages. The development and introduction cycles for new products were quite short, indicating the effectiveness of the on-line infrastructure for product delivery. These are precisely the type of products that can be easily supported by IT and generate additional transactions[14] that increase measured output without consuming commensurate resources.

In the final three-and-a-half-year period (May 1984 to October 1987) productivity leveled off for a zero gain over the period. Output growth slowed in this period while all inputs grew. Now the total growth of information capital almost matched that of production capital and exceeded the magnitude of labor growth. The reduced productivity in 1986–1987 may have been related to large-scale corporate restructuring and enlargement of the corporate and investment banking areas to position the organization for banking deregulation in Canada and the trend to globalization of banking. Some of the impact of the ambitious integrated and upgraded branch banking network implemented in this period should be evident. However, this expensive next phase of automation did not initially yield the expected benefits and ran into some technical delays. This was a factor contributing to the failure to maintain the high rates of productivity growth beyond 1984. Much of the impact was forecasted for 1988–1989, beyond the period for which we have data.

In addition, much of the investment in information technology was made for defensive purposes rather than to improve efficiency. This was a factor in many of the major computerization initiatives. Internal business cases in one bank refer to the initial stage in on-line branch automation, on-line savings, as a "defensive system" required to defend the banks market share. Even at this stage of systems development (early 1970s) the expected benefits from the on-line system were limited to "jobless growth," although this was not evident until after the on-line network was complete.[15] The ATM networks replaced the simpler cash dispensers in this period and the initial Interac network of shared ATMs was in place. These IT innovations were not initially cost effective and had little likelihood of future efficiency gains according to detailed internal bank studies. If this is true, the productivity of other technical innovations is greater as the cost of ATM system development, implementation, and operation is absorbed. These large-scale investments result in increased production costs for public image and other competitive reasons.

4. A Simple Cost Model for the Banking Industry

In discussing productivity in the previous section, we have tried to make use of a large volume of internal cases and memos in regard to the banks use of computers. The detail is difficult to translate directly into econometric models that can be estimated.[16] In this section we are interested in two major questions. If we aggregate the data to the four-input level discussed in the productivity section, can we estimate sensible cost function models for the firm? Will these estimates assist us in separating the observed growth of total factor productivity into shifts in the cost function and scale economies?

The existence of scale economies in banking is not supported in most earlier (U.S.) bank studies, see Lawrence and Shay [1986]. There are difficulties in many of these studies. In banking, like many services, there are only limited prices to use in aggregating outputs. We have aggregated the output components using unit costs. If these unit costs were defined so that the sum of unit costs times the output quantities equalled total cost, we would be enforcing a form of constant returns to scale through the aggregation method. Attempting to measure scale effects would not be possible.[17] In our case, we do not enforce this adding up constraint which leaves us free to try to estimate the scale economies. However, we are still forced to aggregate outputs using relatively weak information about the aggregation weights. This may make it more difficult to observe the scale economies.

We use the translog form of the cost function which, for the cost function C is

$$\ln C = \alpha_0 + \sum_i \alpha_i \ln p_i + \frac{1}{2} \sum_i \sum_j \alpha_{ij} \ln p_i \ln p_j + \alpha_Y \ln Y + 1/2\alpha_{YY}(\ln Y)^2 + \alpha_t T$$

$$+ 1/2\alpha_{tt}T^2 + \sum_i \alpha_{iY} \ln p_i \ln Y + \sum_i \alpha_{it} \ln p_i T + \alpha_{yt} \ln YT. \tag{3}$$

The p_i are the prices of each input, $i, j = K, L, E, M$. The aggregate output of the firm is Y and time, T, is a proxy for technical change. This form of the translog cost function has been widely used, see Denny, Fuss, and Waverman [1981] and Sickles [1985].

Linear homogeneity of the cost function in prices, "adding up" and symmetry impose the restrictions

$$\sum_i \alpha_i = 1, \quad \sum_i \alpha_{ij} = 0, \quad \forall j, \qquad \sum_i \alpha_{it} = 0, \quad \alpha_{ij} = \alpha_{ij}, \quad \forall i \neq j. \tag{4}$$

The application of Shephard's lemma yields a system of cost share equations:

$$S_i = \alpha_i + \alpha_{iy} \ln y + \sum_j \alpha_{ij} \ln p_j + \alpha_{it}t. \tag{5}$$

Denny, Fuss, and Waverman [1981] show that growth in *TFP* can be decomposed into the part resulting from scale economies and the part resulting from technical change, using information provided by the cost function.

The effects of scale can be determined from the elasticity of cost with respect to output, ε_{cy}. This can be obtained from the cost function by taking the partial derivative with respect to output, *Y*. For the translog cost function the scale effects can be determined from the equation.

$$\varepsilon_{CY} = \alpha_{yy} \ln Y + \sum_i \alpha_{iy} \ln p_i + \alpha_{yt}T. \tag{6}$$

If ε_{CY} is less (greater) than unity then cost increases are proportionately less (greater) than increases in output indicating scale economies (diseconomies).

The general contribution of technical progress can be determined from the negative of the elasticity of cost with respect to time, ε_{CT}. The negative sign has intuitive appeal because a positive impact from technical change means a reduction or generative growth in cost. This can be determined from the cost function by taking the derivative with respect to time, *T*. Technical change is defined by

$$\varepsilon_{CT} = -(\alpha_t + \alpha_{tt}Y + \sum_i \alpha_{it} \ln p_i + \alpha_{yt} \ln Y). \tag{7}$$

Then measured *TFP* growth can be decomposed as

$$\dot{TFP} = (1 - \varepsilon_{CY})\dot{Y} + \varepsilon_{CT}. \tag{8}$$

If the scale elasticity equals one, then measured TFP growth will be due entirely to technical change, the second term in (8).

5. Model Estimation

The system of equations (3) and (5) was estimated using the SUR procedures in SAS. The constraints, equation (4), were imposed and the share equation for production capital was omitted from the estimation.[18]

The estimated parameters are shown in Table 5. We are particularly interested in estimating the contribution of economies of scale, ε_{CY}, and technical change, ε_{CT}, in TFP growth, see equation (8). In Table 5, the right-hand side shows the annual estimated values of ε_{CY}, ε_{CT}, and *TFP* growth. Below these estimates in the bottom right hand corner are

Table 5. Parameter estimates with all parameters free.

Parameters	Estimate	T Ratio	Obs		ε_{CY}	ε_{CT}	*TFP*
α_0	0.02699	1.04	1974	A	0.066	0.000	0.000
α_L	0.57086	138.91		O	0.098	-0.026	-0.002
α_M	0.03805	21.04	1975	A	0.313	-0.020	0.025
α_E	0.04008	40.07		O	0.586	-0.014	0.019
α_{LL}	0.14854	5.87	1976	A	0.812	-0.008	0.005
α_{MM}	-0.00722	-1.68		O	0.590	-0.011	-0.024
α_{EE}	0.01065	0.88	1977	A	0.525	-0.011	-0.009
α_{LM}	0.01035	1.22		O	0.587	-0.009	0.004
α_{LE}	-0.00189	-0.16	1978	A	0.795	-0.004	0.010
α_{EM}	0.00227	0.87		O	0.879	-0.001	0.004
			1979	A	0.826	0.000	0.001
α_Y	0.06583	0.13		O	0.926	0.003	0.006
α_{YY}	4.41624	0.90	1980	A	0.857	0.003	0.004
α_{LY}	0.03149	0.81		O	1.015	0.007	0.006
α_{MY}	-0.07323	-3.99	1981	A	0.882	0.006	0.005
α_{EY}	0.05441	4.85		O	0.944	0.008	0.010
			1982	A	0.825	0.007	0.005
α_{YT}	-0.08719	-0.75		O	0.858	0.009	0.012
			1983	A	0.844	0.009	0.012
α_T	0.02746	1.73		O	0.964	0.012	0.014
α_{TT}	0.00071	0.27	1984	A	0.739	0.009	0.001
α_{LT}	-0.00148	-2.02		O	0.691	0.009	0.012
α_{MT}	0.00336	11.16	1985	A	0.664	0.010	0.015
α_{ET}	-0.00086	-5.16		O	0.689	0.011	0.019
			1986	A	0.598	0.011	0.010
				O	0.719	0.014	0.027
			1987	A	0.601	0.013	0.010
				O	0.640	0.015	0.024

Equation	Residual Errors			Components of *TFP*, 19740–19870	
	R^2	Durbin-Watson		Scale effects	0.195
				Tech change	0.052
log *C*	0.995	0.855			
L share	0.885	1.507		Estimated *TFP*	0.247
E share	0.727	0.983			
M share	0.976	0.998		Calculated *TFP*	0.293

summaries of the effects of scale and technical change on *TFP* growth. There are large-scale effects in the estimated model and so most of the growth of TFP is due to scale effects and not technical progress. However, these results are based on imprecise estimates of many of the parameters that enter into the calculation of ε_{CY} and ε_{CT} from equations (6) and (7).[19] Unfortunately, this implies that we are not going to be able to adequately sort out the effects of technical change relative to scale economies in our data. The difficulty of separating scale and technology effects is well known. This problem was experienced as well in studies of the telecommunications industry (Denny, Fuss, and Waverman [1981] Fuss [1983]).

Studies of U.S. banks have typically indicated constant returns or diseconomies of scale for banking, particularly so for large multibranch banks. A notable exception to this is the study by Lawrence and Shay [1986] which investigates a sample of 623 U.S. banks over the period 1979–1982. When data for banks of all sizes is pooled, scale economies are found in two of the four years studied (1979 and 1982). With data split into four quartiles based on firm size, there are economies of scale in the two smallest groups every year and in the largest group in 1980 and 1981. Lawrence and Shay attribute the difference from other research to use of pooled data in estimating parameters and to ignoring the scope effects of a multiproduct firm. The inputs and the measure of output they use are considerably different than ours.[20] In other studies (notably Gilligan, Smirlock, and Marshall [1984]) only the number of loans and deposit accounts are used as the output measure.[21] In our data, the liability component of output, usually over 60% of total output, measures transaction activity against deposit accounts. The actual number of accounts did not grow significantly overall and the number of the highest cost type of account (business current accounts) was almost unchanged over much of the period. If this measure of liability output were used there would be significantly less total growth in bank output. Thus the growth of output, and the measurement of productivity, is very sensitive to the choice of output measure.

In Table 6, we demonstrate the sensitivity of our scale elasticity estimates by constraining $\alpha_{TT} = \alpha_{YT} = 0$. This hypothesis would not be rejected in the model estimated in Table 5. The results from this model have much more modest scale elasticities which increase over time. However, the growth of *TFP* is now predominantly due to technical change and not due to scale effects. This is the reverse of the results in the unconstrained model. We did try a much more systematic statistical investigation starting from the model in Table 5. However, there was no final version, dependent on the test results, in which we had confidence. While we do intend further work, our initial attempts at separating scale effects and technical scale effects in determining *TFP* growth were not successful.

5.1. Elasticities of Substitution and Factor Demand

Do the cost models provide sensible elasticities? In Table 7, we present both the elasticity of substitution and the price elasticities for the models of Tables 5 and 6.

All own demand elasticities are negative as expected. The demand for the two production inputs is very inelastic. The own demand elasticity of information capital is close to one.

There is no complementarity indicated in the elasticities of substitution. Overall, information capital is a substitute for every other factor. As we would expect, it substitutes best for labor. It might be expected that information labor and informaton capital would be complements. In fact they are the best substitutes for each other.

This illustrates the effect of the current information infrastructure. Information labor includes both the systems development personnel and the data processing personnel in the data centers. The on-line network of teller terminals has displaced much of the centralized data processing (particularly data entry) staff. In addition, much more processing power and functionality is embodied in more recent IT. More sophisticated software development

Table 6. Alternative model.

Parameters	Estimate	t Ratio	Obs		ε_{CY}	ε_{CT}	*TFP*
α_0	0.00397	0.16	1974	A	1.128	0.000	0.000
α_L	0.57103	139.26		O	1.109	-0.003	-0.000
α_M	0.03899	20.57	1975	A	1.072	0.003	-0.001
α_E	0.03967	37.27		O	1.016	0.004	0.003
α_{LL}	0.14919	5.90	1976	A	0.969	0.004	0.006
α_{MM}	-0.01329	-3.21		O	0.998	-0.004	0.004
α_{EE}	0.01432	1.05	1977	A	1.000	0.005	0.004
α_{LM}	0.01107	1.31		O	0.985	0.005	0.005
α_{LE}	-0.00854	-0.65	1978	A	0.943	0.005	0.009
α_{EM}	0.00545	1.94		O	0.942	0.006	0.009
			1979	A	0.940	0.006	0.007
α_Y	1.12789	6.83		O	0.923	0.007	0.010
α_{YY}	-0.84643	-1.61	1980	A	0.928	0.008	
α_{LY}	0.02983	0.77		O	0.890	0.008	0.014
α_{MY}	-0.09839	-5.49	1981	A	0.903	0.008	0.007
α_{EY}	0.06568	5.55		O	0.872	0.008	0.012
			1982	A	0.892	0.008	0.007
α_{YT}	0.0			O	0.879	0.009	0.012
			1983	A	0.860	0.008	0.011
α_T	-0.00258	-0.052		O	0.817	0.008	0.017
α_{TT}	0.0		1984	A	0.841	0.008	0.003
α_{LT}	-0.00137	-1.89		O	0.841	0.008	0.010
α_{MT}	0.00350	11.11	1985	A	0.821	0.008	0.011
α_{ET}	-0.00090	-5.06		O	0.806	0.008	0.013
			1986	A	0.813	0.008	0.008
				O	0.777	0.008	0.019
			1987	A	0.785	0.008	0.007
				O	0.776	0.009	0.015

	Residual Errors	
Equation	R^2	Durbin-Watson
log C	0.995	1.035
L share	0.886	1.485
E share	0.688	1.115
M share	0.973	1.111

Components of *TFP*, 19740–19870	
Scale effects	0.053
Tech change	0.198
Estimated *TFP*	0.252
Calculated *TFP*	0.293

tools and increased use of packaged software would have the effect of reducing the proportion of IT systems that are produced internally (information labor) to that purchased or rented (information capital). Production capital is the least elastic while the two labor categories are reasonable substitutes for each other.

Table 7. Partial elasticities of substitution and factor demand.

Factor	Model in Table 5 K	L	E	M	Model in Table 6 K	L	E	M
				Substitution Elasticities				
Production capital, K	-0.4343	0.1762	0.2751	0.6972	-0.4950	0.2039	0.2622	0.8192
Production labor, L		-0.3278 (0.084)	0.9213 (0.479)	1.3703 (0.269)		-0.3256 (0.084)	0.6438 (0.533)	1.3961 (0.268)
Information labor, E			-16.1884 (6.083)	2.0706 (1.028)			-14.2082 (6.848)	3.5674 (1.101)
Information capital, M				-21.8834 (1.312)				-24.5333 (1.301)
				Demand Elasticities				
Production capital, K	-0.1513	0.0970	0.0128	0.0416	-0.1723	0.1122	0.0122	0.0479
Production Labor, L	0.0626	-0.1797 (0.046)	0.0412 (0.021)	0.0761 (0.015)	0.0722	-0.1786 (0.046)	0.0290 (0.024)	0.0774 (0.015)
Information labor, E	0.0953	0.5065 (0.263)	-0.7112 (0.271)	0.1093 (0.059)	0.0908	0.3540 (0.293)	-0.6270 (0.305)	0.1822 (0.063)
Information capital, M	0.2417	0.7541 (0.148)	0.0895 (0.046)	-1.0852 (0.075)	0.2847	0.7683 (0.148)	0.1522 (0.049)	-1.2052 (0.072)

Standard errors (SE) are in parentheses.
For substitution elasticities $SE_{ij} = SE(\alpha_{ij})/S_iS_j$.
For factor demand elasticities $SE_{ij} = SE(\alpha_{ij})/S_i$.

5.2. Other Variations on the Model

Several variations on the basic model were estimated in an attempt to shed more light on the scale and technical effects. The calculated *TFP* in Section 3 indicates that the productivity improvement occurred in the five-year period from May 1979 to April 1984. Prior to this period the major technical innovation of branch automation was being implemented and, despite this large-scale automation, labor input continued to grow. During this period, large investment costs were incurred but the IT was used as a simple substitute for manual processing. Documentation within the bank supports the interpretation that while the major investment and development occurred in the 1970s, the benefits were expected in the 1980s.

To investigate this interpretation several models were estimated with dummy variables representing the possible accelerated technical change after April 1979 (chosen due to the observed pattern of TFP growth). The cost function (3) was augmented,

$$\ln C = \ldots + \Sigma\, \alpha_{id} \ln p_i d + \alpha_{yd} \ln yd + \alpha_{td} td + \alpha_d t_2, \tag{9}$$

with three dummy variables. The first, d equals one from October 1979 to the end of the period and captures any break that occurs after 1979. To preserve degrees of freedom, it only changes the first-order translog price and output parameters after 1979. The second, t_d, equals one from October 1979 until April 1984. This variable could capture the very high rate of technical progress observed during this period. The third variable, t_2, equals one in Ocotber 1979 and increases in unit increments every six months until it reaches 10. The value of t_2 is zero prior to October 1979 and remains at 10, when it reaches this value, until the end of the data.

The model was tested with various combinations of these d coefficients and with and without the t_2 dummy variable. Generally, these parameters were not statistically significant. In some variations that included only α_d this coefficient was significant and one impact was a slight "improvement" in the estimation of ε_{CY} with values closer to 1 (which indicates no scale effects). Overall, however, there was little support in the data for the hypothesis that the impact of technology was systematically different after the initial completion of the on-line branch network.

6. Conclusions

The productivity improvements in a Canadian bank have been measured and the impact of investment in information technology investigated. Productivity improvement was limited to a 5-year subperiod of the 14 years studied. Attempts to separate technical and scale effects are not conclusive. There is evidence to support the hypothesis that the investment in and maturation of large-scale computer and communication networks have introduced economies of scale and facilitated output growth without growth in inputs. There is evidence of substitution effects between information technology and other capital and labor.

All productivity gains may not be due to the impact of investment in IT but it can be argued that the computer infrastructure provided the central means for rationalizing bank operations, particularly after the economic recession of the early 1980s. Other studies have failed to find productivity growth in the banking sector. Although we found a productivity growth (possibly understated) of 17–23% over a period of 13.5 years, this seems to be fairly modest considering the very large value of investments in IT and the great effort and risk that has been expended in putting the information infrastructure in place. The productivity gains all occurred in the five year period just after the completion of the on-line branch network. Throughout most of the period when the investments were being made (during the 1970s) the return on these investments was negative. Other factors should be considered in arriving at an understanding of the banks reasoning.

There was no cost justification of the initial on-line computerization projects. They were started for strategic reasons and because there was a widespread belief that they would provide benefits. As the benefits appeared elusive, cost justification was imposed on systems projects (this did not start until the early 1980s in the bank studied). But, by this time, there were enormous sunk costs and competitive pressures dictated that the current trend in banking technology be utilized. The Canadian banks are not particularly price competitive but they do compete by means of product innovations, access, and public image.

However, internal bank studies on the potential efficiency impacts from innovative use of the IT network suggest that the real impacts on domestic bank operations have not yet been seen.

This study has focused on the collection and analysis of a relatively unique set of bank data. However, the benefits of information technology may largely accrue to the customer. It is not possible with our data to measure these benefits but this type of analysis is necessary to complete the study of the benefits of information technology.

Acknowledgment

We would like to thank two referees for their helpful comments. Professor Denny acknowledges financial support from the Canadian Social Science and Humanities Research Council. An earlier version of this work appears in Parsons [1990].

Notes

1. Useful empirical studies of these successes do not exist.
2. Lawrence and Shay [1986] use computer rentals as in input in their cross-section study of 650 U.S. banks. Their other computer and capital inputs are much more limited than our data.
3. We have used the implicit depreciation rate for the aggregate capital categories from the accounts of the bank. Note that these are not the depreciation rates available for tax purposes.
4. That is, we are capitalizing the type of expense that most accounting systems permit firms to capitalize. On the margin, there are always some judgments involved in this allocation of expenses to current and capital accounts.
5. That is we have suppressed the material input category by aggregating a small volume of material inputs with production capital.
6. All actual bank data shown—the total cost of each input and the number of employees—have been uniformly adjusted by a scaling factor to maintain bank confidentiality.
7. Hours of work, i.e., paid hours, was used as the labor variable in all of the analysis.
8. As a mnemonic aid, think of E as engineers (although software "engineers" make up only a small portion of the information labor category) and M as machines.
9. The quantity of labor is an index of manhours weighted by wages and hence will not change in the same way as the employment series. The latter does not convert part-time workers into full-time equivalent workers.
10. Average wages were constructed for a variety of occupational classes and the aggregate labor price is a Divisia index of these disaggregated wages. Wages include benefits.
11. The production capital input includes property related expenses and other operating expenses. For premises rent, the fixed capital stocks and flows price index for the finance, insurance and real estate, building construction (CANSIM series D883289, Statistics Canada) is used. As producer price indices are not available, consumer price indices are used for Utilities (D484177), property insurance (D484174), property taxes (D484173), postage (D484191), and telephones (D484188). For other miscellaneous components the general consumer price index (D49000) is used as an index for inflation. For stationery, a producer price index for newspaper and other paper stock (D611616) is available quarterly from only 1981. It is extrapolated back to 1974 by comparison with other price series. For price series that are available only annually, semi-annual prices are interpolated.
12. For discussion of the debate on this pricing policy see Gordon [1989], Triplett [1990].
13. This methodology is similar to that used by BLS in measuring bank output for their studies on banking labor productivity.
14. Another element in the possible undervaluation of bank output is that the enhanced value to the customer from new flexible loans and repayment schedules are not factored into the output measure. Numbers of loans and not transactions against loans are used as output.
15. From a feasibility study On-Line Savings Defensive Systems versus Central Posting, dated early 1970s, from another major Canadian bank.

16. This is a common problem when detailed firm specific information is available for only a small number of years.
17. This appears to be a problem in the Daly et al. study.
18. This procedure assumes that output is exogenous. A simple set of instruments (GNP, population, exports, etc., and their lagged values) was tried as an alternative but the estimates did not change significantly.
19. There is also evidence of some first-order serial correlation.
20. Lawrence and Shay use an output aggregate consisting of four components: total dollar value of loans, deposits, and investments, and fee-based services (for which output equals fees charged).
21. In most U.S. studies, the dollar value and not the transactions volume has been used to measure output.

References

Berger, A.N., and D.B. Humphrey. (1990). "Measurement and Efficiency Issues in Commercial Banking." Paper presented at the Conference on Income and Wealth, National Bureau of Economic Research.

Bowen, W. (1986). "The Puny Payoff from Office Computers." *Fortune*, May 26, pp. 20–24.

Binhammer, H.H., and J. Williams. (1976). "Deposit-Taking Institutions: Innovation and the Process of Change." *Economic Council of Canada*, Supply and Services Canada, Ottawa.

Daly, M.J., P.S. Rao, and R. Geehan. (1985). "Productivity, Scale Economies and Technical Change in the Canadian Life Insurance Industry." *International Journal of Industrial Organization* No. 3, 345–361.

Denny, M., M. Fuss, and L. Waverman. (1981). "The Measurement and Interpretation of Total Factor Productivity in Regulated Industries, with Application to Canadian Telecommunications." *Measurement in Regulated Industries*. T.G. Cowing, and R.E. Stevenson (eds.), New York: Academic Press, pp. 179–218.

Fixler, D.J., and K.D. Zieschang. (1990). "User Costs, Shadow Prices and the Real Output of Banks." Paper presented at the Conference on Income and Wealth, National Bureau of Economic Research.

Fuss, M.A. (1983). "A Survey of Recent Results in the Analysis of Production Conditions in Telecommunications." In L. Courville, A. De Fontenay, and R. Dobell (eds), *Economic Analysis of Telecommunications, Theory and Applications*. New York: North-Holland, pp. 3–26.

Geehan, R., and L. Allen. (1978). "Measuring the Real Output and Productivity of Credit and Savings Institutions." *Canadian Journal of Economics* 11, 669–679.

Gilligan, T., M. Smirlock, and W. Marshall. (1984). "Scale and Scope Economies in the Multiproduct Banking Firm." *Journal of Monetary Economics* No. 13, 67–77.

Gordon, R.J. (1989). "The Postwar Evolution of Computer Prices." In D. Jorgenson and R. Landau (eds.), *Technology and Capital Formation*. Cambridge, MIT Press.

Gorman, J.A. (1969). "Alternative Measures of the Real Output and Productivity of Commercial Banks." In V.R. Fuchs (ed.), *Production and Productivity in the Service Industries*. New York: Columbia University Press, pp. 155–199.

Gotlieb, C.C. (1985). *The Economics of Computers: Costs, Benefits, Policies, and Strategies*. Englewood Cliffs, NJ: Prentice-Hall.

Greene, W.H. (1983). "Simultaneous Estimation of Factor Substitution, Economies of Scale, Productivity, and Non-Neutral Technical Change." In *Developments in the Econometric Analysis of Productivity*. Boston: Kluwer, pp. 121–144.

Hoos, I.R. (1982). "Statement of Concern." In *Office Technology and People*, Vol. 1. Amsterdam: Elsevier Scientific, p. 30.

Lawrence, C., and R.P. Shay. (1986). "Technology and Financial Intermediation in Multi-product Banking Firms: An Econometric Study of U.S. Banks, 1979–1982." *Technological Innovation, Regulation, and the Monetary Economy* 1986, 53–92.

Marimont, M.L. (1969). "Measuring Real Output for Industries Providing Services: OBE Concepts and Methods." In V.R. Fuchs (ed.), *Production and Productivity in the Service Industries*. New York: Columbia University Press, pp. 15–52.

McQueen, D.L., and J.R. Savary. (1977). "Economic Significance of the Computerization of Deposit-Taking Institutions in Canada." *Economic Council of Canada*, Discussion Paper No. 87.

Parsons, D. (1990). "Information Technology and Productivity in Canadian Banking." Ph.D. thesis, Computer Science Department, University of Toronto, Toronto.

Sickles, R.C. (1985). "A Nonlinear Multivariate Error Components Analysis of Technology and Specific Factor Productivity Growth with an Application to the U.S. Airlines." *Journal of Econometrics* No. 27, 61–78.

Touche, Ross. (1984). *The Impact of Techology on the Canadian Banking Industry*. Touche Ross Management Consultants.

Triplett, J.E. (1990). "Two Views on Computer Prices." Discussion Paper No. 45, Bureau of Economic Analysis, U.S. Department of Commerce, Washington, DC.

Yap, C.S., and G. Walsham. (1986). "A Survey of Information Technology in the U.K. Service Sector." *Information & Management* 10, 267–274.

The Journal of Productivity Analysis, 4, 115–125 (1993)

Efficiency and Productivity Growth Comparisons of European and U.S. Air Carriers: A First Look at the Data

DAVID H. GOOD
SPEA and INSEAD, Indiana University, Bloomington, IN 47405

M. ISHAQ NADIRI
New York University and NBER

LARS-HENDRIK RÖLLER
INSEAD and CEPR

ROBIN C. SICKLES
University of Michigan, Rice University and NBER

Abstract

In this paper we carry out technical efficiency and productivity growth comparisons among the four largest European carriers and eight of their American counterparts. The time period of our comparisons is 1976 through 1986. This is a particularly interesting period since it begins just after the informal steps toward deregulation in the United States and ends just prior to the introduction of the first wave of reforms by the Council of Ministers in Europe. We also identify the potential efficiency gains of the European liberalization by comparing efficiency differences between the two carrier groups. The reductions in inefficiency describe the amount that inputs can be decreased without altering output.

1. Introduction

In this paper we carry out technical efficiency and productivity growth comparisons among the four largest European carriers and eight of their American counterparts. The time period of our comparisons is 1976 through 1986. This is a particularly interesting period since it begins just after the informal steps toward deregulation in the United States and ends just prior to the introduction of the first wave of reforms by the Council of Ministers in Europe.[1] We also identify the potential efficiency gains of the European liberalization by comparing efficiency differences between the two carrier groups. The reductions in inefficiency describe the amount that inputs can be decreased without altering output.

Our analysis also provides a description of the competitive standing of European carriers relative to one another. As such, it is suggestive of the future success of these airlines once the protection of regulation is relaxed. Moreover, one of the most politically vocal sectors affected by widening competition (and its projected effects on inefficiency) will be labor. Our analysis demonstrates that the potential magnitude of cost savings may more than compensate displaced workers. Further, our analysis is useful because it explains why some airlines have favored liberalization in Europe, such as British Air, while others have been opposed to it.

In the next section we describe the data sources and variable constructions. Section 3 describes alternative estimation procedures for identifying the temporal patterns of inefficiency over the study period. The procedures differ in assumptions regarding the correlation of firm-specific efficiency with factor inputs and other explanatory variables. Estimates are discussed in Section 4 with particular emphasis on their implications for the extent of resource displacement which would result were European carriers to perform at the same level as the deregulated American carriers. The last section provides summary and concluding remarks.

2. Data

Our airline data set consists of a panel of the four largest European carriers: Air France, Alitalia, British Air, and Lufthansa, and the eight largest American airlines: American, Continential, Delta, Eastern, Northwest, Pan Am, TWA, and United. These four European carriers supply approximately half of the international traffic of all airlines based in Europe. The eight U.S. carriers supply virtually all of the scheduled international traffic of the U.S. airline industry. We follow these carriers with annual observations during the period 1976 to 1986. The primary data source is the *Digest of Statistics* from the International Civil Aviation Organization (ICAO). With this we construct a set of three airline input aggregates: labor, energy/materials, and aircraft fleet. In addition, aggregate airline outputs and several of its characteristics are constructed.

Labor input is an aggregate of five separate categories of employment used in the production of air travel. These categories include pilots, as well as copilots and other cockpit crew, flight attendants, mechanics, ticketing and passenger handlers, and other employees. Information on annual expenditures and the number of employees are available for these categories from ICAO's *Fleet and Personnel Series* for each year. The discrete approximation to the Divisia multilateral index number is used to aggregate these subcomponents (Caves, Christensen, and Diewert [1982]).

Fuel expenses are given for each carrier in ICAO's *Financial Data Series*. Unfortunately, there are no carrier specific quantity or price figures given in that source. Contract fuel prices for international traffic in different regions is available through ICAO's *Regional Differences in Fares and Costs*. The airline's fuel price is then estimated as a weighted average of the domestic fuel price (weighted by domestic available tonne-kilometers), and regional prices (weighted by international available tonne-kilometers in the relevant region). This method explicitly recognizes that for international carriers not all fuel is purchased in the airline's home country. Expenditures on supplies, services and ground based capital equipment and taxes are combined into a residual aggregate. Since the purchasing power of a dollar or its market exchange rate equivalent is not the same in all countries, we use the purchasing power parity exchange rates for the carrier's home country in each year constructed from Heston and Summers [1988]. These are adjusted by allowing for changes in market exchange rates and changes in price levels. Use of airport runways is based on landing fee expenses with aircraft departures as the quantity deflator. The service price for owned ground based equipment is constructed using the original purchase price, a 7% depreciation rate, and the carrier's interest rate on long-term debt. As with the labor input, these subcomponents are aggregated using a multilateral index number procedure. Finally, energy and the residual category are aggregated into the materials input using the multilateral index number procedure.

Detailed information for aircraft fleets is provided in ICAO's *Fleet and Personnel Series*. In addition to counts of the total number of aircraft, we construct the percentage of the fleet that is wide-bodied, which is a measure of average equipment size, and the percentage of the fleet that is turboprop, which is a measure of aircraft speed.

Information regarding the carrier's output quantities are obtained from ICAO's *Commercial Airline Traffic Series*. While this source permits several possible disaggregations we consider three components of airline output: passenger service, cargo operations, and incidental services which includes, among other things, equipment leasing and maintenance provided to other carrier's equipment. Revenues for passenger, cargo and incidental outputs as well as explicit subsidies are obtained in ICAO's *Financial Data Series*. The country's purchasing power parity is used as a price deflator for incidental output. Revenue tonne-kilometers (RTK) is used as a quantity deflator for passenger and cargo outputs. As with the inputs, these three components are aggregated using the multilateral index number procedure.

Three characteristics of airline output are also calculated. These include load factor, stage length, and a measure of network size. Load factor provides a measure of service quality and is a widely used proxy for service competition in most airline transportation studies. Stage length provides a measure of the length of individual route segments in the carrier's network. Finally, the number of route kilometers, from the International Air Transport Association's *Statistical Yearbook*, provides a measure of total network size. As the number of route kilometers falls, *ceteris paribus*, route density rises.

A table listing means and standard deviations for American and European variables are in Table 1. One of the more striking differences between these two groups is that while the output of an American carrier is on average 50% larger than that of a European carrier, there is little difference on average in the levels of employment or materials usage. The number of planes used by European carriers, however, is on average only about half that of U.S. airlines. Europeans have clearly chosen a more labor and materials intensive input

Table 1. Summary statistics.

Variable	American Mean	European Mean	American Std. Dev.	European Std. Dev.
Aggregate output (10^6)	3075.54	2022.64	1165.95	735.71
Labor (workers)	30730.76	31693.27	12435.41	10459.30
Materials (10^6)	1690.34	1610.86	569.02	649.48
Number of planes	220.21	108.10	85.74	37.72
Load factor	0.60	0.62	0.04	0.03
Stage length (kilometers)	1295.06	1179.70	422.65	123.48
Percent wide-body aircraft	24.89	24.04	12.18	16.62
Percent truboprop aircraft	0.40	0.26	0.99	0.34
Network size (thous. of kilometers)	302.14	489.51	117.03	143.63

mix than carriers in America. Together with the relatively small differences in load factors and stage length, this may be suggestive of service competition incentives among the European carriers which was extant in the U.S. industry before it was deregulated early in the sample period.

3. Econometric Estimation

Our estimates of efficiency differences among international airline carriers are based on a Cobb-Douglas single output technology and can be interpreted in the neoclassical tradition of static long-run equilibrium. While it would be desirable to estimate a flexible form such as the translog, we limit our initial study to more parsimonious forms.[2] Alternative approaches, such as examining the partial static long-run equilibrium using a variable cost function are not considered here since different objectives of nationalized and private carriers are likely to imply that production decisions are not cost minimizing given market prices for at least some airlines. Multiple output specifications, which include domestic and international traffic or enplanements along with revenue traffic have been considered elsewhere (e.g., Good and Rhodes [1991]) but do not easily lend themselves to the econometric issues considered herein.

Since productive efficiency can be viewed as a residual, we are particularly interested in the specificaton of the error term. Three alternative statistical treatments are considered for the Cobb-Douglas stochastic frontier production model:

$$y_{it} = X_{it}\beta + W_{it}\delta_i + \epsilon_{it}, \qquad \delta_i = \delta_0 + u_i, \tag{1}$$

where the subscripts $i = 1, \ldots, N$ and $t = 1, \ldots, T$ refer to the firm and to time, respectively, y_{it} is the log of aggregate output, X_{it}' is a (K) vector of log inputs and other firm characteristics at time t, and W_{it}' is a (L) vector of explanatory variables which may have different effects for different firms. The unobservable firm effects, δ_i, can be correlated with other explanatory variables and can interact with selected slope and intercept terms. This allows us to consider the endogeneity of such variables as load factor to firm specific statistical error. u_i is asumed to be an i.i.d. zero-mean random vector with covariance matrix Λ. The disturbances ϵ_{it} are taken to be i.i.d. with zero mean, constant variance σ^2, and to be uncorrelated with both the regressors and u_i.

The distinguishing feature of this model, developed by Cornwell, Schmidt, and Sickles [1990], over other panel data models (e.g., Hausman and Taylor [1981] is that W has coefficients that depend on i. Where W_i constant then (1) is the standard panel data firm effect model. In our application, W is expanded to include a time variable (t) which models firm specific productivity growth rates. Consequently, the effect for firm i is $\alpha_{it} = w_{it}\delta_i = \delta_{i1} + \delta_{i2}t$.

It is useful to describe equation (1) in matrix form as

$$y = X\beta + W\delta_0 + v, \qquad v = Qu + \epsilon, \tag{2}$$

where X is $NT \times k$, W is $NT \times L$, u is $NL \times 1$, and $Q = \text{diag}(W_i)$, $i = 1, \ldots, N$, is $NT \times NL$.

The three statistical treatments we consider are the within, or dummy variables estimator, generalized least square (GLS), and efficient instrumental variables (IV). Denote P_Q as the projection onto the column space of Q and M_Q as the projection onto the nullspace of Q. Let (X_1, W_1) indicate the regressors which are exogenous to firm effects and the regressors (X_2, W_2) those which are endogenous to the firm effects. The within estimator is IV with instruments M_Q and is given by

$$\hat{\beta} = (X'M_Q X)^{-1} X'M_Q y. \tag{3}$$

The GLS estimator is

$$\begin{bmatrix} \hat{\beta} \\ \hat{\delta}_0 \end{bmatrix} = [(X, Q)' \Omega^{-1}(X, W)]^{-1}(X, W)' \Omega^{-1}y. \tag{4}$$

The efficient IV estimator uses instruments $A^* = \Omega^{-1/2}(M_Q, X_1, W_1)$ where $\Omega = \mathrm{cov}(v)$ and is given by

$$\begin{bmatrix} \hat{\beta} \\ \hat{\delta}_0 \end{bmatrix} = (G'\Omega^{-1/2}P_{A^*} \Omega^{-1/2}G)^{-1}G'\Omega^{-1/2}P_{A^*} \Omega^{-1/2}y, \tag{5}$$

where $G = (X, W)$. The properties of these estimators differ by the extent to which factor inputs and other regressors are endogenous to firm effects, which in the panel stochastic frontier model are interpreted as technical efficiency. If they are exogenous, then GLS is efficient. If any of the regressors are endogenous to the firm effects, then GLS will be inconsistent. However, the within estimator is consistent regardless. If firm effects are endogenous to some, though not all regressors, then some of the efficiency gains of GLS can be obtained by efficient IV without sacrificing the consistency of the within estimator. These estimators are discussed in depth by Cornwell, Schmidt, and Sickles [1990]). The δ_{i1} and δ_{i2} parameters are estimated by regressing the residuals for firm i on W_{it}. Consistent estimates of the frontier intercept at time t and the firm-specific relative level of technical inefficiency for firm i at time t, μ_{it}, are

$$\alpha_t = \max_j (\alpha_{jt}), \quad j = 1, \ldots, N; \qquad \mu_{it} = \exp\left[\frac{-\alpha_t}{\alpha_{it}}\right]. \tag{6}$$

For firm i, productivity growth at time t is evaluated as the time derivative of α_{it}.[3]

4. Empirical Results

In addition to the standard inputs (capital (K), labor (L), and materials (M)), we augment the production function with several capital, output, and network characteristics (percent turboprop aircraft (PTURBO), percent wide-bodied aircraft (PWIDEB), and load factor (LOADF), stage length (STAGEL), network size (NETSIZE)), time (T), and time-squared.

Parameter estimates for the three treatments of correlations, within, GLS and efficient IV, are given in Table 2. The efficient IV estimator allows efficiency to be correlated with

Table 2. Parameter estimates for within, GLS, and IV models.

	Within Estimates		Eff. IV Estimates		GLS Estimates	
Variable	Estimate	*t* Stat	Estimate	*t* Stat	Estimate	*t* Stat
Intercept	*		1.125	2.100	1.330	2.307
ln K	0.349	3.411	0.339	4.266	0.360	4.741
ln L	0.468	4.887	0.347	4.195	0.355	4.342
ln M	0.221	2.419	0.280	3.161	0.280	3.241
PTURBO	−0.044	−0.163	−0.123	−0.486	−0.143	−0.910
PWIDEB	0.330	1.170	0.186	0.725	0.256	1.067
ln STAGEL	0.024	0.202	0.045	0.433	0.078	0.921
ln LOADF	1.048	7.435	1.053	7.500	1.048	7.970
ln NET	−0.065	−1.041	−0.034	−0.647	−0.055	−1.219
T	*		0.031	2.532	0.028	2.471
$T^2(\times 10^2)$	−0.012	−0.124	−0.031	−0.515	−0.046	−0.365
Model adj R^2	0.999		0.987		0.992	
D.W.	2.091		1.962		1.878	

*The within estimate of the intercept and coefficient on T are not comparable since they depend on the arbitrary choice of which firm dummies to exclude. These parameters are not included in Hausman-Wu tests.

a subset of the regressors. X_2 contains the output and capital characteristics: PTURBO, PWIDEB, STAGEL, LOADF, and NETSIZE, and W_2 is a null matrix. The variables in X_2 were altered significantly by U.S. carriers during the transition to deregulation and may be endogenous to the level of and growth in efficiency. Empirical evidence (Cornwell, Schmidt, and Sickles [1990]) also points to the endogeneity of these variables.

The three sets of estimates describe production technologies with similar properties. For all three procedures returns to density, whose point estimates range from 1.04 for within to 0.97 for GLS, and returns to scale, whose point estimates from 1.10 for the within model to 1.01 for the GLS model, are insignificantly different from unity to the 1% level.[4] Output elasticities for capital fall in the range [0.34, 0.37] while those for the energy/materials aggregate and for labor are in the ranges [0.22, 0.28] and [0.35, 0.47]. Estimated elasticities for network and capital characteristics vary across the within, GLS and IV models. The signs of the point estimates are quite plausible although individually they are not statistically significant. Reducing the size of the network increases route density. In general, more output can be produced with the same level of resources over long, dense route structures with larger aircraft.

Since the primary distinction among these techniques is the imposition of othogonality restrictions, the assumptions underlying the GLS and efficient IV estimates can be tested. At conventional significance levels ($\chi^2_{9,0.05} = 16.9$) the Hausman-Wu test leads to a rejection of both the GLS ($\chi^2 = 22.5$) and efficient IV ($\chi^2 = 20.2$) models for these data in favor of those from the within model which allows for correlation of all regressors with the firm effects. The remainder of our empirical discussion is consequently based on the within estimates.

Technical efficiency estimates are given in Table 3 for each carrier. Table 4 summarizes the European and American efficiency averages as well as productivity growth rates. Among the American carriers, there is generally an increase in efficiency over the study period

Table 3. Estimate of technical efficiency for within model (percent).

Airline	1976	1977	1978	1979	1980	1981	1982	1983	1984	1985	1986
Air France	65.83	66.37	66.00	65.65	65.27	64.91	64.55	64.19	63.83	63.47	63.12
Alitalia	59.93	60.24	59.73	59.22	58.72	58.22	57.73	57.24	56.75	56.27	55.79
American	73.46	74.54	74.61	74.68	74.74	74.81	74.88	74.95	75.01	75.08	75.15
British Air	58.73	60.62	61.72	62.84	63.97	65.13	66.31	67.51	68.74	69.98	71.25
Continental	76.58	78.00	78.35	78.71	79.07	79.44	79.80	80.17	80.54	80.90	81.28
Delta	73.08	74.25	74.41	74.57	74.73	74.90	75.06	75.22	75.38	75.54	75.71
Eastern	66.89	67.81	67.79	67.77	67.75	67.74	67.72	67.70	67.69	67.67	67.65
Lufthansa	66.62	67.02	66.49	65.97	65.46	64.94	64.43	63.93	63.43	62.93	62.44
Northwest	98.63	100.00	100.00	100.00	100.00	100.00	100.00	100.00	100.00	100.00	100.00
Pan Am	100.00	99.65	97.95	96.27	94.62	93.01	91.41	89.85	88.31	86.80	85.32
TWA	72.32	74.12	74.93	75.74	76.57	77.41	78.25	79.10	79.96	80.84	81.72
United	71.07	72.91	73.78	74.65	75.55	76.45	77.36	78.28	79.21	80.15	81.11

Table 4. European and American airline productivity growth rates and technical efficiencies (within estimates).

Productivity Growth (%)			Technical Efficiencies (%)		
Year	Europe	U.S.	Year	Europe	U.S.
76	2.8	2.8	76	62.9	77.0
77	2.7	2.8	77	63.8	78.2
78	2.7	2.8	78	63.8	77.7
79	2.7	2.7	79	64.0	78.3
80	2.7	2.7	80	64.0	79.0
81	2.6	2.6	81	64.1	79.0
82	2.5	2.6	82	64.2	79.0
83	2.5	2.6	83	64.2	79.2
84	2.6	2.6	84	64.5	79.1
85	2.6	2.6	85	64.6	79.2
86	2.5	2.7	86	64.7	79.4

from an average of 77% in 1976 to 79.4% in 1986 (see Table 4). This 0.24% average annual increase in technical efficiency can be added to the 2.4% average annual technological change[5] to yield an average of 2.7% average annual productivity growth. This reduction in heterogeneity (less efficient firms are converging toward the production frontier) is consistent with the deregulatory process. Firms lost both their protected niches and nonsystematic network restrictions. This was especially true for Pan Am. Pan Am had been the designated U.S. carrier for several European and oriental routes. As a part of the deregulatory process, the United States began to open its international routes to other carriers. Without any firm feeder network within the United States (only a very limited network concentrated in New England was provided by the acquisition of National in 1979), Pan Am was severely disadvantaged, and ultimately sold its oriental routes to United in 1986. Northwest, on the other hand, already had a well-developed feeder network with hubs in Minneapolis and Detroit for its oriental routes. This carrier is also one with a reputation for negotiating very flexible work rules with its unions, providing another rationale for the stellar efficiency performance. Another reason for the relatively high efficiency of Pan Am, which ceased operations in 1991, and TWA, which filed for bankruptcy in the same year, is that both have relatively long average stage lengths. Since their network remained relatively unchanged during the sample, very little within variation of stage length remains after the within transformation. The efficiency effect may be an artifact of long haul flights which are not being controlled for adequately due to the low explanatory power of stage length.

The four European carriers had approximately a 0.18% average annual increase in technical efficiency over the sample period. This can be added to the 2.4% average annual technological change to yield nearly the same rate of productivity growth as experienced by U.S. carriers. This finding is potentially misleading, however, as there are considerable differences among firms. British Air shows a 2% annual increase in technical efficiency, while the average for other European carriers is a 0.7% average annual *decline* in technical efficiency. Under the Thatcher government, British Air was reorganized as part of an economy-wide move toward privatization of national industries and was eventually sold in January 1987. During this period, neither the French, German, or Italian governments made significant moves toward increasing private interests in their near total government enterprises. In fact, the French and Italians have maintained a high level of explicit subsidies.[6] The difference also appears to be reflected in the different attitudes toward intra-European bilateral agreements: Great Britain has been a strong proponent of liberalization, while France and Italy have been strongly against it.

There are large differences between the average technical efficiencies of European and American carriers. Table 4 shows that U.S. carriers were nearly 15% more efficient throughout the study period than European airlines (this efficiency gap is nearly the same across all three of our estimated models). Figure 1 dissaggregates technical efficiency scores for the European carriers and compares them to the U.S. average. Technical efficiency levels are also projected through 1996. This provides a reasonable first estimate of the relative competitive advantage of individual European carriers. For Air France, Lufthansa and Alitalia, one possible reason for the declining technical efficiency levels is the loss of feeder

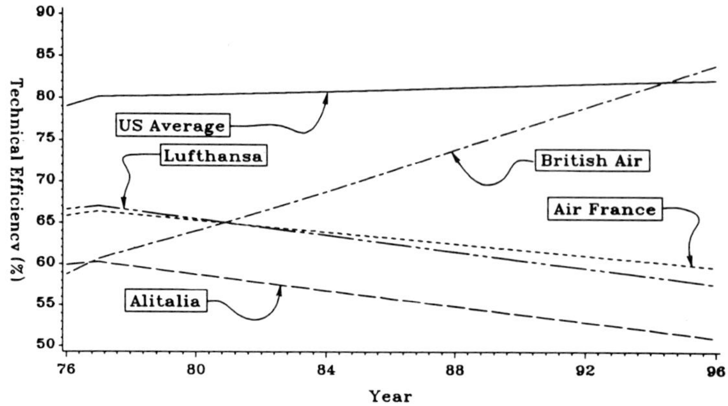

Figure 1. Estimated and projected levels of technical efficiency.

traffic in the United States as American carriers increasingly began offering their own international service. The figure also illustrates British Air's substantial reduction in inefficiency. British Air's technical efficiency passes Air France in 1981, the worst of the U.S. carriers (Eastern) in 1984, and were trends to continue, the U.S. average in 1993.

Although point estimates of time trends in efficiencies suggest heterogeneity among carriers in Europe and in the United States, further examination reveals highly significant differences in levels, but no statistically significant differences in trends among all carriers ($F = 1.28$, $v_n = 11$, $v_d = 99$). Whether additional time periods and a larger number of European firms will provide more precise estimates of heterogeneous firm-specific trends or homogeneous firm-specific trends in efficiency is unclear.

As mentioned (note 2), measurement of allocative distortions is not carried out in this research. The possibility exists that the magnitude of allocative inefficiency is such that it offsets the differences in technical efficiency between the U.S. and European industries. However, evidence on the U.S. carriers suggests that the magnitude of allocative distortions is substantially smaller than the fifteen percent technical inefficiency differences between U.S. and European carriers during our study period (Sickles, Good, and Johnson [1986]; Sickles [1987]; Good, Nadiri, and Sickles [1992]). Comparable studies are yet to be completed for the European carriers. Consequently, the public policy implications of our research are viewed in absence of such large countervailing allocative distortions.

The opening up of competition in Europe is likely to pressure firms to eliminate much of this efficiency gap. Implications of eliminating the gap on the four large European carriers are reported in Table 5. Since these four carriers produce approximately half of the output of Association of European Airlines members, we can double the figures in this table to get a rough idea as to what the implications would be for all of Europe. We find that bringing all European airlines up to the U.S. performance average in 1986 would have saved the entire European airline industry approximately $4 billion (in 1986 prices) annually which is about 16% of total operating costs. This is a *minimum* estimate since it does not include the costs of allocative inefficiency. Were output to remain fixed, such a

Table 5. Within estimates of cost and labor reductions resulting from elimination of technical efficiency gap between U.S. and European carriers.

Year	Total Operating Cost	Explicit Subsidy	Cost of TE	Workers Eliminated	Average Wage ($)
76	5,436.	*	875.64	19,207.	11,873.
77	6,371.	101.31	1,047.62	21,748.	14,989.
78	7,969.	118.22	1,311.92	22,244.	18,297.
79	10,160.	112.23	1,669.74	22,240.	21,706.
80	12,328.	95.84	2,026.60	22,085.	26,094.
81	11.390.	71.75	1,877.01	21,087.	23,453.
82	10,642.	76.43	1,767.41	19,858.	23,001.
83	10,663.	54.49	1,773.57	20,000.	22,646.
84	11,267.	*	1,843.50	20,421.	22,032.
85	11,850.	*	1,944.02	21,086.	21,946.
86	12,433.	*	2,022.27	21,083.	25,342.

*Missing data
All amounts are in $ millions unless otherwise stated.

change could lead to the displacement of approximately 16% of the entire European airline workforce, or about 42,000 workers. Cost savings from such a 16% reduction in labor and other inputs could compensate displaced workers much the way that special provisions in U.S. unemployment insurance were established. However, there are two countervailing forces which should be considered in subsequent analyses. First, the input mix is likely to change. Second, demand for air travel appears to be fairly elastic. There has been a large increase in air travel with accompanying increases in employment in the U.S. airline industry due to fare reductions accompanying deregulation, even though labor intensities have fallen. On the other hand, the potential for output increases in the European airlines may be lessened by the presence of substitute transportation modes, particularly the railroads. Unlike in the United States, these may offer up substantial competition to intra-European air travel which may mitigate the scope for increasing output through fare reductions.

5. Summary and Concluding Remarks

This paper has analyzed technical efficiencies and productivity growth rates for four European and eight American air carriers using three alternative estimators. While nominal efficiency measures are fairly different across these estimators, the properties of technology and the estimation of an efficiency gap between European carriers are rather stable. Eliminating the efficiency gap brings with it a savings on the order of $4.5 billion per year and a displacement of about 42,000 workers across the European industry.

As the title of our paper indicates, this is a first look at a very rich set of data that are continuing to be collected as well as a first look at somewhat reduced form explanations of the sources technical efficiency differences between Europe and America. As our European carrier list becomes more exhaustive, as we extend our time period to the early 1990s, and as we augment the European and American carriers with the remaining major world carriers, we anticipate being able to examine more structural explanations for the presence of technical and allocative distortions. The role that differing regulatory and institutional constraints have on the evolution of the international airline industry and how changes in these constraints will impact the survival propensities of particular carriers is yet another issue on which we will focus subsequent research.

Acknowledgment

A previous version of this paper was prepared for the National Bureau of Economic Research's Summer Workshop on Franco-American Productivity. The authors would like to thank the C.V. Starr Center, INSEAD, and Indiana University for financial support and John Meyer and seminar participants at the University of Toulouse and the Catholic University of Louvain for helpful comments. Special gratitude is extended to J. Mairesse and an anonymous referee for criticism which strengthened earlier drafts considerably. Purvez Captain, Cynthia Huebner and Michaiene Reilly supplied crucial research assistance.

Notes

1. For a survey of the institutional setting surrounding U.S. deregulation, European liberalization, and the international airline industry the reader is referred to Bailey, Graham, and Kaplan [1985], de Murias [1990], and Kaspar [1991]. For an early empirical study of European and U.S. airlines see Barla and Perlman [1989].

2. Substitution elasticities are unity for the Cobb-Douglas. Caves et al. [1984] and Sickles et al. [1986] both estimate elasticities of substitution of between −0.1 and 0.5, although they estimate cost and profit functions and their inputs are defined somewhat differently. Still, Madalla [1979] notes that measurement of technological change and efficiency are quite insensitive to the choice of functional form of production since both of these properties are related to shifts of the isoquants rather than their shapes. This initial study focuses on technical efficiency and leaves the analysis of allocative distortions for future research.
3. The empirical specification outlined in Section 4 includes a quadratic time effect that is common to all firms. All firm-specific productivity growth rates must be adjusted accordingly to also include the common time derivative of this second-order time effect.
4. Returns to density is based on the elasticity of output with respect to a proportionate increase in the inputs, *K, L* and *M*, while holding other variables fixed. Returns to scale, is based on a proportionate increase in inputs and network density which increases when the number of route kilometers in the network (NET) falls. Note that these are not comparable to the returns to density and scale constructed by examining the ray average costs of producing ton miles of service and serving destinations. The interpretation of network in a single output study such as this is a characteristic of the output, which although potentially endogenous to firm effects, is nonetheless not interpreted as a separate output.
5. Following Nishimizu and Page [1982] we use the term technological change to describe the rate of increase of the efficient production technology (in our notation, measured by changes in the α_t over time). Productivity growth includes both technological change and reductions in technical inefficiency.
6. Explicit subsidies include only overt transfers from the government to cover operating losses. Other transfers do occur, such as government purchases of stock at unreasonably high prices, favorable rents for the use of government facilities, etc.

References

Baily, E.E., D.R. Graham, and D.P. Kaplan. (1985). *Deregulating the Airlines.* MIT Press.

Barla, P. and S. Perelman. (1989). ''Technical Efficiency in Airlines under Regulated and Deregulated Environments.'' *Annales de l'Economie Publique Social et Cooperative*, 60, No. 1.

Caves, D.W., L.R. Christensen, and W.E. Diewert. (1982). "Output, Input and Productivity Using Superlative Index Numbers." *Economic Journal* 92, 73-96

Caves, D.W., L.R. Christensen, and M.W. Tretheway. (1984). ''Economies of Density versus Economies of Scale: Why Trunk and Local Service Airline Costs Differ.'' *Rand Journal of Economics* 14, 471–489.

de Murias, R. (1990). *The Economic Regulation of International Air Transport.* Jefferson, NC: McFarland.

Cornwell, C., P. Schmidt, and R.C. Sickles. (1990). ''Production Frontiers with Cross-Sectional and Time-Series Variation in Efficiency Levels.'' *Journal of Econometrics* 46, 185–200.

Good, D.H., M.I. Nadiri, and R.C. Sickles. (1991). ''The Structure of Production, Technical Change and Efficiency in a Multiproduct Industry: An Application to U.S. Airlines.'' National Bureau of Economic Research Working Paper 3939.

Good, D.H., and E.L. Rhodes. (1991). ''Productive Efficiency, Technological Change and the Competitiveness of U.S. Airlines in the Pacific Rim.'' *Journal of the Transportation Research Forum* 31, 347–358.

Hausman, J.A., and W. Taylor. (1981). ''Panel Data and Unobservable Individual Effects.'' *Econometrica* 49, 1377–1399.

Heston, A., and R. Summers. (1988). ''Comparisons of Price and Gross Domestic Product for Several Countries,'' *Review of Income and Wealth,* 34, 1–28.

Kaspar, D.M. (1991). *Deregulation and Globalization: Liberalizing International Trade in Air Services.* American Enterprise Institute. Cambridge MA: Ballinger.

Madala, G.S. (1979). ''A Note on the Form of the Production Function and Productivity.'' In *Measurement and Interpretation of Productivity.* National Research Council. Washington, DC: National Academy of Sciences, pp. 309–317.

Nishimizu, M., and J.M. Page. (1982). ''Total Factor Productivity Growth, Technological Progress and Technical Efficiency Change.'' *The Economic Journal* 92, 920–936.

Sickles, R.C. (1987). ''Allocative Inefficiency in the U.S. Airlines: A Case for Deregulation.'' In Ali Dogramaci (ed.), *Studies in Productivity Analysis,* Vol. 7. Boston: Kluwer-Nijhoff, pp. 149–162.

Sickles, R.C., D. Good, and R. Johnson. (1986). ''Allocative Distortions and the Regulatory Transition of the U.S. Airline Industry.'' *Journal of Econometrics* 33, 143–163.

The Journal of Productivity Analysis, 4, 127–144 (1993)

Cost Effects of Mergers and Deregulation in the U.S. Rail Industry

ERNST R. BERNDT
Massachusetts Institute of Technology, Alfred P. Sloan School of Management, Cambridge, MA 02139

ANN. F. FRIEDLAENDER
Department of Economics, Massachusetts Institute of Technology, Cambridge, MA 02139

JUDY SHAW-ER WANG CHIANG
Massachusetts Institute of Technology, Center for Energy Policy Research, Cambridge, MA 02139

CHRISTOPHER A. VELLTURO
National Economic Research Associates, Cambridge, MA 02139

Abstract

We attempt to disentangle the effects of deregulation on rail costs from those directly attributable to mergers and acquisitions, employing a translog variable cost function, based on an unbalanced panel data set of annual observations for major U.S. Class I railroads from 1974 to 1986. We find that both deregulation and mergers contributed significantly to cost savings. However, of the accumulated cost savings achieved by the six major firms involved in mergers postderegulation, we estimate that by 1986 about 91% of the reduction in accumulated costs is due to deregulation, and about 9% is directly due to mergers and acquisitions (which in turn were facilitated by regulatory reforms).

1. Introduction

In the decade since the passage of the Staggers' Act—legislation that substantially deregulated U.S. railroads—considerable change has occurred. The number of Class I railroads has diminished through bankruptcies, consolidations and mergers; concentration has risen concomitantly, with seven carriers now accounting for over 70% of rail freight traffic. Over 25,000 miles of track have either been sold or abandoned; and rates of return have risen substantially, with several railroads now achieving revenue adequacy.

While the impacts of deregulation on the railroads are widely recognized, the sources of the changes that have occurred in this industry have not been fully analyzed. Because deregulation gave the railroads substantial freedom in rate setting, track abandonments, and mergers, it provided them with a number of avenues through which costs could be reduced and revenue could be enhanced.

As part of an ongoing research project, we have attempted to disentangle the various effects of deregulation upon the railroads. In particular, the impact of deregulation upon rates and revenues, on the one hand, and costs and capital adjustments, on the other, have been respectively analyzed by Friedlaender [1992], Friedlaender et al. [1991], and Vellturo et al. [1992]. In this paper we attempt to disentangle the effects of deregulation on real costs and productivity from those directly attributable to mergers and acquisitions. Our empirical analysis employs a short-run variable cost function, and our econometric estimates are based on an unbalanced panel data set of annual observations for major Class I U.S. railroads from 1974 to 1986.

This paper takes the following form. Section 2 discusses the nature of rail mergers, specifies an econometric model based on a translog short-run variable cost function, and then outlines how the effects of deregulation and mergers on costs and productivity growth can be distinguished and quantified. Section 3 describes the data set, while Section 4 provides a discussion of a number of econometric issues related to the specification and estimation of the cost function equations. Our principal empirical findings are given in Section 5, and in the final section we briefly summarize our conclusions and suggest issues for future research.

2. Rail Mergers and Productivity Growth

Prior to the onset of deregulation, rail mergers typically involved unions of systems having a great deal of parallel trackage.[1] Under such circumstances, hearings at the Interstate Commerce Commission (ICC) typically focused on the traditional welfare trade-off that mergers could provide between the cost efficiencies occasioned by consolidation and economies of scale on the one hand, and the potential for noncompetitive pricing on the other. These hearings were often lengthy, and judgments were typically complex.[2] Most approvals required that extensive trackage rights be granted others to ensure competition, and/or that smaller satellite roads be included to guarantee service.

In contrast, proposed mergers in the post-Staggers' era have principally been end-to-end unions,[3] in which the proponents have cited significant economies through the elimination of freight transfer, the implementation of joint marketing agreements, the consolidation of tracking and maintenance systems, increased run-through operations and more efficient car utilization. While such economies are certainly available in principle, it is also possible that they may be offset and outweighed by organizational issues related to consolidation and merger. Thus, whether these potential economies produce any net efficiency gains in costs or productivity is unclear.

In this context, the potential efficiency gains from mergers fall into three categories: reduced short-run variable costs; reduced long-run costs due to adjustments in way and structure capital stocks toward allocatively efficient levels; and enhanced service quality. Cost functions provide a useful framework in which these efficiencies can be studied.

Consider a total cost (TC) function for railroad h in year t, in which short-run operating and long-run total costs are related as follows:

$$TC_{ht} = SRVC[y_{ht}, w_{ht}, \tau_{ht}, t; K_{ht}] + R_{k,ht}K_{ht}, \tag{1}$$

where $SRVC$ is a short-run variable cost function with capital K_{ht} fixed in the short-run, y_{ht} is ton-miles of revenue freight,[4] w_{ht} is a vector of prices for variable inputs (labor, equipment, fuel, materials, and supplies),[5] τ_{ht} is a vector of technological factors (route miles, average length of haul, traffic mix), t is a vector of time-related variables (an annual time counter to accommodate disembodied technical change, as well as time counters for years since deregulation occurred, and years since firm h was last involved in a major merger), and $P_{K,ht}$ is an *ex ante* cost of capital for firm h.

Note that the cost specification in (1) does not include measures of a given railroad's network configuration—factors that embrace the logistics of a firm's route structure such as end-to-end versus hub-and-spoke, its track grade, population density over routes, etc. It is of course true that such factors may be important in specifying cross-sectional variations in variable costs. However, specifying a cost function that fully captures these effects would involve introducing a very large number of right-hand-side variables into the analysis, many of which would suffer from significant measurement errors. As a practical matter, therefore, we assume that these poorly measured and/or unobserved network configuration effects are invariant for a given railroad over time, and we will attempt to capture the aggregate impact of such network effects on costs by introducing a series of firm-specific dummy variables into the cost function and input share equations; these are discussed further in Section 4.

Other important measurement issues concern modeling the effects of changes in service quality, and the effects of adjustment toward optimal capital stocks. Service quality measures are typically market specific; for example, Levin and Weinberg [1979] employed market shares in point-to-point markets, while Harris and Winston [1983] used the mean and variance of transit time for specific point-to-point shipments. In both these studies, the network size and capital stocks were implicitly held fixed. This study relies upon firm-level data rather than point-to-point shipment data. Although we will model the effects of capital adjustment toward optimal long-run levels, we will not be able to account for service quality improvements. In related papers we quantify the cost savings and capital adjustments of the past 15 years.[6] In this paper we focus on the issue of measuring the differential effects of mergers and deregulation upon costs and productivity in the rail industry.

We analyze this issue by utilizing a short-run translog variable cost function, written as

$$
\begin{aligned}
\ln C_v = {} & A_0 + \sum_{i=1}^{n} A_i \ln w_i + B_1 \ln y + \sum_{j=1}^{m} C_j \ln t_j + D_1 t \\
& + M_1 t^m + R_1 t^r + 0.5 \sum_{i=1}^{n} \sum_{c=1}^{n} AA_{ic} \ln w_i \ln w_c + 0.5\, BB_{11} (\ln y)^2 \\
& + \sum_{i=1}^{n} AB_{i1} \ln w_i \ln y + \sum_{i=1}^{n} \sum_{j=1}^{m} AC_{ij} \ln w_i \ln t_j + \sum_{i=1}^{n} BC_{j1} \ln t_j \ln y \\
& + 0.5 \sum_{j=1}^{m} \sum_{k=1}^{m} CC_{jk} \ln t_j \ln t_k + \sum_{i=1}^{n} AD_{i1} t \ln w_i
\end{aligned}
$$

$$+\sum_{i=1}^{n} AD_{i2}t^{r} \ln w_i + \sum_{i=1}^{n} AD_{i3}t^{m} \ln w_i + AD_4 MDUM$$

$$+ 0.5D_{11}t^2 + 0.5M_{11}t^{m2} + 0.5R_{11}t^{r2}, \tag{2}$$

where C_v is variable costs, $C_v \equiv \Sigma_i w_i x_i$, w_i and x_i are input prices and quantities, respectively, $i = 1, \ldots, n$, y is output, the t_j are technological variables, $j = 1, \ldots, m$, t is an annual time counter having the value 1 in the first year of the sample (1974), t^m is an annual time counter on the number of years since the company has last been involved in a merger, *MDUM* is a dummy variable taking on a value of 1 if the railroad was involved in a merger in that year (else it is zero), and t^r is another annual time counter measuring years since the 1978 deregulation occurred (1979 = 1, . . . , 1986 = 8). According to this specification, mergers may have a one-time positive "adjustment cost" effect on costs as measured by AD_4 (the coefficient on the *MDUM* dummy variable), but after that costs can diminish over time, depending on the values of the M_1 and M_{11} parameters.

For the translog restricted cost function to be well behaved, it is necessary that symmetry and homogeneity restrictions be imposed. These take the form

$$AA_{ic} = AA_{ci}, \quad CC_{jk} = CC_{kj}, \quad i, c = 1, \ldots, n; j, k = 1, \ldots, m,$$

$$\sum_{i=1}^{n} A_i = 1, \quad \sum_{i=1}^{n} AA_{ic} = \sum_{i=1}^{n} AB_{i1} = \sum_{i=1}^{n} AC_{ij} = \sum_{i=1}^{n} AD_{ip} = 0,$$

$$i, c = 1, \ldots, n; \quad j = 1, \ldots, m; \quad p = 1, 2, 3. \tag{3}$$

Logarithmically differentiating (2) with respect to input prices and using Shephard's lemma yields n cost share equations, only $n - 1$ of which are linearly independent. The ith share equation is of the form

$$\frac{\partial \ln C_v}{\partial \ln w_i} = \frac{w_i x_i}{C_v}$$

$$= A_i + \sum_{c=1}^{n} AA_{ic} \ln w_c + \sum_{j=1}^{n} AC_{ij} \ln t_j + AB_{i1} \ln y$$

$$+ D_{i1}t + D_{i2}t^r + D_{i3}t^m, \quad i = 1, \ldots, n. \tag{4}$$

We analyze productivity growth by differentiating the cost function (2) with respect to time, which yields the following expression for the rate of cost diminution (the negative of the rate of productivity growth):

$$\frac{\partial \ln C_v}{\partial t} = D_1 + M_1 FM + R_1 FD + \sum_{i=1}^{n} (AD_{i1} + AD_{i2} FD + AD_{i3} FM) \ln w_i$$

$$+ D_{11} t + M_{11} FMt^m + R_{11} FDt^r, \tag{5}$$

where FM and FD are dummy variables indicating whether the firm was ever involved in a merger ($FM = 1$ if yes), and if the observation is in a year after deregulation has occurred ($FD = 1$ if yes). According to (5), productivity growth differs depending on whether the observation comes from a regulated time period (in which case the R_1, AD_{i2}, and R_{11} terms are zero) or a deregulated era (these terms become nonzero), and, for firms having been involved in a merger or acquisition, the number of years since the last merger (the M_1, AD_{13}, and M_{11} terms become nonzero).

The effects of deregulation and mergers on costs and productivity can be partially quantified as follows. If deregulation and mergers have no effects on costs and productivity, then $M_1 = R_1 = AD_{i2} = AD_{i3} = AD_4 = M_{11} = R_{11} = 0, i = 1, \ldots, n$. But if deregulation has differential effects on costs and productivity while mergers do not, then $M_1 = AD_{i3} = AD_4 = M_{11} = 0$ and some of the R_1, AD_{i2}, and $R_{11} \neq 0, i = 1, \ldots, n$. Finally, if mergers have differential effects on costs and productivity while deregulation does not, then $R_1 = AD_{i2} = R_{11} = 0$, and some of the M_1, AD_{i3}, AD_4, and $M_{11} \neq 0$. Hence, within this framework, one can distinguish in part the effects on costs and productivity of deregulation from those directly due to mergers and acquisitions.

3. Data Sources and Econometric Issues

The estimation of a short-run variable cost function and its input demand equations requires the following firm-specific data: short-run variable costs by input, input factor prices, output measures and output composition; technological factors; and way and structures capital stock. We now provide a brief overview of our data set and its construction; further details are given in Vellturo [1989].

We begin with a discussion of firms in our sample. Fifty-six railroads had Class I status in 1974, but only 21 reported data in 1986.[7] From these systems, 27 railroads were deemed to have sufficiently accurate data to be included in the sample. A large number of railroads lost Class I status, others had incomplete bond histories (which made it impossible to generate correct capital equipment costs), while others went bankrupt for significant portions of the sample and their data was deemed unreliable. Since certain roads ceased to exist upon consolidation into other new systems, the panel is not balanced; if it were balanced, our panel would have 351 observations (27 firms times 13 years), but for us only 229 observations are available. The names of the firms used in our sample, and their abbreviations, are given in Table 1, while firms involved in major mergers are listed in Table 2.

In order to adjust for the effects of inflation, we estimate the cost function in which all dollar magnitudes are expressed in real dollars.[8] Thus variable costs, input expenses and prices, and the capital stock are deflated and measured in constant 1971 dollars.

Table 1. U.S. class I railroads, 1974–1986.

Railroad/System	Abbreviation	Years Observed in Data Set
Ann Arbor	AA	
Atchison, Topeka & Santa Fe	ATSF	74–86
Baltimore & Ohio	BO	
Bessemer, Lake Erie	BLE	
Boston & Maine	BM	
Burlington Northern	BN	74–79
Central of New Jersey	CNJ	
Chesapeake & Ohio	CO	
Chicago, Northwest Transit	CNWT	74–86
Chicago, Milwaukee & St. Paul	MILW	
Colorado Southern	CS	74–81
Delaware & Hudson	DH	
Denver, Rio Grande Western	DRGW	74–85
Detroit, Toledo Shore Line	DTS	
Detroit, Toledo & Ironton	DTI	
Duluth, Missabe & Iron Range	DMIR	
Elgin, Joliet & Eastern	EJE	
Erie Lackawanna	EL	
Florida East Coast	FEC	
Fort Worth, Denver	FWD	74–81
Grand Trunk & Western	GTW	75–86
Illinois Central Gulf	ICG	74–86
Kansas City Southern	KCS	74–86
Lehigh Valley	LV	
Louisville & Nashville	LN	
Missouri-Kansas-Texas	MKT	74–86
Missouri Pacific	MP	74–82
Norfolk & Western	NW	74–81
Penn Central	PC	
Pittsburgh, Lake Erie	PLE	
Reading Railroad	RDG	
St. Louis, San Francisco	SLSF	74–79
St. Louis, Southwestern	SSW	
Seaboard Coast Line	SCL	
Soo Line	SOO	74–86
Southern Pacific	SP	74–86
Southern Railway System	SOU	74–81
Union Pacific Railway	UP	74–82
Western Maryland	WM	
Western Pacific	WP	74–82
Consolidated Rail Corp.	CRC	77–86
Clinchfield & Ohio	CLINCH	
Chessie System	CHES1	74–80
Seaboard System	SBD	74–80
CSX Corporation (1981–82)	CSX1	81–82
CSX Corporation (1983–86)	CSX2	83–86
Burlington Northern–St. Louis System	BNSL	80–81
Burlington Northern System	BNSYS	82–86
Union Pacific System	UPSYS	83–86
Norfolk-Southern Corporation	NS	82–86

Table 2. Major U.S. class I rail consolidations, 1979–1984.

Baltimore & Ohio Chesapeake & Ohio Western Maryland	=>	Chessie System (CSX1)	=>	CSX Transport Corp. (CSX2)
Seaboard Coast Line Louisville & Nashville	=>	Seaboard System (SBD)		
Burlington Northern St. Louis–San Francisco	=>	BN System (BNSL) Colorado Southern Fort Worth–Denver	=>	BN System (BNSYS)
		Union Pacific Missouri Pacific Western Pacific	=>	Union Pacific System (UPSYS)
		Southern Railway System Norfolk & Western	=>	Norfolk Southern RR (NSC)

For each firm in the sample, data series on operating expenses as reported by Class I railroads annually to the ICC required two significant adjustments before they could be used as variable costs. First, equipment costs are reported to the ICC through depreciation of the rolling stock. Instead, we constructed a rental price for equipment, allowing both for economic depreciation and the cost of floating equipment trusts, the most common form of rolling stock financing. We then multiplied this rental price measure times an estimate of the replacement value of the rolling stock for each firm, to obtain an estimate of the annual cost of equipment services. Second, prior to 1983, rail firms expensed maintenance on way and structures capital in the year such maintenance was undertaken.[9] Instead, we removed these maintenance charges from variable costs and added them to net capital investment in the construction of the replacement value of each road's way and structure stock.

For factor prices, our goal was to obtain as disaggregated a series as possible, cross sectionally. For fuel and "materials and supplies" we took published regional prices by the ICC and assigned them (or a weighted sum of them) to individual railroads; thus for differing railroads operating entirely in the same region, the price of materials is the same for the various firms, but for firms operating in more than one region, the materials price is firm-specific.[10] For wage rates, a Divisia index was constructed for each road, based upon labor compensation data for 78 wage categories.[11] The equipment factor price represents the user cost of capital, and incorporates firm-specific costs of capital, as noted earlier.

A single output measure, total ton-miles of revenue and nonrevenue freight, was deemed the most reliable measure available. Since AMTRAK handles the overwhelming majority of noncommuter passenger traffic, it is reasonable to use only freight as a measure of output.[12] Another multiproduct option we considered involved freight output by type of traffic (e.g., coal, agriculture and manufactured goods). Unfortunately, railroads only account for tons of traffic by commodity type, not ton-miles. As a result, we included percent of tons carried for each commodity type (coal, agriculture and other) as technological factors in the short-run cost function specification.[13] Other technical factors include average length of haul (total ton-miles divided by tons carried), and miles of main and secondary track owned and operated by each system.

As noted, way and structures capital stocks for each road have undergone significant accounting restructuring at the ICC over the sample period. Independent of these changes is the fact that ICC measures of capital are book values. Constant-dollar capital stocks, measured using reproduction value concepts, is clearly a more appropriate capital measure in assessing the effect a marginal unit of capital has on variable costs. Fortunately, Nelson [1974] has provided estimates of reproduction values of way and structure stocks for each major Class I road in 1971. Using Nelson's figures and subsequent investment data, a geometric depreciation schedule based upon capital lifetimes, and maintenance expenditures, we have constructed estimated capital stocks in constant dollars for each major Class I road. Further details of this procedure are given in Vellturo [1989]. Sample means and standard deviations of variables in our data set are given in Table 3.

With this information as background, we now move on to a discussion of some econometric issues associated with the estimation of this cost function.

Table 3. Means and standard deviations of variables used in econometric analysis of railroad costs, 1974–1986.

Variable	Units	Mean	Std. Dev.	Min Value	Max Value
Variable costs	$ Billion	1.141	1.148	0.019	5.040
Price of labor	$/hour*	9.677	2.843	5.390	17.740
Price of equipment	Index**	0.396	0.131	0.190	0.674
Price of fuel	Index***	1.637	0.742	0.684	2.844
Price of M+S	Index***	1.173	0.260	0.652	1.495
Ton-miles	Billion	45.245	41.876	1.910	203.000
Percent Ag	% Points	19.117	9.025	6.298	69.175
Percent coal	% Points	26.403	17.816	0.291	79.378
W&S capital	$ Billion	1.906	1.923	0.118	8.303
ALOH	1000 miles	0.392	0.145	0.173	0.780
Route mileage	1000 miles	7.930	6.428	0.543	25.810
Time (year)	Year–1973	6.476	3.594	1.000	13.000
Labor expenses	$ Billion	0.460	0.464	0.004	1.940
Equipment expenses	$ Billion	0.373	0.416	0.003	2.175
Fuel expenses	$ Billion	0.116	0.123	0.003	0.547
M+S expenses	$ Billion	0.192	0.205	0.001	1.137
Labor share		0.397	0.081	0.105	0.664
Equipment share		0.333	0.091	0.068	0.585
Fuel share		0.105	0.039	0.036	0.301
M+S share		0.165	0.064	0.008	0.459

*Variable costs, the price of labor, and input expenses are in constant 1971 dollars.
**Indexed to 1977 = 1.000.
***Indexed to 1971 = 0.100.

4. Specification of Cost Function and Issues in Econometric Implementation

We begin with a discussion of the stochastic specification of our equation system, one that explicitly incorporates the notion that variables not observed by the econometrician are important to the economic agent; in turn, the actions of this economic agent on input demands and variable costs reflect cost minimization in a coherent manner. Specifically, we assume that the cost equation and its associated input share equations have additive error component structures of the following form:

$$\ln C_{v,ht} = F(w, y, t, \tau, K; \beta)|_{ht} + \epsilon_{ht}, \tag{6}$$

$$S_{iht} = G(w, y, t, \tau, K; \beta)|_{ht} + \mu_{iht}, \qquad i = 1, \ldots, n, \tag{7}$$

where the variables have their previous definitions and β represents the vector of parameters associated with the estimated equations. We decompose each of these error terms into three components: a firm-specific error (α_h and α_{ih}); an error that exhibits first order autocorrelation within a given equation (δ_t and γ_{it}), but no error autocorrelation across equations; and a normally distributed disturbance term that is only contemporaneously correlated across equations (ϕ_{ht} and ω_{iht}). These errors are therefore written as

$$\epsilon_{ht} \equiv \alpha_h + \delta_t + \phi_{ht}, \qquad h = 1, \ldots, H, \quad t = 1, \ldots, T, \tag{8}$$

$$\mu_{iht} \equiv \alpha_{ih} + \gamma_{it} + \omega_{iht}, \qquad i = 1, \ldots, n. \tag{9}$$

To motivate this stochastic specification, we begin by considering the origin of the firm-specific error terms (α_h and α_{ih}). We interpret these firm-specific disturbances as reflecting unobserved fundamental network differences among Class I railroads (e.g., the spatial configurations of their routes, whether networks are primarily hub-and-spoke, end-to-end, etc.). Since it is reasonable to assume that this network configuration effect is fixed over time for a given railroad, we can eliminate this firm-specific error component by introducing indicator variables for each firm. We assume that these network attributes are known to the railroads but are not observed by the econometrician, that the underlying network configuration influences input utilization decisions by firms, and therefore that these unobserved effects enter into their cost-minimizing behavior.

We implement these assumptions by introducing dummy variables into the linear term of the input share equations, and, since the share equations are derived as logarithmic derivatives from the variable cost function, we also introduce interactive dummy $*$ ln w_i slope coefficients into the variable cost function equation, constraining their coefficient values to equal those in the input share equations; our interpretation of the unobserved variables therefore implies that cross-equation restrictions should be imposed on the fixed-effect parameters.[14]

Thus the coefficients given in the cost (2) and input share (4) equations should be interpreted as follows:

$$A_0 = A_0' + F_h, \qquad h = 1, \ldots, H - 1, \tag{10}$$

$$A_i = A_i' + F_{ih}, \qquad i = 1, \ldots, n; \quad h = 1, \ldots, H - 1, \tag{11}$$

where A_0' and A_i' respectively represent the intercept and linear coefficients on the input price variable for the base railroad (denoted H); F_h is a zero-one intercept dummy for railroad h in the cost function, and F_{ih} is both a zero-one intercept dummy for railroad h in the ith share equation *and* a multiplicative dummy variable on the ln w_i term in the variable cost function equation.

In the context of mergers, we define new firm-specific fixed-effect dummy variables for merged firms; obviously, the component firms of the merger are dropped from the sample once a merger occurs. Given the nonlinear nature of the translog variable cost specification (2), it is not possible to relate analytically the fixed effects of merged firms to those of their premerger constituent firms. As a result, we can only perform a partial parametric test on the effects of mergers. In particular, although appropriate restrictions can be tested on merger dummy variables and merger-related slope coefficients, it is not possible to establish and therefore test for relationships between the fixed effect of a merged firm and those of its premerger constituent firms.

Given this fixed effect specification, appropriate adding-up conditions must also be imposed on the fixed effects coefficients. These turn out to take the form

$$F_{nh} = -\sum_{j=1}^{n-1} F_{jh}, \quad h = 1, \ldots, H-1, \qquad \text{and} \qquad F_{n0} = 1 - \sum_{j=1}^{n-1} F_{j0}. \tag{12}$$

Returning to our stochastic specification, we introduce intraequation intertemporal effects by permitting the δ_t and γ_{it} terms to follow first-order autoregressive processes. Although equal across firms, we specify that the first order autoregressive parameter in the cost function disturbance term δ_t differs from that in the share equation disturbance terms γ_{it}, but to ensure adding-up consistency, we also specify that the autoregressive parameter for each share equation is equal across shares.[15]

Cross-equation contemporaneous correlation of the ϕ_{ht} and ω_{iht} terms is expected, due to the adding up of the share equations. Therefore, we specify that the n-element disturbance vector consisting of thc ϕ_{ht} and $n - 1$ ω_{iht} terms is independent and multivariate normally distributed, with mean vector zero and covariance matrix Ω_{ht}. Finally, on the basis of preliminary examination of residuals, it was determined that in both the share and cost function equations, heteroskedasticity occurred, with the variance of residuals being positively related to the $(\ln y)_{ht}$. To transform the model so that the disturbance terms became homoskedastic, we therefore divided all variables by the square root of $(\ln y)_{ht}$.

One other matter deserves particular attention in the context of stochastic specification, and that concerns the exogeneity of output (ln y), ALOH, and the output composition variables %AG and %COAL. Because of the rate-setting freedom introduced by the Staggers Act, it is reasonable to ask whether output and its composition should be treated as being exogenous, particularly after 1978. If they are endogenous, output and its components may well be correlated with the cross-equation error terms, so that estimates based on the assumption of exogeneity of these regressors could be biased and inconsistent. To test for the validity of the exogeneity assumption, we have utilized the specification test procedure due to Hausman [1978] and Hausman et al. [1988].

Specifically, insofar as output and its components are determined endogenously through the profit-maximizing behavior of railroads, they should be related to demand variables that do not enter the cost function. Consequently, in implementing the Hausman specification test, we utilized as instruments appropriate firm-specific demand-related variables, including coal production, mine-mouth prices, oil rates, farm income, and value of shipments from manufacturing.[16] We now turn to a discussion of empirical findings.

5. Econometric Implementation and Results from Estimation

We begin by implementing a system version of the Hausman specification test, estimating the equation system consisting of the variable cost function (2) and $n - 1$ of the cost share equations (4), first by the 3SLS procedure assuming that ln y, ALOH, %AG, %COAL, and their transforms are endogenous, and then by maximum likelihood (ML) under the assumption that all regressors are uncorrelated with error terms. Note that under the null hypothesis, ML estimation is efficient while 3SLS is consistent, and if the alternative hypothesis is true, then only the 3SLS estimates are consistent.[17] The χ^2 test statistic corresponding to the null hypothesis that $\beta_{3SLS} = \beta_{ML}$ is 1252.988, which is much larger than the critical value with 38 degrees of freedom at any reasonable significance level. We conclude that ln y, ALOH, %AG, and %COAL are not exogenous variables, but instead are endogenous. All subsequent estimation results that we report are therefore based on the assumption that these output-related variables are endogenous (i.e., we only report the 3SLS estimates).

Using the residuals from the 3SLS model, we estimated a common autoregressive parameter for the three share equations, and another autoregressive parameter for the cost function; the null hypothesis that these two autoregressive parameters were simultaneously equal to zero was not rejected at usual significance levels.[18] Hereafter we set these autocorrelation coefficients to zero.

The 3SLS estimated model had one additional drawback, in that curvature restrictions involving way and structures capital were frequently violated.[19] Inspection of our parameter estimates revealed that the CC_{11} coefficient was positive but very imprecisely estimated. We therefore constrained this parameter to zero.[20] Once this restriction was imposed, curvature restrictions were satisfied at 195 of our 229 observations. Parameter estimates and t-statistics (based on heteroskedasticity-robust standard errors) for the common parameters are given in Table 4, firm-specific effects estimates are presented in Table 5,[21] and the merger-deregulation parameters and test statistics are highlighted in Table 6.[22]

We begin our discussion of results by examining the differential effects on costs and productivity growth of deregulation from those of mergers and acquisitions. In Table 6 we summarize time-related parameter estimates for a model in which both deregulation and merger variables are incorporated (Model I), a model in which deregulation variables are excluded but merger variables are included (Model II), and a model in which the merger variables are excluded but the deregulation variables are included (Model III). As is seen in the Model I column of Table 6, the linear and the squared time counter estimates for the merger (M_1 and M_{11}, see top panel) parameters are significant, as are both deregulation (R_1 and R_{11}, see bottom panel) parameters. Both M_1 and R_1 are negative, but R_1 is about

Table 4. 3SLS parameter estimates for restricted translog short-run cost function ("*t*-stat" is the ratio of parameter estimate to its asymptotic standard error): U.S. Class I railroads, 1974–1986.

Parameter	Variable	Estimate	*t*-Stat	Parameter	Variable	Estimate	*t*-Stat
B_1	y	5.5726	3.09	AA_{11}	$P_L \cdot P_L$	0.1654	2.89
C_1	K	1.3454	1.26	AA_{22}	$P_E \cdot P_E$	0.1530	3.26
C_2	ALOH	−3.1596	−1.20	AA_{33}	$P_F \cdot P_F$	0.0791	8.04
C_3	MILES	−7.1830	−3.00	AA_{44}	$P_{M+S} \cdot P_{M+S}$	0.1253	2.10
C_4	%AG	4.6114	2.88	AA_{12}	$P_L \cdot P_E$	−0.1298	−4.52
C_5	%COAL	−2.0086	−3.39	AA_{13}	$P_L \cdot P_F$	−0.0128	−0.80
AB_{11}	$y \cdot P_L$	0.0442	1.68	AA_{14}	$P_L \cdot P_{M+S}$	−0.0228	−0.40
AB_{21}	$y \cdot P_E$	−0.2042	−10.00	AA_{23}	$P_E \cdot P_F$	0.0064	0.35
AB_{31}	$y \cdot P_F$	0.0766	3.69	AA_{24}	$P_E \cdot P_{M+S}$	−0.0296	−0.80
AB_{41}	$y \cdot P_{M+S}$	0.0835	2.12	AA_{34}	$P_F \cdot P_{M+S}$	−0.0728	−3.39
AC_{11}	$P_L \cdot K$	0.0860	1.26	BC_{11}	$K \cdot y$	0.6115	3.01
AC_{21}	$P_E \cdot K$	0.0567	0.90	BC_{12}	ALOH $\cdot y$	0.0375	0.11
AC_{31}	$P_F \cdot K$	0.0519	1.89	BC_{13}	MILES $\cdot y$	−0.5425	−1.95
AC_{41}	$P_{M+S} \cdot K$	−0.1945	−3.20	BC_{14}	%AG $\cdot y$	0.1882	0.98
AC_{12}	$P_L \cdot$ ALOH	−0.0032	0.07	BC_{15}	%COAL $\cdot y$	0.0130	0.21
AC_{22}	$P_E \cdot$ ALOH	0.1228	3.11	BB_{11}	$y \cdot y$	0.0899	0.25
AC_{32}	$P_F \cdot$ ALOH	0.0219	0.61	CC_{11}	$K \cdot K$	0.0000	
AC_{42}	$P_{M+S} \cdot$ ALOH	−0.1415	−1.90	CC_{12}	ALOH $\cdot K$	−0.5618	−2.25
AC_{13}	$P_L \cdot$ MILES	0.0437	1.24	CC_{13}	MILES $\cdot K$	−0.4126	−2.27
AC_{23}	$P_E \cdot$ MILES	0.0095	0.31	CC_{14}	%AG $\cdot K$	0.5892	3.47
AC_{33}	$P_F \cdot$ MILES	−0.0226	−1.53	CC_{15}	%COAL $\cdot K$	−0.1630	−3.85
AC_{43}	$P_{M+S} \cdot$ MILES	−0.0306	−0.72	CC_{22}	ALOH · ALOH	1.0303	2.27
AC_{14}	$P_L \cdot$ %AG	0.0487	1.87	CC_{23}	ALOH · MILES	0.2689	0.65
AC_{24}	$P_E \cdot$ %AG	−0.0404	−2.02	CC_{24}	ALOH · %AG	−0.5902	−2.92
AC_{34}	$P_F \cdot$ %AG	0.0023	0.85	CC_{25}	ALOH · %COAL	−0.1494	−1.37
AC_{44}	$P_{M+S} \cdot$ %AG	−0.0106	−0.23	CC_{33}	MILES · MILES	1.0130	2.86
AC_{15}	$P_L \cdot$ %COAL	−0.0144	−2.11	CC_{34}	MILES · %AG	−0.6779	−3.13
AC_{25}	$P_E \cdot$ %COAL	0.0161	3.16	CC_{35}	MILES · %COAL	0.1947	2.52
AC_{35}	$P_F \cdot$ %COAL	−0.0205	−3.63	CC_{44}	%AG · %AG	0.1160	0.58
AC_{45}	$P_{M+S} \cdot$ %COAL	0.0188	2.00	CC_{45}	%AG · %COAL	−0.0759	−1.17
AD_{T1}	$P_L \cdot$ TIME	0.0009	0.27	CC_{55}	%COAL · %COAL	−0.0199	−1.30
AD_{T2}	$P_E \cdot$ TIME	0.0009	1.32	DT	TIME	−0.1284	−4.10
AD_{T3}	$P_F \cdot$ TIME	−0.0125	−5.13	DTT	TIME · TIME	0.0509	5.37
AD_{T4}	$P_{M+S} \cdot$ TIME	0.0107	2.50	M_1	t^m	−0.0718	−2.40
R_1	t^r	−0.0909	−2.96	M_{11}	t^{m2}	0.0097	2.29
R_{11}	t^{r2}	−0.0537	−6.25	AD_4	*MDUM*	−0.0724	−3.14
AD_{12}	$P_L \cdot t^r$	−0.0064	−1.35	AD_{13}	$P_L \cdot t^m$	−0.0029	−0.83
AD_{22}	$P_E \cdot t^r$	0.0009	0.20	AD_{23}	$P_E \cdot t^m$	0.0009	0.20
AD_{32}	$P_F \cdot t^r$	0.0108	3.52	AD_{33}	$P_F \cdot t^m$	0.0108	3.52
AD_{42}	$P_{M+S} \cdot t^r$	−0.0053	−0.94	AD_{43}	$P_{M+S} \cdot t^m$	−0.0053	0.94

Prices, output quantity, *K*, ALOH, MILES, %AG, %COAL are all logarithmically transformed. TIME, t^m (years since last merger) and t^r (years since deregulation) are all in natural units. Standard error estimates employ the Halbert White [1980] heteroskedasticity-robust computation.

Table 5. 3SLS parameter estimates for firm-specific cost and factor share terms translog short-run cost function: U.S. Class I railroads, 1974–1986 (asymptotic t-statistic based on robust standard errors).

	Cost Function		Labor Term		Equipment Term		Fuel Term	
Firm	Estimate	t-Stat	Estimate	t-Stat	Estimate	t-Stat	Estimate	t-Stat
Base firm								
ATSF	21.027	2.43	−0.708	1.92	1.500	5.57	0.003	0.02
Other firms								
BN	−0.095	−0.47	−0.033	−0.73	−0.027	−0.68	−0.038	−2.04
CNWT	−1.724	−6.17	0.238	3.70	−0.130	−2.63	0.128	3.05
CS	−2.906	−3.62	0.266	1.19	−0.268	−1.33	0.404	3.59
DRGW	−1.964	−3.50	0.357	2.25	−0.220	−1.47	0.256	2.96
FWD	−4.152	−5.41	0.594	2.85	−0.485	−2.52	0.413	4.50
GTW	−2.062	−3.26	0.498	2.73	−0.241	−1.49	0.249	2.41
ICG	−0.828	−3.69	0.107	1.88	−0.023	−0.74	0.081	1.86
KCS	−2.213	−3.56	0.355	2.00	−0.114	−0.71	0.229	2.56
MKT	−1.994	−3.45	0.312	1.92	−0.093	−0.64	0.237	3.07
MP	−0.734	−4.46	0.090	2.30	−0.008	−0.25	0.054	1.91
NW	−0.020	−0.09	0.073	1.52	0.081	2.09	0.026	0.64
SLSF	−1.473	−4.18	0.236	2.53	−0.158	−1.90	0.163	3.35
SOO	−1.933	−4.73	0.259	2.29	−0.165	−1.61	0.150	2.65
SPTC	0.152	1.52	−0.044	−2.10	0.072	4.01	−0.068	−3.79
SOU	−0.022	−0.10	0.016	0.32	0.097	2.70	0.038	0.85
UP	0.054	0.55	0.005	0.24	0.007	0.40	0.011	0.96
WP	−2.459	−3.81	0.323	2.11	−0.350	−2.42	0.204	3.07
CRC	0.025	0.06	0.068	0.66	−0.190	−2.11	−0.054	−0.99
CHES1	0.116	0.34	0.073	1.10	0.069	1.52	0.003	0.05
SBD	−0.347	−1.29	0.009	0.17	0.138	4.06	0.009	0.16
BNSL	−0.147	−0.57	−0.039	−0.74	−0.011	−0.22	−0.024	−1.09
BNSYS	−0.014	−0.05	−0.070	−1.22	0.018	0.32	−0.052	−2.20
CSX1	0.194	0.44	−0.068	−0.74	0.202	2.65	−0.073	−1.18
CSX2	0.292	0.71	−0.052	−0.59	0.147	2.00	−0.077	−1.32
NS	0.502	1.74	−0.055	−0.89	0.203	3.95	−0.049	−1.08
UPSYS	0.305	1.46	−0.067	−1.40	0.131	2.94	−0.057	−2.34

BNSL and BNSYS represent the Burlington Northern System over two phases, 1979–80 (before the acquisition of FWD and CX), and 1981–86 (after the acquisition). CSX1 and CSX2 represent the two phases of the CSX merger, 1981–82 and 1983–86.

27% larger in absolute value; interestingly, M_{11} is positive and small (0.0097), while R_{11} is negative and quite large (−0.0537). Together with the substantial negative estimate of the merger dummy variable MDUM (equals one if the firm was involved in a merger that year), these results imply that mergers appear to have had a cost reducing impact, but that in our sample this effect diminishes with time; by contrast, while the negative effect of deregulation on costs is also substantial, the large negative estimate of R_{11} indicates that in our sample, the cost-reducing effects of deregulation increased over time. In brief, the cost-reducing effects of mergers are smaller and shorter-lived than are those due to deregulation.

Table 6. 3SLS estimates of deregulation and merger coefficients alternative model specifications: Class I railroads, 1974–86 (absolute value of coefficient estimate to heteroskedasticity-robust asymptotic standard error in parentheses).

Parameter	Variable	Model I	Model II	Model III
M_1	t^m	−.07183 (2.4008)	−.06848 (2.2334)	.00000
M_{11}	t^{m2}	.00973 (2.2950)	.00959 (2.1659)	.00000
AD_4	*MDUM*	−.07238 (3.1368)	−.06666 (2.8824)	.00000
AD_{13}	$t_m w_1$	−.00291 (0.8319)	−.00335 (1.6291)	.00000
AD_{23}	$t_m w_2$	.00055 (0.1937)	.00144 (0.4964)	.00000
AD_{33}	$t_m w_3$	.00150 (0.9775)	.00440 (2.2175)	.00000
AD_{43}	$t_m w_4$	.00087 (0.1504)	−.00249 (0.3587)	.00000
R_1	t^r	−.09087 (2.9597)	.00000	−.06777 (2.2322)
R_{11}	t^{r2}	−.05373 (6.2501)	.00000	−.05110 (5.7998)
AD_{12}	$t_r w_1$	−.00640 (1.3516)	.00000	−.00716 (2.1372)
AD_{22}	$t_r w_2$	.00089 (0.1998)	.00000	.00096 (0.2264)
AD_{32}	$t_r w_3$	.01077 (3.5215)	.00000	.01093 (3.6587)
AD_{42}	$t_r w_4$	−.00526 (0.9360)	.00000	−.00473 (0.8669)
$E'HH'E$		481.779	581.522	493.849

The cross-product terms involving the time and factor price variables are also of particular interest here. From Table 4 we see that the estimate of AD_{T1} is positive, very small, and statistically insignificant, implying that in the absence of deregulation and mergers, the effects of time on labor demand are approximately neutral. Recall that estimates of AD_{13} and AD_{12} indicate whether the effects of time on the labor share are different in the presence of deregulation (AD_{12}) or mergers (AD_{13}). As is seen in Table 6, deregulation has a nonneutral labor-saving effect on costs, but so too do mergers; the estimated effect of deregulation (−0.00640) is more than twice as large as that due to mergers (−0.00291). The precision with which these labor bias effects are measured is not great, although the 1.35 t-value on the deregulation labor coefficient is larger than the 0.83 t-value on the merger labor coefficient.[23]

We then tested Model II (deregulation does not matter) as a special case of Model I; the quasi-likelihood ratio test statistic is 99.74, which is greater than the chi-square test statistic with five degrees of freedom at any reasonable significance level. We also tested Model III (mergers do not matter) as a special case of Model I. This too was rejected, although not nearly as decisively; the chi-square test statistic with 6 degrees of freedom is 12.07, which implies rejection of the null hypothesis at all significance levels less than 0.06043.[24] We conclude that both mergers and deregulation had significant cost-reducing effects on railroads in the United States from 1974 to 1986, although our estimates of effects of deregulation are measured more decisively.

To obtain some idea of the relative quantitative magnitudes of mergers and deregulation on costs and productivity, we simulated costs of all firms involved in mergers since 1980,[25] we predicted what their costs would have been had they not merged,[26] and we predicted what costs would have been had deregulation not occurred. By 1986, of the total cumulative cost savings achieved by merged firms since 1980, that due to deregulation is estimated at 91%, while those due directly to mergers is estimated to be 9%. We conclude, therefore, that while mergers and deregulation both had substantial cost-reducing effects in our 1974–1986 sample, those due to deregulation are much larger.

6. Concluding Remarks

In this paper we have sought to disentangle the effects of deregulation on rail costs from those directly attributable to mergers and acquisitions. Our empirical analysis has employed a translog short-run variable cost function, based on an unbalanced panel data set of annual observations for major U.S. Class I railroads from 1974 to 1986. In our econometric implementation, we specify that the fixed effects reflect variables not observed by the econometrician, but are known and important to the cost-minimizing firm; this interpretation implies that the traditional fixed effect model should be modified to incorporate cross-equation restrictions on the fixed effect parameters.

Our first empirical finding is that both deregulation and mergers contributed significantly to cost savings; hypotheses of the form that "deregulation has no effect" and "mergers have no cost effects" were both strongly rejected, although the former was rejected much more decisively than the latter.

Second, although mergers accounted for some of the cost savings observed in firms that have consolidated during our sample period, by 1986 the bulk of the accumulated cost savings achieved by merged firms since 1980 appears to be due to deregulation (about 91%). Moreover, the cost-reducing effects of mergers are short-lived than are those due to deregulation.

Third, in terms of factor biases, we find that both deregulation and mergers resulted in a substantial labor-saving bias; although our point estimate of this labor-saving effect for deregulation is more than twice as large as that for mergers, we were not able to estimate the magnitude of these bias coefficients precisely.

These findings suggest that while mergers contributed modestly to the cost and productivity improvements that occurred during our 1974–1986 sample period, deregulation has also had an enormous impact; indeed, its impact appears to have been much larger.

Acknowledgments

Research support from the National Science Foundation and the MIT Center for Energy Policy Research is gratefully acknowledged, as is the research assistance of Mark H. Showalter. We have benefited from the helpful comments of Zvi Griliches, Jacques Mairesse, Joshua Rosett, and Mohammed Sassenou.

Notes

1. For example, major mergers such as the formation of the Penn-Central railroad (from the New York Central and Pennsylvania roads), and the Burlington Northern (from the Great Northern, Northern Pacific, and Burlington railroads) all involved consolidations of parallel trackage.
2. As an example, the Burlington Northern application was originally presented to the ICC in 1959. Final approval was granted 11 years and three resubmissions later. The infamous Penn-Central application spanned seven years. For details, see Saunders [1978].
3. One notable exception involved the proposed consolidation of the Southern Pacific and Atchison, Topeka and Santa Fe Railways, brought to the ICC in 1984. Both roads had extensive trackage that ran virtually parallel to one another throughout the southwest. The merger was rejected.
4. A number of previous studies have specified a multiproduct variable cost function with ton-miles of freight and passenger miles treated as distinct outputs (e.g., Friedlaender and Spady [1981]). Since the advent of AMTRAK, however, passenger traffic has comprised less than 1% of total car-miles for Class I railroads. Hence we ignore passenger traffic in this study. An entirely different issue, however, is the distinction with ton-miles by type of traffic, such as coal, agriculture, and manufactured goods. We address this issue later in this paper.
5. In this study fixed capital refers to way and structures capital, as it is known in the industry. Such capital includes track, grading, bridges, buildings, etc. Equipment capital (commonly referred to as "rolling stock") is treated as a variable input in the short-run, since an active rental market exists for such equipment.
6. See Friedlaender et al. [1991], and Vellturo et al. [1992].
7. During this period, the ICC changed the minimum freight revenue required to be considered a Class I railroad from $1 million to $5 million in 1978, and to $10 million in 1983. Non-Class I railroads are required to file far less detailed cost schedules with the ICC.
8. To deflate costs, we use the producer price index, taken from the Economic Report of the President.
9. In 1983, the ICC recognized that this approach led to a severe miscalculation of the replacement value of the way and structure capital for most roads. This form of accounting (known as "betterment accounting") was replaced with a depreciation-based accounting procedure, and way and structure replacement values underwent a one-time adjustment to capture the misclassified maintenance expenditures.
10. Until 1985, railroads were classified into the east, south or west region, but mergers prompted the ICC to consolidate the east and south regions in 1985.
11. The relative values of this price index for labor among firms was set equal to relative average values in 1974.
12. Local transportation authorities handle commuter traffic in nearly every major metropolitan area in the United States. The notable exception is the Chicago Northwest Transit Co., which provides a portion of Chicago's rail needs.

13. An alternative approach involved exploiting the relationship between total ton-miles and tons by commodity type, ton-miles = $\Sigma_i \text{ALOH}_{ri} \cdot \text{Tons}_{ri}$ for railroad i for various commodity types i, where ALOH is average length of haul. We estimated this relationship using time series data for each railroad to obtain estimated average lengths of haul by commodity type. Although most estimates were positive, they were very imprecise and we therefore abandoned this effort.
14. In estimating rail costs, Caves et al. [1985] specified that fixed effects enter the cost function, but not the input share equations. By contrast, the specification employed here introduces fixed effects into the input share equations in a logically consistent manner along with cross-equation constraints, thereby permitting unobserved network and related effects to influence input utilization.
15. Hence, we assume a diagonal autocovariance matrix, with the diagonal elements for the share equation autoregressive parameters being equal. For further discussion, see Berndt and Savin [1975].
16. These data were obtained at the state level and were then aggregated for each railroad according to the states through which each firm operates. Although such a method does not account for demand effects arising from interline traffic, any attempt to incorporate interlining would be ad hoc and would reduce the heterogeneity of the instruments. See Vellturo [1989] for a full discussion on the use of these variables and their construction.
17. We deleted the linearly dependent M&S cost share equation from this system.
18. The estimate of ρ in the cost function equation was 0.1535, with a t-statistic of 0.1160, while the estimate of the common ρ in the share equations was 0.1956, with a t-statistic of 0.1090.
19. Specifically, point estimates of either the monotonicity or concavity conditions were violated at 119 of 229 observations (52%).
20. The point estimate of CC_{11} parameter was 0.6775, and dividing by the robust standard error yielded an asymptotic t-statistic of 2.0832.
21. In estimation, the Atchison, Topeka and Santa Fe (ATSF) railroad was treated as the "base case" railroad; thus all other fixed-effects estimates in Table 6 should be interpreted as differences from this base case railroad.
22. The R^2 value for the variable cost function equation is 0.9988, while that for the labor, equipment and fuel share equations are 0.9395, 0.9721, and 0.8719.
23. For further discussion of labor bias impacts, and for estimates by railroad, see Vellturo et al. [1992].
24. Note that this test is partial in the sense that, under the null hypothesis, the fixed effects of merged firms are not related to those of their premerged constituent firms, for this is not possible to do analytically. See Section 4 for further discussion of this issue.
25. The six mergers here involve CSX1 (1981), BNSL (1980), BNSYS (1982), NS (1982), UPSYS (1983), and CSX2 (1983).
26. In these simulations, we assigned the input prices actually faced by merged firms postmerger to their constituent firms, and allocated capital stock and output levels of the merged firms in the same proportion as existed among constituent firms just prior to the merger.

References

Berndt, Ernst R., and N. Eugene Savin. (1975). "Estimation and Hypothesis Testing in Singular Equation Systems with Autoregressive Disturbances." *Econometrica* 43, 937–958.

Caves, Douglas W., Laurits R. Christensen, Michael W. Tretheway, and Robert J. Windle. (1985). "Network Effects and the Measurement of Returns to Scale and Density for U.S. Railroads." In Andrew F. Daugherty (ed.), *Analytical Studies in Transport Economics*. Cambridge: Cambridge University Press, pp. 97–120.

Friedlaender, Ann F. (1992). "Coal Rates and Revenue Adequacy in a Quasi-Regulated Rail Industry." *The Rand Journal* 23, 376–394.

Friedlaender, Ann F., Ernst R. Berndt, Judy Shaw-Er Wang Chiang, and Christopher A. Vellturo. (1991). "Rail Costs and Capital Adjustments in a Quasi-Regulated Environment." Cambridge, MA: National Bureau of Economic Research, Working Paper #3781.

Friedlaender, Ann F., and Richard H. Spady. (1981). *Freight Transport Regulation: Equity, Efficiency, and Competition in the Rail and Trucking Industry.* Cambridge, MA: The MIT Press.

Harris, Robert G., and Clifford Winston. (1983). "Potential Benefits of Rail Mergers: An Econometric Analysis of Network Effects on Service Quality." *Review of Economics and Statistics* 65, 32–40.

Hausman, Jerry A. (1978). "Specification Tests in Econometrics." *Econometrica* 46, 1251–1271.

Hausman, Jerry A., Whitney K. Newey, and James L. Powell. (1988). "Nonlinear Errors in Variables: Estimation of Some Engel Curves." Jacob Marschak Lecture of the Econometric Society, Australian Economics Congress, Canberra.

Levin, Richard C., and Daniel H. Weinberg. (1979). "Alternatives for Restructuring the Railroads: End-to-End or Parallel Mergers?" *Economic Inquiry* 17, 371–388.

Saunders, Richard. (1978). *The Railroad Mergers and the Coming of Conrail.* Westport, CT: Greenwood Press.

Vellturo, Christopher A. (1989). "The Deregulation of the U.S. Rail Industry: Efficiency and Equity in Attaining Rail Viability." Cambridge, MA: MIT Department of Economics, unpublished Ph.D. dissertation.

Vellturo, Christopher A., Ernst A. Berndt, Ann F. Friedlaender, Judy Shaw-Er Wang Chiang, and Mark H. Showalter. (1992). "Deregulation, Mergers, and Cost Savings in Class I U.S. Railroads, 1974–1986." *Journal of Economics and Management Strategy* 1, 339–370.

White, Halbert J. (1980). "A Heteroskedasticity-Consistent Covariance Matrix Estimator and a Direct Test for Heteroskedasticity." *Econometrica* 48, 817–838.

The Journal of Productivity Analysis, 4, 145-163 (1993)

Provision of Child Care: Cost Functions for Profit-Making and Not-for-Profit Day Care Centers

SWATI MUKERJEE
Department of Economics, Bentley College, Waltham, MA 02154

ANN DRYDEN WITTE
Department of Economics, Wellesley College, Wellesley, MA 02181 and National Bureau of Economic Research, Cambridge, MA

Abstract

In this paper, we explore and compare the operation of profit making (PMOs) and not-for-profit (NPOs) day care centers using data from a random sample of Massachusetts day care centers. We find many differences in the characteristics of PMOs and NPOs. Most interestingly, NPOs pay significantly higher wages than PMOs although the staff of NPOs has aproximately the same education and less experience than the staff of PMOs. NPOs also have significantly more staff per child than PMOs. We estimate separate cost functions for PMOs and NPOs and find the parameters of these functions to be insignificant different implying that the higher observed costs for NPOs result from different input (e.g., paying higher wages) and output (e.g., more interaction and larger size) choices and not from differences in methods of operation. Finally, we find that current monetary and in-kind subsidies have no significant effect on the costs of day care centers.

1. Introduction

In this paper, we estimate cost functions for both not-for-profit and for-profit day care centers using data from Massachusetts, testing, in particular, for differences in behavior between the for-profit and not-for-profit firms. Massachusetts was chosen since it has one of the best data sets currently available. In the process, we deal with problems of defining and measuring the output of day care, and also grapple with the difficult issue of measuring quality appropriately in the day care context.

The impetus for this paper arose from the increasing concern regarding the affordability of day care. The need for child care has escalated in recent years as a result of two demographic trends: the rapid, continuing increase in maternal employment in the last decade and a half and an even higher increase in the number of single parent households.[1] Parents have a range of options to choose from. These could include, apart from formal center-based care, family day care whether licensed or unlicensed, care by relatives and baby-sitters at home. The question arises: what determines the price of day care? A complete answer to this question requires an examination and estimation of both supply and demand factors in the context of a full-fledged model of the day care industry. Rising prices may follow from high costs due to output levels, technology, low productivity of factors, high input costs, and/or rapidly increasing demand. This paper investigates the supply aspect of the problem by focusing on the cost determinants in the case of day care centers in

Massachusetts. The latter comprise a significant subset of all day care options caring for 16% of infants, 31% of toddlers, 66% of pre-schoolers and 7% of schoolgoing children in nonparental care.[2]

The day care industry in Massachusetts is characterized by both for-profit and not-for-profit firms. Cost functions were estimated separately for the profit and the not-for-profit sectors and the results analyzed in the context of current literature on NPOs. A major conclusion from the analysis is that the not-for-profit firms do not behave differently from their for-profit counterparts, in that we cannot reject the null hypothesis that their cost functions are the same.

The paper is organized as follows: Section 2 contains the background and literature survey. A discussion of descriptive statistics follows in Section 3. Section 4 contains the theoretical underpinnings in two parts. The first part deals with the functional specification of the model and is followed by a discussion of the conceptual issues regarding the measurement of output and quality in the second part of the section. The data and empirical formulation of the model is discussed in Section 5. Results and concluding remarks are in Sections 6 and 7.

2. Background and Literature Survey

Economists are well versed in the operation of profit-making organizations, but may be less familiar with not-for-profit entities and the literature that relates to them. The crucial property that distinguishes a not-for-profit (NPO) firm from its for-profit counterpart (PMO), is that it is legally prohibited from distributing any profits that may be earned. This is now widely known in the literature as the "nondistribution constraint" following Hansmann [1980]. Note that there is no bar to the earning of profits per se. Hansmann notes that there are limitations to policing the adherence to such a constraint and some NPOs circumvent the requirement through various means such as "excessive salaries, low interest loans from the organization, personal services and amenities paid for out of the organization's funds." The nondistribution constraint results in special tax treatment for NPOs by both federal and state governments. These concessions (which can vary amongst NPOs) apply to individual and corporate taxes, estate and gift taxes, and some excise taxes. Within the not-for-profit sector, a distinction may be drawn between those that are "donative" (donations comprise a large proportion of earnings), and those that are "commercial" (sales of goods and services provide a major or only source of income).[3] These two categories are not mutually exclusive and an NPO day care center can be a bit of both.

Bearing in mind the special features of NPOs in general, we turn to the theories on nonprofit organizations. These theories fall into two categories. One deals with the *role* of NPOs (e.g., why NPOs have arisen in particular industries) and the second category deals with the *behavior* of NPOs.[4] In explaining why NPOs have risen in particular industries, it is generally agreed that it is due to market failure (e.g., contract failure or public goods)[5] which was strong enough to overcome the inherent disadvantages of NPO firms in regard to their access to capital, the efficiency of their operations, and the rapidity with which they can respond to demand (Hansmann [1980]).[6]

There are a number of theories related to the behavior of NPOs. A major set of theories assume maximizing behavior. However, these theories disagree concerning exactly what is maximized, e.g., quantity, or service.[7] Most of these models imply cost-minimizing behavior on the part of NPOs. The second group of models asserts that due to certain problems inherent in the nondistribution constraint, NPOs, especially entrepreneurial ones, cannot be minimizing costs (see Alchian and Demsetz [1972]; Hansmann [1980]).

We follow the first literature and assume that NPOs are minimizing costs (see Hansmann [1980]). We recognize that this can only be a first step toward evolving appropriate models for different types of NPOs providing child care. We do not assume that NPOs are profit maximizing but only cost minimizing. Cost minimization is less restrictive and consistent with many different objectives.[8]

Turning finally to the literature on day care, most previous work has focused on modeling the demand for child care (e.g., Robins and Spiegelman [1978]; Henriques and Vaillancourt [1988]). Two exploratory studies analyzing the costs of providing day care are now over a decade old. Hall [1978] sought to determine the factors affecting the price (rather than the cost) of day care. The second study (Ruopp et al. [1979]) is the 1977 National Day Care Study by Abt Associates, which analyzes costs of a random sample of licensed centers. Both studies adjusted for heterogeneity in output by including a staff/child ratio as an indicator of quality. They also included the average experience and educational levels of the staff. A more recent study on costs has been done by the GAO [1990]. Their purpose was to examine determinants of the cost of centers which satisfied criteria comparable to those laid out in the "Smart Start" bill. The sample therefore included only high-quality centers. They included a child to adult ratio and an average children group size as partial indicators of center quality. Education and experience were taken to be reflected in higher input price and not considered separately. Preston (1993) compares (using 1976–77 data from the Abt study) costs of for-profit and nonprofit firms controlling for quality and social externalities. In the present paper we have estimated cost functions for both profit and nonprofit day care centers separately, refining further the measurements of quality. The results are then compared and interpreted in the context of current literature.

3. Descriptive Statistics

Tables 1a and 1b present, separately, the descriptive statistics for the for-profit and not-for-profit firms in our data set. The data are from a random cross-section sample taken in 1987–88 of day care centers in Massachusetts. Further details regarding the data set and on the construction of each variable are given in Section 5 which deals with the empirical formulation of the model. The comparison of the statistical profiles of the two sectors reveals differences and similarities, expected and unexpected. A significant difference exists (at the 10% level of significance) in the output per week variable, with NPOs producing more output. The average cost per child-hour is higher in NPOs but not significantly so. Analyzing the cost components, the major portion of costs in both sectors is labor, with the NPOs having a significantly higher (0.77 as opposed to 0.63) proportion of their costs accounted for by labor. Capital, on the other hand, represents a significantly higher share of costs in PMOs. As regards provision of materials and services as well as shares of insurance costs, the difference in the shares between the two sectors is insignificant.

Table 1a. Descriptive statistics for day care centers in Massachusetts.

Variable	PMO Sample Mean	PMO Sample Std Dev	NPO Sample Mean	NPO Sample Std Dev	T^*	Variable Definition
CHRS	943.086	724.861	1385.170	1505.630	1.74	Total number of hours children cared for per week
PLAB	6.809	2.585	9.571	7.656	2.28	Labor costs per hour
PCAP	333.997	312.390	291.198	632.778	0.40	Capital costs per room per month
PINS	245.565	123.137	250.368	156.854	0.15	Liability costs per month
MSP	61.366	271.407	17.801	16.272	0.95	Materials and services provided per child per month
INTER	0.543	0.500	0.814	0.583	2.24	Ratio of paid staff class hours per weighted child
EDUC	14.877	1.691	14.700	1.426	0.50	Average education of staff
EXPER	5.764	2.511	4.659	2.229	2.06	Average experience of staff
WKLYEXP	1768.290	1841.980	3409.570	3440.200	2.76	Total weekly expenditure
AVGCOST	2.691	3.705	4.115	5.278	1.43	Cost per child hour
SUB	46.488	155.188	4705.370	12773.300	2.47	Subsidy funds received per month
SUBDUM1	0.514	0.507	0.674	0.474	1.44	Parents and volunteer hours
SUBDUM2	0.657	0.482	0.565	0.501	0.84	Food brought by parents
TOTRMS	3.971	2.162	5.783	3.960	2.63	Total number of rooms
LABCOST	4620.660	3962.830	11252.700	10961.200	3.79	Total labor costs per month
MATCOST	1869.960	6484.230	1123.830	1139.430	0.67	Total material costs per month
CAPCOST	948.619	778.006	1340.410	3182.470	0.80	Total capital costs per month
INSCOST	245.565	123.137	250.368	156.854	0.15	Total liability costs per month
SHCLAB	0.632	0.167	0.769	0.164	3.68	Share of labor costs
SHCCAP	0.170	0.112	0.096	0.111	2.98	Share of capital costs
SHCMAT	0.137	0.146	0.095	0.062	1.60	Share of material costs
SHCINS**	0.059	0.058	0.040	0.071	1.36	Share of liability costs
WTCHLD	294.259	147.074	353.6	232.815	1.40	Weighted children
STCHR	0.135	0.085	0.206	0.152	2.66	Staff/child ratio

*Absolute *T*-value for test of difference in means.
**Share of other costs for PMO: mean = .00113, std dev = .00448; for NPO: mean = .00006, std dev = .00043; (T = 1.41).

Table 1b. Descriptive statistics for children in day care centers in Massachusetts.

Variable	PMO Sample Mean	PMO Sample Std Dev	NPO Sample Mean	NPO Sample Std Dev	T^*	Variable Definition
INF	0.800	2.447	1.804	4.113	1.37	Number of infants
TOD	7.371	8.882	6.543	9.955	0.39	Number of toddlers
PRE	35.171	19.326	35.478	25.462	0.06	Number of preschoolers
KIN	2.543	6.128	4.848	9.573	1.32	Number of kindergartners
SCH	2.371	8.222	9.587	23.922	1.90	Number of school age
TOTCHLD	48.257	21.618	58.261	36.668	1.53	Total children enrollment
RINF	0.018	0.052	0.042	0.092	1.47	Ratio of infants to total enrollment
RTOD	0.158	0.168	0.135	0.204	0.55	Ratio of toddlers to total enrollment
RPRE	0.745	0.231	0.644	0.335	1.60	Ratio of preschoolers to total enrollment
RKIN	0.046	0.108	0.078	0.157	1.07	Ratio of kindergartners to total enrollment
RSCH	0.033	0.103	0.102	0.231	1.80	Ratio of school age to total enrollment

*Absolute *T*-value for test of difference in means.

NPOs pay significantly more in wages, though in terms of education, on the average, neither has an edge over the other. PMO staff are, however, more experienced. The variable INTER is designed to reflect the degree of interaction between child and staff and is measured by paid staff class hours per weighted child. A comparison reveals that INTER is significantly higher for NPOs than PMOs.

The range of subsidies available to PMOs and NPOs are captured in the subsidy variable that includes all the funds the centers receive from various sources, such as United Way funding, state food funding, etc. NPOs receive on the average, significantly higher subsidies. In terms of food and supplies brought in by parents, or in terms of hours that parents and/or volunteers contribute, (indicated by the two dummy variables), the nonprofit sector has no significant edge over its for-profit counterpart.

4. The Cost Model

4.1. The Functional Specification

At its simplest, a firm's total cost function may be denoted as

$$TC = f(Q, P_i),$$

i.e., total expenditures (TC) are related to the level of output Q, the cost of its inputs P_i, and the type of production technology represented in the functional form, f. Specification of a cost function does not imply any restriction on the market structure. However, the derivation of a supply curve from a cost function involves the assumption of competitive conditions which, *prima facie*, does not seem appropriate in this subsector of the day care industry. Thus, we make no attempt to estimate a supply curve. The latter would require a careful formulation of the appropriate model for the day care industry and a simultaneous estimation of both supply and demand.[9] This simple formulation of the total cost function involves certain restrictive assumptions. Output must be homogeneous, all differences in factor inputs fully reflected in their price, and factor-embodied technology absent. The day care industry does *not* fit this mold. Output is not homogeneous, either within or between firms, and it is possible that total costs are affected by the education and experience of the staff even after controlling for wage level. The technology of day care production is the manner in which day care is provided. Though some of the technology may be disembodied (i.e., independent of the level of education and experience of the staff) some may not be so separated from the factors of production.

In selecting a functional form, we considered the different restrictions that various functional forms impose. The simplest, the usual Cobb-Douglas production function, allows returns to scale to be increasing or decreasing for all output levels, but does not let them depend on the output level. Further, the elasticity of substitution is constrained to be unity. Functional forms that allow returns to scale and/or the elasticity of substitution to vary with output are available. We chose our functional form from the class of homothetic functions which allows returns to scale to vary with output.[10] We chose a homothetic, CES functional form, first proposed by Zellner and Revankar [1969].

The cost function that was estimated is the dual to this production function and has the following specification:

$$\ln TC = B_0 + B_1 Y_i + B_2 \ln Y_i + (\ln P_i)' B_3 + (\ln X_i)' B_4 + E_i,$$

where TC is the dependent variable denoting total costs; Y_i is output; P_i is the vector of explanatory price variables; X_i is the vector of non-price explanatory variables; B_0, B_1, B_2 are parameters to be estimated; B_3, B_4 are vectors of parameters to be estimated; and E_i is a random disturbance term.

4.2. The Measurement of Output and Quality

Two methods of measuring the output of service industries are discussed in the literature (see Searle and Waite [1980]; Ross and Burkhead [1974]; Bradford *et al.* [1969]). Output may be measured as either "D-output" or "C-output" (using the terminology of Bradford *et al.* [1969]). D-output consists of direct services produced (e.g., the number of hours a child is cared for). C-output measures the consequences (e.g., the cognitive ability of the child cared for). The latter measure creates the difficulty of not differentiating the output from its consequences (e.g., a child's cognitive ability is also a function of the home environment).[11] Measuring D-output, on the other hand, has the advantage of separating the output from an evaluation of its effectiveness.

D-output, the direct services produced, has been measured for many service industries. For example, the output of hospitals can be measured as the number of patient-days in the hospital, with the caveat that the product has to be a function of the diseases treated. (See Newhouse [1970].)[12] When firms such as hospitals produce different types of output, an aggregation problem is inevitable. Day care centers are like hospitals in that both the type of child cared for and the quality of care provided can differ widely.

The ultimate output (C-output) of day care has an impact on both the children and the parents. High-quality day care may increase the productivity of parents as they are freed of concern for the welfare of their children.[13] The impact of day care on children has been measured through test scores and such direct measures as the Prescott SRI Child Observation System (Stallings and Wilcox [1978]). This paper, while recognizing the desirability of measuring the ultimate impact of day care, focuses on the direct output of day care centers.[14]

Physical direct measures of output have been used by researchers studying the nature of production in day care centers.[15] For example, Ruopp *et al.* [1979] use the number of full-time equivalent chidlren enrolled at the center.[16] In the case of day care centers, it appears to be more appropriate to take one child hour as the unit of measurement rather than one child. This is because different children are enrolled for different hours, and these hours can vary from day to day. The total output of a center is taken to be the total number of hours all children spent at the center per unit of time. Recognizing the heterogeneity of output of a day care center, even more appropriate would be a measure that adjusts for this by weighting child hours according to whether a child is an infant, toddler, preschooler, etc. Unfortunately, this measure of output was not available in our data set.

Output is heterogeneous not only in terms of children of different age groups and therefore different needs, but also in terms of varying quality of care. The concept of quality is a difficult one to define and to reduce to measurable indices. Historically, the concept of what constitutes "quality" shifted from post-WWII to the present times as the earlier emphasis on the nurturing aspect of care shifted in the 1960s to a stress on cognitive skills. From the 1970s a more balanced consideration has prevailed in the recognition that both cognitive and social skills are needed to enhance both physical and emotional development.[17] This perspective can be discerned in the various approaches to quality in accreditation criteria, federal and state regulations, as well as in other studies.[18]

Today, the National Association for the Education of Young Children (NAEYC),[19] which accredits child care programs, defines a high-quality early childhood program as:

> one that meets the needs of and promotes the physical, social, emotional, and cognitive development of the children and adults—parents, staff, and administrators—who are involved in the program. Each day of a child's life is viewed as leading toward the growth and development of a healthy, intelligent, and contributing member of society. (NAEYC [1989, p. 7])

Among the integral criteria in the establishment of a "high-quality early childhood program" as cited by the NAEYC are the following components: interactions among staff and children, a well-rounded and developmental curriculum, frequent staff-parent interaction, effective administration, sufficient and highly qualified staffing, a nurturing and spacious physical environment, a high degree of health and safety, a well-balanced nutrition and food service program, and continual evaluation of the program to assess its strengths and weaknesses.

Federal and state regulations of U.S. day care centers relate mainly to enrollment policies, staff quality, group size and staff-child ratios (Ruopp et al. [1979]). The Federal Interagency Day Care Requirements (FIDCR) were suspended in 1981 and the regulation of child care services came under the jurisdiction of individual states.[20] In spite of a gradual tightening of regulations by the states since the mid-1970s, individual state regulations can and do vary a great deal.[21] In addition, the existence of these regulations does not necessarily imply that they are actually followed or enforced, since monitoring is poor (see Hayes et al. [1990]). An important component, nevertheless, in both federal and state regulations has been the staff-child ratio the requirements which usually vary with the age of the child.

Measures like the staff-child ratio, however, can only be an indication of quality and not be quality per se. The comprehensive NDCS study [22] studied the quality of care by detailed observations and concluded that out of the measurable characteristics, group size and caregiver-child ratio were important indicators of quality, especially for infants and toddlers. This finding is corroborated in subsequent research.[23]

More recently, a Department of Labor report (U.S. Department of Labor [1988]) cited a reader survey from *Working Mother* magazine (March 1988) indicating that parents feel that "warmth, frequency, and kind of interaction" between child and caregiver is important as is imparting values consistent with their own. Other quality factors mentioned in the report were the training level of the staff, wages, and stability of staff. Clearly, the quality of child care is best measured by a vector of attributes.[24]

Beginning with a vector of quality variables that were availble from our data set, we carried out a factor analysis to ascertain the relevant and important quality attributes. The results of the factor analysis are given in the next section.

5. The Data and Empirical Formulation of the Model

5.1. Factor Analysis

Since output of day care centers is not homogeneous, one has to control for quality. As mentioned earlier, quality is a multidimensional concept best captured by a vector of quality attributes. We had available four measurements of what we felt, a priori, were relevant distinct attributes of quality. These were the staff-child ratio discussed previously (INTER), education (EDUC), and experience (EXPER) variables and a measurement of materials and services provided to each child (MSP).

The ratio most often used to measure interaction is the simple staff/child ratio. The interaction ratio (INTER) we use is the number of staff-class hours divided by a weighted index of the number of children.[25] We believe that this reflects the element of interaction and the group composition better than the simple staff/child ratio. By using this measure we take into account the fact that interaction only occurs when the staff is in contact with the children and that children of different ages require different levels of attention. For example, it requires far more time to provide necessary care for an infant than to provide necessary care for a preschooler. Thus a weighted[26] children measure is used instead of the simple number of children.

To reflect the diverse educational levels of the staff in any day care center, we construct a variable (EDUC) that indicates the average education of the staff.[27] The experience variable (EXPER) is created by taking the weighted average of the total years of experience possessed by the staff. This reduces the range of staff experience in any one center to a scalar. Adding up costs of supplies, food, phone services, and transportation, and then dividing by the number of children gives us a measure of materials and supplies provided per child (MSP). These four variables constitute our vector of quality attributes. A factor analysis was carried out using these four variables. The results are reported in Table 2.

Table 2. Factor analysis.

Variable	Factor 1	Factor 2	Factor 3	Factor 4	Commun.*
INTER	0.996	0.034	−0.032	−0.080	1.0
EDUC	−0.032	0.057	0.984	0.168	1.0
EXPER	−0.083	−0.027	0.169	0.982	1.0
MSP	0.034	0.998	0.055	−0.025	1.0
Variance**	0.352	0.272	0.219	0.158	
Eigenvalue	1.406	1.086	0.877	0.631	

*Final communality estimates.

**Explained by each factor. The total variance may not sum to 1 due to rounding off.

Using the varimax rotation method, the rotated factor patterns indicate that each attribute loads heavily on a separate factor. Factor 1 has INTER loading with a weight of 0.996, whereas the other attributes have loadings equal to or less than 0.04. Factor 2 has MSP loading with a weight of 0.998 and the other attributes loading with weights ranging from 0.06 to −0.03. Factor 3 has EDUC loading with a weight of 0.984, and factor 4 has EXPER loading with 0.982 again with relatively very small loadings for other factors in each case. The pattern of factor loadings and the final communality estimates indicate that all the attributes are relevant and can be associated uniquely with one factor. This is usually interpreted in factor analysis to mean that each attribute is unique in measuring quality (in this case) in four different dimensions. Attention is also drawn to the variance explained by each factor which lends support to the conclusion that all the attributes are important. Finally, the eigenvalues indicate (as well as the order of the factors) that of the four factors, the first two (INTER and MSP) are relatively greater in importance than the other two. In view of the results from the factor analysis, we decided to retain all four attributes each of which may be considered as a separate dimension of quality.

5.2. The Data Set and Variables

The data set used for this study was collected by the Affordability Study Team at Wellesley College[28] by conducting telephone surveys during the summer of 1987 and in January 1988. Centers were selected randomly from two sampling frames. The first sampling frame was the licensing lists of the Massachusetts Office for Children. The data were collected for 86 centers from this sampling frame. The second sampling frame consisted of the centers used by a random sample of Massachusetts families with children under the age of 13. Twenty-seven centers were selected from this sampling frame. The addition of the second set of centers in January 1988 tends to overcome well-known deficiences in the licensing list sampling frames (e.g., incomplete and out-of-date lists).[29]

The dependent variable, total costs, is the weekly expenditure of each center summing up all labor, capital, supplies, food, transportation, utilities, phone, liability insurance, and other costs. The independent variables are discussed below.

As discussed in Section 4.2, the output of a center is the sum of the hours spent by all children resident at a center in a week. The price of labor is an hourly rate obtained by taking the personnel costs, fringe benefits, and payroll taxes divided by total paid staff hours. To arrive at the total capital cost for a center, we add up rent/mortgage payments, utilities, equipment, and maintenance and repair costs. This aggregate is divided by the total number of rooms to yield the price of capital. The "price" of insurance is just the monthly liability cost of the centers.

Day care centers receive a range of subsidies: state food program allocations, donations, funds from endowments, supplies brought in by parents, volunteer hours, and DSS funding.[30] The total funds that a center receives in a month from any source, other than parent fees, whether it be from DSS, state food funding, etc., are captured in the SUBSIDY variable. SUBDUM1 and SUBDUM2 are two binary variables. SUBDUM1 is 1 if there are contributions of volunteer or parent hours. SUBDUM2 is 1 if there is contribution of food by parents. Apart from the forms of subsidies mentioned above, centers can also receive subsidies in the form of low or no rent. This is captured in the price of capital.

6. The Results

Before the model was estimated, an outlier analysis of the data was carried out and mild and extreme outliers were identified and the data rechecked. If there were data entry mistakes, these were corrected, but no observation was dropped. Next, an outlier analysis was carried out at the regression stage by examining studentized residuals.[31]

6.1. For-Profit Centers (PMOs)

The model was estimated by OLS. The regression results are reported in Table 3. Note that though a homothetic, CES form was used, the coefficient on the log of the output is insignificant, indicting that it collapses to a Cobb-Douglas production function.[32]

First, consider the coefficients on output and input prices. As would be expected, total expenditures increase as the number of child hours provided increases although the coefficient on child hours is not statistically significant. Increases in either the price of labor or insurance increase expenditures although only the coefficient on the price of labor is significantly different from zero at normal confidence levels. The elasticity of total cost with respect to the price of labor is 0.89. This high elasticity is not unexpected considering labor costs constitute the largest share of total costs. The coefficient on capital costs is negative although insignificant. Consider next the results for our measures of quality: INTER, EDUC, EXPER and MSP.[33] Both the interaction variable and the variable denoting

Table 3. Cost function estimates for day care centers in Massachusetts (dependent variable is weekly total cost).

	PMO Sample		NPO Sample		
Variable	Coefficient Estimate	*t*	Coefficient Estimate	*t*	*t*-Value*
INTERCEPT	7.468	2.54	9.823	3.33	0.56
CHRS	0.000	1.34	0.000	2.79	0.48
LNCHRS	−0.257	0.98	0.069	0.50	1.10
LNPLAB	0.890	4.53	0.619	3.89	1.07
LNPCAP	−0.001	0.01	0.052	0.82	0.42
LNPINS	0.188	1.50	0.086	1.04	0.67
LNINTER	0.295	2.44	0.366	2.64	0.38
LNEDUC	−0.592	0.86	−1.923	1.80	1.05
LNEXPER	−0.279	1.50	0.260	1.31	1.98
LNMSP	0.239	3.27	0.052	0.49	1.45
LNSUB	−0.008	0.16	0.019	0.94	0.51
SUBDUM1	−0.116	0.85	−0.124	0.70	0.03
SUBDUM2	0.206	1.17	−0.051	0.27	1.00
F	14.756	—	12.243	—	—
R^2	0.890	—	0.817	—	—
Adj. R^2	0.829	—	0.750	—	—
N	35	—	46	—	—

*T-value for test of difference of estimates.

materials and services have coefficients that are significantly different from zero. A 10% increase in our measure of caregiver/child interaction (INTER) would lead to a 3.0% increase in total costs. A 10% increase in per child expenditure for transportation, material etc. would lead to a 2.4% increase in costs. While negative, the coefficient on neither education nor experience is significant. The sign of the coefficients on these variables suggest that they may measure staff productivity rather than quality per se.

Finally, consider the results for our measure of dollar (SUB) and in-kind subsidies (SUBDUMl and SUBDUM2). The coefficient on none of these variables is statistically significant. This suggests that subsidies for profit making centers do not change expenditures significantly, cetris paribuis. To summarize, an increase in the price of labor, greater interaction, and greater per child expenditure on material and services affect costs significantly.

6.2. Not-for-Profit Centers (NPOs)

The regression results for the NPOs are reported in Table 3.[34] NPOs share many results with PMOs. An increase in the price of labor increases costs signficantly. The elasticity of expenditures with regard to the price of labor is 0.62, slightly lower than the elasticity for PMOs. Increases in other input prices also serve to increase costs, but not significantly so.

Turning to results for our quality measures, greater staff/child interaction serves to increase costs as it does for PMOs. The elasticity of costs with respect to this measure of quality, 0.37 is higher than for PMOs.[35] This difference however, is not significant. More experienced staff serve to increase costs although not significantly so while more educated staff serve to decrease costs. The latter result is significant at the 10% but not the 5% level of a two-tailed test of statistical significance. Increased per child expenditures on materials and services have no significant effect on costs. Recall the NPOs spend relatively little on materials and services. Results for the variables measuring dollar and in-kind subsidies are like results for PMOs. Neither type of subsidy has a significant effect on costs. In sum, a change in the price of labor, improved interaction and more education affect costs significantly in this sector.

6.3. Comparison of PMOs and NPOs

Since the day care industry gave us an excellent opportunity to study a case where both PMOs and NPOs coexist, we can examine the results further in the light of current literature on NPOs in terms of the following questions. The questions are as follows: are the cost functions of the two types of centers the same or have the two samples been drawn from different populations? Do donations increase costs possibly by encouraging "shirking"? Are NPOs "overproducing" quality? Do NPOs and PMOs differ in remuneration to labor? And, finally, are there any policy implications?

To test for the equivalence of the two cost functions, we used the Chow test and found the relevant F statistic insignificant at the .01 level. Further, comparison of individual coefficients across the two equations does not lend support to the hypothesis that the two sets of firms differ greatly in their behavior. The coefficients on staff experience are the only ones that differ significantly.

Will giving donations worsen matters? In this context, James and Rose-Ackerman [1986] succinctly summarize current theoretical thinking on NPOs:

> Shirking is possible in the long run only if there are barriers to entry, if donations are positive for some organizations, or if some customers prefer nonprofits as more 'trustworthy.' Ironically, donations and trust make things worse rather than better in this respect. In effect, 'shirking' is one possible use of donation and other revenues induced by trust. (p. 38)

Donations in our sample are given in different ways: as direct funding and/or as aid in the form of volunteer hours and food brought in by parents. Our results show that donations have no significant effect on either PMO or NPO expenditure. Note that in both PMOs and NPOs, a reduction in the price of labor would decrease costs. Therefore, any form of subsidy that reduces the price of labor should lead to decrease in costs in both forms of organization. It is interesting that volunteer labor does not serve to decrease costs. There has been much discussion regarding subsidies for space and insurance. Our results suggest that such subsidies will have no significant effect on costs for either PMOs or NPOs.

Overall, our results indicate that only subsidies that decrease the price of labor will lower the costs of day care centers.

Where quality is observable, NPO models usually agree that NPO managers may tend to overemphasize quality which leads to higher costs for NPOs relative to PMOs. On the other hand, where quality is *not* easily observed and measured as in the Hansmann model (see Hansmann [1980, 1987]) consumers are unable to make enforceable contracts in regard to these characteristics. This could be the case in areas such as health and education, and PMOs in these industries would then have a tendency to downgrade quality, whereas NPOs would have an attenuated pecuniary incentive to do the same.

The day care industry can be categorized as one where quality may be observed (with cost), but may not be enforceable contractually. Our results indicate that, increasing staff/child interaction increases costs for both organizations. However, a 10% increase in INTER increases total costs by 3.0% in a PMO, as against 3.7% in an NPO. The increase in costs is not significantly higher for NPOs than for PMOs. However, PMOs do have a significantly lower average level of interaction than NPOs. Our results are consistent with the contention that PMOs and NPOs share a common cost function, but that NPOs operate on a function that is higher than PMOs because they produce day care involving significantly more staff/child interaction.

In our study, NPOs pay significantly higher wages than PMOs for workers of the same average level of education and significantly less experience. This contradicts earlier findings for other industries as described in Steinberg [1987]. A study of nonprofit nursing homes by Borjas, Frech, and Ginsburg [1983] found the nonprofits paid much lower wages than their for-profit counterparts, even for workers at comparable levels of skill. Parallel findings by Weisbrod [1983] found that public interest law firms pay less than for-profit law firms. Goddeeris [1984] confirmed Weisbrod's findings and concluded that this stemmed from difference in earnings potential. Steinberg concludes:

> Thus while nonprofits appear to obtain labor at a bargain price, it may be that these workers are of lower quality and do not impart competitive advantage on the sector. (p. 124)

Our work shows that NPOs pay higher wages for less experienced workers. This needs further analysis. Our results also indicate a wage differential larger than that reported in the recent GAO study [1990]. The latter, as mentioned earlier, is a study of high quality centers. The GAO study found that for-profit centers paid "wages that are 3 percent lower for teachers and 7.2 percent lower for aides . . . than nonprofit centers. No evidence suggests, however, that for-profit centers are any more efficient than nonprofit centers." (p. 37)[36] Preston [1988] found that in the federally financed section of the day care industry in the U.S., there was a positive salary differential of about 5% to 10% in favor of the nonprofit sector. There was, however, no significant differential in the non-federally-financed portion of the industry. Her study supported the hypothesis of the importance of property rights effects in determining efficiency and wages.

Payment of higher wages by NPOs could represent a form of indirect distribution of profits. James [1986] has remarked that paying higher wages is one of various methods NPOs could possibly adopt to accomplish indirect distribution of profits.

7. Conclusion

The present study estimated cost functions for PMOs and NPOs in the day care industry in Massachusetts from cross-section data collected in 1987 and 1988. Our results indicate that there is no significant difference in cost functions for PMOs and NPOs.[37] Thus production in NPOs is similar to production in PMOs. Current types of in-kind and financial subsidies have no significant effect on costs. Our results suggest that only subsidies that lower the price of labor may be effective in lowering day care costs. A recent study in Massachusetts (Wellesley College Center for Research on Women and Center for Survey Research, University of Massachusetts at Boston [1988]) suggests that this may best be accomplished by providing NPOs with wage grants and PMOs with tax credit related to their labor costs.

Raising the level of interaction increases costs of both PMOs and NPOs. As predicted by the NPO literature, PMOs have lower ratios of paid staff class hours to the number of children, indicating that NPOs are, on the average, producing more of this aspect of quality.

Finally, contrary to earlier findings in other industries, NPOs pay significantly higher wages than PMOs do, even though their staff do not, on the average, possess more education and, in fact, have significantly less experience. This finding which is confirmed less strongly by the recent GAO report [1990] deserves further study.

Several issues require further research. The fact that the output in the day care industry requires both client and provider inputs makes this a special case of joint production, compounding the usual difficulties of measuring output in service industries. Further, an analysis of cost functions is only a first step toward building a complete model of price determination to be used for a full examination of the affordability issue.

Appendix

Table 4. Supplementary statistics for day-care centers in Massachusetts.

Variable	PMO Q1(25%)	PMO Median	PMO Q3(75%)	NPO Q1(25%)	NPO Median	NPO Q3(75%)	Variable Definition
CHRS	305.000	760.000	1280.000	536.250	907.500	1488.750	Total number of hours children cared for per week
PLAB	5.310	6.543	8.118	5.300	7.870	10.740	Labor costs per hour
PCAP	150.000	254.167	423.333	64.038	131.250	286.851	Capital costs per room per month
PINS	37.500	58.140	75.000	29.070	58.140	79.162	Liability costs per week
MSP	4.944	9.496	22.933	5.794	15.113	23.818	Materials and services provided per child per month
INTER	0.224	0.409	0.667	0.347	0.694	1.127	Ratio of paid staff class hours per weighted child
EDUC	13.375	14.941	16.333	13.650	14.692	15.256	Average education of staff
EXPER	4.167	5.500	7.500	3.400	4.167	5.288	Average experience of staff
WKLYEXP	755.252	1301.140	2230.210	1262.130	1823.080	4263.690	Total weekly expenditure
AVGCOST	1.232	1.456	2.265	1.611	2.169	3.901	Weekly cost per child hour
SUB	0.000	0.000	0.000	0.000	0.000	3303.380	Subsidy funds received
SUBDUM1	0.000	1.000	1.000	0.000	1.000	1.000	Parents and volunteer hours
SUBDUM2	0.000	1.000	1.000	0.000	1.000	1.000	Food brought by parents
TOTRMS	2.000	4.000	5.000	3.000	4.500	7.250	Total number of rooms
LABCOST	2094.330	3386.250	6000.000	4032.130	6388.750	15953.600	Total labor costs
MATCOST	270.833	395.000	1164.510	301.167	774.012	1407.460	Total material costs
CAPCOST	500.000	813.333	1150.000	188.958	554.167	1208.330	Total capital costs
INSCOST	161.250	250.000	322.500	125.000	250.000	340.397	Total liability costs
SHCLAB	0.539	0.659	0.733	0.720	0.812	0.879	Share of labor costs
SHCCAP	0.099	0.145	0.206	0.027	0.059	0.122	Share of capital costs
SHCMAT	0.056	0.106	0.170	0.058	0.081	0.133	Share of material costs
SHCINS	0.022	0.037	0.085	0.009	0.024	0.034	Share of liability costs
INF	0.000	0.000	0.000	0.000	0.000	0.750	Number of infants
TOD	0.000	7.000	10.000	0.000	0.000	9.000	Number of toddlers
PRE	21.000	30.000	40.000	16.750	26.500	57.250	Number of preschoolers
KIN	0.000	0.000	0.000	0.000	0.000	5.500	Number of kindergartners
SCH	0.000	0.000	0.000	0.000	0.000	0.000	Number of school age
TOTCHLD	35.000	45.000	55.000	30.000	48.500	72.250	Total children enrollment
RINF	0.000	0.000	0.000	0.000	0.000	0.012	Ratio of infants to total enrollment
RTOD	0.000	0.167	0.333	0.000	0.000	0.196	Ratio of toddlers to total enrollment
RPRE	0.545	0.728	1.000	0.356	0.641	1.000	Ratio of preschoolers to total enrollment
RKIN	0.000	0.000	0.000	0.000	0.000	0.095	Ratio of kindergartners to total enrollment
RSCH	0.000	0.000	0.000	0.000	0.000	0.000	Ratio of school age to total enrollment
STCHR	0.067	0.111	0.178	0.100	0.153	0.258	Staff/child ratio

Acknowledgments

The authors wish to thank Jacques Mairesse and Elizabeth Kremp for their valuable comments and suggestions. We are also grateful to Gul Butaney of Bentley College for sharing his expertise.

Notes

1. According to the GAO report 1990, "The percentage of women with children under the age of 6 who are employed has tripled from 20 to 63 percent, however, as compared with three decades ago." (p. 14)
2. Infants .... "under 15 months."
   Toddlers .... "at least 15 months but under 33 months."
   Preschoolers ..... "at least 2 years and nine months but under seven years of age, not yet enrolled in first grade."
   Commonwealth of Massachusetts [1990, p. 102 CMR, 96 and 96.1].
3. See Hansmann [1987]. He actually makes a four-way classification by also distinguishing "mutual" NPOs from "entrepreneurial" NPOs. In the former, patrons exert control over the board of directors whom they elect, whereas in the latter category, the board itself exerts ultimate control. However, the boundaries in this four-way classification can be blurred, e.g., some universities can be both mutual and entrepreneurial.
4. See Hansmann [1987] for an excellent survey of economic theories of nonprofit organizations. We draw substantially on his review.
5. See Krashinsky [1986] for bringing in transaction costs as an explanation for NPOs having an advantage over PMOs where there is a problem of monitoring output.
6. See Easley and O'Hara [1983] for a formal model of contract failure treating it as a principal/agent problem. Examples of other theories are subsidy theories and the consumer control theory. See the survey by Hansmann in Powell [1987].
7. The most common maximand has been the quality and/or the quantity of services produced. Newhouse [1970] and Feldstein [1971] have done this for hospitals, James and Neuberger [1981] for universities, Hansmann [1981] for the performing arts, and James [1983] for NPOs in general. A model maximizing use of certain inputs has been developed by Lee [1971] for a hospital. Maximizing the budget is done by Tullock [1966], for example. Pauly and Redisch [1973] have formulated a model that maximizes financial returns to a hospital's affiliated doctors.
8. This can be seen in the case of hospitals. See Cowing, Holtmann, and Powers [1983].
9. This is the subject of a separate paper by the authors.
10. Even more attractive theoretically are the flexible forms which place few restrictions on technology. See for example, the translog (Christensen, Jorgensen, and Lau [1973]), the generalized quadratic (Denny [1974]) and the generalized Leontief (Diewert [1971]). However, the large number of parameters to be estimated in a flexible form call into question the precision of estimates in a reasonably sized data set. The other problem that arises when there is a wide range of observations in the data set, is that flexible forms may fail to fulfill certain restrictions (e.g., diminishing marginal physical product). These considerations led us to consider the class of homothetic functions as good candidates for selection.
11. See Searle and Waite [1980, p. 336].
12. In the case of symphony orchestras (Lange *et al.* [1985]), output measures have been the number of concerts performed or the concert attendance. However, in a study for the sports industry, particularly for cricket, team victories are often used as the measure of output (Schofield [1988]).
13. This was suggested informally at the Spring 1990 CRIW conference (held under the aegis of the NBER) by Robert M. Coen of Northwestern University, who was concerned that all current studies focused on the output of day care too narrowly, and that the broader perspective was ignored. We agree. In this context Klerman and Liebowitz [1989] have found that higher cost of child care slows the process of women's returning to work.

14. Attempts to provide distinct measures of output for the day care industry began in the mid 1970s. As far as we know, the first attempt to discover the number of children in day care occurred in 1974 (U.S. Department of Commerce [1976]). As part of the Current Population Survey, the Census Bureau asked mothers questions concerning day care arrangements. The Census of Services reports information for child day care services beginning in 1977. Prior to 1977, information on day care was incorporated in Social Service (SIC 83) and could not be examined separately. The Census of Services distinguishes between for-profit ("taxable") and not-for-profit ("tax exempt") establishments. The distinction between for-profit and not-for-profit establishments has been dealt with in various ways by researchers analyzing the cost of day care. Basing its work on the Census of Services, the Bureau of Economic Analysis (BEA) began producing estimates of the dollar personal consumption expenditures on day care in 1977. In accordance with its standard practice for services, BEA used weekly dollar receipts as its measure of output for profit making organizations and weekly expenditures as its measure of output for not-for-profit entities.
15. There is substantial controversy whether the physical or dollar measure provides a superior measure of output. For example, see articles in Inman [1985].
16. Hall [1978] claims to estimate "cost equations" for the day care centers utilized by participants in the Seattle/Denver income maintenance experiments. His dependent variable is the "charge for a forty hour week of care." Assuming that the relationship between the charge and the quantity of care is proportional, he includes no measure of output among his explanatory variables.
17. This discussion is taken from Stallings and Wilcox [1978, pp. 103–104].
18. A thorough and up to date discussion on research and professional practice regarding the quality of care is given in Hayes et al. [1990, Chapter 4 and Appendix B]. The Appendix compares the main features of the major sets of standards that have existed/do exist in programs covering early childhood care. These are six in all, two being federal standards, while the remaining four are standards set by professional bodies. The Head Start program still exists while the FIDCR (Federal Interagency Day Care Requirements) was suspended in 1981. The remaining four sets of standards have been developed for voluntary compliance when applicable. These are the accreditation criteria developed by the NAEYC (National Association of the Education of Young Children); guidelines developed by the NBCDI (National Black Child Development Institute); standards of the ECERS (Early Childhood Environment Rating Scale, developed by child development scholars at the University of North Carolina; and, standards of the CWLA (Child Welfare League of America).
19. According to the GAO Report, the NAEYC, "a membership organization of more than 70,000 professionals in the field of child development and early childhood education, provides the only national voluntary accreditation system exclusively for all types of early childhood centers and schools" (GAO [1990, p. 61]).
20. See Hayes [1990, Chapter 6 and Appendix A].
21. According to the Commonwealth of Massachusetts, Secretary of State [1990], the following staff/child ratios and group sizes are mandatory: Infants: "One teacher for the first three infants and an additional teacher or teaching assistant for four to seven infants." Groups should not be larger than seven. Toddlers: "One teacher for the first four toddlers and an additional teacher or teaching assistant for five to nine toddlers." Groups should not be larger than nine. Preschools at full day centers: "At least two years, nine months but less than four years, nine months:" One teacher or teaching assistant is required for each 10 or fewer children. Groups should not be larger than 20. Schoolage children: "At least four years, nine months, but less than seven years:" One teacher or teaching assistant is required for each 15 or fewer children. Groups should not be larger than 30. For more details for mixed group configurations, etc., please see page 108.2 of 102 CMR.
22. The NDCS measures of quality were based on a dual observation system, where daily behavior of both children and caregivers was observed intensely. This dual approach was supplemented by several standardized tests. Their observations and test measures of quality were then correlated to measurable characteristics of day care centers, like staff/child ratio, group size, etc.
23. Findings for infants and toddlers (six weeks–three years) found both group size and caregiver/child ratio strongly correlated with quality. In the case of preschoolers, the results were somewhat different. In their case, a smaller group size led to better quality and this result was both "strong and consistent." However, the relationship of quality to caregiver/child ratio was "slight." Ruopp *et al.* [1979, p. xxxvii]). For overview of subsequent research, see Hayes et al. [1990, p. 88].
24. This is no different from what the literature has discussed (e.g., in the case of hospitals). See Newhouse [1970].
25. An even better measure would be the staff/class hours divided by a weighted average of the number of child care hours provided. The weights would reflect the differential time requirements of children of different ages.

26. The weights were obtained by regressing the total number of infants, toddlers, preschoolers, kindergartners, and school age children on paid staff class hours.
27. Weighted averages of the categorical variables, education and experience, were taken using standard methods.
28. "The Affordability Study was commissioned by the Office for Children in partnership with the United Way of Massachusetts Bay." To conduct this study "a team of researchers at the Wellesley College Center for Research on Women, working with the Center for Survey Research at the University of Massachusetts" was chosen (p. 2 of Marshall et al.). See Marshall et al. for more details.
29. See Marshall et al. [1987] for details. Out of a total of 113 centers, 82 centers were eventually retained as those with missing values had to be dropped. Note 38 explains why after performing outlier analysis one observation from the for-profit sector was dropped subsequently leaving us with 81 centers in the final sample.
30. The Department of Social Services (DSS) provides funding for families based on need. This subsidy is given directly to the centers.
31. At this stage, it was decided to drop one observation from the for-profits sector. Inclusion of this observation completely changed otherwise insignificant coefficients on the price of capital and subsidy to significant ones. Further examination of the data revealed that this was an extremely unusual firm whose price of capital was four times the average for-profit price of capital. Further, it showed such huge amount of subsidies, that its inclusion changed an otherwise insignificant coefficient to a significant one. In the nonprofit sector, there were three outliers. One was a small center with unusually high quality, the other was small with unusually poor quality, and the third one could not be so easily characterized. We retained all these.
32. The residual plots did not indicate significant heteroskedasticity and therefore no data transformations were made. The adjusted R^2 is 0.83 and the F statistic is significant at any reasonable level of statistical significance. The collinearity diagnostics using eigenvalues (following Belsley et al. [1980]) do not show any significant collinearity.
33. The Pearson correlation coefficients for the quality attributes for the for-profit sector are as follows: The correlation coefficients between INTER and EDUC is 0.05, between INTER and EXPER it is −0.06, and between INTER and MSP it is 0.16. The correlation coefficients between EDUC and EXPER is 0.42, and between EDUC and MSP 0.20. The correlation coefficient between EXPER and MSP is −0.12.
34. The adjusted R^2 is 0.75 and the F statistic is significant at any reasonable level of statistical significance.
35. The Pearson correlation coefficients for the quality attributes for the for-profit sector are as follows: The correlation coefficients between INTER and EDUC is −0.18, between INTER and EXPER it is −0.04, and between INTER and MSP it is 0.45. The correlation coefficients between EDUC and EXPER is 0.50, and between EDUC and MSP −0.21. The correlation coefficient between EXPER and MSP is −0.21.
36. However there is a slight discrepancy between the results reported in the text and in Appendix IV dealing with the technical descriptions. The Appendix reports that there was "no statistical difference in the teachers' wages" though wages paid to aides were lower in for-profit centers.
37. Preston [1992] gets the same result from 1976 to 1977 data even after controlling for social externalities. Our results show that even a decade later in Massachusetts, NPOs and PMOs share the same cost function.

References

Alchian, A., and H. Demsetz. (1972). "Production, Information Costs, and Economic Organization." *American Economic Review* 62, 777–95.

Belsley, D.A., E. Kuh and R.E. Welsch (1980). *Regression Diagnostics: Identifying Influential Data and Sources of Collinearity.* New York: John Wiley & Sons.

Borjas, G.J., H.E. Frech III, and P.B. Ginsburg. (1983). "Property Rights and Wages: The Case of Nursing Homes." *Journal of Human Resources* 17, 231–46.

Bradford, D.F., R.A. Malt, and W.E. Oates. (1969). "The Rising Cost of Local Public Services: Some Evidence and Reflections. *National Tax Journal* 22(2).

Christensen, L.R., D.W. Jorgensen, and L.J. Lau. (1973). "Transcendental Logarithmic Production Functions." *Review of Economics and Statistics* 55, 28–45.

Coelen, C. et al. (1979). *Day Care Centers in the U.S.: A National Profile 1976–1977.* Cambridge, MA: Abt Associates.

Commonwealth of Massachusetts, Secretary of State. (1990). Office For Children, 102 CMR 7.00 Standards for Licensure and Approval of Group Day Care Centers.

Cowing, T.G., A.G. Holtmann, and S. Powers. (1983). "Hospital Cost Analysis: A Survey and Evaluation of Recent Studies." In *Advances in Health Economics and Health Services Research*, Vol. 4. JAI Press, pp. 257–303.

Denny, M. (1974). "The Relationship between Functional Forms for the Production System." *Canadian Journal of Economics* 7, 21–31.

Diewert, W.E. (1971). "An Application of the Shepard Duality Theorem: A Generalized Leontief." *Journal of Political Economy* 70, 481–507.

Easley, K., and M. O'Hara. (1983). "The Economic Role of the Nonprofit Firm." *Bell Journal of Economics* 14, 531–538.

Feldstein, M. (1971). "Hospital Price Inflation: A Study of Nonprofit Price Dynamics." *American Economic Review* 61, 853–872.

GAO. (1990). *Early Childhood Education: What are the Costs of High Quality Programs?* Washington, D.C.: United States General Accounting Office.

Goddeeris, John H. (1984). "Compensating Differentials and Self-Selection: An Application to Lawyers." Econometrics Workshop Paper no. 8405, Dept. of Economics, Michigan State University, East Lansing.

Hall, A. (1978). "Estimating Cost Equations for Child Care." In P.K. Robins and S. Weiner (eds.), In *Child Care and Public Policy.* Lexington, MA: Lexington Books.

Hansmann, H. (1980). "The Role of Non-profit Enterprise." *Yale Law Journal* 89, 835–898.

Hansmann, H. (1981). "Nonprofit Enterprise in the Performing Arts." *Bell Journal of Economics* 12, 341–361.

Hansmann, H. (1987). "Economic Theories of Nonprofit Organizations. W. Powell (ed.), In *Between the Public and the Private: The Nonprofit Sector.* New Haven: Yale University Press.

Hayes, C.D., J. Palmer, M. Zaslow (eds.) (1990). "Who Cares For America's Children? Child Care Policy for the 1990s." Panel on Child Care Policy, Committee on Child Development Research and Public Policy, Commission on Behavioral and Social Sciences and Education, National Research Council. Washington, D.C.: National Academy Press.

Henriques, I. and F. Vaillancourt. (1988). "The Demand for Child Care Services in Canada." *Applied Economics* 20, 385–394.

Inman, R. (ed.) (1985). *Managing the Service Economy: Prospects and Problems.* Cambridge: Cambridge University Press.

James, E. (1983). "How Nonprofits Grow: A Model." *Journal of Policy Analysis and Management* 2, 350–365.

James, E. (1986). Comments in Rose-Ackerman (ed.) (1986).

James, E., and E. Neuberger. (1981). "The University Department as a Non-Profit Labor Cooperative." *Public Choice* 36, 585–612.

James, E., and S. Rose-Ackerman. (1986). *The Nonprofit Enterprise in Market Economics.* New York: Harwood Academic.

Klerman, J., and A. Leibowitz. (1989). "Child Care Costs and Return to Work." Prepared (revised version) for Western Economic Association Meetings.

Krashinsky, M. (1986). "Transaction Costs and a Theory of the Nonprofit Organization." In S. Rose-Ackerman (ed). *The Economics of Nonprofit Institutions, Studies in Structure and Policy, Yale Studies on Nonprofit Organizations.* Oxford University Press.

Lange, M., J. Bullard, W. Luksetich, W. Jacobs and P. Jacobs. (1985). "Cost Functions for Symphony Orchestras." *Journal of Economic Literature* 9, 71–85.

Lee, M.L. (1971). "A Conspicuous Production Theory of Hospital Behaviour." *Southern Economic Journal* 38, 48–59.

Marshall, N.L., and A.D. Witte et al. (1987). *Report of the Child Care Affordability Study.* Center For Research on Women, Wellesley College.

National Academy of Early Childhood Education. (1989). Accreditation Pamphlet. Washington, DC: NAEYC.

Newhouse, Joseph. (1970). "Toward a Theory of Non-Profit Institutions: An Economic Model of a Hospital." *American Economic Review* 60, 64–74.

Pauly, M.P., and M.R. Redisch. (1973). "The Not-For-Profit Hospital as a Physicians' Cooperative." *American Economic Review* 63, 87–99.

Powell, W.W. (ed.) (1987). *The Nonprofit Sector: A Research Handbook.* New Haven: Yale University Press.

Preston, Anne E. (1988). "The Effects of Propety Rights on Labor Costs of Nonprofit Firms: An Application to the Day Care Industry." *The Journal of Industrial Economics* 36, 337–349.

Preston, Anne E. (1993). "Efficiency, Quality and Social Externalities in the Provision of Day Care: Comparisons of Nonprofit and For-Profit Firms. This volume.

Robins, P.K., and R.G. Spiegelman. (1978). "An Econometric Model of the Demand for Child Care. *Economic Inquiry* 16, 83–94.

Robins, P.K., and S. Weiner. (1978). *Child Care and Public Policy.* Lexington, MA: Lexington Books.

Rose-Ackerman, S. (ed.) 1986. *The Economics of Nonprofit Institutions, Studies in Structure and Policy, Yale Studies on Nonprofit Organizations.* Oxford University Press.

Ross, J.P., and J. Burkhead. (1974). *Productivity in the Local Government Sector.* Lexington, MA: D.C. Heath.

Ruopp, R., and J. Travers et al. (1979). *Children at the Center.* Cambridge, MA: Abt Associates.

Schofield, J.A. (1988). "Production Functions in the Sports Industry: An Empirical Analysis of Professional Cricket." *Applied Economics* 20, 177–193.

Searle A.D., and C.A. Waite. (1980). "Current Efforts to Measure Productivity in the Public Sector: How Adequate for the National Accounts? In J. Kendrick and B. Vaccara (eds.), *New Developments in Productivity Measurement and Analysis.* NBER Studies in Income and Wealth, Vol. 44. Chicago: University of Chicago Press.

Simon, J.G. (1987). "The Tax Treatment of Nonprofit Organizations: A Review of Federal and State Policies," in W.W. Powell (ed.), *The Nonprofit Sector: A Research Handbook.* New Haven: Yale University Press.

Stallings, J. and M. Wilcox. (1978). "Quality of Day Care: Can It Be Measured? In P.K. Robins and S. Weiner (eds.), *Child Care and Public Policy.* Lexington, MA: Lexington Books.

Steinberg, R. (1987), "Nonprofit Organizations and the Market." In W. Powell (ed.), *The Nonprofit Sector: A Research Handbook.* New Haven: Yale University Press.

Tullock, G. (1966). "Information without Profit." In G. Tullock (ed.), *Papers on Non-Market Decision Making.* Charlottesville, VA: Thomas Jefferson Center for Political Economy, University of Virginia.

U.S. Department of Commerce. (1976). *Daytime Care of Children:* October 1974 and Februrary 1975. Washington, DC: U.S. Government Printing Office, Current Population Reports, Series P-20, 298.

U.S. Department of Labor. (1988). *Child Care, a Workforce Issue.* Report of the Secretary's Task Force.

Weisbrod, Burton. (1983). "Wage Differentials between the Private For-Profit and Non-Profit Sectors: The Case for Lawyers." *Journal of Labor Economics* 1, 246–263.

Wellesley College Center for Research on Women and Center for Survey Research, University of Massachusetts at Boston. (1988). *Caring for our Commonwealth: The Economics of Child Care in Massachusetts.* Boston, MA: Massachusetts' Office for Children.

Zellner, A., and N. Revankar. (1969). "Generalized Production Functions." *Review of Economic Studies* 36, 241–250.

The Journal of Productivity Analysis, 4, 165–182 (1993)

Efficiency, Quality, and Social Externalities in the Provision of Day Care: Comparisons of Nonprofit and For-Profit Firms

ANNE E. PRESTON
Harriman School and Department of Economics, SUNY at Stony Brook, Stony Brook, NY 11794-3775

Abstract

Efficiency comparisons of nonprofit and for-profit day care centers reveal that, in 1977, production functions of nonprofit and for-profit day care centers were similar. Cost levels were also similar for centers providing identical services. However, on average, nonprofit centers offered costlier services than for-profit centers. In the segment of the industry not subject to federal regulations, nonprofit centers offered services with higher social externalities than for-profit centers. In the federally regulated segment, nonprofit centers offered higher quality services than for-profit centers. Therefore the important difference in economic outcomes of nonprofit and for-profit day care centers involved product selection rather than efficiency levels.

1. Introduction

Recent policy debates over the child care bills before Congress have focused on how to distribute money to needy families and whether the federal government should be regulating state programs. Despite the public attention on developing a national child care bill, there has been surprisingly little attention paid to performance in the market for day care.

The economic analysis needed to inform this policy debate must acknowledge inherent market failures in day care provision and the institutional regulations which already exist in the industry. Two important market failures ensure that socially optimal levels of day care will not be provided in a free market. First, in addition to the private benefits enjoyed by families using day care, day-care services generate social externalities such as care and education of children and labor productivity of young women. Second, the nature of day care makes evaluation of the quality of the service by parents and policy makers difficult. In particular, third party purchasing by parents for children creates natural informational asymmetries. Furthermore, the quality of care has long-term effects on the development of the child that are difficult to observe at the time of provision.

Currently the regulatory constraints in the day-care industry include state laws which apply to all organized day-care providers in the state's jurisdiction. However, nonprofit day-care centers face an additional set of state and federal laws which regulate all nonprofit organizations. Any regulatory decisions must acknowledge the effects of institutional differences between nonprofit and for-profit centers on performance in the day-care industry.

Because of the complexity of the service offered by day-care centers, attempts to compare efficiency levels of nonprofit and for-profit day care centers should use extensive controls for quality. Furthermore, in industries with both nonprofit and for-profit firms, self-selection of entrepreneurs into the two sectors should produce higher levels of social externalities in the nonprofit sector than in the for-profit sector (Preston [1990]). Therefore a failure to acknowledge potential differences in social externalities provided by the two types of firms may further bias efficiency comparisons. A comprehensive study of the effects of nonprofit production on efficiency in the day-care industry needs to consider the effects of nonprofit production on product selection as well.

This study begins with a comparative analysis of product attributes for nonprofit and for-profit day-care centers. The results of this analysis are used then to control for quality and social externalities in cost comparisons of nonprofit and for-profit firms. The analysis is especially helpful for policymakers since the comparisons are made for both federally regulated and unregulated segments of the industry.

2. Econometric Specifications

2.1. Nonprofit Production and Its Effects on Product Selection

The specific federal and state regulations that apply to nonprofit firms should result in a self selection of entrepreneurs between the nonprofit and for-profit sectors (Preston [1990]). Federal law prohibits the distribution of profits to nonprofit entrepreneurs. State laws require that costs of nonprofits remain at reasonable levels, and that nonprofits produce a product which generates external social benefits in order to qualify for preferential tax treatment and to receive tax-deductible donations.

Together these laws, which put an upper limit on the size and variance of entrepreneurial income and which put a floor on the social externalities generated by the firm create a selection process among entrepreneurs. Those with a stronger taste for social externalities start nonprofit firms. The extra social externalities generated with the donative revenue received by the nonprofit firm must be more valuable to the nonprofit entrepreneur than the loss of income resulting from the federal restriction of profits. Therefore nonprofit entrepreneurs will produce products which generate a greater amount of social externalities. For-profit entrepreneurs will produce products which have potentially high levels of sales revenue.[1]

I model the process of self-selection using McFadden's conditional logit specification. An entrepreneur starting a day-care center has a utility function which depends on the attributes of the day-care center being created. In addition the prices of these attributes can differ across centers in different sectors. For example, social externalities may be less costly to provide in the nonprofit sector because donations for services with social externalities are available. The choice between sectors is a simple utility comparison of the centers which provide the highest utility in the two different sectors.[2]

Let $DC_{i,j}^{*}$ represent the utility function of the individual entrepreneur i in sector j when operating a center with attributes $Z_{i,j}$:

$$DC_{i,j}^{*} = \beta(\mathbf{Z}_{i,j}) + \epsilon_i. \tag{1}$$

The observed value $DC_{i,np}$ is given by

$$DC_{i,np} = 1 \quad \text{if } DC^{*}_{i,np} > DC^{*}_{i,fp},$$

$$DC_{i,np} = 0 \quad \text{otherwise.} \tag{2}$$

where *np* and *fp* represent the nonprofit and for-profit sectors respectively.

If the ϵ_i's are independently and identically distributed with the Weibull distribution, we can estimate the model with a multinomial logit model which has the form

$$\Pr(DC_{i,np} = 1) = \frac{\exp \beta \mathbf{Z}_{i,np}}{\exp \beta \mathbf{Z}_{i,np} + \exp \beta \mathbf{Z}_{i,fp}}. \tag{3}$$

Because the theory of entrepreneurial self-selection stresses a difference in preferences for social externalities between nonprofit and for-profit entrepreneurs, $\mathbf{Z}_i$ will include a set of variables that should indicate social externalities. Social externalities associated with day care include the care and education of the young and labor productivity of working mothers. These positive benefits to society may increase when the services are offered to underprivileged families, since without day care, these mothers are likely to be permanent welfare recipients. Similarly, since children of underprivileged families are more likely to grow up in situations which lead to poverty and welfare dependence than are children from privileged families, any positive behavioral or educational effects on the child will create greater benefits to society.[3] Therefore, variables used as proxies for social externalities include percentage of children who are black, percentage of children who are other minority, percentage of children from single-parent families, percentage of children whose parents pay tuition, the maximum weekly fee charged for care, and dummy variables representing whether the center provides counseling on child development, counseling on family problems, assistance in obtaining financial aid, and assistance in obtaining community services.

Hansmann [1980] hypothesizes that nonprofit entreprenurs may also self-select along quality dimensions. Because the nonprofit firm is subject to the nondistribution constraint, consumers will perceive it as a trustworthy institution in markets where quality and service provision are difficult to assess. Therefore entrepreneurs with strong tastes for quality will choose the nonprofit form because it becomes a signal that stated quality is equal to actual quality. Furthermore, even if tastes for quality are similar between nonprofit and for-profit entrepreneurs, there may be quality differences between nonprofit and for-profit firms if monopoly profits prevail. Because excess profits of the nonprofit must be reinvested in the firm, as long as the nonprofit manager has a taste for quality, these excess profits will be used to buy quality.

Therefore variables measuring quality will be included in the logit equations. These variables include proxies for labor quality: maximum salary paid, turnover rate of caregivers, child-to-staff ratio, and dummy variables representing employment of a child development specialist, a psychologist, a nurse, a nutritionist, or a social worker. In addition dummy variables are included for centers which offer physical exams; hearing, speech, or vision exams; psychological exams; or dental exams, parental use of the center for social functions, and parental participation in fundraising; staff selection; budget review; and caregiving.[4] The results from the logit specification can be used to test whether there are significant differences in clientele, child and family programs, and workforce and center quality measurements between nonprofit and for-profit centers.[5]

2.2. *Nonprofit Production and Its Effects on Costs*

Following Mukerjee and Witte [1991], I estimate an average cost function derived from a generalized Cobb-Douglas production function proposed by Zellner and Revankar [1969] which allows variable returns to scale.[6]

$$\ln(\text{AVCOST})_k = a + b(\ln \mathbf{P}_k) + c(Q_k) + d(\ln Q_k) + f(\mathbf{X}_k) + g(NP_k) + \xi_k, \qquad (4)$$

where AVCOST = total monthly costs per full-time equivalent child
$\mathbf{P}$ = vector of the price of inputs
Q = number of full-time equivalent children
$\mathbf{X}$ = vector of control variables which are proxies for quality and social benefits
NP = dummy variable representing nonprofit status

Labor costs are the highest costs of day-care centers: in the current sample labor costs constitute 59% of total costs. The monthly salary costs divided by full-time equivalent staff measures the price of labor in the cost function.[7] The nonlabor operating costs include expenses on toys, books, office equipment, and food. Prices for these products, except for the price of food, are not likely to differ for different areas in the United States at a given point in time. However, to account for differences in these prices, the regional CPI is included as a proxy for the price of operating equipment. The dominant capital cost in day care is the rental cost of buildings and land. Rental costs constitute approximately 13% of total costs in this sample. While no data is available on rental prices faced by establishments, I divide the monthly rental cost by the number of children which the center is licensed to serve. Because the number of children which the center is licensed to serve is determined to a great extent by the amount of space in the facility, this variable is a good proxy for rental price per square foot of space.[8] I also include a dummy variable which is equal to one if the center uses donated space.

Given the earlier theoretical hypotheses, nonprofit and for-profit centers may offer services with systematically different levels of quality and social externalities. Failure to control for these differences may result in observed cost differences that are a result of service differences rather than differences in efficiency levels. Because quality and social externalities in day care are difficult to measure, an extensive vector for proxies for these product attributes will be included in the cost equations. The vector is designed to control for the multidimensional aspects of quality and social benefits in day care that are both observed and unobserved.

The measures of quality include staff-to-child ratio, mean education of caregivers, mean experience of caregivers, turnover rate of staff, hours of operation, and dummy variables representing employment of specialists, centers which offer special health exams, and parental participation in center policy. Measures of social externalities include percent of children that are black, percentage that are other minority, percentage that are parent financed, and percentage that come from single-parent families, and dummy variables representing different types of parental counseling.[9]

3. Data and Sample

To study differences in nonprofit and for-profit performance, I use data collected by Abt Associates for the 1976–77 National Day Care Center Supply Study. The data set has several strengths. First, it is a national sample of centers with capacity exceeding 13 children. Second, the data include information on client characteristics and quality of centers that are not available from other data. Finally, the data cover a period when federal regulations were in place for a subset of the industry. Therefore, comparisons of nonprofit and for-profit performance can be made in different regulatory environments.

During 1976–1977, the years of the Abt study, the Federal Interagency Day Care Requirements (FIDCR) regulated all centers which served federally funded children. Centers receiving federal funds were required to comply with the high quality levels imposed by FIDCR.[10] For example, FIDCR established standards for group sizes, child-to-staff ratios, nutrition, medical exams, social services for families, child development counseling, and parental participation. In 1976 the standards were written into law with the Title XX Amendments to the Social Security Act. However, after a series of controversies involving enforcement procedures, the standards were abolished in 1980.

Therefore at the time of the survey, there were two segments of the organized day-care industry. First, there were centers that did not provide care for federally funded children and which were regulated only by state and local regulations. State regulations of program characteristics, enrollment policies, staff qualifications, group size, and staff-to-child ratios were much more lenient than federal regulations. Most analysts have found that these regulations were so lenient that compliance was almost automatic. This segment of the industry may be characterized by a monopolistically competitive market structure where services are differentiated by location, clientele, and quality attributes. Barriers to entry due to economies of scale or absolute costs are low.

Alternatively, centers which did care for federally funded children were subject to the more stringent FIDCR requirements. The complexity of the requirements for federal funding and the regulations themselves probably elevated entry barriers in this segment of the industry. In the early 1970s before the FIDCR regulations were established, the fragmented nature of the federal grant programs and the complex web of funding sources, specifications, and matching requirements probably imposed a large fixed cost of information gathering on firms considering service to federally funded children (Jackson [1973]). Furthermore, compliance with the quality standards established in 1976 probably increased both marginal and fixed costs of centers. Therefore the potential for monopoly profits was probably greater in this segment of the industry than in the less regulated segment.

The empirical analysis was performed on a subsample of 2703 day-care centers which represent the private nonprofit and for-profit centers. Centers affiliated with head-start programs, government agencies, and schools were dropped from the original sample since they may represent government centers rather than private nonprofit centers. Because nonprofit differences in product selection and costs may vary with the different federal regulations, the models are estimated separately for the FIDCR and non-FIDCR centers. The FIDCR subsample includes those centers which enroll federally funded children and which are subject to the regulations. The non-FIDCR subsample includes both centers which serve no federally funded children and centers which enroll such a small number of federally funded children that federal regulations have been waived.[11]

Table 1 gives means of selected center characteristics for non-FIDCR nonprofit (column 1), non-FIDCR for-profit (column 2), FIDCR nonprofit (column 3), and FIDCR for-profit centers (column 4). The table reveals that where center characteristics vary, they tend to vary both by FIDCR status and nonprofit status. For example, maximum fee (row 1) charged by the center is generally higher for FIDCR centers than for non-FIDCR centers. In addition within both of the regulatory categories, for-profit centers charge a higher maximum fee on average than do nonprofits. However this difference is only significant for the non-FIDCR sample. Similarly average costs (row 2) as well as salaries (rows 5 and 6) are higher for nonprofit than for for-profit centers and for FIDCR centers than for non-FIDCR centers. Child-to-staff ratios (row 4) are higher in non-FIDCR centers than in FIDCR centers and in for-profit than in nonprofit centers. The clientele is more likely to be minority, single parent, or from low income families (rows 9–12) in FIDCR centers than in non-FIDCR centers and in nonprofit than in for-profit centers.

There is a large variation in the socioeconomic status of the clients of both nonprofit and for-profit non-FIDCR centers. While the nonprofits serve a higher percentage of disadvantaged, 12% of their clientele (compared to 18% for for-profits) is high income (income greater than $15,000.00), double-parent, and nonminority. Several of the nonprofit centers serve only these clients. In the FIDCR segment of the industry, the variation in types of clientele is not so great, especially for nonprofit centers. In FIDCR nonprofit centers, one quarter of the clients are disadvantaged along all of the three criteria and only 3% are high income, nonminority, and double-parent.

4. Empirical Results

4.1. Product Selection Differences

Table 2 presents the results of the multinomial logit equations estimating nonprofit status for the non-FIDCR and the FIDCR segments of the industry.[12] In both segments of the industry nonprofit centers occupy a different market niche than for-profit centers. In the more competitive, non-FIDCR segment of the industry, the coefficients on the variables measuring social externalities indicate a higher social externality component in nonprofit day-care centers than in for-profit day-care centers. In particular, centers which have a higher percentage of black children and centers which have a higher percentage of other minority children are more likely to be nonprofit. Similarly centers which have a higher percentage

Table 1. Means of selected center characteristics.

	Non-FIDCR		FIDCR	
	Nonprofit	For-Profit	Nonprofit	For-Profit
1. Maximum fee	24.52* (9.88)	25.33 (6.77)	26.00 (11.32)	27.38 (7.44)
2. Average costs	109.68** (99.07)	92.15 (148.76)	161.97** (98.59)	101.06 (62.41)
3. Total enrollment	53.84** (43.42)	44.34 (36.91)	54.74 (36.94)	54.88 (41.31)
4. Child-to-staff ratio	9.24* (7.28)	10.16 (10.01)	6.81** (5.71)	8.36 (4.95)
5. Maximum weekly salary	133.25** (50.88)	121.11 (53.58)	154.99** (52.76)	124.97 (45.50)
6. Average monthly salary	389.93** (268.08)	324.37 (336.65)	462.90** (314.89)	329.57 (235.82)
7. Mean education of caregivers	13.37 (1.51)	13.26 (1.50)	13.49 (1.23)	13.35 (1.35)
8. Mean experience of caregivers	4.56** (4.05)	5.99 (5.15)	3.73** (2.90)	4.52 (3.57)
9. Percentage of centers with donated space	0.40** (0.49)	0.02 (0.13)	0.38** (0.49)	0.02 (0.15)
Percent of Children				
10. Black	0.24** (0.35)	0.14 (0.27)	0.39** (0.38)	0.24 (0.35)
11. Other minority	0.07** (0.18)	0.05 (0.13)	0.10* (0.19)	0.06 (0.13)
12. Single parent	0.28* (0.25)	0.26 (0.22)	0.57** (0.27)	0.47 (0.24)
13. From family with annual income <$6000	0.23** (0.30)	0.09 (0.18)	0.56** (0.30)	0.42 (0.30)
14. *N*	791	1033	644	226

*The nonprcfit mean is significantly different from the for-profit mean at the .05 level.
**The nonprofit mean is signficantly different from the for-profit mean at the .01 level.

Table 2. Logit estimates of the effects of center characteristics on nonprofit status.

	Non-FIDCR	FIDCR
Child-to-staff ratio	0.002	−0.061**
	(0.010)	(0.026)
Maximum fee	−0.022*	−0.019
	(0.009)	(0.014)
Maximum salary	0.002	0.007***
	(0.001)	(0.003)
Staff turnover	−0.242	−0.970*
	(0.277)	(0.576)
Percentage of children		
Black	0.512**	−0.033
	(0.225)	(0.408)
Other minority	0.764*	0.807
	(0.420)	(0.817)
With a single parent	−0.231	−0.191
	(0.299)	(0.506)
Whose parents pay full tuition	−0.021***	−0.006
	(0.008)	(0.005)
Centers which employ		
Nutritionist	0.281	0.597*
	(0.172)	(0.328)
Hearing, speech, and vision specialist	0.018	−0.072
	(0.300)	(0.499)
Child development specialist	−0.226	−0.513*
	(0.152)	(0.263)
Psychologist	0.049	−0.009
	(0.319)	(0.504)
Nurse	0.113	−0.083
	(0.172)	(0.324)
Social Worker	0.011	1.115***
	(0.230)	(0.376)
Centers which give		
Psychological exams	0.056	−0.718**
	(0.159)	(0.289)
Hearing, speech, and vision exam	0.119	0.359
	(0.149)	(0.305)
Dental exam	−0.187	0.078
	(0.217)	(0.311)
Physical exam	−0.027	0.205
	(0.201)	(0.314)

Table 2. Continued.

	Non-FIDCR	FIDCR
Centers assisting parents in		
Child development counseling	−0.208	0.032
	(0.173)	(0.381)
Family counseling	0.237	0.640**
	(0.145)	(0.280)
Obtaining financial aid	0.463***	−0.178
	(0.162)	(0.319)
Obtaining community services	−0.128	0.258
	(0.159)	(0.302)
Parental participation in		
Fundraising	1.273***	1.052***
	(0.203)	(0.330)
Staff selection	1.016***	0.733**
	(0.280)	(0.377)
Budget review	0.585***	1.218***
	(0.175)	(0.307)
Volunteering	−0.257	−0.180
	(0.190)	(0.319)
Center social affairs	0.580***	−0.328
	(0.164)	(0.273)
Northeast	−0.055	1.118***
	(0.222)	(0.370)
South	−0.638***	1.235**
	(0.194)	(0.510)
Midwest	−0.024	0.705**
	(0.173)	(0.297)
Constant	1.589*	−0.480
	(0.881)	(0.808)
N	1314	620

*Significant at the .10 level using a two-tailed test.
**Significant at the .05 level using a two-tailed test.
***Significant at the .01 level using a two-tailed test.

of children whose tuition is paid by parents and centers with higher maximum weekly fees are more likely to be for-profit. Furthermore centers which offer aid to families in obtaining financial services such as food stamps are more likely to be nonprofit.[13] For these non-FIDCR centers, the main difference in quality between nonprofit and for-profit centers comes in the form of more parental participation in fund raising, staff selection, and budget review in nonprofit centers.[14]

In the FIDCR segment of the industry, the differences between the nonprofit and for-profit centers are more closely tied to quality differences than to differences in social externalities. Along the social externality dimension, centers with a smaller number of children whose tuition is paid for by parents and centers which offer family counseling are more likely to be nonprofit. Along the quality dimension, centers with lower child-to-staff ratios, centers which pay higher salaries, centers for which staff turnover is lower, centers which employ nutritionists, and centers which employ social workers are more likely to be nonprofit. On the other hand, centers which employ child development specialists and centers which offer psychological exams are more likely to be for-profit. As with the non-FIDCR centers, centers in which parents participate in fund raising, budget review, and staff selection are more likely to be nonprofit. These results seem to imply that, while for-profits are more likely to offer some services that nonprofits do not, FIDCR nonprofit centers are more likely to invest in the quality of the caregiving service through investments in labor (higher salaries, fewer children per caregiver, and lower turnover rates) than are FIDCR for-profit centers.[15]

The difference in the distinction between nonprofit and for-profit centers in the FIDCR and non-FIDCR samples may be due to the differences in the regulations imposed on the two types of centers. In the non-FIDCR sample where the principal regulations imposed on centers are the federal and state regulations of nonprofit firms, nonprofit centers provide higher social externalities with little difference in quality. This result supports the hypothesis that nonprofit regulations result in a self-selection of entrepreneurs with strong tastes for social externalities into the nonprofit sector. Because there is little difference in quality, the evidence does not show that entrepreneurs are self-selecting along the quality dimension in the non-FIDCR segment of the industry.

In the FIDCR sample the similarity between nonprofit and for-profit centers along the social benefit dimension may be the result of federal regulation of day care. In order to qualify for federal money, a center has to serve a certain number of low-income, disadvantaged children. This requirement for the FIDCR centers may result in less potential variation in the variables which I use to measure social externalities. These same federal regulations may also elevate entry barriers and create a greater potential for monopoly profits in FIDCR centers than in non-FIDCR centers.[16] Therefore, the quality differences between nonprofit and for-profit firms may be due to nonprofit FIDCR centers using potential profits to buy quality since social externalities are already high.

4.2. *Cost Differences*

The estimated coefficients from the cost equations are presented in Table 3.[17] Column 1 gives the OLS estimates of the cost equations for the unregulated non-FIDCR sample. Separate cost equations were estimated for the nonprofit and for-profit centers. However, because an F test could not reject the hypothesis that the nonprofit and for-profit coefficients are equal at the .10 level, only the coefficients from the cost functions for the total sample are presented.[18] Row 1 gives the estimate of the coefficient on nonprofit status which is insignificantly different from zero at conventional significance levels. Unlike previous studies which conclude that nonprofit centers have higher costs than for-profit centers, this analysis,

Table 3. OLS cost equations (dependent variable is the natural logarithm of total costs per full-time equivalent child; standard errors are in parentheses).

	Non-FIDCR		FIDCR	
1. Nonprofit	0.026 (0.033)	0.139*** (0.035)	0.046 (0.044)	0.226*** (0.043)
2. Full-time equivalent children	0.002** (0.001)	0.004*** (0.001)	0.002* (0.001)	0.003** (0.001)
3. ln(full-time equivalent children)	−0.225*** (0.045)	−0.417*** (0.047)	−0.186** (0.060)	−0.311*** (0.063)
4. ln(average salary)	0.465*** (0.018)	0.510*** (0.020)	0.487*** (0.020)	0.501 (0.022)
5. ln(average rent per licensed child)	0.160** (0.013)	0.185*** (0.015)	0.149*** (0.014)	0.171*** (0.016)
6. Center uses donated space	0.054 (0.039)	0.071 (0.044)	0.100*** (0.035)	0.126*** (0.039)
7. Regional CPI	0.076** (0.033)	0.139*** (0.036)	0.109*** (0.037)	0.214*** (0.038)
8. ln(child-to-staff ratio)	−0.335*** (0.026)		−0.308*** (0.036)	
9. ln(mean education of caregivers)	0.363*** (0.124)		0.390** (0.172)	
10. ln(mean experience of caregivers)	−0.049*** (0.018)		−0.075*** (0.024)	
12. Turnover	−0.117** (0.047)		−0.224*** (0.079)	
13. Total enrollment divided by full-time equivalent children	0.124*** (0.035)	0.132*** (0.038)	0.175*** (0.059)	0.108* (0.059)
14. Years open	0.006*** (0.002)	0.006*** (0.002)	0.004* (0.002)	0.004** (0.002)
15. Parent organization	0.115*** (0.031)	0.147*** (0.034)	0.066** (0.030)	0.060* (0.033)
16. Hours operating per week	−0.0004 (0.001)	0.001 (0.001)	−0.001 (0.001)	−0.004** (0.001)
Percentage of children				
17. Black	0.069 (0.043)		0.082* (0.047)	
18. Other minority	−0.058 (0.076)		0.036 (0.083)	
18. Single parent	0.214*** (0.055)		0.054 (0.060)	
20. Parent financed	−0.003*** (0.001)		−0.002*** (0.001)	

Table 3. Continued.

	Non-FIDCR	FIDCR
Centers which employ		
21. Nutritionist	0.363*** (0.124)	0.026 (0.036)
22. Hearing, speech, and vision specialist	−0.003 (0.052)	0.054 (0.055)
23. Child development specialist	0.051* (0.028)	0.018 (0.031)
24. Psychologist	−0.022 (0.059)	−0.017 (0.053)
25. Nurse	0.036 (0.032)	0.095*** (0.036)
26. Social worker	0.059 (0.042)	0.069* (0.035)
Centers which give		
27. Psychological exams	−0.031 (0.029)	0.043 (0.037)
28. Hearing, speech, and vision exam	0.071** (0.029)	−0.038 (0.044)
29. Dental exam	0.017 (0.038)	0.014 (0.037)
30. Physical exam	−0.022 (0.036)	−0.012 (0.037)
Centers assisting parents in		
31. Child development counseling	0.002 (0.034)	0.039 (0.059)
32. Family counseling	0.032 (0.027)	0.041 (0.038)
33. Obtaining financial aid	−0.064** (0.030)	0.016 (0.040)
34. Obtaining community services	0.034 (0.029)	0.059 (0.042)
Parental participation in		
35. Fundraising	−0.030 (0.035)	−0.004 (0.037)
36. Staff selection	0.106** (0.045)	−0.006 (0.038)
37. Budget review	−0.009 (0.033)	0.018 (0.038)

Table 3. Continued.

	Non-FIDCR		FIDCR	
38. Volunteering	−0.040 (0.033)		−0.001 (0.033)	
39. Center social affairs	0.029 (0.030)		0.048 (0.032)	
40. Constant	−5.459* (3.213)	−11.496*** (3.500)	−9.014** (3.583)	−18.569*** (3.666)
41. R^2	0.666	0.540	0.728	0.643
42. *N*	1037	1037	649	649

*Significant at the .10 level using a two-tailed test.
**Significant at the .05 level using a two-tailed test.
***Significant at the .01 level using a two-tailed test.

which controls extensively for quality and clientele differentials, finds no differences in costs between the two types of centers. In addition there is no evidence that the production functions of the nonprofit and for-profit centers are different.

The coefficient on full time equivalent children is positive and significant. Therefore returns to scale in the non-FIDCR segment of the day-care industry are decreasing. Coefficients on the natural logarithm of salary (row 4) and rent (row 5) imply that the elasticities of average costs with respect to the price of labor and the price of land are approximately .47 and .16 respectively. Controlling for rent, the use of donated space (row 6) has an insignificant effect on costs. A one point increase in the regional CPI (row 7) increases costs by 8%, however without a better measure of the price of equipment, the elasticity of costs with respect to the price of equipment cannot be estimated.

In the non-FIDCR segment of the industry, the proxies for quality are generally significant determinants of costs. The elasticity of total costs with respect to child-to-staff ratio is −.34 (row 8). The elasticity of average costs with respect to education of caregivers (row 9) is positive and significant, implying that, even if more educated workers improve productivity, they increase costs through positive effects on quality.[19] In contrast mean experience of caregivers (row 10) has a negative effect on average costs. Controlling for salary, higher levels of employee turnover (row 12) decrease costs, implying that the quality improvement from a more constant labor force is costly. The employment of a nutritionist (row 21) and a child development specialist (row 23) and the provision of hearing, speech, and vision exams (row 28) all increase costs significantly.

Many of the proxies for social externalities are also significant determinants of costs. Higher percentages of children who are black (row 17) and single-parent (row 23) increase costs while higher percentages of children financed by parental revenue (row 20) decrease costs. Minority, single-parent, and low-income children may have special needs which translate into higher cost services. Generally the different types of parental aid do not affect costs with the exception that aid in obtaining financial services (row 33) decreases costs.

As predicted, the more children served per full-time equivalent child, the higher the costs (row 12), probably due to increased administrative expenses. In addition, contrary to the intuition that older centers use knowledge gained from experience to achieve efficiency and centers which are part of a larger organization can enjoy volume discounts on supplies, older centers (row 14) and centers affiliated with a parent or umbrella organization (row 15) have higher costs.

While nonprofit centers do not have higher costs controlling for social externalities and quality, many of the dimensions of quality and social externalities which increase costs are more prevalent in nonprofit centers than in for-profit centers. Therefore the cost equation was reestimated excluding all quality and social externality controls, and the resulting coefficients are presented in column 2. The coefficient on nonprofit status (row 1) reveals that without controls for quality and social benefits, in the unregulated segment of the day-care industry, nonprofit centers have costs 14% higher than for-profit centers.[20]

Columns 3 and 4 give OLS estimates of the cost equation for the FIDCR segment of the industry. Separate cost equations were estimated for the nonprofit and for-profit firms, but, similar to the non-FIDCR results, an F test cannot reject the hypothesis at the .10 level that the nonprofit and for-profit coefficients are equal. Therefore columns 3 and 4 present estimates for the complete FIDCR sample of centers. In this segment of the industry, controlling for quality and social externalities, the nonprofit coefficient (column 3, row 1) is insignificantly different from zero. Therefore, similar to the unregulated segment of the industry, where federal regulations are in place, nonprofit centers are not less cost efficient than for-profit centers and there is no evidence that they operate with different production functions.

The coefficients on enrollment and input prices are similar to those estimated for the unregulated segment of the industry. However, in the FIDCR centers, controlling for rental price, donated space increases costs implying that the availability of free space may lead to costly program additions. The effects of quality and social benefit proxies on costs are similar in the FIDCR and the non-FIDCR sample. With the exception of employment of nurses and social workers, employment of specialists, provision of extra services, and aid to parents do not affect costs in the FIDCR sample.

The cost equation for the FIDCR sample was reestimated excluding quality and social externalities and the coefficients are presented in column 4. Without these service controls, nonprofit centers operate at cost levels 22% higher than for-profit centers.[21]

The general results of Table 3 imply that extensive controls for quality and social benefits may negate the general conclusion that nonprofit day-care centers are less cost efficient than for-profit centers. However the results need to be qualified somewhat. First, while the general selectivity argument and the logit equations are important in pointing out that nonprofit and for-profit firms locate in different market niches, it is also clear from the cost equations that the nonprofit products and services are costlier than the for-profit products and services. These extra costs are due to higher levels of quality or social benefits in the nonprofit firms. Only when we compare nonprofit and for-profit costs for firms within the same market niche can we conclude that nonprofit centers operate at similar costs to for-profit centers.[22]

A related issue remains unaddressed: are nonprofits overinvesting in quality or social benefits? Given the results from the logit analysis one could only conclude that nonprofits are producing inefficiently high levels of quality and social benefits if it were clear that for-profit centers offer the optimal mix of services. However given the inherent market failures in day care, for-profit centers are likely to provide too little quality and social benefits. In particular because, generally, social benefits are not revenue producing, they will be underprovided by for-profit firms. In addition if there are informational asymmetries involved in quality assessment of day care, for-profit centers may be motivated to maintain actual quality levels below stated quality levels.

5. Conclusion

The results of the study reveal that the production functions of nonprofit and for-profit day-care centers are similar, and nonprofit day-care centers operate at similar cost levels to for-profit day-care centers when comparing firms offering similar products and services. However, nonprofit centers offer costlier services on average than nonprofit centers. In particular, where day-care centers are not subject to federal regulations, nonprofit day-care centers offer services with higher levels of social externalities than for-profit centers. On the other hand, where day-care centers are subject to stringent and complicated federal regulations, nonprofit day-care centers provide similar levels of social externalities but higher quality levels than do for-profit centers. Therefore the important difference in economic outcomes of nonprofit and for-profit day-care centers involves product selection rather than efficiency levels.

The conclusions of this study have broad implications. First, simple unidimensional quality measures are probably not sufficient to measure the quality of day care both because quality of day care is multidimensional and because quality is not easily evaluated. Rather a vector of measures associated with different day care attributes is more likely to capture variations in observed and unobserved quality characteristics.

In measuring the economic benefits generated from the provision of day-care services, it is also important to consider social benefits in the form of spillovers to society and to other industries. These spillovers arise from labor productivity of mothers freed from the child care task and any increases in future productivity of the children themselves. Clearly, any productivity analysis of the day-care industry, which does not take into account these spillovers, measures output of the industry incorrectly and therefore may be misleading. The issue of spillovers has been investigated in the context of R&D investment where social returns also exceed private returns (Griliches [1979]; Jaffe [1986]). However, similar to the case of day-care services, according to Griliches [1988], empirical studies "have not yielded a convincing estimate of their global impact."

The results of this study imply that nonprofit day-care centers provide services with higher spillovers to society because they are more likely to serve minority families who, without affordable day-care services, might be permanently in need of government welfare payments. If this difference in social externalities extends to other service industries in which nonprofit and for-profit firms compete, productivity comparisons of nonprofit and for-profit firms which do not control for these spillovers are likely to overestimate the productivity advantage of the for-profit firm. Furthermore, estimates of service sector productivity growth over time will not be accurate if the fraction of firms which are nonprofit change over time or if the makeup of services changes in ways which alter spillovers.

Notes

1. The theoretical arguments concerning self-selction by entrepreneurs between the nonprofit and for-profit sector are made by Preston [1990] in the general context of product and sector choice of entrepreneurs without specifying industry. The alternative to either type of entrepreneurial activity is work as a wage earner. Application to the more specific context within an industry does not alter the theoretical results. Here, given that a worker has chosen to work in day care, he or she must choose between earning a wage, entrepreneurial/managerial activity in a nonprofit firm, or entrepreneurial/managerial activity in a for-profit firm. In the day-care industry of 1977, the focus of this study, federal regulation of a segment of the industry might have further altered locational incentives. However, because of the intense political questioning of the federal regulations at that time, industry participants may have been unsure of the permanence of the regulations and hesitant to alter behavior because of them.
2. In other words, each entrepreneur compares the day care center in the for-profit center which would maximize his utility given prices of center attributes within the for-profit sector to the day care center which would maximize his utility in the nonprofit sector given the prices of attributes in this sector. Whichever center provides the entrepreneur the highest utility will dictate the sector in which he locates.
3. The Perry Pre-school Program longitudinal study (Berrueta-Clement [1984]) showed important social benefits associated with high-quality preschool programs. In particular in the case of disadvantaged youths, participation in the program reduced the probability of being kept back in later grades and reduced the probability of being placed in remedial education classes in later grades. Both of these effects are direct cost savings to taxpayers.
4. According to *Child Care: A Workforce Issue* [1988], frequently cited measures of quality include the presence of a program of developmentally appropriate activities, degree of parental involvement, training of staff, ratio of children to caregivers, the nutritional value of meals, group size, safety of environment, policies affecting the children's health, and the stability of the staff. The measures of quality included in this analysis are proxies for many of these attributes.
5. The logit specification of the sector choice equation was chosen because it falls out of the theoretical model of self-selection by entrepreneurs. If differences in services between nonprofit and for-profit centers arise for other reasons such as donor preferences, alternative specifications might also be used to describe sectoral differences in day-care centers. For example, discriminant analysis could be used to classify centers as nonprofit or for-profit using the independent variables as predictors.
6. The generalized Cobb-Douglas production function has the form $Ve^{\theta V} = \gamma K^{\alpha\delta} L^{\alpha(1-\delta)}$, where V = output; $0 < \delta < 1, \gamma > 0, \alpha > 0, \theta$ determines returns to scale. If $\theta > 0$ returns to scale are declining for positive V. If $\theta < 0$ returns to scale are increasing. The equation to be estimated is $\ln(\text{AVCOST}) = ([1 - \alpha]/\alpha)\ln V + (\theta/\alpha)V + \delta \ln(P_K) + (1 - \delta) \ln(P_L) + C$, where C is a constant. Therefore the sign of the coefficient on V determines returns to scale.
7. Total staff includes paid staff, staff paid by an outside agency, and volunteer staff. In order to calculate the number of full-time equivalent staff, full-time staff are weighted by 1, and volunteer and part-time staff are weighted by .5.
8. Several centers reported a monthly rent of zero, which is plausible in instances where the centers use donated space. Therefore, if monthly rent was reported as zero and the center acknowledges that it uses donated space, I redefine the value of monthly rent to one so that these observations are not dropped when rent is converted to logarithms. If monthly rent was reported as zero and the center does not acknowledge using donated space, I drop the center from the analysis.
9. In addition to full-time equivalent children, I include total enrollment divided by full-time equivalents to get a measure of the number of children on average which make up a full-time equivalent. Here, more children attending the center for fewer hours may increase administrative costs of the center. I also include variables for age of center and whether the center is affiliated with a parent or umbrella organization.
10. At the time of the study, federal funds were distributed through Titles IV-a and IV-b of the Social Security Act, certain provisions of the Equal Opportunity Act, and other federal legislation.
11. Federal law allowed state agencies to waive federal regulations for centers which served no more than five federally funded children (or 20% of enrollment, whichever was lower). The survey identifies centers which operated under this waiver.

12. In addition to the social benefit and quality variables, region dummies are included in the logit equations. A likelihood ratio test rejects the hypothesis that the coefficients are equal for the FIDCR and the non-FIDCR samples. The constructed test statistic is 84, well above the chi-squared statistic with 30 degrees of freedom and significance level of .01.
13. The logit equations were also estimated including percent of families who are poor and percent of families who are rich, as proxies for social benefits. Although the size of the sample fell dramatically, the general results remained. For the non-FIDCR sample, nonprofit centers were more likely to serve poor and minority families and less likely to serve rich families. For the FIDCR sample, nonprofit centers tended to provide a higher quality service. There was no obvious difference in social benefits offered by nonprofit and for-profit firms: nonprofits were more likely to serve low income but less likely to serve black clients.
14. Parental involvement is considered to increase quality because of parental input. However, free access of parents to the center may also signal high quality since managers of centers blocking access are more likely to engage in activities which they prefer to hide. (This second point was brought up by the referee.)
15. The logits were also run with a full set of state dummy variables instead of the regional dummy variables to determine whether state location of the nonprofits generate the difference in center attributes observed between nonprofit and for-profit centers. In the unregulated sample, the coefficients are generally the same except the variable which measures the percentage of children which are other minority becomes insignificant and the employment of a nutritionist becomes positive and significant. In the regulated sample the coefficients are similar across the two specifications except that when state dummies are included, the coefficients on child-to-staff hours and on turnover are significant only at the .20 level. In addition the coefficient on maximum fee charged to parents becomes negative and significant.
16. Average profit rates of FIDCR for-profit centers are 0.15 while average profit rates of non-FIDCR for-profit centers are 0.13. However the difference in the two means is not significant.
17. Cost functions were estimated for the entire sample with dummies for nonprofit and FIDCR status. The coefficient on the FIDCR dummy was insignificantly different from zero. In addition the hypothesis that the coefficients in the cost equations are equal for the FIDCR and the non-FIDCR samples could not be rejected at the .1 level. However, because the logit results signaled that the differences in the nonprofit and for-profit services differed for the FIDCR and non-FIDCR samples, the results are presented for the two different samples.
18. Mukerjee and Witte [1991], in a study of day-care centers surveyed during 1987 and 1988, also find no significant differences in the costs functions of nonprofit and for-profit day-care centers.
19. For example, if the educated worker's goal is to increase the educational component of the day-care service, he or she might require costly educational supplies.
20. The vector of quality control and the vector of social externality controls were also entered separately to the column 2 specification. Both are significant determinants of costs, according to F tests. The nonprofit coefficient falls to .04 with the inclusion of the quality controls and to .09 with the social externality controls.
21. The vector of quality controls and the vector of social externality controls, when entered separately to the column 4 specification, decrease the nonprofit coefficient to .06 and to .14 respectively. Both vectors are significant determinants of costs.
22. A 1990 Report by the GAO presents results from a 1988 survey of 208 early childhood programs accredited by the National Association for the Education of Young Children (U.S. GAO [1990]). Although the cost functions estimated in this study do not include the extensive quality controls that are included in the current study, there is no evidence that the costs of nonprofit day-care centers are higher than the costs of for-profit day-care centers. However, the sample was created from a group of centers which, by their affiliation with the NAEYC, tended to be high quality and high social benefit centers. In particular, 74% of the centers served at least one low-income child, and almost 70% served at least one handicapped child. Furthermore, as predicted from the empirical results in this paper, most of these centers (80%) were nonprofit. The sample identified a small and fairly homogeneous segment of the market which is predominantly nonprofit and high cost. Yet, as in the current study, within this segment of the market, differences in costs of nonprofit and for-profit day-care centers are not significant.

References

Berrueta-Clement, John R. (1984). *Changed Lives: The Effects of the Perry Preschool Program on Youths through Age 19.* Ypsilanti, MI: High/Scope Educational Research Foundation.

Child Care: A Workforce Issue. (1988). Report of the Department of Labor Task Force, U.S. Government Printing Office, Washington, DC.

Griliches, Zvi. (1979). "Issues in Assessing the Contribution of R&D to Productivity Growth." *The Bell Journal of Economics* 10, 92–116.

Griliches, Zvi. (1988). "Productivity Puzzles and R&D: Another Nonexplanation." *Journal of Economic Perspectives* 2, 9–21.

Hansmann, Henry. (1980). "The Role of the Nonprofit Enterprise." *The Yale Law Journal* 39, 835–898.

Jackson, E. (1973). "The Present System of Publicly Supported Day Care." In Dennis Young and Richard R. Nelson (eds.), *Public Policy for Day Care of Young Children.* Lexington, MA: Lexington Books.

Jaffe, Adam. (1986). "Technological Opportunity and Spillovers of R&D." *American Economic Review* 76, 984–1001.

Mukerjee, Swati, and Anne Dryden Witte. (1991). "Provision of Child Care: Cost Functions for Profit Making and Not-for-Profit Day Care Centers." This volume.

Preston, Anne. (1990). "Entrepreneurial Self-Selection into the Nonprofit Sector: Effects on Motivation and Efficiency." Working Paper, Harriman School, SUNY at Stony Brook.

U.S. General Accounting Office. (1990). *Early Childhood Education: What Are the Costs of High-Quality Programs?*

Zellner, Arnold and N.S. Revankar (1969). "Generalized Production Functions." *Review of Economic Studies* 36, 241–250.

The Journal of Productivity Analysis, 4, 183–210 (1993)

On FDH Efficiency Analysis: Some Methodological Issues and Applications to Retail Banking, Courts, and Urban Transit

HENRY TULKENS
CORE, Université Catholique de Louvain, Louvain-la-Neuve, and Facultés Universitaire Saint-Louis, Bruxelles, Belgium

Abstract

The methodology of free disposal hull (FDH) measure of productive efficiency is defined and put in perspective *vis-à-vis* other nonparametric techniques, in terms of the postulates on which they respectively rest. Computational issues are also considered, in relation to the linear programming techniques used in DEA. The first application bears on a comparison between a private and a public bank, in terms of the relative efficiency of their branches. Important characteristics of the data are revealed by FDH that are not by DEA, due to a better data fit. Next, efficiency estimates of judicial activities are used to evaluate what part of the existing backlog could be reduced by efficiency increases. Finally, with monthly data of an urban transit firm over 12 years, the FDH methodology is extended to a sequential treatment of time series, that supplements efficiency estimation with a measure of technical progress.

1. Introduction

In all empirical studies of productive efficiency, a crucial role is played by the choice of the "reference technology," that is, in the sense given to this expression by Grosskopf [1986], the production possibilities set whose frontier is used to evaluate the observed productive activities. In many cases, the results obtained are indeed quite sensitive to alternative specifications of this set. While recognizing this fact, the efficiency literature does not provide much guidance on the issue of how to evaluate the appropriateness of choices in this respect.

In Deprins, Simar, and Tulkens [1984], an effort was made in that direction. In that paper, results were presented regarding a single data set (on post office operations) that were obtained by using first two reference technologies that were standard at that time: one is the production set whose frontier is defined by the graph of a parametric Cobb-Douglas production function, and the other is a convex polyhedral production set (with nonincreasing returns to scale) of the type used in data envelopment analysis (DEA). In addition to noticing the differences just mentioned in the efficiency measures, the paper also stressed that both estimates of the technologies were characterized by an extremely bad data fit. This led the authors to use a third form of reference technology, not much noticed until then and labeled later on[1] as the "FDH (free disposal hull) production set." This yielded again quite different efficiency results, but also fared much better from the data fit point of view.

Several other experiments having been made with this last method, many of which are reported in Tulkens [1986], Thiry and Tulkens [1988], and in Tulkens [1989], the present paper intends to take stock of the significance of this methodology, and to illustrate it further with three representative case studies.[2] As far as "significance" is concerned, I consider in Section 2 successively (i) the economic production-theoretical assumptions on which rest the FDH methodology and its competing ones, (ii) the question of how efficiency computations with FDH compare with the linear programming techniques used in the literature on DEA, and finally (iii) some further issues regarding data fit and managerial relevance, replicability, and outliers.

The three illustrative applications are covered in Sections 3 to 5. Like the original post office one, they all bear on public sector activities. A strong justification for this choice may be found in the observation, made by Bronwyn Hall, that the public sector is one where frontier production analysis is the most useful since, unlike in the private sector, we cannot rely on Darwinian selection to eliminate inefficient units, or we may find that selection operates much more slowly. The method presented here for identifying inefficient units may thus serve as a way either to speed up that process or to pinpoint where to take corrective action.

2. Efficiency Measurement from an FDH Frontier: Methodological Issues[3]

2.1. FDH and the Postulates Required to Construct Reference Sets

The production set that economic theory associates with any productive activity is usually an unknown. Therefore, the efficiency analyst must construct the reference set he needs. When he does this from statistical data on outputs achieved and inputs used, as is usually the case, his method necessarily rests on a relationship between the statistical observations and the elements of the constructed set. As this relationship may be required to have various properties, our main objective here is to point out that *differences in the properties this relationship is postulated to have* are at the root of the differences between the alternative reference sets used, and hence between the results obtained in the efficiency measurement literature.

Expressing these postulates in terms of the elements that are allowed to belong to the reference set, let us consider the following list (we call a "production plan" any vector of input (x) and output (y) quantities). The reference production set should contain as its elements:

1. (determinist postulate): *all the observed production plans.*
2. (free disposal postulate): *any not observed production plan with output levels equal to or lower than those of some observed production plan and more of at least one input; or with input levels equal to or higher than those of some observed production plan and less of at least one output; or still with both of these properties.*
3. (convexity postulate): *any not observed production plan that is a convex combination of some production plans induced by 1 and 2.*
4. (convexity and partial proportionality postulate): *any not observed production plan that is a convex combination of some production plans induced by 1 and 2, or of some such plans and the origin of the input-output space.*

5. (full proportionality postulate): *any not observed production plan that is proportional to some observed reproduction plan induced by 1 and 2.*

Together, postulates 1 and 2 are sufficient to induce a reference set that has all the properties economic theory requires of a production set. As these postulates make this set to be the "free disposal hull"[4] of the observed plans, we denote it henceforth as Y_{FDH}. Notice that postulate 1 rules out stochastic elements, as most of the nonparametric literature does[5] and contrary to the parametric one.[6]

With the third postulate being added, i.e., convexity, one gets one of the convex polyhedral reference sets used in DEA, namely the one proposed in Banker, Charnes, and Cooper [1984]. It is usually interpreted as exhibiting varying (i.e., first increasing and then decreasing) returns to scale, and is therefore denoted here as $Y_{\text{DEA-V}}$. Adding further postulate 4 yields a convex polyhedron with nonincreasing returns, denoted as $Y_{\text{DEA-CD}}$. Finally, with postulates 1 through 5, the obtained reference set is the one used in the original form of DEA proposed in Charnes, Cooper, and Rhodes [1978], which is the same as the one of Farrell [1957]. It has the form of a cone issued from the origin of the space of input and output quantities, implying constant returns to scale; we denote it here as $Y_{\text{DEA-F}}$.

That the above postulates are stated in order of increasing strength[7] can be seen from the formal expressions of the corresponding reference sets, as they can be obtained from using the set-theoretical notation proposed on pp. 249–250 of the Deprins, Simar, and Tulkens paper. Here we shall dispense ourselves with that exercise, and notice instead directly from Figure 1, for the one input–one output case, that these sets appear as nested in one another: Y_{FDH} (whose frontier is the staircase line *ABCDEF*) is contained in $Y_{\text{DEA-V}}$ (whose piecewise linear frontier is *ABCEF*), which in turn is contained in $Y_{\text{DEA-CD}}$ (whose frontier is now $0CEF$), and this one is further contained in $Y_{\text{DEA-F}}$ (whose frontier is $0CG$). Figures 2 and 3 further illustrate the many inputs and the many outputs cases (where the three DEA-type reference sets cannot be distinguished).

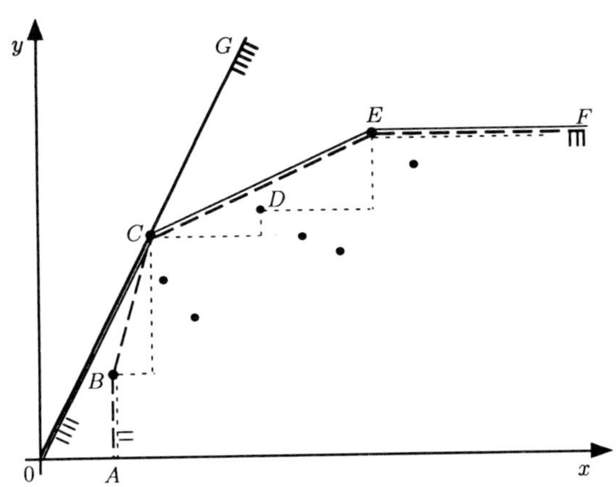

Figure 1. Alternative shapes of the boundary of the reference production set when constructed from observed data by means of the FDH, DEA-V, DEA-CD, and DEA-F methods.

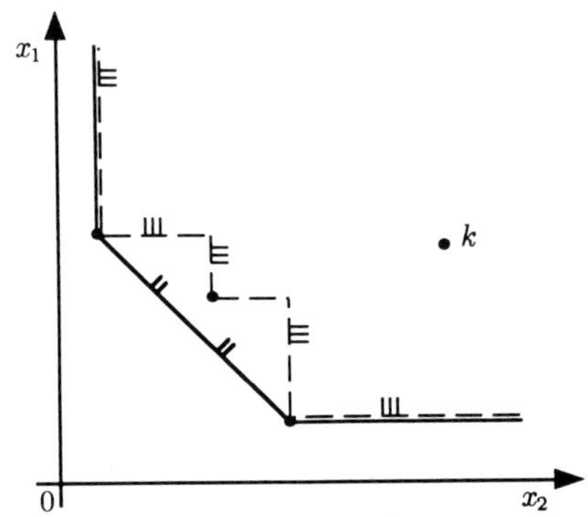

Figure 2. Input requirements reference sets constructed from observed data by means of the FDH vs. DEA-type methods.

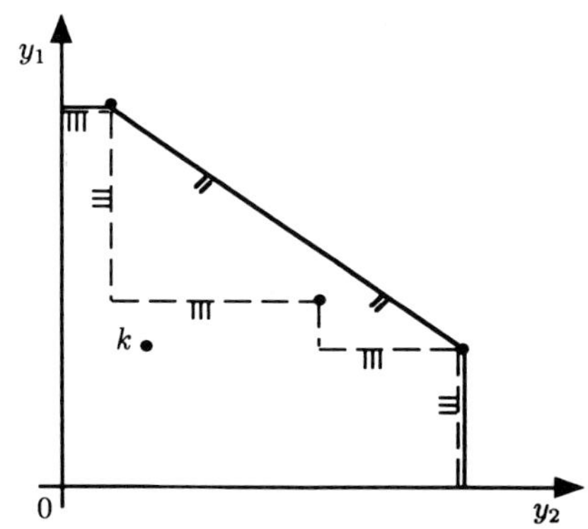

Figure 3. Output possibilities reference sets constructed from observed data by means of the FDH vs. DEA-type methods.

The presentation made so far should make clear what the position is of the FDH methodology *vis-à-vis* the other ones used in efficiency analysis. In particular, it shows that FDH makes the weakest postulates as to how the reference set is constructed from the statistical data.[8]

At this point, we also may offer already one comment on data fit: it is indeed clear that while the Farrell cone is the coarsest way to describe, or "envelop" the data set, the FDH frontier is, at the extreme opposite, the closest one among the four frontiers we have considered. This is due, essentially, to the absence of convexity assumption in the definition of the FDH set.

2.2. FDH Computation of Efficiency Measures and Linear Programming

For computing efficiency measures when the assumed reference production sets are of the type discussed above, the influential paper by Charnes, Cooper, and Rhodes [1978] has rightly popularized the use of linear programming methods—except for the case of the FDH technology which was ignored in that paper. We therefore show here how the programming formulation of efficiency computations also applies (albeit with an important modification) with FDH technologies; this was not seen in the Deprins, Simar, and Tulkens paper, and was apparently not pointed out elsewhere.[9]

Given a set $Y_0 = \{(x^k, y^k) \mid k = 1, \ldots, n\}$ of n observed production plans of a given organization, where x^k is an I-dimensional nonnegative vector of the quantities of I inputs used and y^k is a J-dimensional nonnegative vector of the quantities of J outputs achieved, let us recall that radial efficiency measures *with respect to the DEA-Farrell reference technology*, $Y_{\text{DEA-F}}$, are obtained as follows. The efficiency degree *in inputs* of observation k is the value θ^{k*} of the optimal solution of the linear programming problem (problem P1):

$$\underset{\{\theta^k,\ \gamma^h,\ h = 1,\ \ldots,\ n\}}{\text{Min}} \quad \theta^k, \text{ subject to}$$

$$\theta^k x_i^k - \sum_{h=1}^{n} \gamma^h x_i^h \geq 0, \qquad i = 1, \ldots, I,$$

$$\sum_{h=1}^{n} \gamma^h y_j^h \geq y_j^k, \qquad j = 1, \ldots, J,$$

$$\theta^k, \gamma^h \geq 0, \qquad h = 1, \ldots, n;$$

and the efficiency degree *in outputs* of this observation is obtained as the value of $1/\lambda^{k*}$, where λ^{k*} is the optimal solution of the programming problem (problem P2):

$$\underset{\{\lambda^k,\ \gamma^h,\ h = 1,\ \ldots,\ n\}}{\text{Max}} \quad \lambda^k, \text{ subject to}$$

$$\sum_{h=1}^{n} \gamma^h x_i^h \leq x_i^k, \qquad i = 1, \ldots, I,$$

$$\lambda^k y_j^k - \sum_{h=1}^{n} \gamma^h y_j^h \leq 0, \qquad j = 1, \ldots, J,$$

$$\lambda^k, \gamma^h \geq 0, \qquad h = 1, \ldots, n.$$

It is well known that adding to either one of these problems the constraint

$$\sum_{h=1}^{n} \gamma^h \leq 1 \tag{1}$$

amounts to *take* $Y_{\text{DEA-CD}}$ *as the reference set*; and changing further this constraint into

$$\sum_{h=1}^{n} \gamma^h = 1 \tag{2}$$

implies assuming instead that *the reference set is of the form* $Y_{\text{DEA-V}}$.

It is now a simple matter to see that by substituting for (1) or (2) the $1 + n$ constraints

$$\sum_{h=1}^{n} \gamma^h = 1 \tag{3}$$

and

$$\gamma^h \in \{0, 1\}, \qquad h = 1, \ldots, n, \tag{4}$$

radial efficiency measures are obtained *with respect to the reference set* Y_{FDH}. Figure 4 illustrates the outcome of these alternative computations for an observation such as M, in the one input–one output setting (the multiple inputs and outputs cases are illustrated in Figures 5–6, which the following considerations regarding the computation technique will make clearer).

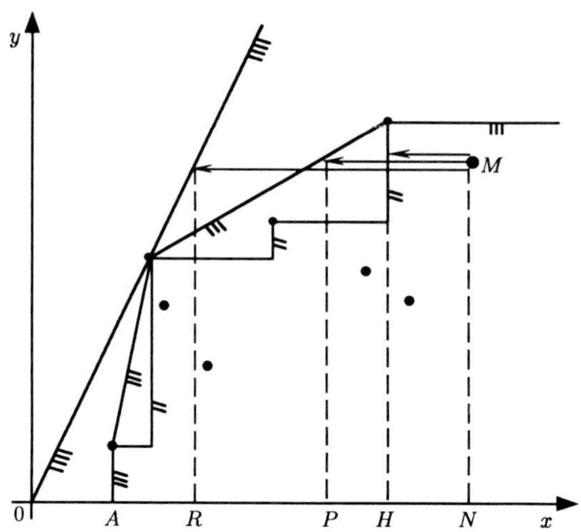

$0R/0N$ = DEA-F measure; $0P/0N$ = DEA-CD and DEA-V measures; $0H/0N$ = FDH measure (all measures in input)

Figure 4. Alternative efficiency measures of observation M with FDH, DEA-V, DEA-CD, and DEA-F reference sets.

For the first three pairs of problems just described, i.e., P1 & P2, P1+(1) and P2+(1), and P1+(2) and P2+(2), the actual computation of solutions requires the apparatus of the standard linear programming algorithms. In the fourth case however, i.e., P1+(3)+(4) and P2+(3)+(4) which is the FDH one, the problems are seen to be ones of mixed integer programming: hence, these standard algorithms do not apply. Solutions are easily obtained, though, by means of a simple vector comparison procedure that amounts to a complete enumeration algorithm. The procedure runs as follows.[10]

Given the observation (x^k, y^k) to be evaluated, associate with it the set $D^i(k)$ containing the indices of the observation (x^k, y^k) itself and of the subset of observations that weakly[11] dominate it *in inputs*, that is, the subset of vectors $(x^h, y^h) \in Y_0$ such that $x_i^h \leq x_i^k$, $i = 1, \ldots, I$, with strict inequality for at least one i and $y_j^h \geq y_j^k$, $j = 1, \ldots, J$. The solution θ^{k*} of the linear programming problem P1 stated above augmented with constraints (3) and (4) then reads

$$\theta^{k*} = \underset{d \in D^i(k)}{\text{Min}} \quad \underset{i=1,\ldots,I}{\text{Max}} \left\{ \frac{x_i^d}{x_i^k} \right\}. \tag{5}$$

That (5) is indeed the solution of P1 with (3) and (4) is easily proved by first observing that all vectors that correspond to the elements of the set $D^i(k)$ are vectors that satisfy the first two sets of constraints of P1. Next, rewriting the first set of constraints as

$$\theta^k \geq \frac{\Sigma_{h=1}^n \gamma_h \, x_i^h}{x_i^k}, \qquad i = 1, \ldots, I,$$

shows that the role of the Max operator in (5) is to satisfy each one of these inequalities. Finally, the Min operator corresponds to what is sought for in the objective function of P1. The observation d in (5), with respect to which the efficiency of k is computed, thus appears to be the one which "most dominates" observation k in inputs.

Let us consider next the measurement in output. To this effect, associate now with (x^k, y^k) the set $D^0(k)$ containing the indices of the observation (x^k, y^k) itself and of the subset of observations that weakly dominate it *in outputs*, that is, the subset of vectors $(x^h, y^h) \in Y_0$ such that $x_i^h \leq x_i^k$, $i = 1, \ldots, I$, and $y_j^h \geq y_j^k$, $j = 1, \ldots, J$, with strict inequality for at least one j. The value $1/\lambda^{k*}$ where λ^{k*} solves the linear programming problem P2 augmented with constraints (3) and (4) is then given by

$$\frac{1}{\lambda^{k*}} = \underset{d \in D^0(k)}{\text{Min}} \quad \underset{j=1,\ldots,J}{\text{Max}} \left\{ \frac{y_j^k}{y_j^d} \right\}, \tag{6}$$

the proof of this assertion being the same as in the previous case. Here again, the observation d retained in (6), with respect to which the efficiency of k is computed, thus appears to be the one which "most dominates" in outputs observation k. Notice that it need not be the same as the one that most dominates in inputs.

Figures 5 and 6 illustrate that radial computations almost always leave a positive slack for all inputs (or outputs) except for those retained in (5) or (6). In that sense, these efficiency

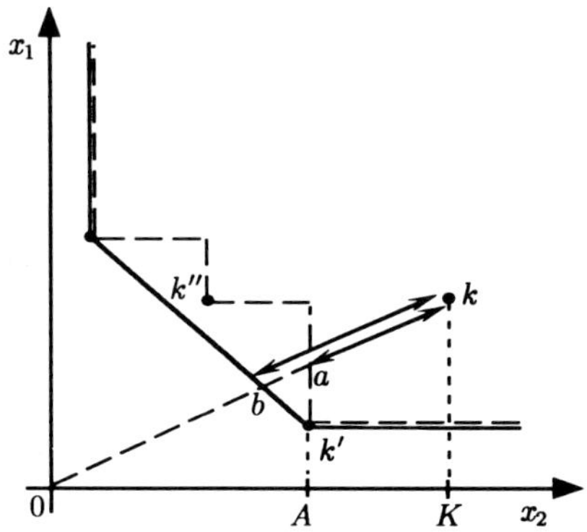

Figure 5. Input efficiency measures with FDH and DEA reference sets.

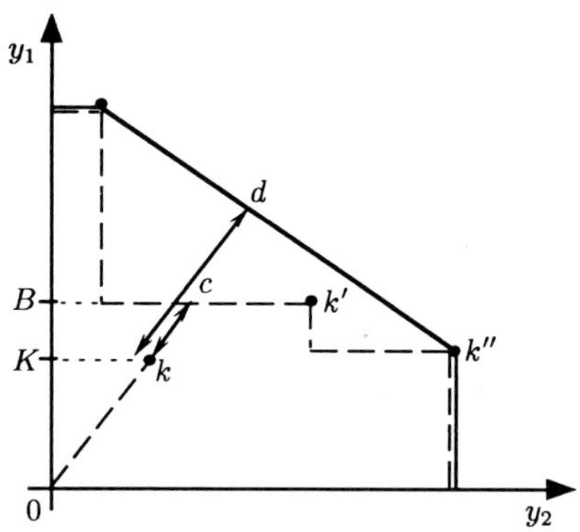

Figure 6. Output efficiency measures with FDH and DEA reference sets.

measures may be seen as underestimates. As no *radial* measure can circumvent this, and in view of the easy interpretability of radial measures, it seems preferable to use them in numerical applications, with slacks recorded separately.

2.3. Dominance, Proportionality versus Replicability and Outliers

Returning to the procedure just described, let us further observe that beyond its computational virtues, the procedure offers the additional interest of putting forward the notion of *dominance* between observations, which is of both theoretical and managerial relevance.

From the theoretical point of view, let us notice that when the sets $D^i(k)$ and/or $D^0(k)$ only contain the index k itself, the corresponding observation has the property of being *undominated*, in inputs and/or in outputs respectively, *by any of the other observations*. This is in fact how, with the FDH methodology, an observation is defined as being efficient (one may also check that the resulting efficiency measures θ^{k*} and $1/\lambda^{k*}$ are then each equal to 1). In this context, efficiency appears to be a property of an observation essentially *vis-à-vis* other observations rather than *vis-à-vis* a predefined frontier. Elaborating on this observation may have far reaching consequences, as explored recently in Tulkens and Vanden Eeckaut [1991].

From a managerial point of view, I should like to point out that the identification of a set of dominating observations, by showing *actually implemented* production plans that are clearly more efficient, gives to the *inefficiency* scores a credibility that they usually lack when reference is only made to an abstract frontier. This argument is illustrated with the observation labeled D on Figure 1: its inefficiency alleged by all forms of DEA measurement is only supported by reference to some fictitious combination of other observations, and not by any real-life production plan. The gain in realism thus claimed for the FDH methodology may be seen as an implication of its already observed virtue of better data fit.

Further conceptual developments are also suggested by the linear programming formulations P1+(3)+(4) and P2+(3)+(4). In Petersen [1990] for instance, other forms of nonconvexities of the reference set than those implied by FDH are obtained by putting an upper or lower bound equal to 1 (but *no* integrality constraint) on the γ^h variables of problems Pl and P2. In particular, he shows how such an upper (lower) bound induces nonincreasing (resp. nondecreasing) returns to scale of a somewhat special form. Although they are called "intensity" variables by the author, it should be clear that the role of the γ^h variables in the construction of the reference set is governed by our *proportionality* postulate 5. In fact, Petersen's bounds amount to postulating restricted forms of proportionality: a restriction on expansion for the upper bound, and on contraction for the lower bound.

Another variant of the proportionality postulate is suggested by replacing (4) by

$$\gamma^h \in \{0, 1, 2, \ldots\}, \qquad h = 1, \ldots, n, \tag{7}$$

by introducing some integer larger than 1 in the right-hand side of (3) and by further substituting therein the weak inequality $\leq$ for the equality. Alternatively, one may dispense with (3) and have an upper bound in the integers allowed in (7), possibly different for each observation h.

The philosophy behind these new specifications is perhaps best expressed by formulating it as a *replicability postulate*, similar in spirit although weaker than proportionality, and running as follows: *the reference set should contain any production plan which is a γ^h-fold replica of the hth observed one* (thus not simply scaled up or down in a continuous way, as full proportionality allows).

As to outliers, finally, we may derive the following general statement from Section 2.1: with nonparametric methods, sensitivity to outliers increases with the strength of the postulates made in constructing the reference production set—"sensitivity" being understood here in terms of the size of the subset of the data whose efficiency measures are influenced by a given outlier. It is lowest with FDH, since this method rests on the weakest postulates.

It is easy to see that the set of observations whose efficiency rating is affected by the presence of an outlier is at least as large (and most often much larger) when convexity assumptions are made, as in all forms of DEA, with sensitivity to outliers being the most extreme one with DEA-F.

3. Retail Banking: Assessing Relative Productive Efficiency Performance for the Branches of a Public and of a Private Bank[12]

3.1. The Public Bank

This application bears upon the activities of 773 branches of a large publicly owned bank operating in Belgium. Our data are a cross section of the output and input quantities of each branch for the month of January 1987. The outputs are measured in terms of the number of operations performed during the month. More than 60 different ones are reported, but we aggregate them into eight categories, the list of which is given in Table 1. Only the number of operations is considered, irrespective of their financial values.[13] As to inputs, the statistics available for each branch consist of data on manpower (in terms of the number of people employed in the branch), on the number of windows operated, as well as on whether or not the branch operates an automatic teller machine. As to methods, we concentrate here on the nonparametric FDH one, and we limit ourselves to input measures of efficiency.

From a managerial point of view, the most interesting results of efficiency computations in such a case are those provided by the complete listing of the efficiency scores of each individual branch, ranked in increasing order. One can thus locate at the top of the list the most severe cases of inefficiency. The size of our data set clearly precludes providing this entire listing here, but an excerpt from its first lines is given in Table 2 as an example, where we present five of the worst cases as determined by the FDH method.

On Table 2, various comments are in order. First, the efficiency degrees provided in column 3 are "radial" ones, i.e., equiproportionate input reductions as suggested on the

Table 1. Description of inputs and of output aggregates for the bank branches.

Inputs	No. 1	Labor (number of hours worked per month; in Tables 3 and 4 this data is converted into number of persons per month)
	No. 2	Windows (number available)
	No. 3	Automatic teller machine (0 or 1)
Outputs	No. 1	Checking and savings accounts operations (deposits and withdrawals)
	No. 2	Automatic teller machine operations
	No. 3	International operations (transactions on foreign exchange and on travelers' checks)
	No. 4	Brokerage activities (stock and bonds)
	No. 5	Credit operations
	No. 6	Opening of new accounts
	No. 7	Special services (e.g., issuing of credit and ATM cards)
	No. 8	Miscellany (e.g., life insurance operations for a public insurance company closely related with the bank)

Table 2. Sample of worst FDH inefficiencies, with dominating unit and underlying data.

Rank	Unit's Code #	Efficiency Score	Dominating Unit's Code #	Input Quantities No. 1	Input Quantities No. 2	Input Quantities No. 3	Output Quantities No. 1	Output Quantities No. 2	Output Quantities No. 3	Output Quantities No. 4	Output Quantities No. 5	Output Quantities No. 6	Output Quantities No. 7	Output Quantities No. 8
1	81832	.648		27,578	4	0	1109	0	231	85	2	17	9	3
			81997	17,857	2	0	1281	0	330	125	31	18	18	21
2	81619	.667		29,178	3	0	2030	0	485	33	0	38	35	5
			81561	19,442	2	0	2096	0	494	73	17	67	108	18
3	82894	.710		25,149	3	0	1159	0	172	75	1	24	10	0
			81997	17,857	2	0	1281	0	330	125	31	18	18	21
4	82753	.740		26,273	4	0	2060	0	368	34	0	18	46	4
			81591	19,442	2	0	2096	0	494	73	17	67	108	18
5	81667	.750		39,811	4	0	2673	0	689	50	18	29	20	7
			81768	29,612	3	0	3133	0	719	71	22	51	37	14

theoretical Figure 5. Thus, with the 0.648 figure mentioned for the first quoted branch it is claimed that had this branch been operating on the assumed efficient frontier, it could have achieved the same output with only 64.8% of all its inputs (and possibly even less for some of them as will be made clear next).

One further notes in column 4 that the method identifies, for each inefficient branch, one which *dominates*[14] it, in the sense that it uses no more inputs and strictly less of some of them, while producing more of *all* of the outputs. As stressed in Section 2, this information is managerially very relevant as it provides *from within the enterprise* factual evidence of better achievement.[15] Of course, it is not an absolute reference, in the sense that it may well be that the dominating branch operates under characteristics (*other* than output and input quantities) that are substantially different from those of the dominated unit. If so, what is measured as inefficiency is rather to be attributed to these characteristics. But if no such characteristics can be identified, the measure then reveals rather convincingly exactly what is sought for, namely situations where inputs are used in larger quantities than elsewhere, with less of all outputs achieved, i.e., pure technical inefficiency. For each branch found inefficient, such a careful case by case examination of characteristics is called for, before the inefficiency diagnosis can be confirmed.

Finally, the table allows one to characterize the importance of the inefficiency in terms of each one of the inputs involved. Thus, for the first quoted branch, the reduction of *all* inputs to 64.8% of their use corresponds to reducing them to an amount such that at least one of them be equal to its usage in the dominating branch (0.648 is indeed the ratio of the usage of input 1 by the dominating branch, namely 17,857 hours of labor, to the 27,578 hours used in the dominated branch). If such a ratio had been computed for input 2, the reduction would even be to 50% of actual use. But this would mean that one would require the inefficient branch to do even better, *in terms of input* 1, than what the dominating branch does. As the dominating branch referred to happens to be an efficient one, this would imply requiring from the dominated branch to perform beyond the assumed frontier, a clearly excessive requirement. However, while a reduction to 64.8% is thus the maximum reduction one can require for *all* inputs, there remains "slack" for some of them since a reduction to 50% is possible for input 2. For the second branch quoted in Table 2, whose efficiency score is 0.667, notice that the slack is with input 1. When more than just two inputs are involved, this inputwise analysis clearly gains importance. However, I doubt that seeking for a single numerical index of efficiency including these "slacks" would be a useful extension. Additional columns exhibiting the values of all slacks would be more informative.

Turning now to aggregate statistics of our results, Table 3 shows on the bottom line of columns 9 and 10 that, out of the total 773 branches, 136 (i.e., 18%) are found to be inefficient in the FDH sense, that is, dominated by at least one other well-identified branch. This leaves of course ample room for the case by case analyses mentioned above—a task surely beyond the grasp of the outside analyst and probably best tackled by the firm itself. A contrario, there are 637 branches found undominated, and thus declared FDH-efficient (column 3). Within this rather large subset, we further distinguish two classes: on the one hand (column 4), the class of efficient branches which do dominate some inefficient one(s): for those, superiority of behavior is hardly questionable. There are 141 such branches (i.e., 18% of the total). On the other hand (column 5), there is the class of branches that we call "efficient by default," defined by the fact that there is no branch in the data set that they dominate. Essentially, the branches in this class are compared to no other branch, and their "efficiency" label actually amounts to one of noncomparability. The number of branches in this class is 496 (i.e., 64%). To sum up, the 773 branches in our data set is partitioned into three groups: the group of worse-than-others, comprising 18%, the group of better-than-others, comprising another 18%, and finally the group of noncomparable ones (64%).

On the first five lines of Table 3 these results are broken down according to branch size, size being measured by manpower input. Typically, inefficiency appears to be more frequent in small scale branches than in large ones. However, efficiency by default is also more frequent in large branches (especially in the largest class).

Finally, the average efficiency scores are given in column 11. They appear to be quite high, due of course to the large percentage of the observations that are 100% efficient. More informative is the frequency distribution of the efficiency scores, given on Figure 7. It exhibits a typical decreasing shape, with the number of inefficiency cases declining gradually with severeness.

Table 3. Summary statistics of FDH efficiency results.

1 Cat. by Size	2 # Obs.	3 # Eff.	4 %	5 # Eff. & Domtg.	6 %	7 # Eff. by Default	8 %	9 # Ineff.	10 %	11 Aver. Degree
0–2	191	141	.74	47	.25	94	.49	50	.26	.976
2–3	243	186	.77	51	.21	135	.56	57	.23	.986
3–4.5	119	106	.89	19	.16	87	.73	13	.11	.995
4.5–7.5	120	108	.90	22	.18	86	.72	12	.10	.991
>7.5	100	96	.96	2	.02	94	.94	4	.04	.997
Total	773	637	.82	141	.18	496	.64	136	.18	.987

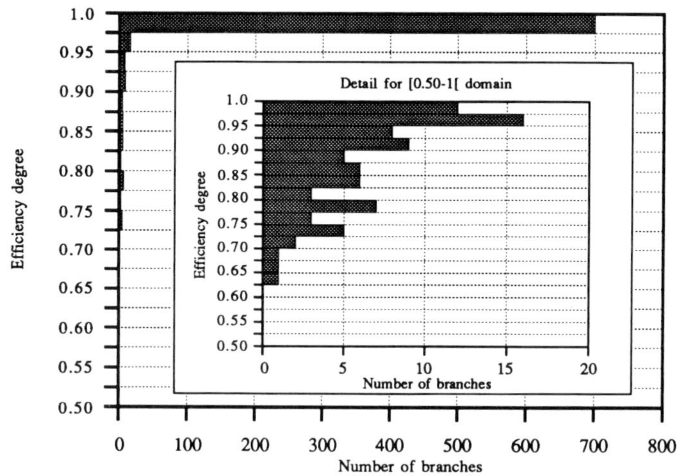

Figure 7. Frequency distribution of FDH efficiency scores of the public bank branches (3 inputs, 8 outputs).

3.2. Comparing with a Private Bank

To put the above results in perspective, it is of some interest to attempt a comparison with similar computations made in the private sector. To this effect, we make use of a fairly similar data set pertaining to the 911 branches of a Belgian private bank—thus an institution of comparable size. The data were compiled and studied by Respaut [1989]. As the setting is somewhat different (outputs are aggregated into seven categories, and only one input—labor—is considered), we modified accordingly the aggregation of our public bank data, and recomputed efficiency scores. The computation methods used are this time not only FDH, but also DEA-F and DEA-V, applied to each bank separately.

Table 4 and Figure 8 report the results and provide the elements for the comparison. First of all, the DEA methods, that impose convexity, yield in both cases strikingly less favorable results than FDH. A difference was to be expected, since we know that the former method less closely envelops the data than the latter; but the importance of that difference is considerable: with DEA-F the frontier is constructed with only about 2% of the observations in either case (since only that percentage is declared efficient; see the bottom line of column 4 in either table), and with DEA-V it is so with about 5% (see bottom of columns 6); but with FDH these percentages are 57.8 and 74.6 (columns 8) for the private and the public banks respectively. Without embarking here in a discussion of the virtues or defects of convexity, and of the merits or demerits of fitting a frontier close to the data, let us just note with this example how important an impact these issues can have.

The difference in the methodological assumptions also has a direct bearing on the public versus private comparison. Indeed, with the two DEA methods, the private bank appears to score somewhat better than the public bank, at least in terms of percentages of efficient units (columns 4 and 6 in either table). With FDH, on the contrary, the public bank scores better, and even much better (compare columns 8). This is strikingly summarized in the total figures: only 57.8% of the private bank's branches make up the FDH frontier, whereas

Table 4. Efficiency results for branches of the private and of the public bank.

Input Categ. (#Pers) (1)	Total (2)	#Br.Dea-F Efficient # (3)	% (4)	#Br.Dea-V Efficient # (5)	% (6)	#Br.FDH Efficient # (7)	% (8)
Public Bank Branches							
0–2	220	7	3.2	11	5.0	143	65.0
av.eff.deg.		0.64		0.69		0.95	
2–3	242	2	0.8	6	2.5	157	64.9
av.eff.deg.		0.70		0.72		0.97	
3–4.5	121	2	1.7	8	6.6	103	85.0
av.eff.deg.		0.72		0.78		0.99	
4.5–7.5	120	1	0.8	6	5.0	104	86.7
av.eff.deg.		0.68		0.78		0.98	
>7.5	101	1	1.0	11	10.9	93	92.1
av.eff.deg.		0.63		0.77		0.99	
Total	804	13	1.6	42	5.2	600	74.6
Private Bank Branches							
0–2	187	9	4.8	13	7	95	50.8
av.eff.deg.		0.6		0.73		0.95	
2.5–4.5	397	10	2.5	11	2.8	201	50.8
av.eff.deg.		0.63		0.66		0.91	
4.5–6.5	174	1	0.6	7	4	116	66.7
av.eff.deg.		0.63		0.67		0.95	
6.5–10.5	93	1	1.1	6	6.5	63	67.7
av.eff.deg.		0.61		0.68		0.96	
>10.5	60	1	1.6	13	21.7	52	86.7
av.eff.deg.		0.59		0.74		0.98	
Total	911	21	2.3	50	5.5	527	57.8

74.6% make it up for the public bank. To the extent that close data fit is considered to be a desirable property of the analysis, which is the case with FDH, one may conclude that these data reveal relative superiority of the public bank in terms of relative productive efficiency of its branches.

This conclusion is reinforced by the information provided by the frequency distributions of efficiency scores appearing on Figure 8: the two diagrams clearly show that the tail of the distribution for the public bank is flatter and stretches less far in the low values than for the private bank. In the public bank, relative efficiency of the branches *vis-à-vis* one another is stronger than in the private bank.

There may be several reasons for the so identified evidence of superior productive performance in this public bank. However, the method used here is not designed to discover such reasons; they must be found in *other* statistical and factual data than inputs and outputs. But the method does seem to achieve what it is designed for, namely to reveal the specific cases and the magnitude of inefficient behavior. In our comparison of a public and a private bank, we can conclude in favor of the former. To further substantiate this finding, however, further data allowing one to repeat the experiment would be desirable.

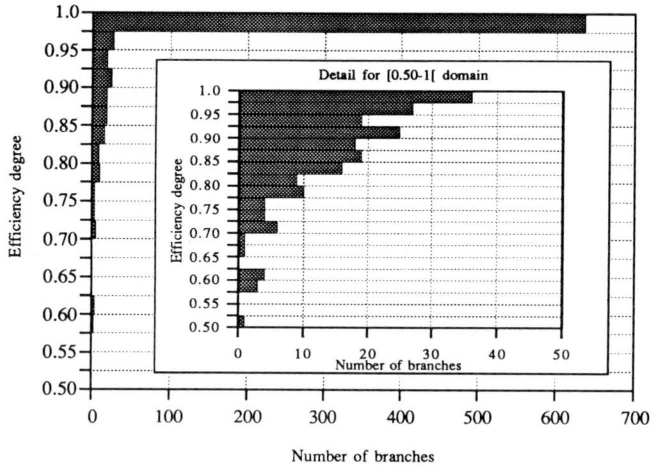

(a) Public bank

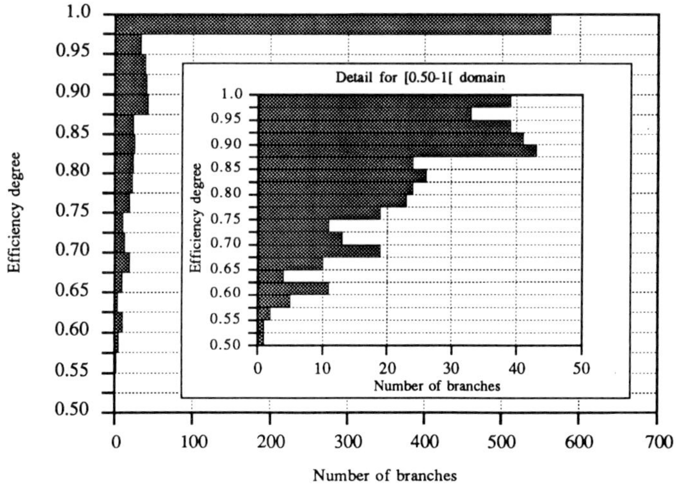

(b) Private bank

Figure 8. Frequency distribution of FDH efficiency scores for the branches of the private and the public bank (1 input, 7 outputs).

4. Courts: Using Efficiency Results to Evaluate the Backlog[16]

In this application we attempt to evaluate productive efficiency in the provision of judicial services, i.e., essentially court decisions, using again the FDH nonparametric method explained earlier. From the results of this analysis, we then derive some implications concerning the phenomenon of the judicial backlog, which happens to have reached important proportions in Belgium.

4.1. The Data

Our enquiry is limited to only one category of courts, the Justices of the Peace ("Justices de Paix;" JPs henceforth), mainly for reasons of easiness of access to statistical data. In Belgium, these are courts with a single judge, dealing with cases of minor monetary value (up to BF 50 000, i.e., about U.S. $1,500) and of local character (i.e., arising within a well-defined geographical area called "canton"). At the time our data were compiled (1983–85), the country was served by 187 such judges.

As to further labor input, each judge is assisted by one or several clerks, the number of them ranging from 1 to 7, depending upon the importance of the canton. Most JPs (about 125 of them) have three or four such clerks. As no statistical material is available on other inputs, we conduct the analysis for the labor input only, actually clerical labor since the number of judges in each canton is a constant.

As to outputs, the competence *rationae materiae*, (i.e., in terms of the nature of the cases they are entitled to deal with) of the Juges de Paix is fairly wide ranging. Available statistical data report their activities in yearly figures of three broad categories, namely

(i) The number of settled civil and commercial cases (denoted CC)
(ii) The number of family arbitration sessions held ("conseils de famille") (denoted FA)
(iii) The number of minor offense cases settled (denoted MO)

Table 5 provides the orders of magnitude of this activity.

Table 6 provides further information as to the backlog of unsettled cases (BL-1), as well as on the number of cases newly introduced each year (CI). Both bear on CC cases only,

Table 5. Summary statistics on outputs.

	C.C.			F.A.			M.O.		
	1983	1984	1985	1983	1984	1985	1983	1984	1985
Min.	172	197	199	0	4	1	115	103	102
Median	1,070	1,068	1,039	83	87	85	506	525	512
Mean	1,162	1,141	1,131	85	85	85	568	570	566
Max.	3,796	4,103	4,095	241	228	237	1,413	1,443	1,176
Total	216,898	212,283	211,592	16,037	15,901	15,985	42,446	42,744	42,571

Table 6. Summary statistics on backlog and new cases.

	BL-1			CI		
	1983	1984	1985	1983	1984	1985
Min.	12	24	12	156	185	181
Median	686	732	773	1,128	1,120	1,088
Mean	890	949	1,008	1,215	1,200	1,178
Max.	8,873	8,738	9,201	3,640	4,566	4,013
Total	167,648	175,635	188,936	225,390	223,133	280,388

as these are the only ones for which a backlog phenomenon occurs. The importance of the backlog problem can be summarily appreciated from the last line of Table 6 where the total backlog is seen to be increasing over the three years under review; from the rest of the table, it also appears to represent more than half of the new cases introduced, and even more than the double in the largest JPs.

4.2. *FDH Efficiency Results*

Table 7 presents summary results of applying FDH efficiency measurement, for each one of the three years separately, to the data just described. The results are presented in successive classes that correspond to increasing sizes of the clerical labor force in the various JPs. Figure 9 shows the frequency distribution of the efficiency degrees obtained for year 1985 only, but the distributions for 1983 and 1984 have approximately the same shape.

Table 7. Summary of results of FDH efficiency measures for years 1983–1986.

	1983			1984			1985		
Clerks (units) (1)	J.P. (units) (2)	Ineff. (units) (3)	(3)/(2) (%) (4)	J.P. (units) (5)	Ineff. (units) (6)	(6)/(5) (%) (7)	J.P. (units) (8)	Ineff. (units) (9)	(9)/(8) (units) (10)
1	6	3	50	6	3	50	6	2	66
2	29	26	90	29	26	90	25	18	72
3	72	66	92	72	65	90	78	67	86
4	56	49	87	56	50	89	56	50	89
5	20	16	80	20	16	80	19	17	85
6	1	0	0	1	0	0	1	0	0
7	3	1	33	3	2	66	2	0	0
Total	187	161	86	187	162	87	187	153	82

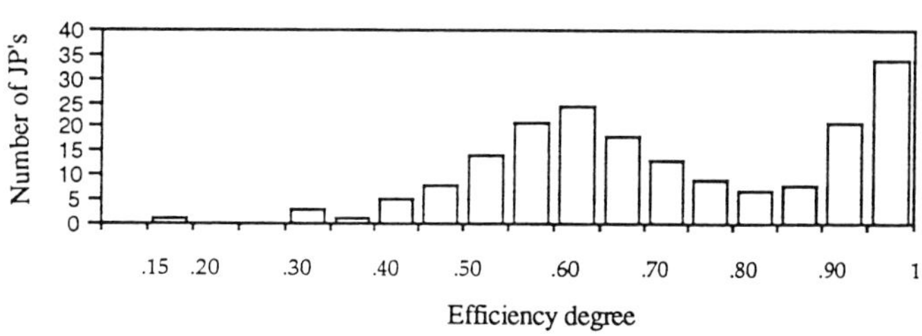

Figure 9. Frequency distribution of efficiency degrees.

Let us highlight two characteristics of the contents of the table. First, one reads from the bottom line that the percentage of inefficient units is in the range of 82% to 87%. This is a rather high proportion, especially in comparison with the FDH results obtained in the previous application, where that proportion was between 18% and 40%. Recalling the characteristically more "generous" nature of this methodology, in comparison with DEA, this high proportion is indeed surprising. Second, one observes in the table that the most frequent cases of inefficiency occur in the middle sized JPs (as measured by clerical staff).

Considering now Figure 9, the frequency distribution of the efficiency degrees exhibits a strikingly different shape than the one such distributions had in the previous application. Indeed, while we found such distributions there to be typically decreasing, of the exponential type, in the present case the shape is bimodal, with a normal shape around the mode of low efficiency (.60–.65) and an exponential decreasing shape around the other mode.

From these various observations we derive essentially two conclusions. On the one hand, the weakness of the criterion that inspires FDH calculations justifies that our results be a matter of concern for whoever cares about productivity and/or efficiency. A serious problem seems to be present here in this respect, in terms of the judges' work organization, as well as motivation, given that almost no agency is monitoring their work.

On the other hand, this is a case where even the free disposal hull lies away from a large proportion of the data. Why is that? Part of the answer might well be in a much stronger heterogeneity of the cases than what is assumed in the simple aggregation in three categories. And even among cases of the same nature, some can be much more difficult to handle than others. Heterogeneity might thus explain the wide dispersion of the output data for similarly staffed JPs. Unquestionably judges themselves would invoke this argument. However, let us mention as a reply that they could not use it all the time. In other words, if over time a same JP were found repeatedly dominated by one or several of its peers, it would come first in line for an examination of the characteristics of its activity, so as to find out whether the evaluation is due to lack of productivity or to a truly different kind of activity.

4.3. Inefficiency and the Judicial Backlog

The fact that figures are available on the number of unsettled cases pending before each JP at the end of each year allows one to connect them with the efficiency results in the following simple way. Consider a JP inefficient (i.e., dominated) at time t, denoted as k, whose inefficiency degree is E_t^k, and whose backlog is BL_t^k. Let $d^*(k)$ denote the JP that most dominates it, with $CC^{d^*}(k)$ the number of CC cases handled by this dominating JP.

If JP k had behaved as its peer $d^*(k)$, it could have reduced its backlog—assuming homogeneity of the cases—by an amount at least equal to

$$X_t^k = (1 - E_t^k)\ CC^{d^*}(k).$$

However, for this to be possible for the JP k, its backlog at time t must of course reach at least X_t^k. Hence, we can define for the JP k the *backlog reducible by productivity increase* as

$$RBL_t^k = \mathrm{Min}[X_t^k,\ BL_t^k],$$

and the complement to the total backlog,

$$NRBL_t^k = BL_t^k - RBL_t^k$$

as the backlog reducible only by an increase in personnel, given the peers' best practice.

Table 8 provides aggregate estimates of the so defined reducible backlogs for all JPs, ranked according to the size of their current clerical staff. In total, about 35% of the prevailing backlog is claimed to be reducible by productivity increases that would match best peers' practice. Naturally, given our previous findings, this percentage is largest with the middle sized JPs, where it reaches 40%. Still on the basis of best peer practice, about 70% of the backlog could not be so reduced. Personnel increases thus seem to be justified, all the more that this figure of course includes the backlog of the efficient JPs, which by construction is not reducible in the sense we have retained.

Without going into further details, this brief account should prove sufficient to see how efficiency analysis can serve, in this case, as a way to evaluate to what extent the backlog figures do justify [17] the repeated claims for increases in personnel in this part of Belgium's judiciary.

5. Urban Transit: Efficiency over Time and Shifts in the Production Frontier[18]

The specific interest of this third application stems from the fact that it deals with time series data of a single firm, in contrast with the cross-sectional nature of the preceding studies. New and interesting problems do indeed arise with the nonparametric methodology[19] when the time dimension is recognized.

Table 8. Summary results of "reducible backlog" computations.

	1983			1984			1985		
Pers	RBL (1) units	BL (2) units	(1)/(2) (3) %	RBL (4) units	BL (5) units	(4)/(5) (6) %	RBL (7) units	BL (8) units	(7)/(8) (9) %
1	476	2902	0.16	486	2,981	0.16	407	3,371	0.12
2	8,669	21,690	0.40	8,803	22,674	0.39	3,336	15,723	0.21
3	26,851	58,422	0.46	24,916	61,291	0.41	29,436	75,663	0.39
4	23,821	58,952	0.40	21,432	62,705	0.34	29,148	66,808	0.44
5	7,095	29,350	0.25	7,342	31,919	0.23	8,375	31,477	0.27
6	0	2,510	0.00	0.00	2,641	0.00	0	2,828	0.00
7	380	2,182	0.17	997	2,644	0.38	0	1,863	0.00
Total	67,292	176,008	0.38	63,976	186,855	0.34	70,702	197,733	0.36

5.1. Sequential FDH Measurement

Letting $Y_0 = \{(x^t, y^t) \mid t = 1, \ldots, T\}$ denote an input (x)–output (y) data set extending over T periods, straightforward applications to such a set of any of the nonparametric techniques explained in Section 2 rest on the implicit assumption of an unchanging production set throughout the T periods—a severe assumption indeed when T is large. In Tulkens [1986] and Thiry and Tulkens [1988], this assumption is avoided by introducing the notion of "sequential free disposal hulls," that is, a time sequence of reference production sets successively constructed at each time t from the observations made thus far.

Formally, recalling the terminology of Section 2, *at each time t*:

(i) A specific reference set $Y^{1,t}$ is constructed from the following subset of the data: $Y^{1,t} = \{(x^\tau, y^\tau) \mid 1 \leq \tau \leq t\}$; and
(ii) The efficiency degree of the observation (x^t, y^t) is computed by referring to the boundary of this constructed set $Y^{1,t}$.

Thus, the efficiency of each successive observation is determined by referring only to those who are preceding in time—hence the expression of "sequential" FDH measurement.

5.2. Measuring both Efficiency and Local Shifts in the Production Frontier

For increasing values of the time index t, the successively constructed production sets necessarily contain each other, i.e.,

$$\gamma_0{}^{1,t} \supseteq \gamma_0{}^{1,\tau}, \qquad t \geq \tau,$$

and a "larger" production set also necessarily has a more (North-West) outward boundary—at least locally—than a smaller one. Such outward shifts are of the nature of technical progress. As they involve a distance between the new frontier and the previous one, one may think of measuring this distance in a way similar to the one used to measure inefficiency. Within the FDH conceptual framework—that is, in terms of the domination relation between the observations—this is easily done as follows.

Consider an observation at some time t that is sequentially efficient in the sense just defined. Among the previous observations that this observation dominates, there may exist some which were themselves declared efficient, because of being undominated *at the time they were made* (see for instance, in a one input–one output setting, observation $t = 8$ on Figure 10, which dominates observations $t = 3$, and also $t = 6$. When an observation has this double property of (1°) being sequentially efficient *and* (2°) of dominating observations previously declared efficient, one may logically conclude that the boundary of the production set has (locally) shifted outwards, in other words, that "local" *technical progress*—call it *FDH technical progress*—has occurred.[20] This is illustrated by the cross-hatched area on Figure 10.

A measure of the degree of FDH technical progress can be formulated in output terms and in input terms, just as it is the case for the degree of efficiency. In output terms, it

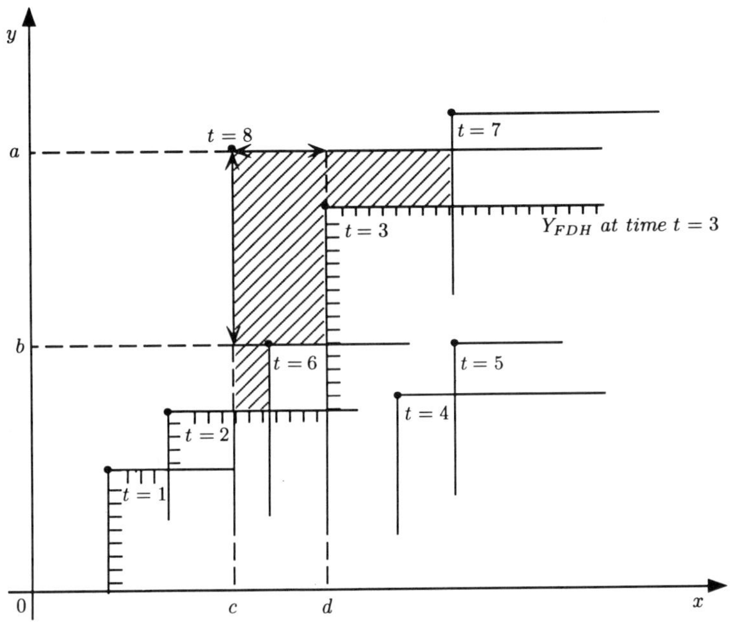

Figure 10. Local technical progress with FDH sequential production sets.

can be defined as the ratio of the output achieved at time t to the output achieved by the previous observation with the smallest input level among those that are dominated and efficient (see the vertical distance indicated below observation $t = 8$). In input terms a similar ratio is suggested by the horizontal distance indicated to the right of observation $t = 8$. Both ways, the ratio is by construction larger than 1, thus indicating a distance away from the previous boundary.[21]

5.3. Urban Transit Data

Our data are monthly observations on quantities of output produced and quantities of inputs used by the Société de Transports Intercommunaux de Bruxelles (STIB). The company operates buses, streetcars and a subway. The observation period covers almost 12 years (from January 1977 to September 1989). We thus have 153 observations.

Output, denoted by Y, is measured by the number of seats-km monthly supplied. This is a standard measure of the output[22] of mass transit firms. This output is considered to be produced by means of three inputs: labor, denoted by H, measured by the total number of hours worked; energy, denoted by E, measured in number of kWh; and vehicles, denoted by PV, measured by the number of seats-vehicles. Our data on output and inputs are graphically shown on the four charts of Figure 11a–d.

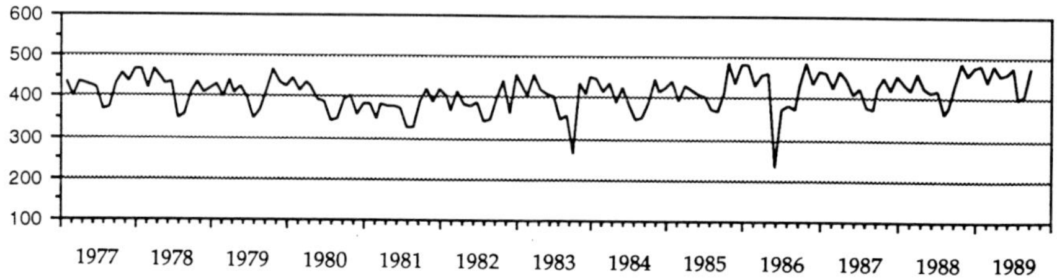

Figure 11a. STIB: output data (monthly seats-km × 1,000,000).

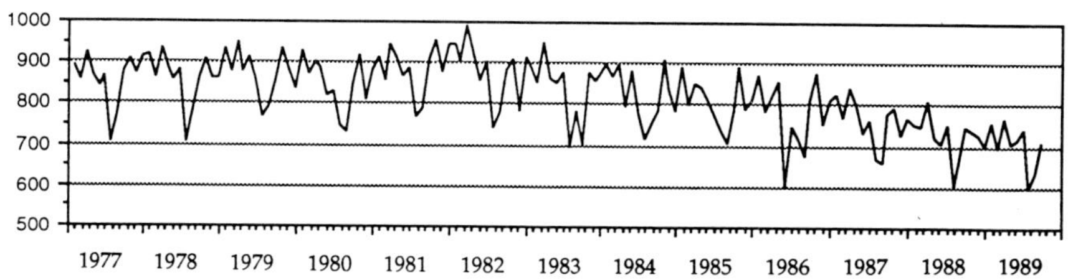

Figure 11b. STIB: labor input (monthly hours (× 1000) worked).

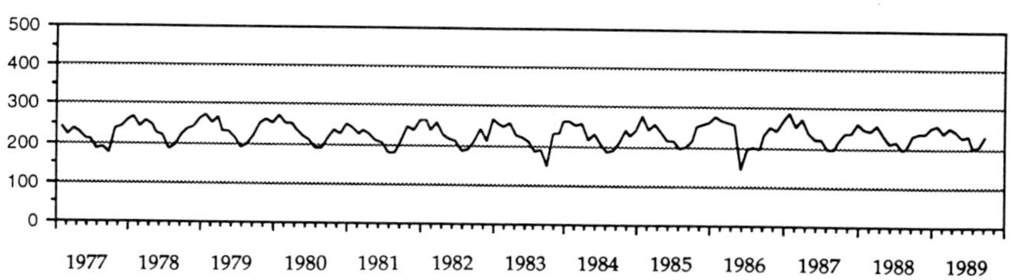

Figure 11c. STIB: energy input (monthly kWh (× 100,000) used).

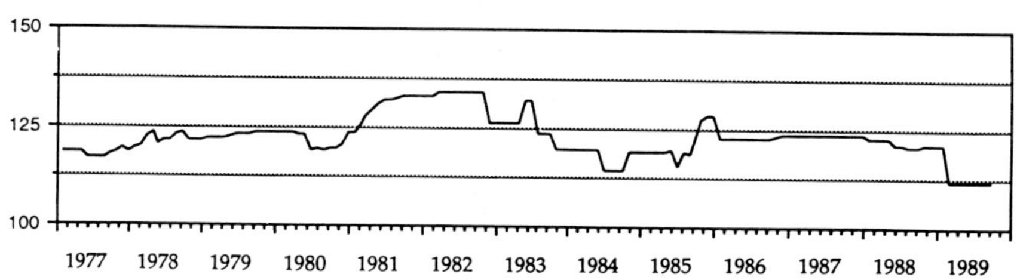

Figure 11d. STIB: vehicle input (number (× 1000) of available seats per month).

5.4. Results of Sequential FDH Measurement of Efficiency and of Local Technical Progress for STIB (1977–1989)

Results of FDH efficiency and technical progress computations in output terms are exhibited graphically on Figure 12. All efficiency and technical progress degrees are multiplied by 100. We note that:

(i) In general, the sequential method implies by construction that at least the first observation is always efficient, and the immediately following ones have a high probability of being so too, because of the paucity of the observations set in early periods. A similar argument can be made also as to (FDH) technical progress when it is observed at early times: it may in fact be only efficiency.
(ii) 61 observations are sequentially inefficient, 73 are efficient, and 19 exhibit technical progress. The inefficiencies occur during the first half of the observation period, reaching a bottom level of 81 in February 1981. On the other hand, technical progress appears occasionally in 1984–85–86, with no more inefficiency; progress occurs even systematically, and in increasing amounts, throughout 1988 and 1989 (the early case in 1977 is negligible in view of the argument made in (i)). The maximum level of technical progress achieved is 111.7 in the month of November 1988.

Beyond a history of the productive performance of the firm that these results provide, and beyond the obvious question they raise as to which factors explain its ups and downs (which have not really been elucidated as yet), I should like to stress the potential interest of the sequential approach from a managerial point of view: the efficiency and progress degrees provide indeed each month a single index evaluation of the current activity, resulting from a comparison with the past one, and based on physical data. The domination criterion which is exclusively used also allows one to precisely identify which periods were better ones, in case of inefficiency, and which periods are improved upon in case of progress.

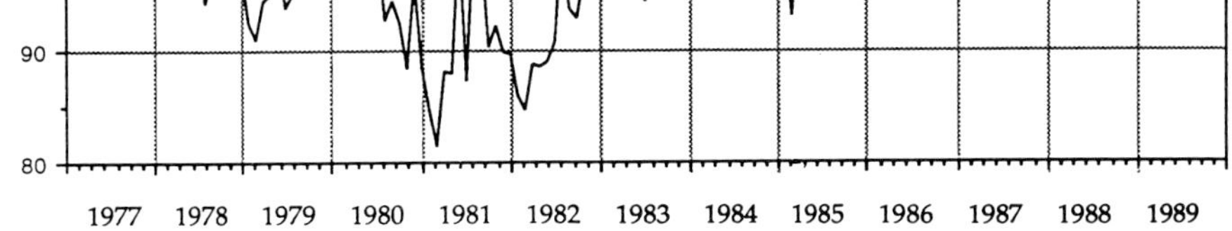

Figure 12. STIB: efficiency degrees and technical progress, 1977–1989 (output measure).

However, the technique presented here characteristically cannot identify technical *regress*, as this phenomenon would be assimilated with inefficiency. This is a severe limitation of the domination criterion (at least in the way it is used here), which does not contain a way to distinguish between the two on the sole basis of input and output data. Recent research on this issue[23] suggests that this difficulty may be circumvented, but at the cost of a rather radical reconsideration of the concepts in which efficiency measurement methods are rooted.

6. Conclusion

To evaluate the FDH method of efficiency measurement, *vis-à-vis* its nonparametric competitors DEA-V, DEA-CD and DEA-FARRELL, let us consider four possible viewpoints: (i) theoretical; (ii) empirical; (iii) managerial; and (iv) computational. In this comparison we leave aside the parametric approaches (except for a brief albeit important remark below) because they have not been dealt with in this paper. They would indeed deserve a separate and systematic treatment.

As far as theory is concerned, it seems natural to evaluate a methodology in terms of the strength (or for that matter, the weakness) of the postulates on which it rests. In this respect, the increasing strength of the postulates listed in Section 2.1 clearly shows that FDH rests on the most parsimonious ones, among the four methodologies here reviewed. Perhaps still more parsimonious postulates could be imagined: but I am not aware of any such, currently existing in the literature, and allowing one to construct frontiers appropriate for efficiency measurement.

From the point of view of empirical analysis, goodness of fit (to the data) of the frontier model used to measure efficiency seems to be a desirable virtue. Here, the nested character (as illustrated on Figures 1–3) of the four alternative frontiers whereby data are enveloped in each of the four methods, does imply that the FDH reference set always fares best: its frontier always lies at least as close (and often lies much closer) to the data than any of the other three frontiers. As a result, efficiency scores are of course always higher with FDH than with all other three reference technologies—a fact perfectly in line with the far reaching observation made recently by Färe and Grosskopf [1991] according to which efficiency measures are actually nothing else than "goodness of fit" measures of the chosen reference technology.

Concerning managerial relevance, i.e., relevance for decision making, our judgment must differ according to whether the results generated by the alternative methods are considered for predictive versus evaluative uses. By "predictive" uses I mean uses relating to decisions concerning the future—thus requiring forecasts, whereas "evaluative" uses are meant to relate instead to decisions that somehow involve the past, the typical example of which being decisions to reward performance.

As to the former, FDH frontiers are of almost no use because of their extremely conservative character. Indeed, whether the needed predictions require extrapolations or interpolations of the productive activity in areas of the input–outupt space where no activity has ever been observed, FDH frontiers provide only trivial answers (precisely due to the weakness of the postulates they rest on). For interpolations, frontiers of the DEA type are somewhat more informative, by suggesting convex combinations of observed realizations;

for extrapolations however, such frontiers cannot do better than FDH, unless the additional assumption of unlimited proportionality is made, as in DEA-FARRELL as well as in one of the methods suggested by Petersen [1990]. Overall, nonparametric methods are, however, rather poor ways of making extrapolations in general, and parametric methods probably are of irreplacable help in this respect.

As to evaluative uses of frontier efficiency estimates, the situation is reversed: because of the tight closeness of the FDH frontier to the data, and because of the fact that another observation is singled out when computing the radial measures of inefficiency as defined in (5) and (6), individual units are always rated in reference to *another one*, belonging to the frontier. Thus, the comparison is *always* a realistic one, and this makes it more convincing than the DEA evaluations, whenever the latter rate the unit by referring to frontier points that are not observed ones (i.e., not vertices of the constructed convex polyhedron).

Turning finally to the computational aspect, there is hardly more to say than highlight the simplicity of the computational requirements of the FDH efficiency measures: they only involve making pairwise comparisons between all observation vectors and then taking appropriate ratios between some of their components. This may be a matter of surprise, if not a source of frustration for some. But the connection established in Section 2 with the linear programs of DEA shows that FDH measures do solve just a mixed integer variant of programs with the same structure: the role of mathematical programming in this area is thus reinforced, albeit in terms that hardly call for the development of new algorithms. Instead, we have here an example of a mixed integer problem where a technique of complete enumeration works easily even with large data sets.

Beyond a confirmation of these general properties, the three empirical illustrations presented in Sections 3–5 do provide each some specific additional information: a more clearcut differentiation with FDH than with DEA between public and private efficiency performance in multibranch retail banking; the effects of the sparsity of observations, due to heterogeneity of the outputs, in the case of courts; and finally, in the case of urban transit time series data, a new possibility of distinguishing nonparametrically between efficiency gains and technical progress.

Acknowledgment

This is a revised version of the CORE Discussion Paper No. 9050 presented, under a slightly different title, at the *Third Franco-American Seminar on Productivity Issues in Services at the Micro Level* held at the National Bureau of Economic Research, Cambridge, MA, July 1990. The author wishes to express his thanks to Bronwyn Hall and Charles Hulten, who discussed the paper in depth, as well as to Marie-Astrid Jamar and Philippe Vanden Eeckaut for excellent research assistance. He also benefitted from comments received at several earlier presentations of various parts of this material (Boston University, LOS Center Bergen, University of Odense, KU Leuven, GREQE Marseille, Journées de Microéconomie Appliquée in Toulouse and Montréal, the *Productivity in Europe* conference of the European Production Study Group held at ENSAE, Paris and the *European Workshop on Productivity and Efficiency Measurement in the Service Industries* held at CORE in October 1989).

Gratefully acknowledged funding sources for the works surveyed here were for one part the Belgian Fonds de la Recherche Fondamentale Collective (under convention No. 2.4528.88 with the author), for another part the Belgian Ministry of Scientific Policy (under its Programme d'Actions de Recherche Concertées No. 87–92 with CORE), and for this revision, the Collège interuniversitaire d'Etudes Doctorales dans les Sciences du Management (CIM), Brussels.

Notes

1. Actually on p. 4 of the 1988 discussion paper on which Thiry and Tulkens [1992] is based.
2. A fourth one, dealing with cost efficiency in municipalites and summarizing Vanden Eeckaut, Tulkens, and Jamar [1993], appeared as Section 4 of the first version of the present paper.
3. Beyond the Deprins, Simar, and Tulkens paper already mentioned, Tulkens [1986] and Thiry and Tulkens [1989] provide extended introductory presentations; in the last paper, the connection is also made with the usual productivity concepts. For a general exposition of efficiency theory in economic terms, the book by Färe, Grosskopf, and Lovell [1985] is a basic reference.
4. A terminology introduced by MacFadden [1978, p. 8].
5. This is of course quite a severe limitation that only recent works such as Land, Lovell, and Thore [1988] and Olesen and Petersen [1989] have attempted to overcome.
6. At least since Aigner, Lovell, and Schmidt [1977] and Meeusen and Van Den Broeck [1977].
7. We have restricted ourselves to postulates inducing reference sets with nonparameteric frontiers. When parametric methods are used, one central postulate is made, namely that the reference set's frontier be the graph of a function with constant parameters, specified *a priori*. Whether any of the postulates 2–5 also apply entirely depends on the properties of this function.
8. FDH thus uses still more parsimonious axioms to characterize a production possibility set than those advocated by Charnes et al. [1985, p. 94].
9. The development that follows originates in a private conversation with Sten Thore from IC² Institute, to whom the author is grateful.
10. We deal here with the general case, i.e., with several inputs and several outputs. On pp. 252–253 of the Deprins, Simar, and Tulkens paper, just the one input–several outputs case was considered, and for input efficiency measures only.
11. An alternative form of *strong* dominance may be defined by letting the inequality that follows be a strict one for *all* inputs. It allows for less observations to belong to $D^i(k)$.
12. This section summarizes the work presented in Tulkens and Vanden Eeckaut [1989].
13. Thus, we consider only the "production" aspect of the banking activity. Financial values are of course no less essential, but they do not lend themselves easily to a treatment in terms of production sets. In fact, the efficiency theory developed above should clearly be reformulated for that purpose, an extension that has not been made so far, to our knowledge.
14. Actually the most dominating one if there are several such.
15. Among all the methods described in this paper, the FDH one is the only to provide such information for *each* one of the activities it declares inefficient.
16. The contents of this section is taken from Jamar and Tulkens [1990]. Other efficiency studies in this area have been made by Lewin, Morey, and Cook [1982] and by Førsund and Kittelsen [1992].
17. A referee has observed that the backlog may serve a substantive role, by reducing demand for the use of the courts since it increases the price of the service they provide. Alternatively, delays may be seen as a decrease in quality.
18. Much of the work reported on here was initiated in collaboration with Bernard Thiry during the preparation of Thiry and Tulkens [1988, 1992]. Earlier (parametric) work on this firm was done by d'Aspremont [1984].
19. Parametric efficiency measures bearing on the same data set are reported, and compared with FDH results, in Chapter 3 (Section IV) of Thiry and Tulkens [1988]. Chapter 2 of that book contains similar comparisons for two other transit companies.
20. Professor Ricottilli has pointed out to me that Atkinson and Stiglitz [1969] have proposed a similar notion in a framework of the DEA-CD type.
21. In more than two-dimensional input or output cases, this ratio is to be defined in a radial way, as was mentioned in Section 2.
22. Passengers-km are often thought of as a more appropriate measure, but they are in fact an expression of the demand rather than the output, with the discrepancy between seats-kms and passengers-km being then to be interpreted as a measure of effectiveness rather than efficiency in the specific sense used here.
23. Reported in Tulkens and Vanden Eeckaut [1991].

References

Aigner, D., C.K. Lovell, and P. Schmidt. (1977). "Formulation and Estimation of Stochastic Frontier Production Function Models." *Journal of Econometrics* 6, 21–37.

Atkinson, A.B. and J.E. Stiglitz. (1969). "A New View of Technical Change." *Economic Journal* 79, 573–578.

Banker, R., A. Charnes, and W. Cooper. (1984). "Some Models for Estimating Technical and Scale Inefficiencies in Data Envelopment Analysis." *Management Science* 30, 1078–1092.

Charnes, A., W. Cooper, B. Golany, L. Seiford, and J. Stutz. (1985). "Foundations of Data Envelopment Analysis for Pareto-Koopmans Efficient Empirical Production Functions." *Journal of Econometrics* 30, 91–107.

Charnes, A., W.W. Cooper, and E. Rhodes. (1978). "Measuring the Efficiency of Decision Making Units." *European Journal of Operations Research* 2(6), 429–444.

d'Aspremont, A. (1984). *Une mesure générale de l'efficacité au sens de Farrell: application au cas de la STIB,* Thèse de doctorat, Intitut d'Administration et de Gestion, Université Catholique de Louvain, Louvain-la-Neuve.

Deprins, D., L. Simar, and H. Tulkens. (1984). "Measuring Labor Efficiency in Post Offices," In M. Marchand, P. Pestieau, and H. Tulkens (eds.), *The Performance of Public Enterprises: Concepts and Measurement.* Amsterdam: North-Holland, pp. 243–267.

Farrell, M.J. (1957). "The Measurement of Productive Efficiency." *Journal of the Royal Statistical Society,* Series A, 120, part 3, 253–281.

Färe, R. and S. Grosskopf. (1991). "Non-parametric Tests of Regularity, Farrell Efficiency and Goodness of Fit." mimeo.

Färe, R. S. Grosskopf, and C.A.K. Lovell. (1985). *The Measurement of Efficiency of Production.* Boston-Dordrecht: Kluwer-Nijhoff.

Førsund, F. and S. Kittelsen. (1990). "Efficiency Analysis of Norwegian District Courts," *Journal of Productivity Analysis* 3(3), 277-306.

Centre for Applied Research, Institute of Economics, University of Oslo.

Grosskopf, S. (1986). "The Role of the Reference Technology in Measuring Productive Efficiency." *Economic Journal* 96, 499–513.

Jamar, M.A., and H. Tulkens. (1990). "Mesure de l'Efficacité de l'Activité des Tribunaux et Évaluation de l'Arriéré Judiciaire." Paper presented at the *European Workshop on Productivity and Efficiency Measurement in the Service Industries* held at CORE, October 19–20, 1989. Available as *Document de travail* No. 90/1, Fonds de documentation statistique et économique sur les services publics belges, CORE, Université Catholique de Louvain, Louvain-la-Neuve.

Land, K.C., C.A.K. Lovell, and S. Thore. (1988). "Chance-Constrained Efficiency Analysis." Paper presented at the National Science Foundation conference on *Parametric and Non-Parametric Approaches to Frontier Analysis* held at the University of Carolina at Chapel Hill, September 30–October 1, 1988; revised April 1990.

Lewin, A., R. Morey, and T.J. Cook. (1982). "Evaluating the Administrative Efficiency of Courts." *OMEGA* 10 (4), 401–411.

MacFadden, D. (1978). "Cost, Revenue and Profit Functions." In M. Fuss and D. MacFadden (eds.), *Production Economics: A Dual Approach to Theory and Applications.* Amsterdam: North-Holland, pp. 3–110.

Marchand, M., P. Pestieau, and H. Tulkens. (1984). "The Performance of Public Enterprises: Normative, Positive and Empirical issues." In M. Marchand, P. Pestieau, and H. Tulkens (eds.), *The Performance of Public Enterprises: Concepts and Measurement.* Amsterdam: North-Holland, pp. 3–42.

Meeusen, W., and J. Van Den Broeck. (1977). "Efficiency Estimation from Cobb-Douglas Production Functions with Composed Error." *International Economic Review* 18(2), 435–444.

Olesen, O., and N.C. Petersen. (1989). "Chance Constrained Efficiency Evaluation." Publication No. 9/1989, Department of Management, Odense University, Odense.

Petersen, N.C. (1990). "Data Envelopment Analysis on a Relaxed Set of Assumptions." *Management Science* 36, 305–314.

Respaut, B. (1989). "Mesures de l'Efficacité Productive des 911 Agences d'une Banque Privée Belge." In H. Tulkens (ed.), *Efficacité et Management.* Travaux et Actes de la Cinquième Commission du Huitième Congrès des Economists Belges de Langue Française, Centre Interuniversitaire de Formation Permanente (CIFOP), Charleroi, Belgium, pp. 53–71.

Thiry, B. and H. Tulkens (eds.) (1988). *La Performance Économique des Sociétés Belges de Transports Urbains.* Centre International de Recherche et d'Information sur l'Economie Collective (CIRIEC), Liège, Belgium.

Thiry, B., and H. Tulkens. (1989). "Productivity, Efficiency and Technical Progress: Concepts and Measurement." *Annals of Public and Cooperative Economics/Annales de l'Economie Publique Sociale et Coopérative* 60(1), 9–42.

Thiry B., and H. Tulkens. (1992). "Allowing for Inefficiency in Parametric Estimates of Production Functions for Urban Transit Firms." *Journal of Productivity Analysis* 3(1/2), 45–66.

Tulkens, H. (1986). "La Performance Productive d'un Service Public. Définitions, Méthodes de Mesure et Application à la Régie des Postes en Belgique." *L'Actualité Economique, Revue d'Analyse Economique* (Montréal), 62(2), 306–335.

Tulkens, H. (ed.). (1989) *Efficacité et Management.* Travaux et Actes de la Cinquième Commission du Huitième Congrès des Economistes Belges de Langue Française, Centre Interuniversitaire de Formation Permanente (CIFOP), Charleroi, Belgium.

Tulkens, H., and P. Vanden Eeckaut. (1989). "Productive Efficiency Measurement in Retail Banking in Belgium." Paper presented at the *European Workshop on Productivity and Efficiency Measurement in the Service Industries* held at CORE, October 19–20.

Tulkens, H., and P. Vanden Eeckaut. (1991). ''Non-Frontier Measures of Efficiency, Progress and Regress.'' Paper presented at the *Second European Workshop on Efficiency and Productivity Measurement* held at CORE, October 25–26, 1991; *CORE Discussion Paper No. 9155*, Center for Operations Research and Econometrics, Université Catholique de Louvain, Louvain-la-Neuve.

Vanden Eeckaut, P., H. Tulkens, and M.A. Jamar. (1993). ''Cost-Efficiency in Belgian Municipalities.'' In H. Fried, C.A.K. Lovell, and S. Schmidt. (eds.), *The Measurement of Productive Efficiency: Techniques and Applications*, New York: Oxford University Press, pp. 300–334.

The Journal of Productivity Analysis, 4, 211-234 (1993)

A Look at Productivity at the Firm Level in Eight French Service Industries

JACQUES MAIRESSE
ENSAE-CREST, 92245 Malakoff Cedex, France
NBER, Cambridge, MA 02138

ELIZABETH KREMP
Banque de France, Centrale des Bilans, 75001 Paris, France

Abstract

In this paper, we take advantage of information collected by the French annual survey of market services to analyze productivity differences and changes among firms in eight major industries (restaurants, hotels, engineering, computer programming, computer processing, legal services, accounting and building cleaning), over the five-year period 1984–1988. We find a pattern of cross-sectional and time-series type estimates of the Cobb-Douglas production function, which is comparable to that typically found in studies of manufacturing industries, thus raising similar issues of interpretation and modeling. Using a capital stock measure corrected for rented equipment and building and taking into account the number of hours of work per employee improve these estimates to some extent. An interesting finding is that the output elasticity seems significantly smaller with respect to hours per employee than with respect to the number of employees.

1. Introduction

The present paper has two main goals. Our first motivation is to contribute to the development of studies of the behavior and performance of firms at the microlevel in service industries. In recent years, an increasing number of studies based on firm panel data have been carried out; these studies have typically concentrated on manufacturing, despite the growing importance of services. One reason is that the most easily accessible microdatabases cover primarily large publicly traded corporate companies, a large portion of which belong to the manufacturing industries. In this work, we take advantage of information collected by the annual survey of the market services sector in France, from which we have been able to construct a balanced panel of medium and large firms in eight major industries over the five-year period, 1984–1988.

The eight industries we selected all belong to the private competitive sector and fall into the category of personal services, where direct relations between providers and customers are essential. Two of them are traditional consumer services, which have been undergoing important changes: restaurants and hotels. The six others are producer services with different characteristics; four of them are advising or consulting-type services: engineering services, computer programming, legal services and accounting services, while two are performance-type services: computer processing and building cleaning services.

Our focus here will be on productivity issues, and more precisely in trying to account for part of the wide variability of differences and changes in productivity at the firm level, and assessing the importance of the contribution of the two traditional main explanatory factors, capital and labor (or equivalently capital intensity and scale). To do so, we rely on a straightforward Cobb-Douglas production function framework. We have also experimented with a more flexible functional form using a translog equation. This extension, however, did not add very much to the analysis on the whole, and raised difficulties of interpretation; we shall not report on it here. Of particular interest with panel data, and of more importance than the question of functional form, is the comparison of cross-sectional and time-series type estimates. We shall document at some length the fact that we encounter a pattern among these alternative estimates, comparable to that typically found in studies of manufacturing industries, and thus raising similar issues of interpretation and modeling.

Our second goal is to attempt to go one step further than in previous panel data analyses of productivity, by improving the usual measures of capital and labor in such studies, using information specifically available in the French survey of services. An increasing part of the physical capital stock of firms in equipment and building is actually not owned but rented by them, and this is generally disregarded in capital measures, which are based on the book values of fixed assets (or on the history of past investment expenditures). Knowing the annual expenditures on rented capital allows us to make a plausible correction to the usual capital measure and experiment whether it improves the basic estimates.

Other important information which is often missing in productivity studies at the firm level is the number of hours of work, the only available measure of labor being the number of employees. Because we have such information in the present case, we can compute the average number of hours per employee and simply include this variable in the Cobb-Douglas equation as an additional factor of productivity. We can thus check again for an improvement in the basic estimates, and explore in some depth the issue of whether changes in labor through variations in the total number of employees, or through variations in the average number of hours of work, have similar or significantly different impacts on productivity.

Still another dimension in the measurement of labor which is of paramount importance, but cannot be directly assessed in most productivity analyses, is the quantity and quality of management. In this work, we cannot really measure such variables, but we can proxy for them to some extent by a ratio of employees in management positions, and include this ratio as an additional factor in the production function.

The present paper is a continuation of a previous one, in which we relied on almost the same sample.[1] For this study, the earlier sample has been extended by one more year, i.e., 1988, but the industry of personnel supply services has been dropped, because of its peculiarities.[2] In a large part of the former paper, as its title indicates, we concentrated on examining the dispersion and heterogeneity of firm performances in terms of productivity and profitability, both in levels and growth rates.[3] We did so for sales per person and value added per person as measures of labor productivity, and also for the ratio of value added to sales and that of operating income to sales as measures of profitability margins. We documented the fact that the differences across industries in average firm performances are usually small when compared to the range of individual differences within industries. We also investigated to what extent, besides the industry effects, the extreme variability in individual performances could be accounted for by three other factors of heterogeneity we could measure: specialization (within the four digit industry), location (Paris versus the provinces) and the form of ownership (corporate firms versus sole proprietorship). We found that, while industry effects are strongly related to productivity levels (and profitability levels as well) and weakly so to productivity growth rates (and profitability changes), the three heterogeneity indicators play only a minor role in explaining the dispersion in levels and practically none in accounting for that in growth rates. What we do here can be viewed as going beyond this previous analysis by focusing on productivity and using a Cobb-Douglas model with a number of explanatory factors, (instead of an analysis of variance with only industry and other types of heterogeneity effects).[4]

We begin in Section 2 by describing the data with necessary explanations on sample construction and variables measurement. The interested reader can find in our previous paper general information on the French survey of market services and more details on the different stages which were involved in constructing a balanced and cleaned sample. In Section 3, we explain our framework and present the basic set of production function estimates, examining the improvements which arise from being able to measure both owned and rented capital. In Section 4, we discuss the results obtained when considering hours of work per person and the managerial ratio as two additional factors of productivity. In these two sections, we comment on both the overall (pooled) estimates for the eight service industries and the individual estimates by industry. Although this comes at the cost of two rather large tables of numbers, we deem it worthwhile to give the industry estimates and confront them in some detail. Our eight industries are indeed a priori very different and, as we shall see, besides a common pattern, the results reveal important contrasts between them.

2. Data

2.1. Sample Construction

Our balanced and cleaned panel data set consists of 1790 firms over the five years, 1984–1988. We have constructed it in three stages from the raw databases available to us at the French National Institute for Statistics and Economic Studies.[5]

In the first stage, we decided to concentrate on firms with 20 or more salaried employees which we will call "large" firms for the sake of brevity. These large firms are covered with certainty in the French annual survey of market services (thus allowing us to construct a panel) and they have to answer a more detailed questionnaire than the smaller firms (providing us with needed information on capital and hours of work). We also selected the service industries which we thought representative (at the four-digit level of the French classification of activities and commodities), and which had at least 200–300 large firms in a given year, in order to get a cleaned balanced sample of about a minimum of 100 firms in each industry over the study period.[6]

In the second stage, we kept only the large "continuing" firms, the ones which have continued answering the survey from 1984 to 1988. We thus took out "leaving" firms which stopped reporting during this period (either because they ceased their activities, went bankrupt or were taken over, or because they shrank in size under the limit of 20 salaried employees). We also left out "entering" firms, which began reporting during the period (because they went into business with already 20 or more salaried employees, or because they increased in size over this limit).

In the third stage (actually done in parallel with the second), we "cleaned" the data set from observations which can be seen as erroneous or which were clearly "outliers." We did so according to three sorts of criteria. First, we dropped out firms with missing values for the main variables. Then, we eliminated firms with extreme outliers in the distribution of a few important ratios (computed from the main variables in levels, such as value added per person, capital per person, average number of hours per person). Last, we cleaned out firms exhibiting huge rates of increase or decrease in the main variables.[7]

By insisting on working with a balanced and cleaned sample, we have, of course, sizeably restricted the actual set of firms in the study, and thus possibly restrained the validity of the results to the population of large ongoing ("continuing") firms. In the eight service industries, large firms (of 20 and more salaried employees) account for about 40% of total employment but only 3% of the total number of firms (with wide differences across industries). Although the discrepancies between small and large firms might not be so important for the main results of the analysis (say for a parameter of interest like the elasticity of capital), evidently we cannot infer that from a sample of large firms only.

The proportion of large continuing firms over the five-year-study period relative to all large firms existing in the first year (1984) is about 70% in terms of employment (i.e., about an 8% annual decrease) and 50% in number of firms (i.e., about a 15% annual decrease). These numbers, which do not vary much across industries, clearly show that the large firm population is changing and renewing itself rapidly over time. However, from the few trials we did, we have the feeling that selectivity should not affect much of our results. This is nonetheless an issue which would need more careful investigation.[8]

The reduction in sample size from cleaning is also rather large, since we are left with about 75–80% of the continuing firms, both in terms of numbers of employees and firms (such reduction varying little by industry). However, contrary to the selection of large ongoing firms, this should not be viewed as possibly affecting our results (and restricting their scope and interpretation), but as improving them by making them more robust and secure. Even a few outliers can, to a large extent, influence estimates and statistical tests, possibly resulting in spurious correlations or conversely masking significant relations.[9]

2.2. *Measurement of Variables*

The key variables of the study are value added, which is our output measure, the (physical) capital stock, the number of employees, the average number of hours per employee and a managerial ratio. The measure of productivity throughout is value added per employee, although, in the last section of the paper where we consider hours of work, it could equivalently be value added per hour of work. In order to be consistent with our measure of both owned and rented capital and except for the regressions with owned capital only, we have corrected the standard accounting value added by adding back to it the rental expenditures on capital.[10]

We have also deflated nominal value added by the price indices at the industry level, which could be retrieved from the national accounts.[11] Since we do not have information on the service prices at the firm level, we cannot, strictly speaking, measure productivity nor draw a sharp distinction between our actual productivity variable and a revenue variable (or a profitability one). Productivity differences and changes among firms, as we measure them in a given year or over a period, do, in fact, incorporate the corresponding price differentials among firms. If we insist on a strict interpretation of productivity in the analysis, we have to assume that these price differentials reflect real quality differences and changes, or (and) that they are randomly distributed across firms (uncorrelated with the explanatory variables in the regressions), or (and) that they are taken care of in the regressions by the heterogeneity indicators such as location (which are included in addition to, or more precisely interacted with the year industry dummies).[12]

The improved measure of capital is computed as the sum of two independent measures of owned capital and rented capital. The first one (the usual or uncorrected measure of capital as we also call it here) is based on the gross book value of the firm fixed assets.[13] The second one is obtained from the available information on the firm annual rental expenditures on equipment and buildings. Since we wanted to get an estimate of the stock of rented capital and since rentals are a flow measure, we had to convert them in a stock measure, and we did so simply by multiplying them by an average length of life coefficient. The problem was to choose a reasonable value for such a coefficient. We did in fact several sensitivity analyses for a large range of values, to find out how the quality of fit of our production function regressions would change with the corrected capital stock measures based on these values. We finally adopted a coefficient of eight years which, on the whole, tended to correspond to the best fits, and which a priori seemed to us a plausible value (perhaps on the low side) for the overall average length of life of rented capital.[14] An important point to note with regard to our capital measures is that we have used beginning of year values, which are more appropriate in principle than end of year values in estimating production functions.[15]

The number of employees variable includes both salaried and nonsalaried persons (self-employed) and full-time as well as part-time employees.[16] It is to be understood as an average number of persons over the year. The hour variable is the average number of hours of work during the year per person (or more precisely per salaried employee); it is computed as the ratio of the total number of hours worked by salaried employees during the year divided by the corresponding average number of salaried employees. The managerial ratio is that of what is called in France "cadres" to the number of salaried employees; "les cadres" in a French firm are the persons in executive or managerial positions who have the responsibility of leading and supervising the other personnel (and those who could be in such positions according to their diplomas and skills).

Table 1 shows the averages of our key variables for the overall sample (pooled industries) and by industry, both in levels (geometric means) and growth rates (arithmetic means of the log first differences). It can be seen for example that computer programming services have the highest average value added per person (about 300,000 1984 francs) and building cleaning services have the lowest one (about 70,000 1984 francs); or that legal services have experienced by far the largest growth in value added per person (6.5% per year) while on the opposite hotels have performed very poorly (−0.4% per year).

Table 1. Industry averages of variables in levels and growth rates (1984–1988).

	Sample Size N	Value Added per Person Q/L	Owned Capital per Person K/L	Owned and Rented Capital per Person KC/L	Number of Employees L	Hours of Work per Person H	Managerial Ratio MR
Levels							
Overall	1790	157.1	30.3	90.5	56.6	1714.7	18.9
6701 restaurants	249	141.6	72.8	146.8	42.2	1946.5	7.1
670R hotels	200	155.1	143.1	290.7	50.3	1941.5	9.3
7701 engineering	239	227.8	31.1	121.8	66.4	1829.5	36.6
7703 computer programming	94	295.4	22.3	144.7	84.7	1856.9	61.3
7704 computer processing	126	199.7	49.0	241.7	51.3	1817.5	21.0
7708 legal services	194	236.4	37.6	90.3	34.7	1813.2	17.4
7709 accounting	328	202.4	26.8	93.0	40.4	1818.0	25.7
8708 building cleaning	360	66.0	6.3	17.0	110.1	1239.8	3.2
Growth Rates							
Overall	1790	2.3	8.1	8.9	1.1	0.2	0.4
6701 hotels	200	−0.4	7.1	8.0	0.1	−0.2	0.0
670R restaurants	249	0.7	7.3	8.5	−0.5	0.1	0.2
7701 engineering	239	2.1	10.0	8.0	0.2	0.5	1.2
7703 computer programming	94	2.8	8.6	8.9	8.1	0.3	1.3
7704 computer processing	126	1.9	8.1	7.7	−0.4	0.0	0.7
7708 legal services	194	6.5	7.8	10.8	0.8	0.4	0.4
7709 accounting	328	3.5	6.0	9.7	1.2	0.1	0.4
8708 building cleaning	360	1.3	9.6	8.7	1.6	0.3	−0.0

The means given in the table for the variables "in levels" (except *MR*) are the geometric means (antilogs of the arithmetic means of the logs) and not very different from the median (the log distribution of the variables being roughly symmetrical, and even normal). They are given in 10^3 francs per person in 1984 prices for productivity (Q/L) and the capital-labor ratios (K/L and KC/L); in number of persons for labor (L) and number of hours per year per person for the average hour variable (H). The mean for the managerial variable (MR) is the arithmetic one and given in percent. The means for the variables "in growth rates" (except *MR*) are the arithmetic means of the log first differences and are approximately equal to the average annual growth rates of the variables (in absolute levels) over the study period 1984–1988; they are given in percent. For the managerial ratio *MR*, the mean is the average annual (absolute) change in percent.

A striking observation is the magnitude of the corrected measure of total capital compared to the usual one; it is about three times larger on average (overall industries), with rented capital appearing to be at least the size of owned capital in restaurants and hotels, and as much as five times this size in computer programming. Although the exact comparison is of course quite dependent on the assumptions underlying such estimates, it seems clear that rented equipment and buildings have become a major part of total physical capital stock in the service industries, and that ignoring them could be extremely misleading.[17] Even when considering both rented and owned capital, it is nonetheless the case that most of our service industries, with the one outstanding exception of hotels, are not very capital-intensive. Such a situation may be gradually changing, since in all eight industries the growth of capital tends to be much higher than that of labor (by roughly 8% per year over the study period, except in computer programming).

The average number of hours of work per employee varies very little across industries, apart from building cleaning services, where the low figure reflects the very large proportion of part time employees but also shorter hours for the full-time employees. The managerial ratio differs widely, on the contrary, from a low 3% in building cleaning to an extreme 60% in computer programming.

Table 2 illustrates the extreme dispersion of the variables, both in log levels and in growth rates (log first differences), and to what extent it is related to the industry and heterogeneity effects and to the firm effects. The standard deviations s_t, s_{wc}, and s_{wf} respectively computed for the overall sample, within industries and the finer categories of a cross-classification according to the three heterogeneity indicators of specialization, location and form of ownership taken from our previous study (these categories being interacted with years and using up $111 \times 5 = 555$ degrees of freedom in levels and $111 \times 4 = 444$ in growth rates), and within firms (within the previous categories, thus using up $1790 - 111 = 1679$ additional degrees of freedom). Their magnitudes speak for themselves. Assuming a roughly normal distribution of the variables (in log levels and in growth rates), about one-third of the firms are outside the plus or minus one standard deviation range around the mean, and most of these ranges are extremely wide indeed. For example, the absolute levels of value added per person for one third of the firms differ by a factor of more than 1 to 3.1; even within category the differ by a factor of more than 1 to 1.8 and within firm by a factor of more than 1 to 1.3. Similarly, the annual growth rates of value added per person diverge by more than 30% for one third of the firms.

Table 2 also displays another distinctive feature of panel data. Most of the variance of the variables in levels (in ratio form such as they are, except log L) arises from the cross-sectional dimension of the data (the share of the between category variability $R_{bc} = 1 - R_{wc}$ being over 50% and that of the between firm variability $R_{bf} = 1 - R_{wf}$ going from about 85–95%), while most of the variance in growth rates is in the time dimension (the share of the within category variability R_{wc} being over 90% and that of the within firm variability R_{wf} of about 80%).[18] The same pattern is reflected in the values of the F-statistics providing simple tests for the existence of category effects and individual firm effects (or heterogeneity tests). There is overwhelming evidence for heterogeneity in levels, for both types of effects, as could be expected, while the hypothesis of homogeneity of individual firm growth rates is never rejected, which is a priori surprising, and that of category growth rates is either not rejected or not strongly so.

Table 2. Total, within category, and within firm standard deviations of variables in log levels and growth rates: corresponding shares and *F*-statistics: pooled industries (1984–1988).

	Value Added per Person Q/L	Owned Capital per Person K/L	Owned and Rented Capital per Person KC/L	Number of Employees L	Hours of Work per Person H	Managerial Ratio MR
Log levels						
Standard deviations						
total s_t	0.569	1.250	1.184	0.941	0.232	0.221
within category s_{wc}	0.281	0.772	0.717	0.766	0.159	0.151
within firm s_{wf}	0.130	0.294	0.398	0.143	0.100	0.107
Within shares						
within category R_{wc}	22.9	35.8	34.4	62.3	44.1	44.1
within firm R_{wf}	3.9	4.1	8.5	1.8	14.0	17.5
F statistics						
category effects F_c	51.4	27.4	29.2	9.2	19.4	19.4
firm effects F_f	18.4	17.3	8.1	42.3	4.6	3.6
Growth rates						
Standard deviations						
total s_t	0.162	0.349	0.485	0.144	0.129	0.141
within category s_{wc}	0.159	0.348	0.484	0.141	0.129	0.139
within firm s_{wf}	0.172	0.372	0.521	0.139	0.142	0.154
Within shares						
within category R_{wc}	90.5	93.6	93.7	90.6	94.6	91.1
within firm R_{wf}	79.7	80.3	81.3	65.6	85.6	83.6
F statistics						
category effects F_c	1.6	1.0	1.0	1.6	0.9	1.5
firm effects F_f	0.2	0.2	0.2	0.4	0.1	0.1

For the variable y_{it} (with i going from 1 to $N = 1790$, and t going from 1 to $T = 5$, if y_{it} stands for a variable in log level, or t going from 1 to $T = 4$, if y_{it} stands for a variable in log first difference), the total variability (within year) VART_t, the between and within category variabilities VARB_c and VARW_c the between and within firm variabilities VARB_f and VARW_f are respectively defined as

$$\text{VART}_t = (N - 1)Ts_t^2 = \sum_{t=1}^{T} \sum_{i=1}^{N} (y_{it} - y_{.t})^2,$$

$$\text{VARW}_c = (N - S)Ts_{wc}^2 = \sum_{t=1}^{T} \sum_{i=1}^{N} (y_{it} - y_{.t}^{(c)})^2,$$

$$\text{VARB}_c = (N - 1)Ts_{bc}^2 = \sum_{t=1}^{T} \sum_{i=1}^{N} (y_{.t}^{(c)} - y_{.t})^2,$$

$$\text{VARW}_f = (N - S)(T - 1)s_{wf}^2 = \sum_{t=1}^{T} \sum_{i=1}^{N} (y_{it} - y_{.t}^{(c)} - y_{i.} + y_{..}^{(c)})^2,$$

$$\text{VARB}_f = (N - 1)Ts_{bf}^2 = \sum_{t=1}^{T} \sum_{i=1}^{N} (y_{i.} - y_{.t})^2,$$

Table 2. Continued.

where $y_{.t}^{(c)}$ and $y_{.t}$ are respectively, the year t mean for the firms in category (c) and for all firms, and $y_{i.}$ and $y_{..}^{(c)}$ are respectively the firm i mean and the category c mean (for all years). By construction, we have the two following decompositions of total variability in the category and firm dimensions: $\text{VART}_t = \text{VARB}_c + \text{VARW}_c = \text{VARB}_f + \text{VARW}_f$.

The standard deviations total s_t, within category s_{wc} and within firm s_{wf} given in the table are directly computed from the corresponding variabilities. The shares of variability within category R_{wc} and within firm R_{wf} (in the total variability) are $R_{wc} = \text{VARW}_c/\text{VART}_t$ and $R_{wf} = \text{VARW}_f/\text{VART}_t$, while the corresponding shares of variability between category R_{bc} and between firm R_{bf} (not given in the table) are $R_{bc} = \text{VARB}_c/\text{VART}_t = 1 - R_{wc}$ and $R_{bf} = \text{VARB}_f/\text{VART}_t = 1 - R_{wf}$. The F-tests of heterogeneity F_c and F_f for the significance of category effects and firm effects are respectively $F_c = s_{bc}^2/s_{wc}^2$ with $(S - 1)$ and $N - S)T$ degrees of freedom and $F_f = s_{bf}^2/s_{wf}^2$ with $(N - 1)$ and $(N - S)(T - 1)$ degrees of freedom. For $N = 1790$, $S = 111$, and $T = 5$ or 4, the critical values of F_c and F_f at the 5% confidence level are respectively 1.25 and 1; at the 1% confidence level they are 1.40 and 1.

3. Framework and Basic Results

3.1. Model and Stochastic Assumptions

Our model is the simple Cobb-Douglas production function, which can be written in logarithmic form as the following linear regression:

$$q_{it} = a_t^{(c)} + \alpha k_{it} + \beta \ell_{it} + e_{it}.$$

The subscripts i and t refer to the firm i and the current year t. The variables q, k, and ℓ are the logarithms of the output, capital, and labor variables; while $a_t^{(c)}$ denotes the set of year-category dummy variables (capturing year effects interacted with industry and other heterogeneity effects for specialization, location and form of ownership).[19] The parameters α and β are the capital and labor elasticities of interest, and e is the disturbance or error term in the model.

For interpretative reasons, this regression can also be rewritten in terms of a labor productivity and capital intensity equation:

$$(q - \ell)_{it} = a_t^c + \alpha(k - \ell)_{it} + (\alpha + \beta - 1)\ell_{it} + e_{it},$$

where the coefficient of the logarithm of labor now measures the departure of the elasticity of scale ($\alpha + \beta$) from constant returns (and can be more conveniently estimated with its standard error).

The stochastic assumptions about the error term in the model are of course crucial for its estimation. The error term reflects all the many inevitable imperfections of the model, such as the omission of relevant variables, errors of measurement in the available ones, heterogeneity across firms and unstability over time of the production function, and approximations in its functional form. In order for the ordinary least squares estimates of the elasticities of capital and labor (and possibly other factors) to be consistent, it is necessary to assume that our measures of capital and labor (and possibly other factors) are exogenous, i.e., uncorrelated with the error term (or in practice weakly correlated).

The usual route in panel data econometric analyses is to consider that the error term can be broken into two independent components: a permanent firm effect u_i and a time varying firm effect w_{it}, for which separate exogeneity assumptions can be made. In the production function case, u_i may represent managerial ability (which we shall attempt to proxy), or specific characteristics of the firm economic environment, while w_{it} may reflect changes in hours of work (which we shall consider explicitly), or changes in capacity utilization. These two error components may also respectively correspond to systematic and transitory errors of measurement in the variables, such as the ones we investigate by using an improved measure of capital.

The usual and convenient way to deal with the error components u_i and w_{it} is to transform the variables, and the regression among them accordingly, in such a way as to give relatively less weight to one of these components or to abstract from it completely. The two basic transformations consist in going "within firm" and "between firm," generating "within and between firm regressions." The within firm regression is based on the deviations of the original observations y_{it} from the individual firm means $y_{i.}$ (i.e., $y_{it} - y_{i.}$), which is equivalent to including firm dummy variables in the "total regression" using the original observations (y_{it}). The firm effects (the u_i's) are eliminated from the error term of the within firm regression and the within estimates are thus free from the biases arising from the potential correlations of these effects with the regressors. The between firm regression is performed on the individual firm means $y_{i.}$, thus downweighting the w_{it}'s (more so the longer the study period) and providing estimates which should be less affected, by the biases from the potential correlations of these errors with the regressors, than the total estimates (based on the original observations y_{it}). With variables in levels (or in ratios of levels) such as ours, for which most of the variability comes from the between firm dimension rather than the within firm dimension (as documented in Table 2), the total estimates tend to differ little from the between estimates, and both should be robust to the biases resulting from correlated w_{it}'s. These two types of estimates being actually very close, we only present here the total estimates.

Another way to view the within firm regression on the one hand, and the total and between firm regressions on the other, is to consider them as providing respectively time-series and cross-sectional type estimates, since the within estimates are only based on the changes of the variables over time, and the total and between estimates mostly based on their differences among firms. Similarly to the within firm regression, the regressions performed on the first differences of the variables and on their long differences (usually from the first to the last year of the study period), abstract from the firm effects (the u_i's) and provide time-series type estimates. The first and long differences estimates, as the within firm ones, are often used in panel data econometrics; we shall report here on all three of them, since they tend to be differently affected by the various possible sources of correlation of the w_{it}'s and since they are actually different. The long difference and within firm estimates are more robust than the first difference estimates to random errors of measurement in the variables. They are also more robust to errors in the dynamic specification of models in general, and in our case to the timing and synchronization of the output, labor and capital measures and the omission of hours of work and capacity utilization variables.

3.2. Overall and Industry Estimates with and without Rented Capital

The different types of estimates: totals, within, long and first differences for the eight industries pooled together are shown in Table 3, using both the usual capital measure (owned capital only) and the improved one (owned and rented capital). The corresponding industry estimates are given in Table 4. Three key findings emerge from these sets of estimates.

The most evident finding is the pattern of the alternative capital, labor and scale elasticities estimates, which is also characteristic of similar estimates from panel data studies of manufacturing industries.[20] There are large, significant and remarkably consistent decreases in the elasticities α and β of capital and labor, and hence also in the elasticity of scale $(\alpha + \beta)$, when we go from the total estimates (in the cross-sectional dimension of the data) to the other types of estimates (in the time dimension). The decreases are particularly marked when we compare the total estimates to the first difference ones, the within and long difference estimates usually falling between them; they also tend to be relatively (percentage-wise) much more pronounced for the capital elasticities than for the labor elasticities (though smaller in absolute magnitudes). The scale elasticities are typically close to one in the cross-section (near constant returns to scale), while they are decreasing in within and long differences (by about −20% overall), and even more so in first differences (−50% overall). Such a striking configuration of estimates is true for the two measures of capital, and carries over, with not very many exceptions, for the eight industries taken separately.

The second finding is that using the more extensive measure of both owned and rented capital has indeed an economically sensible and statistically significant impact on most of our capital elasticities estimates, while not changing much the estimated labor and scale

Table 3. Alternative pooled industries estimates with or without rented capital.

	Owned and Rented Capital				Owned Capital Only			
	α ( )	β ( )	$\alpha + \beta - 1$ ( )	R^2 (σ)	α ( )	β ( )	$\alpha + \beta - 1$ ( )	R^2 (σ)
Totals	.187	.808	−.005	.228	.133	.860	−.007	.136
	(.004)	(.005)	(.003)	(.239)	(.004)	(.005)	(.004)	(.250)
Within	.122	.672	−.206	.203	.098	.705	−.197	.116
	(.003)	(.009)	(.009)	(.113)	(.004)	(.010)	(.010)	(.119)
Long differences	.086	.756	−.158	.138	.058	.786	−.156	.079
	(.007)	(.017)	(.016)	(.050)	(.010)	(.018)	(.017)	(.051)
First differences	.084	.473	−.442	.264	.024	.495	−.481	.199
	(.003)	(.011)	(.012)	(.132)	(.005)	(.012)	(.013)	(.139)

The estimated elasticities of capital (measured by K or KC), labor and the departure of the estimated elasticity of scale from unity are given in columns α, β, and $(\alpha + \beta - 1)$, respectively. The estimated standard errors are given in ( ). The R^2 are the multiple coefficients of correlation of the regressions as performed on the transformed variables. The σ's given in ( ) are the estimated standard errors of the error terms in these regressions. The regressions: Totals, Within, Long differences, and First differences are performed respectively on the original observations (y_{it}), the deviations from the firm means: $(y_{it} - y_{i.})$, the differences between the last year (1988) and the first year (1984), and the differences between consecutive years $(y_{it} - y_{it-1})$.

Table 4. Alternative industry estimates with and without rented capital.

	Owned and Rented Capital				Owned Capital Only			
	α	β	$\alpha + \beta - 1$	σ	α	β	$\alpha + \beta - 1$	σ
6701 restaurants								
T	.13**	.89**	.02	.263	.08**	.94**	.02	.279
W	.11*	.53**	−.36**	.114	.08**	.56**	−.36**	.120
LD	.14**	.72**	−.14**	.057	.10**	.77**	−.13*	.060
FD	.10**	.36**	−.54**	.137	.07**	.36**	−.57**	.145
670R hotels								
T	.27**	.76**	.03**	.220	.13**	.90**	.03**	.249
W	.11**	.52**	−.37**	.109	−.05**	.56**	−.49**	.115
LD	.11**	.61**	−.28**	.050	−.07*	.70**	−.37**	.049
FD	.16**	.30**	−.54**	.134	.02	.29**	−.69**	.144
7701 engineering								
T	.17**	.83**	.00	.224	.09**	.90**	.00	.241
W	.11**	.81**	−.08**	.118	.09**	.84**	−.07**	.126
LD	.10**	.84**	−.06	.053	.09**	.85**	−.06	.056
FD	.08**	.70**	−.22**	.148	.02	.73**	−.25**	.159
7703 computer programming								
T	.13**	.86**	−.01	.221	.07**	.91**	−.02	.232
W	.08**	1.02**	.10**	.115	.06**	1.05**	.11**	.120
LD	−.01	1.11**	.10	.049	.06	1.07**	.13*	.052
FD	.06**	.90**	−.04	.150	.01	.94**	−.05	.157
7704 computer processing								
T	.32**	.75**	.07**	.265	.24**	.82**	.06**	.275
W	.14*	.79**	−.07**	.102	.09**	.86**	−.05	.112
LD	.10**	.95**	.05	.048	.07	1.00**	.07	.051
FD	.13**	.62**	−.25**	.126	.00	.71**	−.28**	.137
7708 legal services								
T	.10**	1.01**	.11**	.219	.07**	1.04**	.11**	.227
W	.11**	.91**	.02	.139	.13**	.92**	.05	.143
LD	.01	.66**	−.33**	.044	.00	.68**	−.32**	.045
FD	.04**	.33**	−.63**	.119	.02	.34**	−.64**	.122
7709 accounting services								
T	.15**	.86**	.01	.194	.10**	.91**	.01	.202
W	.12**	.72**	−.16**	.082	.08**	.79*	−.13**	.088
LD	.05**	.74**	−.21**	.030	.02	.77**	−.21**	.031
FD	.05**	.56**	−.39**	.097	.00	.57**	−.43**	.100
8708 building cleaning								
T	.20**	.74**	−.06**	.248	.18**	.77**	−.05**	.254
W	.14**	.51**	−.35**	.111	.14**	.52**	−.34**	.115
LD	.16**	.59**	−.25**	.052	.16**	.62**	−.22**	.054
FD	.10**	.36**	−.54**	.135	.06**	.38**	−.56**	.139

See Table 3—*T, W, LD, FD* stand respectively for the regressions in totals, within, long differences, and first differences. * and ** denote the estimated parameters being significantly different from zero as the 5% and 1% confidence levels, respectively.

elasticities. Capital elasticities are mainly raised in totals and first differences (with the discrepancies between the two remaining), less so in within and long differences. These increases are of about 0.05 for the pooled total and first difference estimates, and they are quite sizable in most of the industries (as much as 0.10 to 0.15 in hotels and computer processing). The size of such increases actually does not appear to be related to the average magnitude of the correction for rented capital (relative to owned capital), which may not be too surprising since what really matters are the (partial) correlations. The fact that the increases are (relatively) large for the total and first difference estimates may be restated and rationalized by viewing owned capital as a proxy or error-ridden measure of both rented and owned capital. In the cross sectional dimension of the data (in totals), the deviations between the "true variable" and its proxy mainly reflect the more "permanent" differences in the relative importance of rented capital among firms, and these, as could be expected, are positively correlated with the productivity differences. In the time dimension, for the first differences, these deviations reflect mainly short run adjustment of the capital stock to changes in output, which are achieved by renting buildings and equipment (in addition to purchasing them).[21]

Our third point concerns the magnitudes of the capital elasticities per se. Even when using the better capital measures, the total estimates for our service industries tend to be lower than the comparable estimates usually obtained for manufacturing industries. At best, the overall total estimate of capital elasticity is about .20, while corresponding average estimates in manufacturing are more of the order of .30. This is what might be expected since firms in services are generally less capital intensive than in manufacturing. The first difference estimates are more comparable in services and in manufacturing, and implausibly low in both cases. The within and long difference estimates are again in an intermediate position, usually with more reasonable values, though still on the low side.

In addition to such evidence as can be gathered from directly estimating the production function, the main sources of our knowledge of what are plausible values of capital elasticities derive from considering factor shares and from computing rates of return. Under the common assumptions of perfect competition and constant returns to scale (which a priori seem more sensible in services than in manufacturing), the capital share (s_k) is the complement of the labor share (s_ℓ) in value added, and is equal to the elasticity of capital α (the labor share being equal to that of labor β). This can be written as:

$$s_k = 1 - s_\ell = 1 - \frac{wL}{Q} = \frac{r^*K}{Q} = \alpha = 1 - \beta$$

where w is the unit cost of labor (or wage rate) and r^* the implied rate of return on capital. Since we have information on total labor costs, we can compute the industry labor shares s_ℓ and derive the capital shares s_k, and hence confront these with the estimated capital elasticities α. This is what is done in Figure 1, where the industries are displayed on the x-axis and the capital share s_k and both the total and first difference estimated α are given on the y-axis. Figure 2 presents the same evidence, cast in terms of the three corresponding implied rates of return r^* (computed at the industry medians, or geometric averages, of the firms capital-output ratios K/Q).

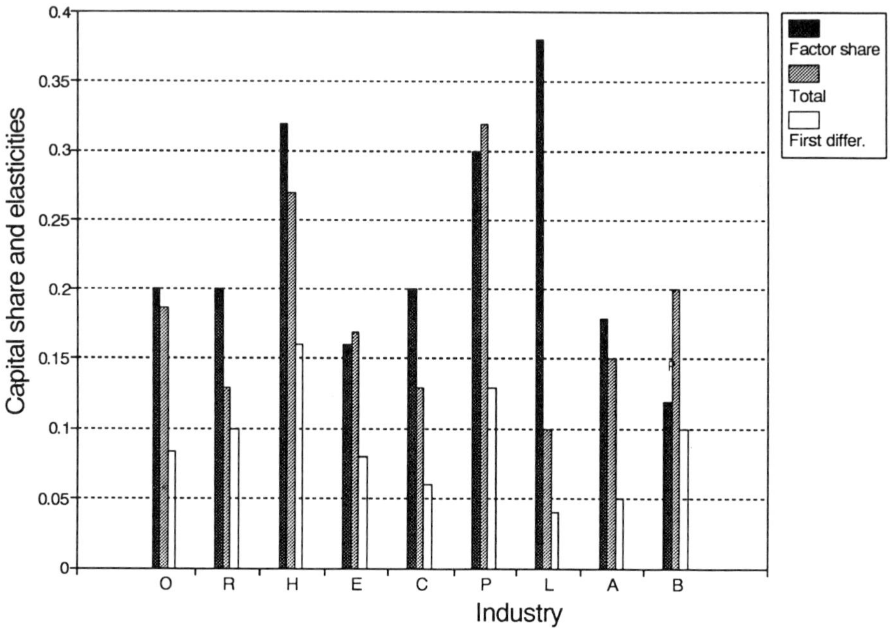

O: Overall
R: Restaurants
H: Hotels
E: Engineering
C: Computer programming
P: Computer processing
L: Legal services
A: Accounting services
B: Building cleaning

Figure 1. Capital share and capital elasticity estimates.

What can be seen here is twofold. On the one hand, the capital shares and the total estimates agree quite well overall and in half of the industries, the main discrepancy arising for legal services where the computed capital share is the highest (s_k = .38 as against α = .10). The first difference estimates, on the contrary, are much too small compared with the capital shares, excepting only building cleaning services (where s_k = .12 is the lowest).[22] On the other hand, the (gross) rates of return r^* implied by both the shares and total estimates appear to be very high, of the order of .40 overall (and as much as 1.0 for legal services!). Those implied by the first difference estimates look more reasonable, of the order of .15 overall.[23] It is important to realize, however, that such inferences as the present ones, based on the equality of the factor shares and elasticities, are very much conditional on the maintained hypotheses of competition and constant returns; even moderate degrees of market power and (or) small economies or diseconomies of scale will be enough to overturn them.[24]

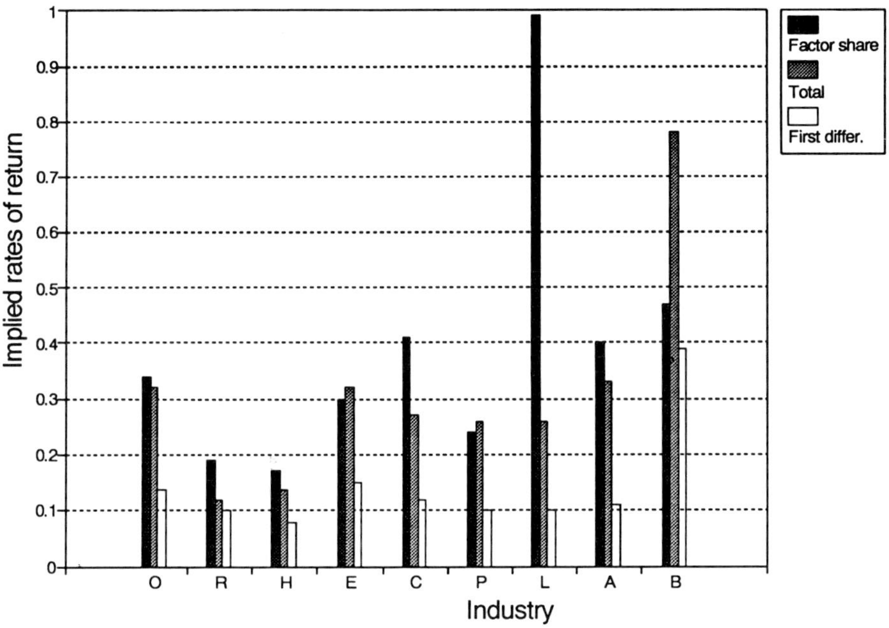

O: Overall
R: Restaurants
H: Hotels
E: Engineering
C: Computer programming
P: Computer processing
L: Legal services
A: Accounting services
B: Building cleaning

Figure 2. Implied rates of return.

4. Further Estimates

4.1. Observed Divergences in the Estimates and Possible Misspecifications

There are three possible responses when confronted with divergences between alternative estimates such as the ones we observe here for the capital, labor, and scale elasticities. The first one is to interpret the different estimates in an intuitive and somewhat loose way, usually considering the cross-sectional estimates as long-run type estimates by opposition to the time series ones of a more short-run nature. A second is to choose one set of estimates as closer to consistent (less biased) and to ignore the other sets of estimates which are, or may be, largely biased. The general tradition in panel data econometrics is to favor time-series estimates, such as the within ones, which are free of the biases possibly arising from correlated individual effects.[25] A third response is to improve the estimated model by investigating some of the various misspecifications which could possibly account for the major discrepancies between the different estimates. This is an ambitious option and in principle a more fruitful one than the other two, but it is also more demanding to implement in practice. It requires having some knowledge of the plausible errors of specification and making specific hypotheses about them, so that it becomes possible to learn more from the existing data. Otherwise, it requires having access to new data providing additional (or more accurate) information and exploring the actual relevance of such information for improving the model specification and reconciling the different estimates. We pursue this approach here by considering the number of hours of work per employee and the managerial ratio as two additional factors in the production function.

The fact that a management variable could not be measured and included as a specific factor of production has been viewed, for a long time, as a major misspecification in production function studies. If this variable is conceived of as a more or less permanent (unobservable) individual firm effect, one of the advantages of panel data is that it makes it possible to abstract from it by "going within" or "taking differences." This is what is actually done in many panel data productivity analyses in order to be protected against management biases. However, the cost of such protection is quite high since it amounts to discarding all the cross-sectional information in the data (which accounts for most of its variability), and since measurement errors tend to much more seriously affect the (remaining) time series information.[26] Whenever feasible, it seems much preferable to try to retrieve and use some direct real measure or proxy measure for management. Although our managerial ratio may not be a very good proxy for the "true" quantity and quality of management, examining how it performs in the regressions is a priori worthwhile.

Besides random errors in variables, there are other reasons why time series estimates of the production function could be biased, more than cross-sectional estimates. One of them is the omission of the utilization rates of labor and capital, and especially the number of hours of work per employee. It can be shown that, under certain conditions, such an omission could result in an upward bias in labor elasticity and a negative (transmitted) bias in capital elasticity.[27] This is strong enough motivation for being willing to experiment with the hours of work variable. But trying to assess the magnitude of the elasticity of the number of hours per employee is also a matter of substantial interest. This issue has important policy implications for productivity and employment, which have given rise, for example, to recurrent debates among French economists.[28] The current view is that the elasticity with respect to the number of hours per employee is smaller than one, and even smaller than the elasticity with respect to the number of employees. Assuming output and capital constant, this would imply that a reduction in the average number of hours will have a positive impact on the productivity per hour and will tend "to create jobs" less than proportionally. Such a view, however, has no strong empirical support and can be challenged.[29]

Using the same notation as before, we can write the production function with the number of hours per employee variable (h in logarithmic form) and the managerial ratio (MR)

$$q_{it} = a_t^{(c)} + \alpha k_{it} + \beta \ell_{it} + \delta h_{it} + \theta \mathrm{MR}_{it} + e_{it}$$

or

$$(q - \ell - h)_{it} = a_t^{(c)} + \alpha(k - \ell - h)_{it} + (\alpha + \beta - 1)(\ell + h)_{it} + (\delta - \beta)h_{it} + \theta \mathrm{MR}_{it} + e_{it}$$

It can easily be seen that unity and β, the elasticity with respect to the number of employees, are two critical magnitudes for the elasticity with respect to the number of hours per employee δ. If δ is less than unity, the returns to the length of work are diminishing; thus, for fixed employment and capital, a reduction in the number of hours per employee (of $\Delta H/H = \Delta h\%$) will increase the productivity expressed in terms of hours of work (by $(1 - \delta)\Delta h\%$), and decrease that in terms of employees (by $\delta\Delta h\%$). If δ is less than β, the returns are diminishing more for hours than for employees. Hence, assuming a given output and capital constant, a reduction in the number of hours per employee (of $\Delta H/H = \Delta h\%$) will be offset by a less than proportional increase in the number of employees (by $\Delta L/L = \Delta \ell = (\delta/\beta)\Delta h\%$).[30]

4.2. *Overall and Industry Estimates with Hours of Work and a Managerial Ratio*

Tables 5 and 6 present the four types of estimates with the hours of work per employee variable and the managerial ratio in the same format as Tables 3 and 4. We first consider whether our expectations about a partial reconciliation of the different estimates are fulfilled. This is at best only very weakly so.

What we see in the cross-sectional dimension (in totals) is that the capital elasticity estimate goes down slightly overall (by .03), which reflects parallel decreases in four of the industries: engineering, computer processing, accounting services and mainly building cleaning services (with practically no changes in the other four industries). If anything, there is a counterbalancing increase in labor elasticity. In the time dimension (in within and in long and first differences), we see a sensible rise in both the labor and scale elasticities overall (by almost .10), with no effect on capital elasticity. These increases result in fact from similar but larger changes (by about .20), in building cleaning services mainly (and much smaller changes or none in the other industries). It is also possible to conclude more precisely that the rise of the labor and scale elasticities in within and in first and long differences

Table 5. Alternative pooled industries estimates with hours of work per employee and a managerial ratio.

	α ()	β ()	δ ()	θ ()	$\alpha + \beta - 1$ ()	$\beta - \delta$ ()	R^2 (σ)
Totals	.155 (.003)	.849 (.005)	.651 (.015)	.378 (.016)	.004 (.003)	.197 (.015)	.401 (.211)
Within	.112 (.003)	.754 (.009)	.410 (.014)	.034 (.012)	−.134 (.009)	.343 (.014)	.281 (.107)
Long differences	.074 (.007)	.829 (.017)	.491 (.029)	.060 (.030)	−.097 (.016)	.338 (.030)	.256 (.046)
First differences	.081 (.003)	.565 (.012)	.269 (.013)	.006 (.012)	−.354 (.012)	.296 (.014)	.305 (.129)

See Table 3. The estimated elasticity with respect to the number of hours per employee is given in column δ, and the estimated coefficient of the managerial ratio in column θ.

Table 6. Alternative industry estimates with average hours of work per employee and a managerial ratio.

	α	β	δ	θ	$\alpha + \beta - 1$	$\beta - \delta$	σ
6701 restaurants							
T	.12**	.92**	.72**	.15**	.04**	.20**	.234
W	.10**	.67**	.43**	.04	−.23**	.24**	.107
LD	.11**	.82**	.70**	.07	−.07	.12	.050
FD	.10**	.44**	.19**	.05	−.46**	.25**	.135
670R hotels							
T	.26**	.77**	.27**	.01	.03**	.50**	.217
W	.11**	.55**	.16**	−.04	−.34**	.39**	.108
LD	.10**	.61**	−.04	.01	−.29**	.65**	.050
FD	.16**	.36**	.18**	−.00	−.48**	.19**	.133
7701 engineering							
T	.13**	.88**	.03	.45**	.01	.85**	.207
W	.11**	.81**	.08	.05	−.08**	.73**	.118
LD	.09**	.86**	.24	.15	−.05	.62**	.053
FD	.08**	.70**	−.01	.00	−.22**	.71**	.149
7703 computer programming							
T	.13**	.85**	.42**	.28**	−.02	.43**	.207
W	.08**	1.02**	.29**	.00	.10**	.73**	.114
LD	−.01	1.11**	.26	.01	.10	.85**	.050
FD	.07**	.91**	.22*	−.02	−.02	.69**	.149
7704 computer processing							
T	.27**	.76**	.06	.68**	.03*	.70**	.232
W	.13**	.79**	.22**	.07*	−.08**	.57**	.100
LD	.09**	.98**	−.18	.17*	.07	1.15**	.048
FD	.12**	.64**	.20**	.04	−.24**	.44**	.124
7708 legal services							
T	.10**	1.00**	.50**	.22**	.10**	.50**	.211
W	.11**	.96**	.34**	.07	.07	.62**	.137
LD	.01	.63**	−.08	−.04	−.36**	.71**	.044
FD	.04**	.36**	.06	.02	−.60**	.30**	.119
7709 accounting services							
T	.12**	.88**	.43**	.43**	.00	.45**	.179
W	.12**	.74**	.19**	.04	−.14**	.55**	.082
LD	.04**	.78**	.22**	.05	−.18**	.56**	.030
FD	.05*	.58**	.14**	.00	−.37**	.44**	.096
8708 building cleaning							
T	.08**	.89**	.81**	.16**	−.03**	.08**	.147
W	.10**	.72**	.49**	.05	−.18**	.22**	.093
LD	.11**	.79**	.60**	−.08	−.10**	.20**	.040
FD	.09**	.56**	.36**	.16**	−.35**	.20**	.121

See Tables 3–5.

is entirely due to the inclusion of the hours variable, and that the fall of capital elasticity in totals is also mostly related to the inclusion of this variable (and very little to that of the managerial ratio).[31]

On the whole, it appears that taking into account the managerial ratio does not change our estimates, and in particular does not significantly decrease the capital elasticity in totals, contrary to what could be expected. Including the hours of work variable does better, partly reducing the gap between the cross-sectional and time-series estimates, at least in one industry and overall. It does so, however, in a different way from what we thought. We expected that this will mainly reveal a positive bias on labor elasticity, rather than the opposite (and probably a negative bias on capital elasticity).

In fact what we observe in most industries (and particularly in building cleaning) are negative (partial as well as simple) correlations between changes in the number of employees and their hours of work, instead of positive ones as we assumed, There is a possibility, though, that these surprisingly negative correlations could be spurious. Since the hours of work per employee variable is obtained by dividing the total number of hours by the number of employees, one would think that random measurement errors in this last number could account for such a finding. Considering the order of magnitudes involved, this is not at all unlikely. For example, in building cleaning, random errors amounting for only about 1% of the observed variance in the number of employees (in levels) would account for about half of the observed variance in the changes in this variable, and would be enough to generate the observed (simple) correlation of $-.5$ with the changes in hours of work per employee.[32]

What we find is thus a different story from the one we were looking for. Including hours of work per employee in the Cobb-Douglas regression, in addition to the number of employees, is in fact equivalent to introducing the total number of hours separately. Assuming that this variable is more appropriate to measure labor than the mere number of employees (and is not itself too severely affected by measurement errors), the fact that we can take it into account in the regression has the effect of correcting for the bias due to the errors in the number of employees.[33]

Once more, in conclusion, errors of measurement in variables seem to provide a plausible reason for the divergence between the cross-sectional and time-series estimates. They do so not only in the case of the elasticity of capital (as we have seen), but also for the elasticity of labor and that of scale, explaining in part why the estimates appear too low in the time dimension, especially the first differences ones.

The second matter to be considered is the evidence provided by the elasticity of hours per employee and the managerial ratio coefficient estimates themselves, and whether their magnitudes make sense. The picture is a mixed one, but some of the results are interesting and seem strong enough not to be too much affected, hopefully, by the error in variables problem.

Not too surprisingly perhaps, the managerial ratio does not show up (or very little) in the time series regressions; but it comes in cross-sectionally overall and in all the industries, except hotels, with a coefficient θ ranging from 0.2 to 0.7 (0 in hotels). This implies an average efficiency of managers relative to the other employees of 1.5 overall and going from a low 1.2 to 1.3 in restaurants, building cleaning, legal services, and computer programming up to about 1.6 in accounting services and engineering and about 2 in computer processing. Such values appear not unreasonable, although probably on the low side if compared to wage differentials.

The average number of hours of work per employee variable enters very significantly in all four types of regressions, overall and for most industries (the one clear exception being engineering). Across types of regressions, the estimated elasticities δ exhibit, however, a pattern of differences very similar to that of the estimated labor elasticities β, being highest in totals (.65 overall), lowest in first differences (25 overall), and intermediate in within and long differences.[34] Across industries, the estimated δ tends to be more widely spread than the estimated β. What is quite remarkable is that in all industries and for all estimates the estimated δ are very significantly smaller than the estimated β. It is also remarkable that for a given industry and whatever the estimates the estimated gaps $(\beta - \delta)$ between the two elasticities are not that different.[35] They are the smallest, about .20, in restaurants and building cleaning, and the largest, about .70, in engineering, computer programming and computer processing, and in the .30 to .60 range for the other three industries. Considering what are the very different characteristics of the organization and the nature of the work in these industries, this is more or less what one might have guessed a priori.

On the whole, it seems clear from such evidence that, even allowing for sensible biases from measurement errors, there are diminishing returns to hours per employee. These returns vary a great deal across industries, but remain smaller, in all of them, than the returns to the number of employees. On the basis of these estimates, it appears that a policy of cutting down on the length of work in order to create jobs is likely to have a very different outcome in the various industries." Under the extreme (and irrealistic) assumptions that "other things remain equal," and in particular that output would be unchanged (and hourly wages not increased), this hypothetical outcome would range from no impact on employment in engineering and little in computer programming and computer processing, up to almost an 80% off-setting increase of employment in restaurants and building cleaning services.[36]

5. By Way of Conclusion

This study of medium and large firms in eight French service industries could warrant a number of specific remarks. However, by way of conclusion, we shall end with a general comment on the similarity of the problems of productivity analysis in the market services and the manufacturing goods sectors, and the necessity of making efforts to improve the data if we hope to solve them.

Considered in terms of a standard productivity analysis at the firm level such as the present one, service industries are not much different from manufacturing industries. They exhibit distributions of productivity differences and changes among firms, which are comparable and in particular extremely dispersed. In both cases, labor and capital appear to be major factors in accounting for such large productivity variability, much being left, however, to be explained. The patterns of alternative estimates for the elasticities of capital and labor (and scale) that we find in the cross-sectional and time-series dimensions of the data, are also strikingly similar, strongly suggesting comparable misspecifications in the econometric modeling of the production function. The results based on the information specifically available in this study, on rental expenditures on capital, hours of work and a managerial ratio, confirm that there is not one single specification issue involved, but probably many of them. The fact that the available variables usually suffer from measurement errors of various origins is a pervasive problem, which can be specially severe for the time-series type estimates. Not being able to observe or not knowing how to measure various characteristics of firms and their behavior (such as levels of human and knowledge capital, innovations in equipment, technique, and products, labor relations and production organization, work effort and managerial ability, pricing and marketing policies, . . .) raises questions of even greater magnitude. We are left with the feeling that progress in our understanding of productivity issues will not come primarily from more powerful and sophisticated techniques; it will instead depend on the quality, relevance and scope of our data and on our efforts to improve them.

Acknowledgment

We thank Zvi Griliches, Bronwyn Hall, Sarah Lane, Catherine Morrison, and Don Siegel for comments at various points when preparing and revising this paper. We are also grateful to Jean Albert, Jean Marie Chanut, Marc Tajan, and Philippe Trogan for their help in having access to the data of the French annual surveys of market services.

Notes

1. See Kremp and Mairesse [1992].
2. Personnel supply services are not readily comparable to the other service industries in the sense that temporary workers are actually recorded together with permanent employees in the survey data, whereas it would be preferable to consider them as an intermediate input. For this reason also, the figures recorded in that industry for the number of hours of work are meaningless.
3. In the previous paper, we also tried to illustrate the different perspectives of macro and micro economists, even when they investigate the same issues. We thus contrasted the different choices they typically make in constructing a sample and computing average characteristics from it.
4. The analysis of profitability differences and changes is pursued in Kremp [1992].
5. INSEE = Institut National de la Statistique et des Etudes Economiques.
6. The numbers of firms by industry of the balanced and cleaned sample we actually use are given in the first column of Table 1.
7. More precisely we used the following criteria. If m and σ are the mean and standard deviation of the log of the ratio variable in year t: ($\text{Log } R_t = \text{Log}(Y_t/X_t)$), an observation was considered to be an "outlier" if $|\text{Log } R_t - m| > 4.4\sigma$ (i.e., a value which will have a probability of less than 1 in 100,000, for a normal distribution of Log R, or lognormal distributions of both X and Y). For the variable X in log first differences (approximately equal to the growth rates for small enough changes), an observation was taken as an "outlier" if $|\text{Log } X_t/X_{t-1}| > 1$ (i.e., an increase or decrease in one year by a factor of more than 2.7 times).
8. What we found was that firms leaving and entering are much smaller in size than continuing ones, but have surprisingly similar productivity and profitability levels (Kremp and Mairesse [1992]). A serious study of the issue would, in fact, require being able to distinguish firms really leaving or entering the industry and those crossing the limit of 20 salaried employees. For a panel data productivity study in which selectivity seems to matter quite significantly, see Olley and Pakes [1991].
9. In this sense, it is less of a problem to clean "too much" than "not enough." There is a limit to cleaning, however, which comes rapidly if one insists on cleaning on many variables (and/or with strong criteria), since the sample size goes down quickly (and the dispersion in variables dwindles away). If one encounters

difficulties in that respect or has reasons to be especially careful, it seems better to remain rather conservative on cleaning a priori, and then control for possible influential observations a posteriori, and report on them if need be. In the present work, we did some a posteriori checks for influential observations, to no avail.

10. This correction is relatively small on average (about 5%), and by itself does not practically affect our estimates. Hence, we shall not report on it.
11. The value-added price indices at the four-digit industry level are usually not published, but are inputs to the more aggregated national accounts published figures. Since we are including industry year dummies in our regressions, such deflation at the industry level does not in fact change our estimates, and we could have done without it. It allows us, however, to interpret the average industry growth rates in value added per person (in Table 1) as (more) truly reflecting productivity changes.
12. It is plausible that this is the case to a large extent. Location, for example, is clearly related to wages differentials, and hence very likely related to price differentials too. Going within firms or considering differences in estimating the production function (as we shall see below) is also a way to be protected from permanent price differentials. The impact of correlated (and varying over time) price differentials still remains of potential importance on such estimates as ours. The only direct way to know would be to observe the prices at the firm level, together with relevant output quality attributes.
13. In the present work, the gross book value has not been adjusted for inflation (since we have no information about the net book value or on past investments). Similar investigations using firm panel data have found that such an adjustment had little effect on the production function estimates.
14. An average length of life coefficient of eight years "corresponds" to an average annual rate of depreciation of 12.5%. The differences in fit arising from different values of the average length of life coefficient in the plausible range are in fact quite small, implying that this coefficient is rather poorly "estimated." In this range (from 6 to 10, or even 4 to 12), the basic capital and labor elasticity estimates are not much affected either. The imprecision is such also that it did not make sense to try to use different lengths of life by industry (or year).
15. Using beginning-of-year capital stock allows an average six months lag for new investment to be fully productive; it also mitigates the potential simultaneity problem between output and investment decisions. In fact both the value added and capital stock measures correspond to the fiscal year, and our labor measures to the calendar year, and there is a mismatch in timing for the firms for which the two do not coincide. The proportion of such firms, however, is not large, and we have eliminated the firms for which the length of the fiscal year was less than 9 months or more than 15 months and those which were off by more than 5 months from the calendar year. Attempts to find out whether this timing problem could affect our estimates have shown (as in some previous work) that it has a negligible impact.
16. The proportion of nonsalaried persons for the large service firms in the sample is a mere 2% on average. The proportion of part-timers is higher, on the order of 5–10% in all industries, apart from building cleaning services where it is as much as 55%. It can be estimated that part-time employees work an average number of hours per year which is roughly two-thirds of that of full-time employees. In the regressions with the average number of work per person (as considered in Section 4), we have also included the ratio of nonsalaried employees as a variable correcting for the fact that the information on the number of hours of work concerns the salaried employees only, and that it may be different for nonsalaried persons. This ratio does not show up very significantly nor does it affect the other parameters estimates; we do not report on it.

    The ratio of part-time employees can also be included in the regressions and interpreted in a similar way to the average hours of work per person variable. It usually comes in the regression significantly (at least in the cross-sectional dimension of the data, for the so-called total estimates), and the magnitude of its impact seems to be sensible (in the cross-sectional dimension). However, we did not think it really worthwhile to document this finding here; and since our estimates of interest were not much changed, we preferred not to include the ratio of part-timers as an additional factor in the regressions. Cross-sectional production function regressions including both hours of work and the ratio of part-timers are presented and discussed in Kremp [1993].
17. The size of the adjustment for inflation of owned capital would be much too small to change this conclusion. Taking a low value for the length of life coefficient, of 4 instead of 8, will still leave us with a corrected measure of total capital twice the uncorrected measure, i.e., an estimated rented capital stock of the same average order of magnitude than owned capital stock.

18. Employment (log L) being a size variable behaves somewhat differently from the ratio variables. As could be expected, the share of between firm variability is even higher (98%) in levels, and not as small (35%) in growth rates.
19. The basic estimates do not change much, if we do not fully interact the year, industry and other heterogeneity effects.
20. See for example, Mariesse [1990], and other studies cited there.
21. Rented capital alone seems to be actually a somewhat better proxy than owned capital alone; providing a slightly better fit in the regressions, in totals as well as in first differences.
22. Note, however that these first difference estimates correspond to large decreasing returns to scale, and that there is some inconsistency in comparing them to capital shares computed under the assumption of constant returns. The first difference estimates of the elasticity of capital that we obtain when imposing constant returns to scale ($\alpha + \beta = 1$) (and using the measure of both rented and owned capital) are not much higher (about .11 overall, instead of .08).
23. The implied rates of return are, of course, directly dependent on the average magnitude of the estimated capital stocks. In order to derive a more likely rate of return, of about .20, from the overall capital elasticity estimate in totals, we would need, however, a capital stock which should be two times greater than the present evaluation (i.e., an average capital output ratio of one instead of one half).
24. With a mark up ratio ν and an elasticity of scale μ, the labor elasticity should be $\beta = \nu s_L$ and the capital elasticity $\alpha = \mu - \nu s_L$. If we consider, for example, the extreme case of legal services, it will be enough to take $\mu = 1.10$ (+ 10% as estimated in totals) and $\nu = 1.60$ (+ 60%) to explain away the very large apparent discrepancy between the capital share and the capital elasticity estimated in totals. For discussion of such issues, see for example Hall [1990].
25. A number of panel data studies also favor cross-sectional estimates, which often tend, as in our case, to look more plausible than the time-series-type estimates. There is, of course, not such a choice for the studies only based on cross-sectional data, which are many.
26. See Griliches and Hausman [1986] on this general issue. See also Mairesse [1990], where it is shown that errors in variables can go a long way in explaining the pattern of divergences among production function estimates.
27. However, one would not expect a negative bias on the elasticity of scale and could not account in this way for the estimated decreasing returns. The basic assumption here is that changes in the number of hours per employee are positively correlated with the changes in the number of employees (and uncorrelated or weakly correlated with the changes in capital). See Griliches and Mairesse [1984].
28. See, for example, Malinvaud [1973], Charpin and Mairesse [1978], Oudiz and Sterdyniak [1979], Cette, Durand, and Tyl [1986].
29. See Feldstein [1967] for an argumented critique and some evidence for increasing returns to hours.
30. It is also easy to see that θ, the coefficient of the managerial ratio reflects the efficiency (or marginal productivity) of managers ("cadres") relative to that of the other employees. Our present equation can be interpreted as a direct approximation of the Cobb-Douglas production function in which labor is expressed in efficiency units: $L^* = LO + \psi\ LM = L(1 + (\psi - 1)MR)$, LM and LO standing respectively for the numbers of managers and other employees, (with $L = LO + LM$ and $MR = LM/L$), and ψ measuring (average) relative efficiency. We get simply (and approximately) $\theta = \beta(\psi - 1)$ or $\psi = 1 + \theta/\beta$.
31. This is easily checked by running the regressions including only one of these two variables at a time, which we did.
32. Another reason contributes in part to this negative correlation in building cleaning. In this industry (and also in restaurants), firms tend to rely on part-time employees (with shorter hours than full-time employees), in order to meet shifts in their demand.
33. The bias is proportional to $\beta - \delta$ and not any more to β. There would be of course no bias if the number of employees would not be entering the regression (i.e., $\beta - \delta = 0$), and if the total number of hours entering alone would itself be free from measurement errors.
34. Including the ratio of part-time employees as an additional variable in the regression tends to lower somewhat the estimate of δ in totals.
35. One cannot exclude that errors specific to the measurement of hours of work, which would be different from the errors concerning the number of employees, could result in a downward bias on the estimated δ. Such errors on the hours of work variable would have to be large, and much larger than the ones on the number

of employees variable (in proportion to the observed variances in these variables), in order to account for our systematic finding of an estimated δ much smaller than the estimated β.

36. For a simple macroeconomic model in which the short-run and long-run implications of a policy of reducing hours of work on unemployment, growth and prices, are discussed, see for example Charpin and Mairesse [1978]. It is shown there that these implications are very different, depending whether there is compensation on wages or not, and an increase in capital utilization or not. Of course, in the real world, much also depends on the specific ways in which shorter hours are implemented (for example whether such reduction concerns the annual, weekly or daily length of work, overtime or normal hours, work in shifts, full-time or part-time employees, . . .).

References

Cette, Gilbert, Brigitte Durand, and Thaddée Tyl. (1986). "Réorganiser le Travail: Une Solution pour l'Emploi?" *Economie et Statistique*, 184, 3–23.

Charpin, Michel, and Jacques Mairesse. (1978). "Réduction de la Durée du Travail et Chômage: Éléments de Réflexon en Forme de Modèle," *La Revue Economique* 19, 189–206.

Feldstein, Martin S. (1967). "Specification of Labor Input in the Aggregate Production Function." *The Review of Economic Studies* 34, 375–386.

Griliches, Zvi, and Jerry Hausman. (1986). "Errors in Variables in Panel Data." *Journal of Econometrics* 31, 93–118.

Griliches, Zvi, and Jacques Mairesse. (1984). "Productivity and R&D at the Firm Level." In Zvi Griliches (ed.), *R&D Patents and Productivity*. Chicago: National Bureau of Economic Research and the University of Chicago Press.

Hall, Robert. (1990). "Invariance Properties of Solow's Productivity Residual." In Peter Diamond (ed.), *Growth, Productivity, Unemployment*. Cambridge, MA: MIT Press.

Kremp, Elizabeth. (1992). "Sector and Firm Effects in the Explanation of Profitability in Nine French Market Service Sectors: 1984–1988." Banque de France Working Paper.

Kremp, Elizabeth. (1993). "La Productivité dans les Services." *Economie et Statistique*, to appear.

Kremp, Elizabeth, and Jacques Mairesse. (1992). "Dispersion and Heterogeneity of Firm Performances in Nine French Service Industries, 1984–87." In Zvi Griliches (ed.), *Output Measurement in the Service Sectors*. Chicago: National Bureau of Economic Research and the University of Chicago Press.

Mairesse, Jacques. (1990). "Time-Series and Cross-Sectional Estimates on Panel Data: Why Are They Different and Why Should They Be Equal?" In J. Hartog, G. Ridder, and J. Theeuwes (eds.), *Panel Data and Labor Market Studies*, Amsterdam: North-Holland.

Malinvaud, Edmond (1973). "Une Explication de L'Évolution de la Productivité Horaire du Travail." *Economie et Statistique* 48, 46–50.

Olley, Steven, and Ariel Pakes. (1991). "The Dynamics of Productivity in the Telecommunications Equipment Industry." Yale University Working Paper.

Oudiz, Gilles, and Henri Sterdyniak. (1979). "Réduire la Durée du Travail: Quelles Conséquences?" *Economie et Statistique* 111, 3–26.